Russia          GI

$9.⁰⁰

# RED MUTINY

# RED MUTINY

❖

Eleven Fateful Days on the
Battleship *Potemkin*

Neal Bascomb

HOUGHTON MIFFLIN COMPANY
*Boston • New York*
2007

For information about permission to reproduce selections
from this book, write to Permissions, Houghton Mifflin Company,
215 Park Avenue South, New York, New York 10003.

Visit our Web site: www.houghtonmifflinbooks.com.

*Library of Congress Cataloging-in-Publication Data*
Bascomb, Neal.
Red mutiny : eleven fateful days on the battleship *Potemkin* /
Neal Bascomb.
p.   cm.
Includes bibliographical references and index.
ISBN-13: 978-0-618-59206-7
ISBN-10: 0-618-59206-7
1. Bronenosets "Potemkin." 2. Russia — History — Revolution,
1905–1907. I. Title. II. Title: Eleven fateful days on the battleship
*Potemkin.* III. Title: 11 fateful days on the battleship *Potemkin.*
DK264.B37 2007
947.08'3 — dc22    2006030210

*Book design by Melissa Lotfy*

*Map by Jacques Chazaud*

Printed in the United States of America

MP 10 9 8 7 6 5 4 3 2 1

*For My Grandparents,*

LESTER AND BETTY LINCK

SUMPTER AND HELEN BASCOMB

# Contents

AUTHOR'S NOTE · viii

PROLOGUE · xi

PART I · 1

PART II · 73

PART III · 229

DRAMATIS PERSONAE · 317

ACKNOWLEDGMENTS · 320

RESEARCH NOTES AND BIBLIOGRAPHY · 321

NOTES · 334

INDEX · 372

# Author's Note

Mutiny is a high military crime and — alongside treason — the gravest of crimes against the state. Its perpetrators risk court-martial and almost certain death. Rarely, however, is the act important in the sweep of history. The isolated bands of sailors or soldiers who rebel against their officers seldom warrant a place in a country's, let alone the world's, collective memory. Then there is the mutiny on the battleship *Potemkin*.

In June 1905 on the Black Sea, the crew aboard the *Potemkin* killed their captain and took control of the most powerful battleship in the Russian fleet. The insurrection had begun over a protest against maggot-infested meat, but stale borsht was little more than a pretext for mutiny, an action planned months in advance by sailors turned revolutionaries. All of Russia was on the verge of insurrection against the despotic rule of Tsar Nicholas II, and these sailors hoped to bring the battleship to the people's side, leading to the tsar's fall from the throne.

Flying the red flag of revolution, the *Potemkin* ruled the Black Sea for eleven days. Hunted by battleship squadrons and individual destroyers from port to port, the sailors incited revolts on land, inspired other crews to mutiny, battled on land and sea, and revealed the rotting foundations of the Russian Empire. The sailors also captured international attention, dominating front-page news for weeks and compelling other heads of state to urge the tsar to resolve the situation before it upset the world's fragile balance of power. Pressured from within Russia and abroad to accept peace with Japan and agree to reforms that violated his sacred oath to uphold the autocracy, the tsar found *Potemkin* weighing heavily on his thoughts. Given telegrams from his naval commanders that "the sea is in the hands of mutineers" and reports that wholesale revolution might soon follow, his concern was understandable.

Remarkable events, as evidenced in the famous Russian film *Battleship Potemkin* created by director Sergei Eisenstein in 1925, not to mention the scores of books written about the mutiny by participants and by Russian scholars. However, all of these sources, to one degree or another, were influenced by politics, particularly politics after the Bolshevik Revolution. Over a century has passed since that first shot aboard the *Potemkin* sparked the uprising, and its story deserves to be freed of the myth and bias that have clouded it for so long. I have endeavored to tell this history through the eyes of the *Potemkin* sailors, hoping to reveal who they were, what drove them to dare mutiny, how they succeeded in surviving for eleven days while Russia and the world turned against them, and what ultimately brought their journey to an end. Furthermore, to draw a complete picture, I have woven in the views of the crews on other ships within the fleet, the naval officers who tried to suppress the uprising, the generals facing unrest throughout the region, Tsar Nicholas himself, and others.

It is clear now in hindsight that the events of 1905, including the *Potemkin* mutiny, served only as a "dress rehearsal" for the revolution that would eventually sweep the tsar from power. Twelve years and the misery of a world war would pass before these changes transpired. We also know that any chance for a more democratic government to replace the tsar's regime ended when the Bolsheviks seized the reins in October 1917, much as we are familiar with the terror and suffering that Lenin and his successors would inflict on the Russian people in an attempt to realize their political theories. Inevitably, these facts, as well as volumes of propaganda, color our perception of these sailors, their ambitions, and their chances of achieving some kind of victory.

The truth is, the *Potemkin* sailors were not struggling to advance some stage of history set forth in political philosophy; rather, they were acting against a ruinous autocratic regime that viewed them solely as vassals of the state, existing only to serve — and suffer, as was most often the case. The mutiny showed the willingness of some to face great odds and near-certain death to end oppression. Like those who stormed the Bastille against Louis XVI's reign or fought against King George III in the American colonies, the *Potemkin*'s leaders were ordinary, flesh-and-blood individuals at the forefront of a battle to win personal liberty and a voice in how their daily lives and their country would be led. Alone on the Black Sea, uncertain whether anyone would join them in their fight but sure the tsar of Russia would leverage all of his considerable powers to crush them, the sailors dared revolution. They acted while others stood by to judge and attempt to use the sailors' efforts for their own ends.

# Prologue

History does nothing, possesses no enormous wealth, fights no battles. It is rather man, the real, living man, who does everything, possesses, fights. It is not "History," as if she were a person apart, who uses men as means to work out her purposes, but history itself is nothing but the activity of men pursuing their purposes.

—KARL MARX

AT 91 RUE DE CAROUGE in the city of Geneva, in a tiny apartment stacked with dusty magazines and books, with packing cases for chairs, two men spoke of revolution. It was the end of July, the year was 1905, and the focus of their conversation was Russia.

The two had only just met. The first, Vladimir Ilyich Ulyanov, lived in the apartment with his wife. He went by the pen name Lenin. When he spoke of his rivals, the Mensheviks, his dark eyes hardened, he jabbed his fingers through the buttonholes of his vest, and then he drew back as if he was gathering venom before a strike. Although the Russian secret police, Okhrana, tracked his movements, considering him an enemy of the state, Lenin was largely an unknown figure outside socialist circles. One day he would lord over Russia, but his deeds as of July 1905 were limited, and he acted more as a journalist than a revolutionary leader.

Okhrana agents in Geneva were also watching his guest that afternoon, but his deeds and name were known throughout the world. Hero to some, treasonous villain to others, Afanasy Nikolayevich Matyushenko was the leader of the mutiny on the battleship *Potemkin,* a rebellion that had occurred only a month earlier and had made Tsar Nicholas II question his very hold on power. Lenin, who was as stunned at its outbreak as anyone else, had already written that the eleven-day Black Sea mutiny, led by Matyushenko, marked the first important step of the Russian Revolution. "The Rubicon has been crossed," he declared in the socialist journal *Proletary*.

To many, stories of Matyushenko summoned up a picture of a titan, but the twenty-six-year-old sailor sitting across from Lenin looked far from such. Short in frame, he had a lean, muscular face, pronounced Slavic cheekbones, and a slight upturn on the right side of his mouth, giving him the expression of someone in on a secret. His eyes, which many of his closest comrades knew could darken into a horrible rage, were largely hidden underneath thick red eyebrows. But it was not his appearance, nor his background as a peasant from a small Ukrainian village, that made him a giant; it was his presence. Men instinctively looked to him for direction. He was intelligent, a gifted speaker, and recklessly brave. Perhaps most important of all, people recognized, as one of his comrades said, that "he lived not for himself, but for others."

After the mutiny's end, Matyushenko had escaped the Black Sea shores for Bucharest, where he stayed with Professor Zik Arbore-Ralli, a Russian émigré who was once close to revolutionaries Mikhail Bakunin and Sergei Nechayev. Okhrana agents in Romania kept Matyushenko under the strictest surveillance, but they were forbidden to seize him on foreign soil. Worried these Russian agents might act precipitately, Arbore-Ralli and several *Potemkin* sailors pooled their money to send him to Switzerland to join the community of Russian revolutionary leaders in exile there.

Traveling with a fake Bulgarian passport, Matyushenko arrived by train in Geneva in early July. He sought financial support for his former crewmates and guidance on where he should next take his struggle against the tsar. The Russian secret police soon picked up his trail in Geneva after he met with several individuals on their watch list. Again, they could do nothing but watch. While in Switzerland, he became close with Father Georgy Gapon, the champion of St. Petersburg workers who had marched on the Winter Palace at the first of the year, but Matyushenko could barely stand any of the other revolutionary figures he met. Each party head attempted to recruit him. In the most direct terms, Matyushenko refused them all. "It's not for me," he told one party's terrorist wing. "I'm a man of the crowd. Do what you like, I just can't do it."

These intellectual leaders of the revolution professed their love and respect for Matyushenko, but he knew they thought him nothing more than an ignorant sailor who could be taught to dance for their cause. One party chided him for not reading enough Karl Marx. Another proposed he concentrate more on August Bebel. Thinking for oneself was apparently out of the question in Geneva, Matyushenko reflected. He despised their bickering over theory. While they elbowed one another over whose party deserved credit for the *Potemkin* mutiny, sailors who had risked their lives alongside Matyushenko were days away from the firing squad. The starving people of Russia seemed only an afterthought to these revolutionaries. They certainly had not earned the right to even comment on the mutiny — good or bad. The sailors had acted while these men merely talked and scribbled polemics.

In Lenin, Matyushenko found the most combative and vitriolic of infighters, the one who had splintered the Russian Social Democrats and issued polemic after polemic from his apartment concerning the true path to revolution. That afternoon, Matyushenko told him of the *Potemkin*. He had lost several close comrades in the mutiny, and the feelings of despair and triumph were still raw in the telling.

This story, theirs, begins in St. Petersburg in the cold heart of winter, 1905.

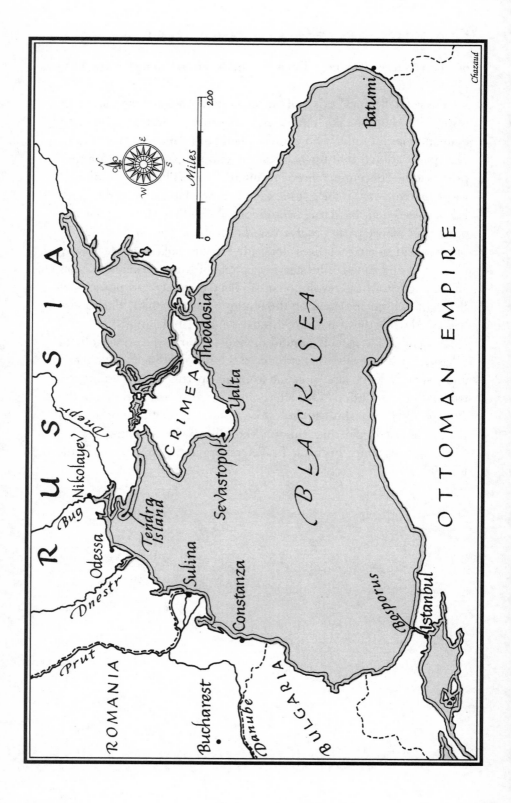

# I

Where there is a lot of water, there
you may expect disaster.

— Russian proverb

Shine out in all your beauty,
City of Peter, and stand
Unshakable as Russia herself
And may the untamed elements
Make their peace with you.

— ALEKSANDR PUSHKIN,
*The Bronze Horseman*

# 1

THE NEVA RIVER cut through the center of St. Petersburg, a mighty artery of ice. On its surface flowed a temporary electric tramway as well as horse-drawn sleighs. The sleigh drivers, bound in sheepskin, their beards white with icicles from their breath, followed paths outlined with pine branches. Police patrols scanned the river for thin spots, marking these with red flags, but in most areas, the ice was now thick enough for workers to cut out piano-sized blocks that would be stored for the hot summer months. Skating rinks dotted the river, enjoyed by those fortunate enough to have leisure time. Below the frozen surface, the water surged inexorably toward the Gulf of Finland, but that was a distant thought to the people of St. Petersburg who had gathered on the Neva and its banks to celebrate the Blessing of the Waters. It was January 6, 1905.

Nicholas II began the day's ceremonies with an inspection of the troops in one of the many grand vaulted halls of the Winter Palace. In his dark blue, gold-studded uniform of the famed Preobrazhensky Guards Regiment, he walked smartly along the lines of men, stopping now and again with the greeting, "Good morning, my children," to which came the swift reply, "Good health to Your Majesty." A slight man, five foot, seven inches tall, the Emperor and Autocrat of All the Russias was known for his tender smile and remorseful blue eyes. At thirty-six years of age, he radiated little of the authority of his father, Alexander III, in whose shadow he perpetually fell. Although Nicholas was weighed down with concern over Russia's war with Japan, now almost a year old, he could expect the day's ceremonies, a blend of religious observance and military pageantry, to lift his spirits.

After the inspection, he proceeded through the 1,054-room baroque palace, a quarter-mile-long monument to the immense, and outrageously concentrated, wealth of the nation. The route through the vast, richly adorned chambers was crowded with people hoping for a glance or a nod from the tsar: Imperial Guards in white gala uniforms with gold and silver helmets crested with the double-headed Russian eagle, Cossacks in long blue robes holding drawn sabers, senators in bright scarlet coats, diplomats and dignitaries in their finest regalia, admirals and generals nearly toppling over with medals, and ladies of the court in flowing dresses of pale green and pink.

Nicholas escorted his mother, the dowager empress, by the arm. His uncle, Grand Duke Alexis, accompanied Tsarina Alexandra, followed by the rest of the royal family. The empresses and grand duchesses wore velvet robes and glittered with diamonds, pearls, and other precious stones. Led by the imperial court's grand marshal, who walked backward and carried a golden staff, they marched from hall to hall, accompanied by the national hymn. Finally, they passed through the 1812 Military Gallery, a long corridor with 332 portraits of Russian officers who fought against Napoleon, and into the palace cathedral. Icons of the patron saints of the imperial family lined the gilded chamber, and the brilliant morning sun shined through the circular windows of the cupola.

In a robe laden with gold and silver, the metropolitan of St. Petersburg, the head of the city's Russian Orthodox Church, began the mass at noon. Nicholas bowed his head and prayed; a heavy incense of cloves and rose oil saturated the air. Surrounded by so many symbols of his power, and the people invested in its continuance, Nicholas might have believed his prayer to God of January 1, that "in the coming year He will give Russia a victorious end of the war, a firm peace and quiet life without disturbances," would soon be answered favorably. After all, the previous year, God had finally blessed him with a son, Alexis.

But centuries of history had shown that the people of Russia, not God, had fulfilled most of the tsar's wishes. The city of St. Petersburg, for instance, raised to give Peter the Great his foolhardy "paradise," came at the cost of the lives of tens of thousands of serfs who drowned or died of cholera while digging the foundations of its first buildings in low marshland prone to serious floods.

In his private life, Nicholas liked to play the part of a common Russian, dressing in a peasant blouse, eating *borscht,* and taking up modest rooms within his grand palaces, but he understood little of peasant lives. Another St. Petersburg existed beyond the towering gold cupolas, elegant mansions, and richly maintained government and military buildings that lined the Neva's granite quays. In this St. Petersburg, as in other Russian cities, workers trudged through dirty snow to labor at factories, where fourteen-hour days yielded only meager wages. Their bosses treated them no better than slaves, and the workers lived in windowless bunkhouses, up to eleven to a room, with wooden benches for beds, rags for pillows, and walls covered with soot from kerosene lamps. They wanted better pay and living conditions — and they had recently grown willing to strike for them.

Across the breadth of the Russian Empire — one-sixth of the world's landmass at that time, stretching from the Gulf of Finland east across Siberia to the warm Pacific waters, from the icebound Arctic in the north down to the Black Sea and the borders of the Ottoman Empire — lived the tsar's 135 million subjects, the majority of whom were peasants who worked the land and never left their villages, except perhaps to serve as cannon fodder for their tsar's wars. None of these people would ever see the good Tsar Batyushka (Father-Tsar) that folktales and tradition held him to be, this individual selected by God himself to care for them. All they knew, however, was that many of their sons led off to war never returned, that the land they tilled barely kept them from starving even in the best of years, and that the tsar never appeared to hear their pleas for help.

At 12:45 P.M., the metropolitan finished the mass and the great doors to the cathedral swung open. Nicholas joined another procession, this one led by chanting clergy down the white Carrara marble staircase and outside to the Neva for the Blessing of the Waters. Bareheaded and cloakless, as tradition dictated, Nicholas was struck by the cold like a slap across the face.

As he walked down crimson carpet to the open-air pavilion on the Neva, specially erected for the ceremony with a blue, star-encrusted dome topped with a cross, he could only see devoted throngs around him. They lined the quays, the palace bridge, the steps of the stock exchange, and the river itself. Soldiers kept them at a proper distance. From the windows of the cherry-red Winter Palace, members of his court pressed their noses to the glass, watching with quiet reverence.

A hole had been cut into the ice underneath the pavilion. The flowing water underneath, warmer than the air outside, caused steam to rise from the opening. The ceremony began. Nicholas kissed the hand of the metropolitan and the Holy Book. A choir sang solemn liturgical hymns, and then the metropolitan carried a large gold cross, linked to a chain, to the hole in the ice. After he blessed the Neva by dipping the cross three times into the water, he gave his benediction. Then, across the river, a cannon from the Fortress of Peter and Paul thundered in salute. Its report rattled the Winter Palace's windows. Blue smoke drifted across the river. Simultaneously, church bells rang throughout the city.

Then from across the river, quickly, came another flash of light and a boom. This time the cannon's report was distinctly different, "more rolling and peculiarly warlike," as one witness described it. Panes of glass shattered in the upper windows of the Winter Palace. Someone had loaded a cannon with live rounds instead of blanks. Nicholas crossed himself, believing someone was trying to kill him, but he did not move for cover. Not even a step.

Nicholas was morbidly unafraid of dying. His younger sister Olga once commented that he was resigned to losing his life on the throne. Murder had been the fate of his grandfather and almost half of the other tsars since Ivan the Terrible ruled Russia. After all, Nicholas was born on May 6, making his patron saint Job, who suffered horrible trials by God's hand. Nicholas believed in the significance of such things.

The cannon fire stopped. A policeman at the pavilion's edge had fallen; blood stained the snow by his head. Shrapnel had cut a nearby banner in two. In the palace's Nicholas Hall, ladies and their escorts trembled; several were seriously wounded, many covered in shards of glass. Admiral Fyodor Avelan, minister of the navy, bled from a cut in his face. Yet while shouts of alarm rang throughout the palace and guards scrambled to see what had happened, the tsar completed the ceremony, received his blessing with the sanctified water, and only then returned to the palace. His entourage and the palace court waited for some reaction: anger, a tremble of fear, a hint of gladness that he had survived — anything. He offered none. Eyes downcast, he walked back inside the palace, not stopping or even turning to inspect the damage.

The guard around the palace was doubled, the police hurried to the fortress to investigate, but otherwise the event was soon put out of mind. A state banquet was held while the pavilion, now embedded with shrapnel, was disassembled. The hole in the ice soon closed in the cold. The investigation never discovered whether the Imperial Guard loaded live rounds by accident in a cannon directed at the pavilion where the Romanov family was clustered.

At 4 P.M., Nicholas left the Winter Palace in his carriage, heading to his retreat at Tsarskoye Selo, a half-hour's drive outside St. Petersburg. The day's event represented a bad omen for the coming year. A tide of discontent was rising among his people, and the Russo-Japanese War was going badly: with the surrender of Port Arthur, a strategic Russian naval base on the Yellow Sea, in December, and with the loss of numerous battles in the Far East, Nicholas needed a military success to calm the people and restore Russia's chances for victory over Japan.

His hope for such a success rested in a squadron of Russian ships, led by Zinovy Petrovich Rozhestvensky, traveling eighteen thousand miles around the globe to crush the Japanese navy.

That same day, Admiral Rozhestvensky and the nearly ten thousand men under his command were waiting, quite literally, in Hellville, a town set on the island Nossi-Bé, off the coast of Madagascar. His Second Pacific Squadron, a motley collection of eight battleships, seven armored cruisers, nine torpedo-boat destroyers, and a number of auxiliaries (tugboats, transports, a water-condensing vessel, a hospital ship, and a floating repair shop), stood in the harbor.

Rozhestvensky's orders from St. Petersburg were to remain at anchor in Hellville and await reinforcements in the form of the Third Pacific Squadron. The First Pacific, the squadron that Rozhestvensky had been sent to connect with in the first place, had been lost when Port Arthur fell. On hearing the news, two weeks before, that he was to stay in Hellville, the admiral told his chief of staff to cable the Naval Ministry: "Tell them I wish to be relieved of my command," he ordered. Then he shut his cabin door, bolting it for good measure, and proceeded to have a mental breakdown.

By most accounts, the fifty-five-year-old Admiral Rozhestvensky was one of the Russian navy's brightest lights. At his squadron's review before departure from Revel in September 1904, standing by the side of Nicholas II, he certainly looked the part. As one attendant described him, "His broad shoulders were decorated with epaulets bearing monograms and black eagles. Medals and stars glittered on his chest. . . . His stalwart figure dominated not only the tsar but all the members of his suite and his piercing black eyes seem to indicate a dauntless will. . . . He stood straight as a ramrod, looking so resolutely at Nicholas that it seemed as if nothing could stop him." Rozhestvensky had excelled at the Naval Academy, he had shown his mettle during combat in the Russo-Turkish War of 1877–78, and, despite a reputation for bluntness and a fast, sometimes cruel temper, he had climbed the naval ranks with his penchant for discipline and exactness, as well as his clever hand at court politics.

When he accepted the command of the Second Pacific Squadron, a position that would require him to travel from the Baltic to the Far East along a route without Russian bases and at imminent risk of attack, to take on the superior Japanese fleet in its own waters, he was falling on his own sword — and he knew it. "We're now doing what needs to be done, defending the honor of the flag," he said publicly before he departed. He understood well that this squadron would either never reach its destination, or, if it did, would likely face a massacre. Nonetheless, Nicholas was determined they should go.

The tsar's execution of the war with Japan was as haphazard as the reasons for its occurrence in the first place — ostensibly, asserting territorial control in Korea and Manchuria. Nicholas had been led into the easily avoidable conflict by his ministers: some were flattering his ambitions of expanding the empire, others were mindful of their commercial interests in the Far East, and a few thought a "little victorious war" would hold back a revolution. These ministers found a welcome listener in Nicholas. In 1890, as a young tsarevich on a grand tour of the East, he narrowly survived an attempted assassination in Otsu, Japan, when an assailant leapt out of a crowd with a sword, slashing Nicholas in the forehead; the assassin's second thrust was parried, but Nicholas was left with a permanent scar. The incident fostered a deep-seated loathing of the Japanese people, whom he dismissed as "monkeys." His bellicose cousin, Kaiser Wilhelm II, also goaded him toward war; a telegram sent to the tsar from the kaiser's yacht reveals his attitude: "The Admiral of the Atlantic greets the Admiral of the Pacific."

When war broke out after a surprise Japanese naval attack at Port Arthur on January 26, 1904, the Russians rallied around the tsar in a fit of patriotism. "We will only need to throw our caps at the enemy to make him run away" was a common expression in the streets. But soon disaster followed disaster on the battlefield. The military campaign was underfunded, ill equipped, and poorly led. Russian generals fought a nineteenth-century campaign, bayonet charges included, against a well-positioned enemy armed with artillery. "Lambs brought to the slaughter," said one observer of the Russian soldiers. For his part, Nicholas sent icons to his troops to boost morale. They would have preferred more modern arms and perhaps fewer officers feuding with one another or drinking champagne on the eve of battle.

Rozhestvensky knew that his mission was just another in a long series of mistakes by the Russian high command, but if there had to be a squadron, he believed he was the best man to lead it. He was not the only one to suffer from this burden. Few of the sailors aboard the armada had any clear understanding of why they were being sent to fight the Japanese. They had been drafted into the navy from peasant farms or derelict warrens in the cities' slums. Many could not read, and they viewed these battleships as "iron monsters." On the first half of their journey from Libau, down the western coast of Africa and around the Cape of Good Hope, to Madagascar, they endured hardships beyond imagination. In the best of circumstances, the Russian navy was cruel to the lower ranks — sailors faced abusive officers, tasteless food, cramped quarters, and back-numbing work — but this journey descended to a different ring of hell altogether.

Forbidden to stop in most ports because assisting the Russians would violate a country's neutrality, Rozhestvensky made sure the squadron took on as much coal as possible from German merchant colliers that met the ships along the way. Coaling at sea was dangerous in its own right, but living with it stacked on the decks and in cabins, corridors, bathrooms, workshops — everywhere — while steaming through the suffocating, 120-degree tropics, was daily torture. Coal dust stung the eyes and choked the lungs. Men collapsed from heat stroke or simply went mad from the daily strain. Other horrors included the ravenous shipboard rats, the dysentery, the decks so hot that they blistered bare feet, and the hurricanes, during which forty-foot waves washed sailors overboard, never to been seen again.

Somehow, Rozhestvensky managed to arrive in Madagascar with most of his crew, though his orders to wait in Hellville destroyed the entire crew's morale more than the heat and coal dust ever could. Rozhestvensky was crushed. For several weeks afterward, his officers heard him moaning in his locked cabin. When he next appeared, he looked twenty years older, haggard and listless. Some of his staff wondered whether he had experienced a stroke, since he now dragged his left leg. What they did know for sure, as January turned into February, then March, was that their fleet was falling apart.

Each day, black torpedo boats carried out to sea those stricken dead by malaria, typhoid, or their own hand. After a single cannon shot, the bodies, sewn in cloth, were let off the side. Those remaining in the harbor suffered a host of illnesses, as well as rotten food, cloying heat, and torrential rain. Many had tropical eczema, scratching themselves until they bled and treating their weeping grazes with kerosene or eau de cologne. At night they slept naked on mats on the decks. Monkeys, chickens, cows, hares, and pigs, brought on board by the sailors, overran every ship. Their stench was overwhelming. Cockroaches and rats swarmed through cabins. Moss and barnacles grew thick on the ships' hulls, and sharks circled around the fleet, eager to consume any bad meat thrown overboard.

Discipline collapsed. Men got stupefyingly drunk, gambled, stole from the local Malagasies, and disobeyed their officers. Signs of mutiny abounded, yet Rozhestvensky, who was reputed to have punched out a sailor's teeth for a minor transgression, let them off easy. "How can I intimidate men ready to follow me to the death by condemning them to be hanged?" he asked his chief of staff. Order deteriorated further upon receiving reports of mass strikes throughout Russia and how the tsar allowed the butchery of his own people, women and children included, when they marched on the Winter Palace to appeal for a better life. Revolution seemed imminent. What was more, the newspaper editorials were pessimistic about the squadron's own mission — writing that the armada was doomed to the same fate as the one Spain sent against England in 1588.

Finally, on March 4, Rozhestvensky, who through sheer force of will had taken back command of his ravaged fleet, decided that he had had enough. He could no longer stand waiting for a fleet of ancient "self-sinkers" — as he called the Third Pacific — that would likely prove a hindrance in a sea fight. Defying his orders, the admiral left Hellville to steam across the vast Indian Ocean. Unbeknownst to him, that day, thousands of Russian infantry troops died in a rout south of the Manchurian city of Mukden. The battle, where over half a million men confronted one another, was the largest of the Russo-Japanese War, and of modern history. The Russians sacrificed ninety thousand men at Mukden.

Proceeding at a sluggish six knots, experiencing engine break-downs and other severe mechanical problems such as one battleship's loss of steering, the squadron made its way across the ocean. Lost to Japanese scouts and the Russian high command for three weeks, the squadron finally appeared off Singapore's coast in four columns; several days later, it anchored in Camranh Bay off French Indochina. On direct orders, this time from Nicholas himself, Rozhestvensky waited again for the Third Pacific. A month later, the squadron arrived. Before dawn on May 14, the combined fleet set out for the naval base in Vladivostok, where Rozhestvensky hoped to service his battleships and restore his sailors' spirits before facing the Japanese fleet. The squadron charted a course through the Korea Strait, the narrow waters between the Japanese coast and Tsushima Island. Rozhestvensky prayed they would elude their enemy in the mist and fog, but his fortune, now in the hands of famed Japanese admiral Togo, would not accommodate his wishes.

"Enemy squadron square 203 . . . apparently bearing eastern passage." The 4:45 A.M. message from a Japanese scout came as welcome news aboard *Mikasa,* the Japanese fleet's flagship. Admiral Togo Heihachiro, who was five foot, three inches tall and weighed a scant 130 pounds, had been waiting for the appearance of the Russians for months. At last, this hero of the Japanese navy, responsible already for several brilliant triumphs over the Russians, could finish off his enemy in one decisive battle. His Zeiss binoculars around his neck, his black uniform buttoned tight under his chin, and his beloved sword in a gold scabbard on his left hip, he calmly began to give orders to his officers on the bridge. Sprays of saltwater splashed over the decks as his fleet moved southeast from its base. A lone sailor sang, "And raging storms dispel the morning dew. . . . So shall the triumph by our vessel won . . . Scatter the Russian ships and all their crew."

By late morning, back on the *Suvorov*, Rozhestvensky watched four Japanese cruisers shadow his fleet's movements like wolves scouting their prey. There would be no slipping through to Vladivostok. Radio intercepts indicated that Togo was on his way. The night before, the mood throughout the Russian fleet had been one of nervous expectation. Sailors slept by their guns or looked out over the railings into the black sea; in the shadows cast by the moon they perceived torpedo boats that never materialized, and they shared their fears. "She'll never get over it if I get killed," said one. "Brrr! It's horrible on the bottom," said another. Rozhestvensky had managed a couple of hours of sleep in an armchair on the forward bridge but had been hunched over his charts from an early hour. Despite the approaching battle, he ordered every ship to pay their respects to the anniversary of the tsar's coronation. Priests moved quickly through the prayers. Tots of vodka were raised: "To the health of His Majesty the Emperor and Her Majesty the Empress! To Russia!"

Before the ceremony's end, action stations were called throughout the fleet. After crossing themselves, sailors hurried to their posts to await the battle. The morning mist cleared, and Tsushima's cliffs towered above them to the west.

At 1:19 P.M., the admirals of the two fleets spotted black smoke on the horizon and, minutes later, each other's fleets. At ten miles' distance, the Japanese were a streak of uniform gray against the heavy, rolling seas. The Russians, their battleship funnels painted yellow, made easy marks. On paper, the two fleets were more or less evenly matched. They each had twelve line-of-battle ships, and although the Japanese had more guns, the Russians boasted heavier weapons. Togo held an advantage in speed and in numbers of destroyers and torpedo boats, but this challenge was by no means insurmountable if Rozhestvensky played his hand right. However, the Russian admiral was no longer the bold, resolute leader who had left Libau eight months previously.

From the day's beginning, Rozhestvensky, who was leading a total of forty-eight ships into battle, weakened his chances by muddling the chain of command and offering the sparest of battle plans. Throughout the engagement, he issued only two orders, both before the first shot was fired. His first order, given even before sighting the Japanese fleet, deployed Rozhestvensky's fleet in a line-abreast formation (perhaps because the admiral feared an attack from the east and did not want to be exposed). His second order, delivered after spotting Togo's ships directly ahead of him, remanded the first order, instructing his fleet to return to single-file, line-ahead formation. This order came too late and only furthered the advantage of the Japanese, who seized upon the Russians' confusion by perfectly executing one of the most daring maneuvers in naval history.

At 1:55 P.M., as the two fleets jockeyed for position before engaging, Togo lifted his right hand and cut a semicircle in the air. The shout "Hard to port!" was raised throughout his ships. Due to the heavy seas and smoke, Togo had misjudged the Russians' initial approach and found himself poorly placed to follow his original plan of isolating two of his enemy's divisions. After his ships passed from starboard to port in front of Rozhestvensky's fleet, heading in the opposite direction, he gave the order to completely reverse direction. For several minutes, his fleet would be exposed at a single spot for the Russians to focus their fire. It was a gamble, but if the ships survived the turn, his fleet could run on a parallel course, and then, with their superior speed, the Japanese could cross in front of the enemy's formation, an ideal vantage point from which to rake them with fire.

During the execution of the turn, guns roared from the flagship *Suvorov*, but most of its shells fell wide and short. Worse, most of Rozhestvensky's fleet, which should have been blanketing the *Mikasa* with shells, was in chaos because of his second order to return to single-file formation. Ships had to slow down, some to a complete stop, so as not to ram those ahead of them. This also made them easy targets for the devastatingly accurate Japanese gunners.

"Open fire! Open fire!" First Togo's *Mikasa*, then each ship coming out of the turn, directed salvos from over five hundred guns at the Russian flagship and at the *Oslyabya*, which spearheaded the fleet's second division and was one of the ships that had pulled to a standstill. Within minutes, the range of the Japanese shells closed. The *Oslyabya*, a modern yet oddly shaped battleship with a high, sloping hull and tall stacks, received a large-caliber hit at the waterline near the bow. The sea poured into the ship's compartments, and soon it began to list dangerously to port, bow down. The Japanese exploited their advantage, showering the *Oslyabya* with shell after shell. The bow turret was ripped away, decapitating one sailor and crippling the rest inside. While being carried below on a stretcher, a sailor with his foot shorn off cried, "Monsters! Bloodsuckers! You see what you've started! May you be swept off God's earth!" An officer stumbled about nearby, his chest ripped open. Most of the shrieks and moans of the dying were lost in the continuing barrage that turned the ship's hull and decks into confetti of twisted steel. Fire leapt across the ship, the acid in the Japanese shells feeding off the paint. The *Oslyabya* shook from bow to stern as it was struck again and again. Soon most of the guns aboard were silenced. Dense black smoke rose from every quarter, and the air bent in the intense heat. Chunks of flesh scattered the decks where there had once been men. As the ship's second officer ran about in a panic, the bow eased deeper and deeper into the water. Still the shells came. The captain, who had died three days before, was lying in a coffin in the ship's chapel, the only one to enjoy peace that day.

Admiral Togo stood unprotected on his upper bridge, one foot forward, lips pursed, watching his fleet advance on the Russians and firing as quickly as his crews could reload the guns. His staff officers tried to get him to move to a safer position — twelve Russian shells had already hit the *Mikasa* — but Togo liked his view. On the foremast to his side battle flags, raised at the engagement's start, signaled that THE RISE OR FALL OF THE EMPIRE DEPENDS UPON THIS ONE BATTLE. DO YOUR UTMOST, EVERY ONE OF YOU.

In the *Suvorov*'s cylindrical conning tower, Rozhestvensky watched the battle unfold through the sliver of a porthole cut in the ten-inch-thick steel structure. The *Oslyabya* had fallen out of line. Most of the fleet was in disarray from the savage Japanese attack, and Togo's ships had closed to within two miles. The distance tightened every minute.

"Your Excellency, we must change the distance," yelled Rozhestvensky's commander, over the roar of explosions. "They've got our range already and they'll make it hot for us."

The admiral turned, a gleam in his eye. "Not so fast. We've got the range too."

Above and all around him, the four-foot-long Japanese shells wailed through the air before hitting. Outside Rozhestvensky's armored tower, the *Suvorov* was in desperate shape. Men scrambled through smoke and over slick pools of blood to help the injured, to escape the fires, or simply to take cover from the rain of hot metal. The gunners continued at their task, but most of the range-finder operators had been killed and the gunners were essentially aiming in the dark. The main mast had disappeared. The signaling halyards were gone. Throughout the ship, separate conflagrations began to join into one leaping inferno.

At 2:30 P.M., the conning tower — the ship's brain, as one observer put it — was hit. Twice. The armor deflected the force of the broadside, but shell splinters ricocheted about the small chamber until they sliced through flesh. Rozhestvensky and his commander suffered cuts on their faces and arms. The helmsman and flag gunnery officer were killed and now lay face-down at their instruments, blood coating the panels. On his knees, the admiral stayed in the tower, but his telegraph and voice tubes were damaged, his rudder was jammed, and he could see nothing through the smoke and flames enveloping his ship. Less than half an hour into the battle, Rozhestvensky had completely lost control of his fleet. The Russian armada disintegrated, every man and ship for himself. Togo maintained his attack in formation, knowing he had won.

At 2:50 P.M., the *Oslyabya* was the first battleship to sink. With its engines stopped, guns silent, and bow underwater, the ship took an eight-hundred-pound shell on the already-listing port side. Then another. Then another. Water gushed through a hole "big enough to drive a troika through," as a survivor described it. As the ship went vertical, sailors spilled over the sides into a sea of flame. An officer yelled, "Get away from the ship, the devil take you! If you don't, you'll go down in the suck! Away!" Over two hundred men never had even that small chance of escape. Locked under shellproof hatchways and forgotten by their comrades, those in the engine rooms and stokeholds went down with the ship, screaming for help in the darkness until the cold sea closed over them.

By that time, Togo's fleet had already turned its broadsides on the other Russian battleships. By 7 P.M., the battle was effectively over. Through the night, Togo's torpedo boats and destroyers picked off those ships that had avoided the day's annihilation. By the morning of May 15, the bodies of thousands of Russian sailors littered the waters of the Korea Strait. With his entire fleet, Togo surrounded the surviving four Russian battleships and demanded their surrender. A few vessels had escaped during the night, including a torpedo boat carrying a blood-smeared, delirious Admiral Rozhestvensky, who had abandoned the *Suvorov* before it sank. A Japanese destroyer captured him later that day.

In winning one of history's biggest naval battles, comparable in scope and significance to Admiral Horatio Nelson's victory at Trafalgar, Togo had lost a sum of three torpedo boats.

Word reached St. Petersburg the next day.

On the morning of May 16, the frozen surface of the Neva River was breaking up. From the quays and surrounding streets, it sounded as if some invisible force was striking the ice with a giant ax. First, cracks had appeared across the surface, then gaps widened between chunks of ice. The river's surface, a smooth blanket of white throughout the winter, was now crowded with clumps of soot-gray ice. Slowly, the current began to move these enormous floes downriver. They collided, spun, and broke apart into smaller pieces, loosening the stubborn ice on the riverbanks. In the weeks ahead, the Neva's flow would finally run clear into the Gulf of Finland. It was a relentless, inevitable process.

Fifteen miles south of St. Petersburg that same morning, Nicholas was horseback riding through Tsarskoye Selo. The air smelled of wet lilacs. Nicholas treasured his country estate. Set behind a tall iron fence and guarded by mounted Cossacks, Tsarskoye Selo was a paradise far removed from the city's chaos. On the eight-hundred-acre park where Nicholas galloped stood two palaces with extensive gardens, a zoo, triumphal arches, numerous chapels, paths weaving through forest groves, an artificial lake dotted with sailboats — even a Chinese pagoda and Turkish baths.

Nicholas finished his ride in front of Alexander Palace, where he had retreated after the Blessing of the Waters ceremony in January. Built a century before, the hundred-room palace was modest compared to the nearby Catherine Palace, which rivaled Versailles in size and opulence. Even so, Nicholas and his family were not at a loss for luxury amidst the long gilded halls and mauve boudoirs lit with crystal chandeliers and scented with fresh-cut flowers. There, hundreds of smartly dressed servants tended to their needs. As Nicholas walked through the palace that morning, however, the luxurious surroundings must have been lost on him. He desperately awaited news of Rozhestvensky's squadron.

The night before, he had shut himself away with his war council in the walnut-paneled study, poring over charts to ascertain where the fleet could be. His naval minister, Admiral Avelan, had reassured him that even if Togo attempted to elude the Russian fleet, Rozhestvensky would draw the Japanese out completely, even if he had to bombard one of their ports. Such was the bravado of Nicholas's inner circle.

Wild rumors ran throughout St. Petersburg. Some talked of a great Japanese victory. Others said that the Russian fleet had arrived in Vladivostok unscathed; the newsboys in St. Petersburg were already selling that story in the streets. But if Nicholas believed every wire report or consul message, then Rozhestvensky had already successfully waged his fight a month before in the Strait of Malacca off Indochina, and the tsar's worries were over.

But they were not; he was very worried. The past four and a half months had trampled his hope for a quiet, peaceful year. On January 9, three days after he escaped death on the Neva, 120,000 workers and their families, dressed in their Sunday best, had converged on the Winter Palace to petition him to ease their oppression. The defenseless crowd, carrying icons and his own portrait, refused to disperse, and his soldiers led cavalry charges against them, killing 130 and wounding many more. "Bloody Sunday," many were calling it.

Mayhem erupted in the days and weeks that followed. As one of Nicholas's faithful described it at the time: "Strikes are rolling over Russia as feathergrass over the steppe, outrunning each other, from Petersburg to Baku, from Warsaw to the heart of Siberia. Everybody is engaged . . . workingmen, students, railway-conductors, professors, cigarette-makers, pharmacists, lawyers, barbers, shop-clerks, telegraphists, schoolboys . . . The atmosphere is overcharged. . . . People cross themselves asking 'What is going to happen? What is going to happen?'" In the countryside, Nicholas's "dear" peasants either ransacked their landowners' manor houses or simply torched them to the ground. Most high officials feared for their lives. On February 4, a terrorist assassinated the governor-general of Moscow, Nicholas's uncle, Grand Duke Sergei, by throwing a bomb into his carriage as he left the Kremlin. Noblemen-turned-liberals pressed for a voice in ruling the country. Meanwhile, revolutionaries made it clear they would be satisfied only with the tsar's head. By May, even though Nicholas could not expect outright victory against Japan, he had to question what would happen within Russia if Rozhestvensky failed.

As he walked through Alexander Palace after his ride, Nicholas received his first reliable piece of information, a cable from the captain of the cruiser *Almaz,* which had managed to elude the Japanese and had recently arrived in Vladivostok. He reported that the *Suvorov,* the *Oslyabya,* and the cruiser *Ural* were lost and the battleship *Alexander* crippled. The *Almaz* had departed the Korea Strait before the battle had ended, but no other ships were in Vladivostok. The captain asked in his cable, "Could it be that none of the squadron's ships has reached Vladivostok?" It was inconceivable that all the others had been lost.

Over the next two days, however, the terrible facts of the battle arrived from the Far East. History has recorded different anecdotes depicting Nicholas's reaction to the developing news. One account had him at a court dinner receiving a telegram about the fleet, taking out his gold cigarette case, and having his master of ceremonies announce, "His Imperial Majesty permits smoking." In another story, he was riding on the imperial train with his minister of war and reacted to the grim reports with élan, formulating new plans for the war within minutes. Still another had him opening the dispatch while playing tennis. "What a terrible disaster," he apparently said, then was handed his racket and finished his game.

One or none of these may be true, but Nicholas was indeed famous for retreating into himself, never exposing his emotions when dealing with problems. Yet in his diary, usually reserved for pedantic accounts of his meals, leisure activities, and the weather, he was forthcoming. On May 16 and 17, he was "depressed" and frustrated at the inadequate, often contradictory news. On May 18, he wrote of a "difficult, painful, and sad" feeling in his soul. The next evening, he seemed to come to terms with the truth: "Now finally the awful news about the destruction of almost the entire squadron in the battle has been confirmed. Rozhestvensky himself is a captive!" In the same entry, he lamented how the gorgeous spring day had only deepened his sorrow.

Government ministers, liberal groups, exiled revolutionaries, and world leaders rushed to assign blame, forward their agenda, and predict the tsar's political future. The Russian and international press followed every move, often unabashedly pushing their own viewpoint. Yet nobody spoke directly for the roughly 4,830 sacrificed at the Battle of Tsushima, nor for twice that number wounded and captured. Until, that is, a band of sailors from the Black Sea Fleet made their voices heard.

# 2

AFANASY MATYUSHENKO, a torpedo quartermaster of the battleship *Potemkin,* climbed the steep incline of Malakhov Hill, east of Sevastopol, on the morning of June 10, 1905. Now covered with cypress and acacia trees, the hill was once a wasteland pocked with mines and fortified trenches, the site of a 349-day siege of Russian forces by the British and French during the Crimean War. That conflict had left the entire Black Sea Fleet scuttled in the harbor. Only a scarred remnant of the tower that had defended the hill fifty years before remained.

By the hill's crest, Matyushenko came across a woman resting against a tree. "Do you have any water to drink?" he asked.

"Go straight ahead. Turn right at the spring," she answered, in code.

After a few minutes, following a narrow path that was nearly lost in the underbrush, Matyushenko heard voices and smelled the drift of cigarette smoke through the trees. Finally, he came to a clearing by one of the graveyards on the hill. Over one hundred sailors in white-and-blue-striped jerseys and a handful of men and women in street clothes stood in the clearing, speaking among themselves. This was a secret meeting of Tsentralka, the revolutionary sailor organization. Scattered about the surrounding area, sailors were on the lookout for the police or naval patrols, who were desperately trying to capture any Tsentralka members.

Vice Admiral Grigory Chukhnin, the Black Sea Fleet commander, had made it clear in speeches aboard each ship that he considered any revolutionaries among his sailors to be a disease like leprosy: they needed to be cut out before their ideas spread. He ordered frequent, surprise searches of crew quarters, looking for sailors with seditious literature. His officers kept constant watch for secret meetings. Spies and informants were everywhere. Even a ship's priest was discovered trying to flush out those sympathetic to revolution, asking sailors during confession, "And now, my child, who do you feel malice toward . . . maybe your officers insult you?" Sailors suspected of revolutionary activities were transferred off battleships to auxiliary ships such as transport or training vessels. Those caught with literature or conducting propaganda campaigns were imprisoned and often sent to hard labor camps.

For Matyushenko, looking down on Sevastopol from the clearing, this was a risk he accepted in order to fight against the tsar and the type of life forced on him in the navy. The base of the Black Sea Fleet stood in the heavily fortified northern section of the city. While many of the captains lived in private houses, Matyushenko and the others were packed like cattle into poorly ventilated barracks, suffering nightly swarms of bedbugs and rats. The windows were barred and their beds were little better than planks of wood. Latrine pipes leaked filth between the walls, and the brackish river water they showered in left its own stench and a dirty film on their skin. Although the "august city," as Sevastopol was nicknamed, was primarily a military town, evidenced by the seven battleships and host of destroyers, torpedo boats, and auxiliary vessels anchored in the harbor, a sign on the city's main boulevard read: NO ENTRY TO DOGS. LOWER RANKS PROHIBITED.

These oppressions aside, the obliteration of Rozhestvensky's fleet forcefully reminded Matyushenko and his fellow revolutionaries that they were struggling for the right cause. Some had friends who had died in the battle, and the sailors understood better than anyone the incompetent and reckless leadership that had sent so many to their graves. It was also clear to them that they might be next. "If we must sacrifice our lives against the Japanese," one Black Sea Fleet sailor noted after learning of Tsushima, "we might as well sacrifice ourselves for the liberation of Russia." Matyushenko, one of the fleet's early revolutionaries, spread this sentiment among the sailors.

Three days before the meeting on Malakhov Hill, an incident in Sevastopol proved to Matyushenko that sailors throughout the fleet were prepared to revolt. When some garrisoned soldiers in the Sevastopol fortress struck out against their officers, Vice Admiral Chukhnin ordered his ships in the harbor to prepare to shell the fortress. Crews aboard two of the battleships refused the command. On the *Holy Trinity,* a sailor informed his watch officer, "Enough blood, we won't fire at those who protest. We ask you, Your Excellency, to inform the commander that we won't fire. Are the soldiers not our brothers?" On the *Ekaterina II,* the crew threatened the officers that they would scuttle the ship before firing on the fortress. Although the garrison commander managed to quell the unrest on his own and seventeen sailors were arrested for their disobedience, the incident showed the strength of feeling among the crews. Soon after, Tsentralka called its members together.

From the beginning, the meeting on the hillside was combative. Usually at these gatherings, the sailors sang revolutionary songs, decided organizational tactics, talked politics with workers and local leaders from various revolutionary parties, and vented their frustrations with their officers. On occasion, they would draft resolutions demanding an end to the war and stating their goals. In March, they had proclaimed these goals in detail in a document called "The Resolution of the Black Sea Sailors," revealing their hopes for the "abolition of the autocratic regime and the creation of a democratic republic." This republic was to be led by a constituent assembly, with representatives elected by the direct, equal, secret, and universal vote of the people.

These were noble ambitions — and treasonous in substance — but writing resolutions was only the first step toward realizing such goals. Today, however, the meeting participants were to decide, after months of debate, whether to take action and launch a fleetwide mutiny to begin the revolution.

Everyone wanted to be heard; few wished to move toward consensus. Some revolutionary leaders talked only of theory — how "the revolution can't be made. . . . It must happen on its own." Others spoke of boldness and armed uprisings as if no lives would be put at risk by choosing this path. Matyushenko despised this back-and-forth general talk, but he was quiet. A radical from Sevastopol named Pyotr argued that a fleetwide uprising was premature. With Chukhnin purging the ranks of revolutionaries even as their group met, Pyotr urged delaying their plans until their numbers were strengthened. His words were met with shouts of protest from all quarters, each voice trying to drown out the others.

Then Aleksandr Petrov, a machinist recently expelled from the *Ekaterina II* after its crew disobeyed the order to fire on the fortress, stood to speak. Tall, with a broad, square face, Petrov held his chin high as if he had been born an aristocrat. From a family of clerks in Kazan, the twenty-three-year-old machinist had benefited from a proper education and from older siblings who had versed him in revolutionary politics and songs from a young age. Once conscripted into the navy, he set about agitating sailors, and his battleship was widely known as the "Red Kate" because of his success.

"We see how difficult it is to create a general uprising. After starting in one place, it risks losing momentum by dying down in another," Petrov began, the words coming easily; they had been waiting for years. "The army will only go over to the people's side when they have confidence in the general uprising. For this it's necessary that the uprising engulf a vast region. And don't we have this vast region? The Black Sea?! Who, if not we, the sailors, after launching a revolution in Sevastopol, might carry it over into the Caucasus and from there to Odessa to Nikolayev? Who, if not we, will be able to immediately draw in the army to take part in the revolution?"

Many others echoed his words. Next to Matyushenko, his friend and fellow *Potemkin* sailor Grigory Vakulenchuk called out: "To delay means to fail the revolution. At this very moment, everywhere, workers and peasants are striking out. We must join the common fight."

The debate swayed in their favor, and the sailors swiftly shifted the discussion to tactics. Many agreed that the mutiny should occur right after the fleet came together for maneuvers off Tendra Island later that month. Matyushenko wanted to move sooner. "Why wait for the journey out to sea?" he asked the gathering. "The mutiny must be started immediately. Tomorrow itself!" But he was shouted down for his usual impetuosity. When the discussion turned to the ship that should signal the start of the uprising, Matyushenko pitched the *Potemkin*. But most felt that the battleship *Rostislav* had symbolic strength as the fleet's flagship.

At the meeting's end, the Tsentralka sailors congratulated themselves on their plan of action: when the fleet met on June 21 and the

*Rostislav* fired from its main battery, the fleetwide mutiny would begin. "Here's to the tsar meeting his father sooner than he thought!" called out a sailor as the meeting disbanded. The clearing emptied, and the sailors returned on foot to Sevastopol, Matyushenko among them. Although his ideas had not carried the day, he was glad that the Tsentralka leaders had at last moved to join the revolution in deed. He had set this goal for himself since his earliest days.

In 1879, in a hut with clay walls and a thatched roof, Afanasy Nikolayevich Matyushenko was born. He shared the living quarters, a space only fifteen feet by fifteen feet, with his parents and five siblings. The hut contained a stove for cooking, a large table for eating, and, in the corner, icons to pray before. The family slept on top of the stove and on bare wooden benches that ran along the walls. During the long winters, they squeezed in their pigs, calves, and geese. The door and windows always were shut to keep out the cold, and the air grew almost poisonous with the stench of the animals.

Outside the hut, the village of Dergachi in "Little Russia," or the Ukraine, was like every other peasant community in the empire, run by village elders. The peasants lived a communal existence isolated from the rest of the world. They dressed in the same bast shoes and cotton tunics that peasants had worn for centuries. Roads leading into the village were often mired in mud, and any outsider who did enter found little of interest. The village was stripped of most trees and bushes. The well for drinking water stood near the horse pond. The surrounding fields of wheat, barley, beets, and other crops were divided into thin, overworked strips of land; each village household tilled some. It was a violent, primitive life based on communal responsibility, attachment to the land, and a deep-seated fear of authority, whether held by the elders, the tsar, or God.

Afanasy's father, Nikolai, was born a serf, bound to his landlord until the Emancipation of 1861, one of several reforms initiated by Alexander II in the wake of the Crimean War. The grant of freedom came as a great burden on an already threadbare existence. The redemption payments Nikolai owed to the government for his land were high, and since he was bound to the village council, Nikolai could not sow the crops he wanted. Nor could he leave the village to find other work without the council's permission.

When Afanasy was a young boy, his father couldn't support his family by farming. He became a shoemaker, earning barely enough to eke out an existence. At nine years of age, Afanasy enrolled in a Sunday church school to learn to read, an uncommon (albeit expanding) opportunity for peasant children at the time. Afanasy was headstrong and eager to learn, so his parents gave him the chance to attend the school. He split his free time between reading and fishing, but both activities were taken from him at the start of the great famine of 1891, when grain fields throughout Russia turned to dust, leaving whole villages devastated by starvation and diseases such as cholera and typhus. His father, always a heavy drinker, became a useless drunkard. Afanasy had to work to help feed his family. He was twelve when he began repairing shoes in the dark room after his father had passed out.

At fifteen, Afanasy decided that there had to be more to life. Eight miles southeast of the village, the city of Kharkov was rapidly industrializing and served as southern Russia's transportation hub. He found a job during the day as a janitor, then as an oilman at the steam-engine depot — one of the legions of peasants who followed a similar path in order to survive. There he experienced the life of an urban worker, breathing the black smoke that spewed from factory chimneys. When foremen were displeased with the pace of work, they struck the faces of their men; when the workers left for the day, they were searched, as if they were assumed to be petty criminals. They had few identifiable rights. Most, like Matyushenko, worked six days a week, twelve or more hours a day, and barely took home six rubles a month. (A decent dinner at one of the city's hotels cost two rubles.) At the day's end, men, women, and children left the factories sallow and weary, only to head to overcrowded barracks with low ceilings and lavatory stalls not fit for animals. The conditions crippled one out of seven workers with a serious illness every year.

For his part, Matyushenko returned to his village every night. There he found moments to still be a teenager, reading books he had borrowed from the library near the depot. He also learned to play music. With the spare kopecks he did not give his family, he bought an accordion. After work, he played his new instrument to the delight of his friends, who would sing and dance to the songs.

One night, a village watchman living nearby grew tired of the accordion. He marched over and confiscated the instrument. Matyushenko tried to fight him, risking arrest, but his father held him back and then pleaded with the watchman not to report the incident. For the rest of his life, Matyushenko remembered his feeling of helpless rage. A few months later, he attempted revenge. Groups of boys were not allowed to gather at night for fear of mischief, and it was the watchmen's job to break up any such gatherings. One summer's night, Matyushenko and several other boys lured a patrol with boisterous singing and then ambushed them with sticks and rocks. The watchmen ran away but later discovered that Matyushenko was the ringleader. They had him arrested and then beat the teenager senseless in a prison cell. When Matyushenko finally awakened, the welts on his face stung to the touch. A deep bitterness welled up within him.

In Kharkov, Matyushenko began to stay after his shift's end to meet with other depot workers and talk about the injustices they saw all around them. Once he even invited them back to his home in Dergachi. The talk around the table turned to how the tsar must be overthrown. Matyushenko's father overheard the discussion from outside the hut and later angrily took his son aside.

"It's not possible that there will be no tsar. It will never happen. Remember, son, just as there is no world without God, there can be no land without the tsar!"

Matyushenko looked at his father and at the rags he wore for clothes. "Do you know the tsar owns more land than anyone in Russia? Do you know there are other countries that are *not* governed by a tsar, and that the people in those countries live better than we do?"

A few months shy of eighteen years, Matyushenko had already left his father and his traditions far behind. There was a world outside Dergachi, and even outside Kharkov, one that he had read about in stories of the French Revolution, Oliver Cromwell, and the adventures of Giuseppe Garibaldi. Like many young men who had come to the city from their villages, he wanted to better himself. He had made friends with people who had suffered terribly, like him, and they had ideas about life that relied on reason and independence rather than blind faith in the tsar's benevolence. Some were willing to fight against rich landlords and factory owners.

In a naive manner, Matyushenko shared this insight with his child-hood friends back in the village. Dergachi's elders heard about this blasphemous talk and arranged for his arrest. The village watchmen came to take custody of him on a Sunday afternoon after church. Matyushenko ran into the church's bell tower to escape. His pursu-ers followed, and he climbed down the rope attached to the bell. His friends screamed, "Fire!" emptying the church directly into the watchmen's path, and Matyushenko slipped away. Unable to return to the village or to go to the Kharkov depot, he left for Odessa. In 1896, he was already on the run, with scarcely a hope of going back.

Several months later, after working in Odessa's port, Matyushenko signed up to be a coalman on a steamboat traveling to Vladivostok. It was a dirty, thankless job deep within the recesses of the ship, but at least he was traveling, witnessing life beyond his village. The steamboat stopped in Turkey, Egypt, and other ports along the way before reaching its destination in the Far East. After his arrival in Vladivostok, Matyushenko spent two years in the port city, working as a machinist assistant on the railroad. He endured debilitating work hours and conditions similar to those in Kharkov.

As Matyushenko matured, he increasingly resented being treated as ignorant chattel with no self-worth. He was now very well read, had learned many new skills since leaving Odessa, had seen more of the world than most, and felt that he deserved some respect from his bosses. But nothing changed: he had no rights or means to redress grievances. He shared the disgust of the worker who said, "We're not even recognized as people, but considered as rubbish that could be thrown out at any moment." In 1898, Matyushenko decided to return to Dergachi to see his family. He traveled by train across Siberia and the breadth of the Russia. On his arrival at his home village, the bitter-ness he first felt after his beating years before had hardened into a ha-tred of the poverty and repression he witnessed everywhere.

After a brief visit, he left his family again and moved to Rostov-on-Don, taking a job as a dockworker. He soon found those who felt the way he did: workers who spoke of revolution. They invited him to join a study circle — a more organized but clandestine form of the discussion groups he had known in Kharkov, where they read Marx and pamphlets by exiled intellectuals between toasts of "Down

with the tsar!" and "Long live socialism!" The circle's leader was
Vladimir Petrov, a future Bolshevik leader. With the aim of bringing
Matyushenko fully to their side, they indoctrinated him in the history
of revolutionary thought, pushing Social Democrat views as the best
path to revolution.

Russia had been moving along this path since a handful of nobles attempted to install a constitutional government after Alexander I's
death in 1825. These nobles, who plotted "between the claret and
champagne" — as Pushkin characterized it — were executed for their
trouble. In the eighty years that followed, a cast of Russian revolutionary leaders emerged. Primarily intellectuals, they steeped themselves
in the study of European philosophical movements (and the French
Revolutions of 1789 and 1848) and then laid plans to remove the tsar
and create a social utopia.

Early radicals such as Sergei Nechayev, who at age nine had worked
in a factory, called for a dedicated group of revolutionaries to seize
control of the government and then see to the people's well-being.
Rivers of blood would have to flow, since a revolutionary needed to
"destroy everyone who stands in his way," as Nechayev wrote. He em-
bodied this ruthlessness: when a member of his organization argued
against his putschist strategies, Nechayev and three others pummeled,
strangled, and then shot him.

But by the time his imprisonment for this crime ended, Nechayev's
ideas had lost favor. Another set of intellectuals — this time inspired
by Aleksandr Herzen, an exiled Russian writer — turned to a bottom-
up approach to realizing social revolution. They divined that the
source of the people's freedom was the Russian peasant. In the early
1870s, students bent on revolution journeyed to the countryside to
persuade the peasants to take up their cause, but they found them
hostile (occasionally physically so) to outsiders. Some radical leaders
returned to violence as the means to gain power; others found enlight-
enment in Karl Marx's *Capital*. Its focus on the industrial working
class (the proletariat) as the force that could bring about a socialist
state had a profound effect, particularly given the failure to marshal
the peasants to the cause.

But Russia had not yet evolved into the mature capitalist state that, according to Marx's theory, must precede the people's liberation. Radical intellectuals, once again, tailored his ideas into a plan for action in Russia. In 1895, Georgy Plekhanov paved the way with his theory of a two-stage revolution. First, the proletariat would ally itself with the middle-class bourgeoisie, who were advancing the capitalist state, to fight against the tsar. Once the workers had gained democratic freedoms — namely, the ability to organize and speak freely — and the market economy had sufficiently developed, then the revolution's second stage would occur, leading to a socialist state. There would be no need for the terror campaigns and wide-scale executions propounded by Nechayev.

Never a cohesive group, radical Russian intellectuals began to splinter into separate, competing factions near the end of the century, frustrated that the tsarist government maintained its hold on Russia. Several revolutionary leaders, Plekhanov among them, formed the Social Democratic Party to enlighten the workers with propaganda and politicize them with labor strikes, creating a revolutionary vanguard that would grow and grow until they realized the two-stage revolution. While the Social Democrats concentrated on the workers, the Socialist Revolutionaries believed in the power of the peasants to bring about revolution, combining this with terror attacks to undermine the government. Other groups fought strictly for the improvement of the workers' lot, rather than using them as a means of revolution. Still others abandoned their more radical ideas, hoping to establish a parliamentary democracy: liberal reform rather than revolution was their new slogan.

A young firebrand named Lenin would have none of this tempered approach. He dissected his opponents' arguments in his writings and with the sheer force of his personality. Compromise with the bourgeois liberals, which some of his own Social Democrats believed in, was anathema to Lenin, as was compromise with anybody else, for that matter, especially those seeking only reform. Lenin argued that Russia was already prepared for revolution. To lead the workers in overthrowing the tsar and bringing about the socialist state, the Social Democrats needed the leadership of an iron-fisted group of devoted revolutionaries. Otherwise, the revolution would disintegrate. This hard-line view eventually split the Social Democrats into two groups:

the Bolsheviks, who rallied around Lenin, and the Mensheviks, a largely leaderless faction who believed in a more democratic revolution, fearing their rival's path would simply descend into another form of dictatorship.

As an uprooted peasant worker who loathed authoritarian rule and enlightened himself through books and study circles, Matyushenko was an ideal candidate for the revolution's rank and file. Yet the philosophical tracts and competing ideologies discussed in Rostov sounded like empty talk to him. In an abstract way, he understood that the tsar was the source of the oppression he had experienced as a peasant, then as a worker, but he had not yet joined the revolutionary cause. Only after coming face-to-face with the instruments of the tsar's regime did he come to despise it enough to risk his life to see it overthrown. Then, on his twenty-first birthday in May 1900, he received his draft notice.

Bound by conscription laws, Matyushenko returned to his birthplace at the summer's end to receive his seven-year sentence to active service: in the army or the navy, assigned by drawing lots. With no money to bribe his way to an exemption and no faith in "wise old women" to cast a spell that would make the doctors turn him away, he had to accept his obligation. In his village, the evening before they drew lots, the scene was riotous: others of his age drowned themselves in vodka, chased girls, and danced in the streets between the farewell dinners thrown by their families. It was as if the young men were celebrating the last day before their doom. Some in Dergachi were old enough to remember the old twenty-five-year conscription requirement and seeing their fellow serfs led away in chains, funeral chants following them as they left the village. To a young man like Matyushenko, however, even seven years seemed a lifetime. One could have forgiven him for feeling "naked, exposed, and trembling" — one recruit's thoughts on departure day.

The next day Matyushenko and the other men from his village, along with their families, traveled by wagon into Kharkov. The elders had given each of them a quart of vodka and five rubles as sustenance for the days ahead. Many arrived drunk as idiots. At the drafting center, a city clerk called out their names one by one. Mothers

threw themselves on the ground, wailing for their sons. Finally, Matyushenko heard his name, stepped forward, and drew his lot — the
navy. Well, he thought, at least he already had some experience on the
sea and liked its open spaces.

He arrived at Sevastopol by train, carrying everything he owned
slung over his shoulder in a canvas bag. At the base, an officer assigned him to the Thirty-sixth Naval Company of the Black Sea Fleet.
Surrounded by former peasants and workers who had known the
same brutal life that he had, he gave his oath of allegiance: "I promise
and do hereby swear before the Almighty God, before His Holy Gos-
pels, to serve His Imperial Majesty, the Supreme Autocrat, truly and
faithfully, to obey him in all things, and to defend his dynasty, without
sparing my body, until the last drop of my blood."

At that moment, Matyushenko stepped into a different world, one
designed, as fellow Black Sea sailor Ivan Lychev wrote, to "dislodge
every last bit of humanity from one's soul." First he became ac-
quainted with how he was to be addressed over the next seven years:
by the Russian *ty*, or "you," commonly used to get the attention of
young boys or animals, instead of the formal *vy*. His father, a former
serf, was once addressed in this way by his master. Then Matyushenko
learned how to address officers according to rank: "Your Honor,"
"Your Excellency," "Your Most High Radiance," and so on, up the
chain of command. To spare himself punishment, he had to answer
his superiors with exactly prescribed phrases in a loud voice: "Quite
so, Your Honor," "Not at all, Your Honor," "Glad to serve you, Your
Honor." Minor violations were met with a rifle butt to the head, a slap
across the face, or an order to stand guard with a heavy sack hung
from the shoulders for eight hours before running barefoot up and
down a ship's rope ladder until the feet bled. If really angered, an officer could always order a discreet flogging or fifteen days of isolation
in a dank, unlit cement cell. In the Russian navy, discipline meant
fearing the corporal's staff more than the enemy itself.

The four-month training regimen consisted of long days and nights
of marching, performing parade-ground drills, learning basic naval
skills, and memorizing useless details and military ranks of the tsar's
extended family. Sailors said they aged decades in this short span of
time. Those from provinces unfortunate enough not to speak Russian

bore a heavier weight; they were struck mercilessly until they learned what was "right" and "left." Some understood only after a visit to the naval hospital.

Any hopes that new sailors such as Matyushenko had of finding relief in the barracks or mess halls were sadly dashed. The food amounted to gruel. "Breakfast of porridge, boiled in large iron kettles, lies there during the day fermenting into thick layers," grumbled a sailor in a letter home. "It is prepared from rotten grain, salt and water and gives one heartburn. . . . The bread cracks teeth, and its taste makes one's eyes burn." At dinner, the borscht, absent of all but the worst cuts of meat, if there was any at all, was likened to pigs' slop. If a sailor complained about the food, the unit doctor prescribed heavy doses of castor oil. As for the crowded, grotesquely maintained barracks, one never enjoyed a moment of privacy.

In the six hours per month that Matyushenko had off duty, he found himself restricted by rules seemingly intended to degrade him. First, he had to beg for a pass to leave the base, placing himself at the whim of whoever was on duty. Once in Sevastopol, he was forbidden to smoke in public, eat in restaurants, attend the theater, ride the tram, or sit in any train compartment other than third class. If he were to meet a girl in one of the few places he was allowed entrance to and they wanted to marry, regulations prohibited this throughout his entire term of service.

Then there were the "dragons," as Matyushenko quickly took to calling his officers. Almost to a rule, they came from noble families, though most were old naval families who had earned their titles through service. The navy typically attracted the worst of this lot, the ones who had failed to be accepted into a better-paying, more prestigious career outside the military. Those who chose to become officers often looked to the navy as a refuge from a changing Russia. In this branch of the military, strong, autocratic principles and old traditions still rigidly held sway. Naturally, there was plenty of room for womanizing, gambling, flagrant drunkenness, duels over injured honor, and outright theft, usually at the sailors' expense. Many officers were boorish tyrants with a cruel streak. They treated their sailors as serfs or as "wild animals" in need of taming, or sometimes a combination of the two.

Matyushenko weathered the four months of training, followed by a specialized course in torpedo machinery, and then he attended an advanced school for the same specialty near St. Petersburg. In 1902 he was promoted to quartermaster and assigned to the battleship *Potemkin,* then under construction at a Black Sea shipyard. Considered a fine, faithful sailor by his superiors, they selected him to serve on Nicholas II's 337-foot private yacht, the *Polar Star,* which the tsar used on his annual vacation in the region.

Since the day he arrived in Sevastopol as a new conscript, however, another Matyushenko was boiling up from within. A revolutionary was being forged under the strain of the persecution that he felt himself subjected to and witnessed around him, the persecution of those whom the officers called "scum" and "scoundrel" and "dirty peasant." Just like the radical intellectuals jailed in the tsar's prisons, Matyushenko found that the fight against Nicholas II had become personal and white hot. He despised how peasants and workers were robbed blind, then marched out to serve the regime that had done the stealing; he loathed how the officers who punished sailors for nothing expected obedience in return and how the tsar ordered his own troops to fire on their brothers and sisters. Then Matyushenko found a way to channel his fury when he met Ivan Yakhnovsky, a fellow sailor who was organizing his own fight against the tsar's navy with a printing press hidden in his father's basement and an ability to inspire.

Ivan Yakhnovsky had a square forehead and chin, brooding eyes, and an air of stoicism. As a metal caster at a locomotive-manufacturing plant in Kharkov (where his family had moved after facing starvation as peasants), he had joined a Social Democrat study circle, learned the art of agitation, and participated in several worker strikes, one resulting in his arrest. In summer 1902, he was drafted into the navy. His friends suggested going underground in Kharkov, but he had a different idea: enter the navy and bring sailors into the revolutionary struggle.

He found the fleet primed for his efforts. The Russian navy required many more literate, better-skilled individuals than the army did because of the complex technology involved in the modern battleship's operation. The navy needed machinists, boilermakers, pipe fitters, electricians, and telegraphers, not simply absent-minded deck hands. With this in mind, they specifically recruited workers from the cities (though they still drew many peasants because of the sheer number of sailors required). Often these workers had already been exposed to propaganda and were sympathetic to the revolutionaries, particularly since their officers treated them as peasants who had not seen a light bulb before their conscription. Furthermore, the nature of basic training, forcing conscripts to subjugate their individuality to work together, unified the sailors and gave them a common identity. Ironically, this perfectly laid the groundwork for revolutionary goals.

By this time, Matyushenko was unable to hide his disgust and must have been easy to spot as a potential agitator. He openly befriended several workers connected to revolutionary parties in Nikolayev. At the slightest provocation, he launched into tirades about "What truth could exist in our society under the existing rules when [the sailor] is considered to be a mere animal." Matyushenko also stood out because others looked to him as their protector. Whenever the sailors had to stand guard during the winter without a proper coat or boots, Matyushenko found the money, often his own, to buy them.

Soon after his arrival in the navy, Yakhnovsky formed a study circle and Matyushenko was one of the first to join. Matyushenko energetically took to the fight, often without concern for arrest while recruiting sailors. He would boldly walk into the lower decks where sailors slept and ask, "Is there anyone here from Kharkov?" If there was no reply, he turned to the nearest sailor to see where he was from. "Podol, really? My dear brother, I'm looking for someone from that area! How long have you been here?" Conversation came easily to him, and soon he would gather a group around him. Then he would begin to mention the harsh treatment of the sailors. After receiving a few nods in agreement, he would bring out illegal literature that could have gotten him hanged. "He was that brave," Yakhnovsky said.

Within months, the former Kharkov agitator and his first recruits developed a network of study circles, five to seven sailors in each, across the fleet. They smuggled illegal pamphlets and newspapers aboard in sacks of sugar or wrapped around their calves, later concealing them in lifeboats and under weapons caches until they were distributed. Often sailors would awaken to find pamphlets stuck under their pillows. They held meetings in the engine rooms, while swimming, and under the guise of prayer sessions. They devised signals to alert sailors of an approaching officer: a cigarette tossed into a water bucket or a rapid series of coughs. Even as the Black Sea Fleet command tried to stamp out their activities, the circles expanded. The leaders of each were connected through Tsentralka, which held group meetings, recruited speakers, coordinated dissemination of literature, cooperated with revolutionary groups in Sevastopol, and directed the overall activities of the sailors. By the time Yakhnovsky was arrested in mid-1904 and shipped off to prison, the revolutionary movement within the fleet had taken on a life of its own. The war with Japan and the arrival of Chukhnin, the Black Sea Fleet's new commander who instituted a harsh crackdown in discipline, only furthered their efforts.

Throughout, Matyushenko maintained his bold recruiting methods, somehow managing to never even come under suspicion. But the sailors knew his views. Some Tsentralka leaders feared his strident hatred of the regime. Nothing else seemed to matter to him, and if a sailor talked of anything but revolution, Matyushenko challenged his dedication or even accused him of being a spy.

Much of Tsentralka's work — and the strength of the movement — was focused on improving the sailor's lot: higher pay, better food, shorter conscription terms, abolition of salutes, and juries made up of their peers in courts-martial. Matyushenko, however, mostly spoiled for a fight. His loyalty as a Social Democrat was, at best, questionable. He followed his emotions, not ideological tracts. "To me every party looks good," he wrote. "The harder a party beats on the regime, the better it looks to me."

In those days, the revolutionary sailors spoke of Matyushenko's revolutionary fervor, raw temper, and inability to remain indifferent to injustice. Once when a petty officer was overzealous in berating a sailor, Matyushenko went instantly crimson in the face, his dark eyes narrowed, and his wiry frame tightened as if he was ready to throw a fist. No fear of authority or punishment held him back as he defended the sailor, speaking fast and harshly to the petty officer about treating the men under his command fairly. His fellow crew members loved Matyushenko for these qualities, but they did not speak of him as their leader.

For the rebels aboard the *Potemkin,* Matyushenko's close friend Grigory Vakulenchuk played that role, particularly after the life-and-death decision on the morning of June 10 to mutiny. Matyushenko might be the one to turn to if things got rough ("he would go through fire for his brother sailor," said one), but Vakulenchuk had the respect of all the men around him. With his distinguished black handlebar mustache, stentorian voice, and preternatural calm, he was a natural leader. Though near the end of his conscription term, he still risked himself for the other sailors. In effect, Matyushenko was Vakulenchuk's second in command.

When Matyushenko and the others returned to the naval base after the Tsentralka meeting, they had much to prepare before the fleetwide maneuvers a week and a half later. Apart from strategizing how to take over the ship — from seizing guns to manning the conning tower and engine rooms — they had, most important, to spread further propaganda among the sailors. Crew members sympathetic to their cause numbered 200 at most. Only 50 of these were absolutely reliable. Of the 763 sailors aboard the *Potemkin,* the majority were raw recruits, indifferent, or blindly faithful to the tsar's authority. By instinct they would follow their officers and petty officers (these former sailors, who had reenlisted and been promoted, were called "self-seekers" because their loyalties most often lay with their superiors and their own advancement). Therefore, the revolutionaries had to convert as many sailors as possible to their cause before departure from Sevastopol. Immediately setting to the task, stoker Fyodor Nikishkin, one of the better agitators, called for "Bible meetings" throughout the ship's crew.

The next day, June 11, the *Potemkin*'s captain, Yvgeny Golikov, informed his crew that they would be leaving early to test the ship's guns before fleet maneuvers. Then came another surprise. On the quarterdeck he announced the names of forty sailors to be removed from the *Potemkin* for reassignment; this came on the heels of a major reshuffling of the Black Sea Fleet's crews earlier that spring to disrupt revolutionary activities. He also dispatched a young officer who was sympathetic to that cause; someone must have betrayed their plans. Fortunately, of those expelled, the officers missed all but one of the *Potemkin*'s revolutionary leaders. Matyushenko and Vakulenchuk remained, although they worried about what Golikov might have planned for the ship once they departed. He obviously knew something was brewing.

Late that evening, in the dark of night, Vakulenchuk sent notes around the base barracks to his fellow Tsentralka leaders. From Yakhnovsky and other revolutionaries he had learned to write in cipher and glue messages inside book bindings. In this most important matter, the notes must not be seen by prying eyes. In them he urged that the *Potemkin* be elected to start the mutiny instead of the flagship *Rostislav*, much as Matyushenko had wanted. Taking this responsibility would help inspire more *Potemkin* sailors, and it would be critical to the fleetwide uprising for participants to see that the *Potemkin*, the most formidable battleship among them, was on their side. The strength of its guns outweighed the importance of a symbolic flagship.

By morning, Vakulenchuk and Matyushenko had their answer: the *Potemkin* would launch the revolt. Their orders were to prepare an advance list of officers and petty officers who might resist and to assign a sailor to deal with each in the mutiny's opening moments. The uprising should occur after the change of the watch at 1 A.M. and, most important, only after the entire fleet came together. Once they took over the ship, their orders then instructed that they "weigh anchor, move beyond the horizon, inform the rest of the crew of the event, and wait for daybreak. If any ships do not join the *Potemkin*, open fire on them." After the revolutionary squadron was formed, it would capture Sevastopol, marshal its forces, and move to bring down the tsar.

Some called the plan reckless, premature, and doomed to fail, but the alternative to sailors like Matyushenko — a torturous existence, death in the Far East, and continued oppression of their countrymen — was far worse to endure.

# 3

DOWN IN THE BOWELS of the *Potemkin,* the men shoveled coal into the furnaces and raised the steam. The cavernous engine room was illuminated by electric lights, but most of the machinists moved in the shadows cast by the enormous boilers and piston-rod engines, their uniforms soiled black, their eyes stinging from the slack in the coal. A mix of oil and water slicked the decks, and the noise made conversation a matter of hand gestures and shouts directly in the ear. As for the heat, the scattering of fans only helped concentrate blasts of moist, scalding air. Outside the engine room, sailors clambered about the decks, following the barked orders of their watch officers as they prepared for departure on Sunday afternoon, June 12, 1905. Finally the command came to weigh anchor.

"Anchor is starting!" Its chain ground through the hawsehole. "Anchor away!" Sailors hosed off the silt that clung to the chain. "Anchor in sight. . . . Anchor is clear." Then a screech of metal against metal. "Anchor secured!"

Bells rang in the conning tower, alerting the captain that the battleship was ready. Fifty-one years old, with a cone-shaped beard and the short, thick neck of a bulldog, Captain First Rank Yvgeny Golikov appeared at ease, speaking with his officers and the few visitors who had come from St. Petersburg to witness the testing of the ship's guns. But he was far from calm, aware of the stirrings of a rebellion among his crew — perhaps even plans for a mutiny.

He had received an anonymous letter alluding to the rebellion, and another fleet captain had found a leaflet aboard his ship, warning him: "Remember, the hour of revenge is coming. Our hands won't

shake when we tighten the loop around your neck." Golikov had
tried to expel all the discontented, revolutionary-minded sailors his
officers had targeted, but it was a scattershot approach, since they
had little information about who was in charge. The day before,
Golikov had asked for a shore leave to avoid the fleet maneuvers, but
Chukhnin denied his request on insufficient grounds. Meanwhile,
three of Golikov's warrant officers suspiciously took sick leave only
hours before departure, suggesting they knew exactly what awaited
them if they went on the voyage. There was nothing Golikov could do
other than keep a close watch on his men and take the *Potemkin* to
Tendra Island.

"Low ahead. . . . Right full rudder" came his command from the
conning tower.

Slowly the battleship began to move forward, its screws churning
through the water and causing a dull vibration through the hull. Sig-
nalmen exchanged protocols with the Black Sea Fleet command.
Drummers and buglers played on the quarterdeck. Those not on duty
gathered along the rails and waved their caps in farewell. A crowd had
assembled along the quays of Sevastopol to watch the battleship's departure. Wives and lovers blew kisses goodbye to their men. Children
watched in awe as the behemoth cut through the water, the bronze
double-headed eagles on the bow looking to spy the way. As the
*Potemkin* gathered more speed, the white and blue–crossed St. Andrew's flag on the mast went stiff in the breeze, and water began to
slap against the sides of the ship. The three square funnels belched
thick dark clouds of smoke into the clear blue sky.

The *Potemkin* steamed out of the harbor and past the Kher-
sonessky Lighthouse, on a northwest course for Tendra Island. A
torpedo boat followed in escort, looking like a child's toy compared
to the *Potemkin*'s massive black hull. Soon the white houses of
Sevastopol disappeared from view, then Konstantin Fort, and finally
St. Vladimir Church faded into the blur of green hills cradling the city
on the Crimean Peninsula. As the battleship ventured farther into the
Black Sea, squalls blew, clapping canvases and whistling through the
handrails. The winds strengthened and violent waves crashed against
the ship. The *Potemkin* drove easily forward, unperturbed, a titan in
the water.

• • •

Named after the beloved minister of Catherine the Great, Prince
Potemkin Tavrichesky, the 12,600-ton battleship was a triumph of
modern shipbuilding and without peer in the Russian navy.

Ever since the Minoans of Crete ruled the seas with twenty-oared
galleys in 1500 B.C., battleships had been slowly evolving. Minoan
sailors carried spears for fighting, so vessels fitted with rams marked
a significant advance in early naval warfare; the sleek fleets of the
ancient Greeks followed, their two-hundred-oared triremes operating
in tactical formation. Then Alexander the Great contributed stone-
throwing catapults to sea battle. By the time Peter the Great founded
the Russian navy in the 1690s, three-rigged warships with batteries of
cannons were squaring off in battles that could determine whether an
empire rose or fell. In the nineteenth century, wooden-hulled men-of-
war gave way to steam-driven ironclads, and then those built of steel.
Decade after decade, rulers built bigger ships with greater destructive
force. By the time Nicholas II ascended to the throne in 1894, the essential relation between naval might and a nation's strength, codified
by Alfred Thayer Mahan in his famous treatise *The Influence of Sea
Power upon History,* had gained universal favor. Nicholas doubled the
expenditures his already profligate father had allocated to the navy,
giving Russia the world's third-strongest fleet (albeit a distant third
behind England and France) before the war with Japan had begun.

The battleship *Potemkin* was the apex of a rebuilding program for
the Black Sea Fleet after its complete destruction in the Crimean War.
In 1897, Russian engineer Aleksandr Shott studied several Russian
battleships, including the American-made *Retvizan,* and improved on
the best elements of each in his design for the *Potemkin.* Although it
would most likely be used to attack land-based forts around the Black
Sea, the battleship was designed to handle itself equally well in sea
battles. Built in Nikolayev, its hull was sprinkled with holy water and
launched on September 26, 1900 — the same year as the light cruiser
*Aurora,* a ship that would play its own role in the coming revolution.
Over the next several years, the *Potemkin* was outfitted with engines,
guns, and operating equipment.

It was faster, better protected, more technologically advanced, and
armed with stronger guns than any other battleship in the Black Sea
Fleet. Its two 10,600-horsepower steam-driven engines, powered by
twenty-two boilers, drove at a top speed of seventeen knots. Twelve

inches of Krupp steel protected its turrets, nine inches of the same its belt line. In terms of firepower, it outclassed the USS *Maine* and HMS *Illustrious* of the same period. Its two twin-armored turrets, fore and aft, carried four twelve-inch guns that could decimate enemies with seven-hundred-pound shells at a range of over six miles. Along its 371 feet, it boasted a secondary battery of sixteen six-inch quick-firing guns, fourteen three-inch twelve-pound guns, an assembly of machine guns, torpedo tubes, mine-laying equipment, and two torpedo launch craft. The *Potemkin* was an armed fortress, and with its three yellow funnels sitting forward amidship, it looked like a terrible beast, crouched and eager to attack.

In October 1903, it took its first sea trials. Two months later, Captain Golikov took command and shepherded the ship to completion in April 1905. The ship's log specifically records two bad omens during this period: first, a towline ripped the double-headed eagles, the symbol of the Romanov family, from the ship's bow; second, Nicholas's portrait fell off the wall in Golikov's cabin, shattering the glass in the frame. It is unknown whether Golikov took much meaning from these omens, but the captaincy of the *Potemkin* was to be his final post and the journey to Tendra Island his final voyage.

While the battleship moved out of Sevastopol, Golikov turned to his second officer, Ippolit Gilyarovsky. "Once away from the revolutionary dockworkers, we'll manage to get rid of these heretics in our own ranks." How little he understood the crew after two years at their command. Neither as stringent a disciplinarian as his fleet commander, Vice Admiral Chukhnin, nor as vicious as his second officer, Gilyarovsky, Captain Golikov was, in a word, middling.

Born into a high-ranking noble family from Moldova (his father was an architect and state councilor), Yvgeny Golikov joined the Naval Cadet School at eighteen years of age in 1872. At that time, professors continued to glorify the age of the sail, looking down on steam-driven warships and the "mechanics" who drove them. He studied mathematics, navigation, three languages, and leadership techniques — a curriculum as frozen in time as the Table of Ranks that Peter the Great had instituted for nobles in 1722. Graduating a guarde-marine, he was promoted to ensign after the typical two-year period and then found himself on board a mine-cutter in the Russo-Turkish War in

1877, guarding a supply bridge over the Danube. It was the only action he would see.

Once the war had ended, Golikov served for the next twelve years aboard the tsar's yachts (first for Alexander II, then his son), gaining little naval experience but rather a good deal of the royal family's favor during their long vacation voyages. He counted among his close friends Konstantin Nikolayevich, cousin of Tsarevich Nicholas. Despite this advantage, he ascended at only a typical pace through the ranks, remaining a lieutenant for eleven years until promoted to captain second rank in 1892. Seven subsequent years aboard a grab bag of transport vessels, steamers, and coast-defense ironclads earned him first-rank status. After several naval staff positions, he was appointed to the *Potemkin*. At the time, he preened because of the "special favor" he enjoyed from Nicholas II and the General Admiral of the navy, Aleksei Aleksandrovich, and he was festooned with twelve separate medals and ribbons, most of them honorary. Golikov had never distinguished himself, in service or ability, but naval promotion was based on seniority and loyalty to the tsar. In his new position, he earned one hundred times a typical sailor's yearly salary.

When Golikov took command of the *Potemkin,* the Black Sea Fleet was beginning to face a crisis: the spread of revolutionaries (or "half-educated Godless traitors," as the senior flagman called them) among the sailors. Golikov was told to conduct periodic searches for illegal literature among his sailors, especially new recruits and those returning from overseas cruises, and to limit sailors' interaction with local workers. As long as he kept his sailors insulated from outside agitators, he was told, there would be no trouble. That sailors may have been open to radicalization as a direct result of their service conditions occurred neither to him nor to his superiors, nor did it inform their actions. Yet, try as Golikov might to eliminate this revolutionary influence, he discovered increasing amounts of literature, especially as the war in Japan began to go poorly. One seized pamphlet, titled "To All Sailors on Patrol," revealed the nature of the threat:

So to arms, comrades! We know you have them loaded. Turn against your oppressors, fire at your blood-thirsty commanders. . . . Show them you know how to die not as slaves in an unnecessary war, nor to protect the bloodstained throne of the tsar-executioner, but for the freedom of your comrades, as true citizens. Down with autocracy! Long live the democratic public! Down with war!

Deeply troubled over the gathering strength of revolutionaries in the fleet, the Naval Ministry appointed Vice Admiral Grigory Chukhnin in July 1904 to rescue Golikov and the other officers from these threats. An old campaigner, Chukhnin made marble look warm and malleable. Raised from the age of seven by the navy, he was strictly devoted to the tsar's motto: "Orthodoxy, Autocracy, Nationality." A stern, decisive man with a wide-ranging knowledge of naval life and an exacting intelligence, he stood out as one of the tsar's best officers. Although he had recently reformed the Naval Cadet School, to great acclaim, he was passed over in favor of Rozhestvensky to lead the squadron heading to the Far East. Instead, the ministry chose him for the Black Sea Fleet.

Chukhnin roared into Sevastopol with his own methods of rooting out the "revolutionary hooligans" and "illiterate sailors who blindly repeat words they can't possibly understand." His measures included additional and more frequent searches, the enlistment of spies, and the placement of undercover agents among the sailors. He demanded obedience to traditional naval discipline — no exceptions. He instructed Golikov and the other captains to put the men in their place, no matter how strenuous their efforts needed to be.

Four months into this new regime, the Black Sea Fleet sailors went on a rampage at the naval base after being refused passes into the city. This was one of several new repressive measures, along with longer shifts and limited fraternization, that Chukhnin had instituted. After breaking down the gates while shouting "Beat them! Hurrah!" several hundred sailors turned their fury on the base, breaking windows, destroying furniture, and torching their barracks and the courthouse. Some officers shot blindly into the dark at the sailors; others simply hid in cellars until relief arrived. The onset of a thunderstorm dispersed most of the sailors; the arrival of a large police force several hours later dealt with the rest. The brief uprising was met with serious consequences. Thirty-six sailors were tried by court-martial, all but seven receiving sentences of hard labor or transfer to disciplinary battalions — despite Chukhnin's attempt to have several hanged. Those suspected of ties to radical organizations were transferred out of their unit; those caught reading illegal pamphlets or participating in secret meetings faced court-martial, and if insufficient evidence was found to convict them, they simply remained in prison until Chukhnin ordered their release. Sevastopol soon ran out of jail cells, so Chukhnin petitioned St. Petersburg for money to build more prisons. He ordered each ship captain to keep a secret log of sailors suspected of revolutionary activity and to periodically deliver this list to him, so he could arrange for arrests.

After Bloody Sunday, unrest in the fleet worsened still. Pamphlets, which Chukhnin saw after they had been seized, urged sailors to fire on their officers and ridiculed the tsar for finally managing to score a "mighty victory" — not in Manchuria or Port Arthur, but in front of the Winter Palace. In February, Chukhnin lost his patience and delivered a harsh speech to his sailors on life's realities, much as a father might resort to scolding his child after other efforts had failed. Then he had his lecture posted throughout the naval base for good measure.

He made clear he would brook no compromise nor listen to complaints about service conditions. Any such grumbling was wholly the product of "pernicious traitors and cowards" trying to drive a wedge between the sailors and their love for Tsar Nicholas. Although the speech foretold how the revolution would end in dictatorship ("The radical will promise the people a better life. . . . This is only the means to get power"), it would have been an empty diatribe, had Chukhnin not believed passionately in its truth. He intended to discipline his sailors until they turned away, as he said in his speech, from the "path of vileness and disgrace of the Russian name."

Still the sailors refused to toe the line. When Chukhnin sent hundreds of unreliable sailors from the fleet into service in the Far East, they revolted again. While changing trains midway through their journey, the sailors refused to reboard and a riot broke out. Eventually they had to be sent back to Sevastopol. As Chukhnin noted in a letter to the ministry in St. Petersburg, a missive unusual in its bluntness, this cycle of rebellion was rooted not only in revolutionary unrest but also in the fleet's idleness (because of the 1856 Treaty of Paris, Russian warships were restricted from passing through the Bosphorus Strait) and in the worthless officers he had inherited from his predecessor.

Legend has it that Admiral Nelson could "in ten days' time restore most mutinous crews," but he had the advantage of good officers at his side. Chukhnin was burdened with the likes of Golikov, whose efforts to enforce discipline and stamp out radicals on the *Potemkin* included barging into sailors' quarters in the middle of the night and demanding to know why a particular hammock was empty — only to discover that the sailor was on duty; bribing his own men to spy on other sailors, then having them arrested for not bringing enough information; inviting musicians on board to sing patriotic songs about obeying one's officers and the tsar; and making a big show of interrogating and then punishing a sailor for possessing an illegal pamphlet even though he was illiterate. Few sailors escaped some kind of punishment from the captain, whether for staining the deck, arriving late for roll call, or simply reading a book that his officers were unfamiliar with. Corporal punishment was not his style, but even for the most minor offense, he would dock a sailor's pay, throw him in the brig for twenty-four hours, make him stand at attention with a fifty-pound bag of sand around his neck, or keep him on duty for three straight shifts.

Golikov was also prone to speeches that resonated with misplaced romance and sheer stupidity. On April 15, to celebrate the final completion of the *Potemkin,* he gathered his sailors together and said, "It took nine years to build this ship. It was dead all that time, but now is endowed with life, like a man, to have arms, legs, a head, and eyes. You should love and cherish this ship as a mother loves her children." After the defeat at Tsushima, he took the opportunity to opine about a mutiny he had experienced aboard the cruiser *Svetlana,* after which several sailors were executed: "This is what happens to sailors who ignore discipline." Hearing the speech, his engineer officer, Aleksandr Kovalenko, muttered under his breath, "Lord, Lord, is he ignorant." These were Golikov's only words of so-called inspiration to his crew after hundreds of their fellow sailors had died in that battle.

Golikov may have been useless, but he was not mean-spirited. However, allowing his second officer, Gilyarovsky, full expression of his viciousness toward the sailors confirmed the captain's unfitness for command. Decorated for bravery at the Battle of Chemulpo against Admiral Togo at the start of the Russo-Japanese War, the tall, rail-thin Gilyarovsky had the personality of a cocked fist. He told his fellow officers that he planned on taking an ax to those "St. Petersburg liberals" for opposing the war as soon as he was finished with his

Sevastopol duties. He treated his sailors with a similar penchant for violence. Once when a new recruit passed him on the street, Gilyarovsky stopped him: "Do you know me?"

"Yes, Your Honor," the recruit replied.

"So what is my name?"

The recruit did not know.

"You don't know my name?"

"No, Your Honor."

"Well, then let me introduce myself," Gilyarovsky said, before striking the recruit repeatedly in the face. This was the man Golikov charged with discipline and order.

As the *Potemkin* steamed toward Tendra Island for maneuvers, any opportunity for Golikov to earn his sailors' respect and address their concerns had long since passed. With the short-fused Gilyarovsky at his side and the imminent threat of mutiny after months of Vice Admiral Chukhnin's misguided measures, trouble could come from any quarter. Inevitably, on a ship of 763 ill-fed sailors, tightly grouped in hot weather on a choppy sea, it would.

Late that night of June 12, Matyushenko looked out over the ship's side, catching occasional flashes of light from signals ashore. He could not sleep, agitated by the day's activities and his desire to make a move on the officers straight away. Finally he went to look for Vakulenchuk to talk about accelerating their plans.

Since they left Sevastopol, he and the other revolutionary sailors had brought as many of their comrades to their side as possible, cornering them on the foredeck, in the engine room, and in the sleeping quarters, on duty and off. Only an officer or petty officer walking by gave pause to their efforts. The revolutionaries beat the drum on the miserable lives they shared before joining the navy: hardship in their villages and exploitation by parasitic factory owners in the cities. Then they turned the discussion to life in the navy, describing how Golikov owned three fine houses in Sevastopol paid for by money siphoned from the sailors' food budget; how Nikolayev's mayor had ordered that sailors passing his house must stop and salute; how the caskets of the dead were streaming into Russia from the Far East; and how an officer had sent a sailor who had been awarded the St. George

Cross, Russia's highest military honor, to the hospital with a serious beating after merely getting in the officer's way on the street.

Once they had infuriated the sailors with these examples, Matyushenko and his fellow revolutionaries urged them to join the cause: "Taking care of these dragons depends on you" or "If we all get together, we can get rid of these dragons."

Word of the planned uprising spread among the crew, but many spoke out against it. They hated their officers, but surely the tsar was not to blame. He would address their troubles, if he only knew. As for mutiny — this took matters too far, much too far.

"It's not the tsar's fault, but the people surrounding him," one sailor said. "Why shed blood if we can come to an agreement with the tsar?"

Matyushenko had listened to similar arguments throughout the day, and he was convinced they must act immediately before someone betrayed them. Too many sailors now knew of the mutiny; it would no doubt reach the captain's ear eventually. They had enough sailors on their side — now — to take over the ship. Only twenty officers and an equal number of petty officers stood in their way — half of them asleep in their cabins. Every minute they waited increased their chance of arrest or Golikov's returning the battleship to Sevastopol.

As the *Potemkin* steamed through the night, Matyushenko found Vakulenchuk, who, as an artillery quartermaster, worked near the weapons cache, where the two often met in secret. Because of the firing exercises, the *Potemkin* was loaded with approximately ten thousand high-explosive and fragment shells, enough to lay waste an entire city. The stacks of ammunition provided ample hiding places where they could speak privately.

"We've got to start now," Matyushenko insisted.

"Rushing matters will only hurt us," Vakulenchuk replied evenly, having heard this plea many times from his friend. "Look, could you break a gun over your knee if I gave you one?"

Matyushenko shook his head.

"You're right; it's impossible. But you can take it apart — piece by piece," Vakulenchuk said.

"Go on."

"Think, Afanasy! It's difficult to fight a whole squadron, but a single ship is a different story. The tsar could easily take back one battleship. Soon, Matyushenko. Very soon. The rest of the ships will arrive, and then we'll strike out."

"I'll try and tolerate it some more," Matyushenko reluctantly agreed. "But I wish it could be now."

He turned and walked away, placated at least for the moment. His friend had as much reason as he did to hate his officers. One of nine children, Vakulenchuk had worked from a young age at a sugar factory with the rest of his family, eating sugar beet and sleeping on a straw floor at night, until conscripted into the navy. A few years into his service, he received a letter from his mother, telling him that the family was starving. There was nothing he could do to help. "Animals live better this," he shouted, knowing well that other sailors had received similar letters. Soon afterward, he was invited to a sailor study circle; then he met Yakhnovsky. When informed that joining the Social Democrats might land him in jail, get him exiled for hard labor, or even shot, Vakulenchuk said, "If I'm to suffer, I know that it's for the people."

By the time Vakulenchuk received his assignment to the *Potemkin,* the sailors idolized him. Although he could barely read when he entered the navy, he had become one of its most informed radicals, thanks to diligent study and the tutoring of Aleksandr Petrov. He organized study circles of his own, and sailors constantly looked to him for guidance. "Believe Vakulenchuk," a revolutionary named Stefan Bessalayev said to a new conscript when asked what role the artillery quartermaster played on the ship. "Obey his requests and know that he will lead us on the correct path."

Stories of his cleverness and equanimity were legend. In order to protect revolutionary gatherings, he asked the Sevastopol gendarmes if he could lead one of the sailor patrols that looked out for such activities. One afternoon, the mounted police came across a meeting. Vakulenchuk stood forward in his patrol uniform, informing the officers that he had already put the group under arrest. The ruse worked and propelled his authority to new heights among the men, Matyushenko included. Now, with their fight reaching its most critical stage, he was resolved to follow Vakulenchuk because he trusted him above anyone.

As dawn approached on June 13, Matyushenko remained awake.

The ship's movement through the sea made his hammock, attached
to the overhead by two hooks, sway back and forth. Dozens of sailors
closely surrounded him in the space below the gun deck on the ship's
bow. The air smelled of sweat and toil, and over the din of the engines, he could hear his crewmates breath, some shallowly, others
deeply, and still others with a steady snore. In the darkness, they
looked like bats hanging from the roof of a cave. Their officers enjoyed private cabins with washbowls on the better-ventilated spar
deck at the stern, typical of the divide between the sailors and the
"stars of the nation," as the officers were considered by St. Petersburg
society. Matyushenko's dream of seizing from these officers control of
the tsar's most powerful weapon and bringing it to the side of revolution was too big for sleep.

# 4

E ARLY IN THE MORNING on June 13, the *Potemkin* arrived
off Tendra Island. Apart from a black-and-white-banded lighthouse and a ramshackle fishing village, the island was nothing more than a long, thin stretch of deserted beach besieged by the
waters of the Black Sea, which stretched to the horizon and beyond.

Connected to the Mediterranean by the Bosphorus Strait and
sourced by five rivers, including the mighty Danube, the Black Sea
stretches over 262,000 square miles, roughly twice the size of the
North American Great Lakes. The kidney-shaped sea is bordered to
the south by steep hills and the lands of the former Ottoman Empire;
to the southwest by the low cliffs of Romania; to the southeast by the
majestic Caucasus Mountains; and to the north by the fertile steppes
of what was the Russian Empire. From the steppe, the Crimean Peninsula juts like a shovel's blade into the sea. Below a depth of six hundred feet, these waters, by a twist of ecology, are anoxic and without
sea life — dead. The sea's bottom is a dense black muck, suffused
with hydrogen sulfide, a toxic gas that smells of rotten eggs. Only the
top layer of saltwater sustains sea life.

Called Pontos Axeinos by the Greeks, "the somber sea," its dark,
bluish waters had been used as a profitable trading route for centuries
in spite of its notoriously tempestuous weather. Beset by strong cur-
rents, abrupt storms, soupy fogs, and swirling winds, many travelers
yearned for shore after a few hours on its waters. An American correspondent came up with a recipe for the experience of taking a steamer
from Constantinople to Odessa during wintertime: "Import a typhoon from the South Seas, mix judiciously with a blizzard from

North Dakota and turn it loose. Add a frosting of snow and sleet, garnish with white-caps, and serve the whole from a tugboat, and you have a fair conception." On these perilous waters that Russia considered its own — regardless of several other bordering countries — the Black Sea Fleet protected the empire's southern borders and the region's rich exports.

The lone battleship dropped anchor off Tendra Island, near the northern coast. Golikov sent an ensign with six sailors on a launch to shore to telegraph Sevastopol that they had arrived but would delay firing exercises until the next day because of rough seas. While on the island, the ensign checked into acquiring meat, bread, and vegetables for the ship. He returned to the *Potemkin* with a list of prices, but the supply officer, A. N. Makarov, decided to buy provisions in Odessa, the four-hour journey notwithstanding. He gave no explanation for his decision or whether he was motivated by lower prices or by mutually beneficial arrangements with Odessa's merchants.

At 1 P.M., Makarov boarded the *Potemkin*'s torpedo boat escort, No. 267 (*Ismail*), commanded by Lieutenant Pyotr Klodt von Yurgensburg. The supply officer brought along with him the *Potemkin*'s junior surgeon, Dr. A. S. Golenko, two cooks, and a handful of sailors to carry the provisions. One among them was Pyotr Alekseyev, a sandy-haired orphan from Kazan, who was a revolutionary close to Matyushenko and Vakulenchuk.

The *Ismail* steamed westward toward Odessa, moving low across the water. Armed with two 37-millimeter guns and a pair of torpedo launchers, the small boat, 127 feet long by 11 feet wide, held a crew of three officers and twenty sailors; its quarters were claustrophobic, to say the least. That afternoon, with the additional company and a fierce sun overhead, they could not arrive at Odessa soon enough. Finally at 5 P.M., the *Ismail* passed around Langeron Point and entered the busy harbor.

Tugboats and transport vessels crisscrossed the waters as the torpedo boat moved toward one of the quays. The port district hummed with activity. Stevedores loaded and unloaded cargo ships carrying grain, sugar, tallow, canned fish, white iron, leather goods, cork, glue, and jute sacks. Customs officials scooted about, checking ship manifestoes. Merchant sailors gathered on the wharves for one last drink before their captains corralled them onto their ships. Weary travelers disembarked from steamers, only to be shuffled aboard horse-drawn carriages that rattled the passengers' bones as they made their way past warehouses and underneath elevated train tracks, out of the port.

Once Lieutenant Klodt docked the torpedo boat, Makarov and his sailors left the *Ismail* to buy provisions. They discovered the city above in the grip of chaos.

Two hundred feet above the harbor on the bluff of a limestone cliff stood Odessa, the Russian Empire's third-largest city and the jewel of the Black Sea. In 1794, only a Tatar trading village named Hadji-bey existed on the site, but Catherine the Great wanted a great imperial city built above the deep harbor and, thanks to efforts of the duc de Richelieu, a future French prime minister, she was granted her wish. Designed with grand parks, chestnut-tree-lined boulevards, and monumental Italianate architecture, Odessa looked more like a sister to Paris than a provincial Russian city.

Connecting the port to the city were the Richelieu Steps — or the *escalier monstre,* as some residents deemed them. With ten landings and 192 granite steps spanning a distance of 465 feet, the designers had not needed optical tricks to give the staircase an appearance of great height, but they had played with perspective nonetheless. As one climbed the staircase, the steps became narrower, from 70 feet wide at the port level to 41 feet wide at its summit, where a statue of Richelieu stood. Looking down from the top step, one saw only landings, whereas looking up from the bottom, one saw only a long line of steps leading to the sky. More than an access route to the city from the harbor, the staircase was also a symbolic gesture to the source of Odessa's wealth and character: the port.

Over the decades since its founding, Odessa had become the El Dorado of the Black Sea. The epicenter of Russian exports and an industrial giant in its own right, Odessa blossomed from a population of a few thousand when Richelieu arrived to half a million people by the nineteenth century's end. The wealthy built mansions along Primorsky Boulevard, which ran in a crescent along the cliffs overlooking the harbor. The city streets were filled with elegant storefronts, fine restaurants, bawdy taverns, and a jumble of residents from across the Russian Empire and around the world.

According to a Swiss tourist of the time, in Odessa "the Russian jostles against a Turk, a German against a Greek, an Englishman against an Armenian, a Frenchman against an Arab. . . . Everything surges and mixes together: the dress coat, the swallow tail coat of the West European mixes together with the kaftan and robes of the Orient . . . the high towering cap of a Persian and the turban of an Anatolian and the fez of a Morean and a Dutch sailor in a wide-brimmed low hat."

Despite its cosmopolitan, festive air, the city had deep-seated troubles that surfaced after two years of recession brought on by the Russo-Japanese War. Impressive colonnaded mansions lined the clifftops, but hidden in the outlying districts stood the homes of the poor, who worked the ports, rail depots, granaries, workshops, and factories.

Isaac Babel, the famed Russian writer who was a ten-year-old living in Odessa in 1905, later described these back streets. "Could we even grace with the name of a town the place where we then were and the streets we beheld? It was a great open space without houses filled with carts and oxen rolling in the dust in company with a mob of Russian and Polish peasants, all sleeping together in the sun in a temperature of 98 degrees." Long neglected and now facing the closure of many factories and worse poverty, these workers turned their anger on the factory owners and the police who protected those owners.

Rather than address the problems caused by the war, fundamentally the source of Odessa's economic difficulties, people attempted to scapegoat the Jewish townspeople, adding to the tension. Overall, those of the Jewish faith accounted for 35 percent of the city's population. Although thousands had found success through running small shops and trading enterprises, they were far from the potent force accused of strangling opportunity for everyone else. Nearly half of all Jewish families had trouble putting food on the table. With each passing day, however, threats of violence rose against their community. Similarly, police and military officials blamed the Jews for leading the city's revolutionary movement — whose influence on striking workers they overestimated. As a result, superiors gave their officers carte blanche to quash unrest with indiscriminate force.

In fact, the situation in Odessa mirrored those unfolding in St. Petersburg, Moscow, and other cities throughout the empire. Many Jewish individuals certainly played a role in revolutionary organizations, but they were by no means dominant. Furthermore, the revolutionaries were often playing catch-up with and second fiddle to workers looking for improved wages, shorter hours, better factory conditions, and legal rights, yet who were generally apolitical — they simply wanted a better life. Also, the revolutionary movement had limited supporters, and they were splintered among various groups. In Odessa, Mensheviks and Bolsheviks fought for control of the Social Democrats (and the roughly one thousand workers sympathetic to their views in the city), while squabbling with their offshoot, the Jewish Bund. All three groups faced serious rivalry from Socialist Revolutionaries and anarchists. These revolutionary groups all battled liberal leaders who spoke to the workers of a certain amount of change, but not a thoroughgoing restructuring of society. Above all else, nobody was in control.

Throughout the first half of the year, strikes had escalated in strength and frequency. Although Odessan revolutionaries called for workers to show solidarity with those killed on Bloody Sunday, they were met with skepticism. A few weeks later, however, Odessan workers began to strike for their own concerns. In early February, pharmacist assistants and workers in tailoring and printing shops appealed to their bosses for more money. These efforts were followed by walkouts in sugar refineries and on the docks. By April, leatherworkers, bakers, machinists, and rail-depot mechanics demanded better conditions. For the most part, management tried to negotiate meager concessions with strikers at the urging of city officials, who feared a repeat of St. Petersburg's troubles. Then in May, strikers called for a general assembly of workers to express their concerns to the city government, a move that revolutionary groups encouraged because of its political significance. Odessa's mayor rejected the petition because an assembly represented a little too much liberty of expression, in his opinion. In the next couple of days, ten thousand workers walked off their jobs. Yet a lack of organization among workers and the bullying of strikers by city officials kept the situation in check throughout May.

Their frustrations peaking, workers began to call for a general strike on Monday, June 13. After learning of their plans, the mayor lured thirty-three of their representatives into the police station under the pretense of opening negotiations with the factory owners. Then, to prevent the planned strike, the police arrested these representatives. This move sent Odessa's outlying districts into an uproar. Hundreds marched to the station, chanting, "Down with the police!" and "Long live the general strike!" earning the release of the jailed workers.

These arrests crystallized workers' distrust of factory owners and local officials alike and persuaded the workers to pursue more strident measures. Some connected with the Social Democrats and Socialist Revolutionaries to obtain arms. The night before the scheduled strike, another group of workers was arrested while heading to a meeting with revolutionaries at a dacha on the coast. The following morning in Peresyp, Odessa's northern district, known for its heavy industry and squalid conditions, news of this second arrest became widely known.

At 8 A.M. on June 13, the same morning the *Potemkin* arrived off Tendra Island, Anatoly "Kirill" Berezovsky, an Odessan Menshevik, walked down Peresyp's Moskovskaya Street. The dusty thoroughfare was lined with vegetable and meat shops and the occasional newspaper vendor. Children played on the sides of the streets, many sickly looking and all of them too poor to attend school. The stench that hung in the air came from pipes carrying the city's sewage; they ran parallel to Moskovskaya Street and emptied their contents at the district's edge.

Although Kirill, a university student and the son of a successful shopkeeper, was dressed in the threadbare clothes of a worker, even a dim-witted policeman would have guessed that he was not a local. He had neatly trimmed red hair, a fleshy face, and a stout figure, and he spoke of injustice in an educated, philosophical manner. For months now he had been coming to this district, distributing leaflets and informing workers that their suffering was caused by a "criminal monarchy" undeserving of its power. He had seen their patience with factory owners turn into rage, but like other revolutionaries, he had been unable to channel their rage toward his purpose. That morning, the general strike was to take place, and he wanted to be on hand to help agitate the district's workers.

Walking farther down Moskovskaya Street toward the cluster of factories at its end, he sensed something was wrong. People were huddled on street corners, shaking their fingers and speaking in harsh whispers as to what they should do. Kirill asked someone on the street what had happened and learned of the arrests — and that a crowd had gathered at the gates of the Henn agricultural equipment factory. This factory employed many of the most militant workers, and their leaders were supposed to go there after the previous night's meeting to start the strike. When Kirill arrived, eight hundred workers had already gathered, and more arrived with every passing minute from other outlying districts. Believing this could be the start of a huge strike, Kirill hurried back to the city to retrieve several of his comrades to help him direct the workers. On his way, he passed several police patrols converging on the Henn factory.

An hour later, a detachment of fifty Cossacks on horseback, armed with sabers and revolvers, arrived at the Henn factory. The Peresyp police chief, Parashchenko, led them. He told the workers to clear off and return to their homes. They stood firm, shouting, "Release our comrades. Then we'll leave!" Parashchenko then ordered the workers back into the plant or they would risk the whips of the Cossacks, who, in black breeches, polished boots, and peaked caps, looked eager to deliver on the threat. Given their history of ruthlessness in the tsar's defense, one painted in blood, nobody doubted they were ready to do so. Nonetheless, the workers refused again. The police chief then declared he would attack the crowd unless it dispersed from the factory's gate by the third bugle blast.

One blast from the bugle came.

"If you don't leave," Parashchenko threatened again, "I will fire!"

The bugle sounded again.

The workers, armed with rubble collected by their wives and children, suddenly released a barrage of stones at the Cossacks. Their commander was struck in the face. His horse reared, and he fell off. Gathering his reins, the commander jumped back on his horse and retreated. In moments, the crowd had forced back the rest of the Cossacks. Shouts of premature victory rang out, but, knowing the Cossacks would return, the workers upended two tram cars and some carts to form a barricade. At a distance, the Cossacks re-formed their line and advanced, slow and deliberate, with deadly intent.

A Social Democrat and former Black Sea sailor, Fyodor Medvedev, who had fled the navy after the November 1904 riot in the Sevastopol barracks, stood on top of the makeshift barricade, holding a red revolutionary pamphlet. A rifle shot sounded from a nearby building. Someone had taken aim at the Cossacks. Medvedev raised the pamphlet over his head to rally the workers, surveyed the scene, and then shouted, "Comrades —"

The Cossacks fired at the crowd, killing Medvedev before he managed another word. They urged their horses forward. Some of the Cossacks fired their rifles; others brandished sabers or studded whips. At their advance, the workers fled in every direction. Some fell where they were struck. Others rushed into the factory or dove for cover behind the barricade. Short of suicide, their only option was to retreat from the Cossack guns, their slashing blades, and the stomping hooves of their horses. By the time the Cossacks reassembled, several workers had been killed and dozens wounded. A slight haze of gun smoke settled over the area.

When Kirill returned down Moskovskaya Street, having failed to locate any comrades in the city center, he saw carriages without their horses and stores and street stalls closed. Mothers hid their children behind their skirts while their husbands gestured angrily at the huge police presence patrolling the streets. Kirill sprinted toward the Henn factory.

Outside its gates, Cossacks stood by their horses, some smoking cigars. The police chief, Parashchenko, was huddled in conversation with several factory workers. Someone grabbed Kirill's shoulder from behind. He turned to find one of his comrades, his face white and his hands trembling.

"Fyodor has been shot," he said.

Kirill looked around him, finally understanding that the gathering had turned violent. His comrade began to tell him what had happened when several workers carried a shrouded body through the factory gates. The Cossacks tried to seize it from the workers, but they escaped down Moskovskaya Street. People emptied out of nearby factories, workshops, and houses and followed the macabre cortege, Kirill with them. "Women tore their hair and filled the air with sobs and curses on the murderers," recounted one witness.

As the procession coursed through the muddied streets of Peresyp, news of the killings spread throughout the district and into the city center. One horrified elderly man cried, "This is our government! This is what it has become!" The crowd became more excited. Some shouted, "Guns! Give us guns!" By the early afternoon, thousands marched through Odessa, stopping trams and ignoring the mayor's pleas to return to their homes.

Kirill felt himself carried along by the surging mass of workers. They roamed the streets, pausing now and then to listen to a speaker or to throw rocks at a patrol, but unable to move together with a single purpose. They needed leadership and, more important, they needed guns if they were to stage an effective armed resistance against the government. Otherwise, as soon as the military stepped in with any strength, they could do nothing but scatter in retreat as they had done earlier that morning. More workers would die while government forces suffered mere scrapes and cuts.

Behind the high walls of Odessa's military garrison, General Semyon Kakhanov stood in his office overlooking the harbor. His lieutenants periodically interrupted his reverie with the latest reports from Peresyp and other parts of the city. As military governor of Odessa, he was the last line of defense, and the reports left him troubled.

At sixty-three years of age, with a slow gait and deep crevasses across his brow, Kakhanov was far from the fit, wild-spirited lieutenant who had participated in lightning charges against highlanders in the Caucasus Mountains in 1863. Even his days as a colonel, leading combat assaults on Turkish emplacements and fortresses during the Russo-Turkish War of 1877–78, seemed a lifetime ago. The gold saber and the St. George's Cross he had earned for bravery were both a quarter-century old. He had led the same life as his noble forebears, within the military and the state, at the highest levels. His family boasted a former deputy minister of the interior, several governors-general of various provinces, and members of the tsar's State Council. Only a few short months from retirement, Kakhanov had no intention of allowing a few "rebels" in Odessa to tarnish his pristine record or his family name.

Since the beginning of the year, he had watched strikes flare up and then expire; the workers accepted a few worthless gestures from their owners and went back to their factories. Although the workers' demands were rarely political in nature, despite the urgings of the revolutionary rabble, these strikes concerned him because they proved that the mayor and the police lacked authority over the people. Kakhanov had complained to St. Petersburg that in the past four months "not a single day has passed that my troops have not been called in to help civil officials." This worried him for two reasons: first, the police were powerless to maintain law and order on their own; second, every moment his men spent in Odessa took away from their training and sapped their morale.

Matters had become much more serious of late, though. Odessa's citizens were scared; rumors floated about of Jewish revolutionaries smuggling in weapons and planning assassinations of government officials; and now workers dared march on the city center. Kakhanov knew he was the only one with the leadership and the resources to subdue the city. Under his command in Odessa, he had a regiment of Cossacks and, should he need it, the authority to arm and direct the police. He could call on three more regiments and a brigade in reserve, more than enough troops and enough firepower to crush an opponent armed with rocks and the occasional peasant hunting rifle or antique revolver.

He had ordered the dispersal of Peresyp's strikers, and more troops were surging into the streets as evening fell. His men had advance instructions on where to station themselves to keep transportation channels open and protect crucial civil administration buildings and staff. Any violent protestors were to be arrested on the spot. When the situation warranted, his officers had orders to meet resistance with overwhelming force, as they had that morning. From his window, Kakhanov heard the shouts of marchers. He would treat them like any enemy on the battlefield.

Supply officer Makarov had never expected to confront citywide riots in Odessa, and they made his simple run for provisions anything but simple. Throngs of workers packed the streets, making a short walk to a grocer or butcher like a swim upstream through a strong current. From every direction came shouts of "Down with autocracy!" and "Death to the police!" In this confusion, it had been difficult to find enough meat to buy, particularly since Makarov insisted on haggling for the lowest price. Some of the sailors suggested they return to Tendra Island for provisions, but Makarov ordered them to keep their thoughts to themselves.

At 9 P.M., the lights went off throughout Odessa. Some workers had shut down the city's gas and electricity station. A few minutes later, gunshots were heard in the distance as Cossacks tried to regain control of the streets. Makarov became more and more nervous. Finally, in the Greek bazaar, he came across a butcher willing to sell a few thousand pounds of meat. The assistant ship surgeon, Dr. Golenko, bald and pale as the moon, inspected the meat and concluded it was acceptable.

Sailor Alekseyev took one look at the hanging carcasses of cattle and turned to Makarov. "Your Honor, this meat is tainted. It's not fit to eat."

Makarov gave Alekseyev a fiendish look. "Bastard, be quiet! Otherwise I'll have you arrested and sent to jail."

After accepting a price, Makarov ordered his men to take the meat in sacks down to the torpedo boat. He had run out of time to look for any other provisions. Alekseyev heaved a sack onto his back, eager at least to return to the *Potemkin* to tell Vakulenchuk and the others about the massive strikes.

An hour later, the *Ismail* steamed out of the harbor, the meat stacked below, stewing in the sultry summer night. The torpedo boat made a fast return to Tendra — too fast for a small fishing boat, which it struck on the way. The crew stopped to rescue the fishermen and return them ashore. Finally, the *Ismail* arrived by the *Potemkin*'s side at 4 A.M., June 14. Most of the ship was quiet; only the sailors on the night watch were still awake. In the dark, the meat was brought aboard and hung on hooks on the spar deck, maggots feasting unseen on the flesh.

# 5

TWO BELLS STRUCK at 5 A.M. on the *Potemkin*. A bugler brought his horn to his lips, inflated his cheeks, and then belted out the reveille. A boatswain's whistle preceded the gruff calls throughout the berth decks: "Turn out! Roll up your hammocks!"

Matyushenko extended his legs out of his hammock and dropped to the deck. Other sailors reluctantly turned out as well.

"Quick about it! Lively there! Tumble out, men!"

The sailors hurried, their petty officers forcing them along with curses and shoves. After rolling his hammock into a tight cocoon and dressing himself, Matyushenko moved down the narrow passageway and then climbed a series of ladders to the upper deck. He stowed his hammock under its number plate, and, with the others, obeyed the order to wash. Hundreds of sailors jostled and elbowed alongside him in the narrow chamber lined with a long trough and seawater taps.

"To prayer!"

Water dripping from his face, Matyushenko followed this command, the morning ritual ingrained in him after years in the navy. The ship's priest, Father Parmen, an unkempt man with a straggly beard and a proclivity to drink who also served as Golikov's spy, led the men through their Orthodox prayers and hymns. A breakfast of tea and buttered chunks of black bread lasted a half-hour before the order came to clean the ship. Dressed in freshly laundered blue-and-white jerseys and plain white bell-bottoms rolled up at the ends, the sailors scrubbed every deck and bulkhead and polished brass fixtures until they glowed.

As the sun rose, a sailor swabbing the spar deck smelled something foul. He followed the stench to the hanging carcasses of meat brought on board the night before. Another sailor came to his side and noticed a writhing mass of white maggots on the flesh. "Well — it's full of worms," he said matter-of-factly. Several others came to look at the meat, disgust visible on their faces, but they were soon broken up by the call for all hands on deck. The men assembled for the raising of the colors; whispers about the rotten meat passed through the ranks.

"Attention! Present arms!"

Captain Golikov walked onto the quarterdeck as the marine guards raised their rifles to their sides like torches lighting the way. He greeted Gilyarovsky, received his reports from the rest of his officers on the state of the battleship, and then turned to the flagstaff. The watch commander yelled, "Attention! Hoist flag!" The sailors and officers removed their caps. As the drums rolled, the St. Andrew's flag rose steadily on the flagstaff. Eight bells struck, and the command came for the assembly to break up.

As Golikov disappeared off the deck and the new watch began, sailors crowded around the spar deck to see this rotten meat for themselves. It was an unusually hot June morning, the air still and dense with humidity; the meat would only grow fouler as the sun rose into the sky.

"The Japanese feed Russian prisoners better," one sailor complained.

"I wouldn't give this meat to a pig," growled another.

More men came forward to see the meat that would be thrown into the pots along with beets, cabbage, and carrots to make their lunch of borscht. "Chuck the stinking stuff overboard!" the crowd began to call out in unison. Matyushenko and Vakulenchuk also inspected the carcasses, not surprised at their quality. More of interest to them was the reaction of their fellow sailors. The sight of the worms had obviously triggered the crew's anger toward their officers more than all of the revolutionaries' propaganda efforts had.

After standing by while the sailors vented for a few moments, a petty officer strode over to get them back to work. "Don't you remember your friends in Port Arthur were eating dog's meat? And you're not happy with beef!?"

"Is this Port Arthur?" a sailor returned.

Several others cursed the supply officer, Makarov, demanding that he or the ship's senior surgeon, Dr. Sergei Smirnov, be brought to the spar deck. Worried that the situation might escalate, the petty officer went to inform Makarov, who told the watch commander, Lieutenant N. Y. Liventsev, who went straight to see the captain. In his spacious cabin, Golikov listened to Liventsev's report about the spoiled meat and then sent for Dr. Smirnov to accompany him on an inspection. The seas were calming, and Golikov planned to send out the *Ismail* to set up targets for firing practice later in the day. No distractions were needed, in particular the usual grumbling about the quality of the borscht.

With Golikov at his side, Smirnov headed to the spar deck to deal with the recalcitrant sailors. With the bedside manner of a drill instructor, Smirnov was already despised by most of the crew. Tall, trim, and through-and-through navy in his full-length coat fitted with three black stars on silver epaulettes, he nevertheless walked gingerly on the deck, unsure of his sea legs. On a previous voyage, he had fallen through a hatch after losing his balance during firing exercises.

"Now. What's all this about? What's all this about?" Smirnov demanded loudly, pushing his way through the sailors who surrounded the dangling carcasses. Golikov stood at a distance.

After putting on his pince-nez, Smirnov cut off a sliver of meat, looked at it briefly, brought it close to his nose, and then turned to his captain. "The meat is of good quality."

The crowd of sailors shouted that the meat was riddled with maggots: could Smirnov not see them, or did he not care?

"That doesn't mean anything," the doctor declared. "It's summertime. All the cook needs to do is wash the meat and cut out the parts with maggots."

"You don't even treat us as men," replied a sailor darkly.

Ignoring their protests, Golikov ordered the men to disperse. If the doctor believed the meat was suitable, that was enough for him. Reluctantly the sailors disbanded. For good measure, Golikov assigned a petty officer to make a list of the sailors who approached the carcasses. As far as he was concerned, this ended the matter.

•  •  •

Later that morning, Matyushenko made his way down to the torpedo room for a hastily called meeting of the ship's revolutionaries. He was eager to tell his comrades of the opportunity created by the rotten meat.

His fellow sailors constantly griped about the navy's abominable food; their meals constituted a three-times-a-day reminder of their plight. While the officers dined well in private compartments, some having skimmed funds that were supposed to be used for the crew's provisions, the sailors ate slop. A couple of years before, on the cruiser *Berezan,* sailors had nearly broken into open revolt because of rancid meat. The *Berezan*'s captain avoided a mutiny only by ordering a fresh batch of borscht.

Matyushenko was convinced that the maggot-infested carcasses could incite the crew to mutiny. With this idea in mind, he slipped into the torpedo room, joining Vakulenchuk, Alekseyev, Yfim Bredikhin, and Stefan Denisenko, among several others. To start the meeting, Alekseyev first informed those who had not already heard about the scenes he had witnessed in Odessa: workers protesting in the streets, the police indiscriminately using force, and calls for revolution.

Breaking into the discussion first, Matyushenko shook his fist and said, "First in St. Petersburg, the tsar's troops fired on the people. Now they're doing the same in Odessa. It's no longer possible to delay. We must seize the ship *today* and go to Odessa." The tainted meat formed the perfect pretext for revolt.

Bredikhin, who considered himself more of an anarchist than a Social Democrat, agreed with Matyushenko. Only cowards would allow the opportunity pass.

"We only go to Odessa with the whole squadron," Vakulenchuk insisted. "Then we'll really be as strong as possible and, together with the workers, we'll win an easy victory." He recommended they use the meat solely to further prepare the crew for mutiny. To do so, they would lead a boycott against eating the borscht. This would also test the reactions of the officers and sailors. With each passing day, Vakulenchuk then argued, the maggots would grow bigger and the boycott gather in strength.

Denisenko supported this plan, as did most of the others.

But Matyushenko wanted to move on the officers now. Patience.

Patience. Patience. This was what Vakulenchuk always advised him, but Matyushenko was weary of propaganda. He wanted his revenge and revolution — now. Only his respect for Vakulenchuk kept him at bay. Finally he assented to wait as well.

Vakulenchuk instructed the group to let the crew know of their resolution, and the revolutionaries quickly disbanded, saying, "We won't eat the soup! If Smirnov or Golikov like it so much, let them eat it! We won't eat the soup!"

Troubled over the crew's mood and fearful that the revolutionaries would easily corrupt others over a few maggots, Commander Gilyarovsky headed toward the galley at lunchtime to make sure everything was in order; the rest of the *Potemkin*'s officers were dining in their wood-paneled wardroom.

Gilyarovsky had made it his special mission to crush these revolutionaries. As the executive officer, or "wolf," as men in his position were often called, he was obligated to serve as watchdog on the battleship, but his efforts exceeded his duty. He recruited his own spies, conducted his own spot inspections, and refused to allow the slightest lapses in discipline to go unpunished. Nothing in his noble upbringing or mediocre naval career differentiated Gilyarovsky from his peers in a way that might explain his more overbearing approach to the sailors, yet he was universally known for his hatred of them. Even Golikov had complained to Vice Admiral Chukhnin that his commander needed to learn restraint. Yet nobody punished Gilyarovsky for his excesses.

Gilyarovsky came across the watch commander, asking him if he had personally sampled the borscht before it was served — as per naval regulations.

"The borscht is wonderful," Liventsev replied. "I would've eaten some with pleasure, but unfortunately my throat hurts."

Leaving his ineffectual officer behind, Gilyarovsky arrived at the mess deck several minutes after a boatswain's whistle signaled the start of lunch. He found the wooden barrels of steaming borscht untouched and the men eating bread dipped in water. Storming over to the cook, Gilyarovsky demanded, "Why aren't you serving lunch to the crew?"

"The crew doesn't want to eat the borscht," the cook answered.

"They said we ought to throw it overboard . . . and the rest of the meat as well. They only ask for tea and butter for their bread."

Gilyarovsky approached the group of the sailors nearest him. "What do you think you're doing? This is a disgrace. Why don't you eat your borscht?"

A long silence met his question. Then a few sailors among the hundreds on deck called out, "Because the meat is stinking!" and "Eat it yourself — we'll stick to bread and water."

Gilyarovsky turned on his heel and quickstepped toward the wardroom. He could barely contain his anger at the men's disobedience and — worse — their disrespect. They had to be dealt with harshly, he thought. The watch commander stopped him on his way, making excuses and saying that he had tried to get the crew to take some borscht.

In the wardroom, Gilyarovsky found Dr. Smirnov and the other officers still dining, a waiter refilling their wineglasses. He walked up behind the doctor and bit off the words "The crew refuses to eat the borscht."

Smirnov looked at the commander with irritation; the tone of his reply was bored at best. "I already told them the meat is fine. The maggots are nothing more than larvae eggs that flies had laid there. They simply need to be washed away with salt and water. The cook did this on my instructions. If the crew continues to refuse to eat, then it's they who are spoiled. That's it."

For a few seconds, Gilyarovsky stared at the doctor, while tossing his cap in the air — either disturbed by the answer or considering what to do next; nobody in the wardroom could tell. Then he walked out. He went straight to Golikov, who was eating alone in his cabin, as was customary for captains. After recounting his visit to the mess deck, Gilyarovsky said pointedly, "We have to teach them a lesson, Yvgeny Nikolayevich — one that they'll remember for the rest of their lives."

Golikov called Dr. Smirnov to his cabin. If the men had no reason to grumble, he had to be quite stern with them. But he needed to be sure. He did not want to start an uprising in the course of trying to prevent one. He knew about the threat of revolutionaries since they had left Sevastopol; caution was needed.

When Smirnov arrived with his assistant surgeon, Golenko, he took his third interrogation on the subject of the rotten carcasses with even less patience than the previous two, but his answer was the same.

"Very well, Doctor, and thank you." Golikov nodded reluctantly and then turned to his second officer. "Commander Gilyarovsky, will you please order the drums to be beaten for roll call."

Events had begun to take on a life of their own. By refusing the borscht and standing up to the hated Gilyarovsky, the majority of sailors got a taste for resisting their officers. Matyushenko eagerly looked toward the next step to outright revolt, now that his fellow sailors had shown some mettle. Smirnov could not back down from his declaration that the meat was suitable; Gilyarovsky wanted retribution; and Golikov needed to show he would not cower at the threat to his command — he had to demand obedience.

The *Potemkin* was a few missteps away from mutiny.

The sailors stood stiffly at attention on the quarterdeck, a sea of men in white and blue, with long ribbons hanging from caps embroidered with the name POTEMKIN. Assembled at the port and starboard sides of the deck, their lines stretched from the ship's stern to the hulking black steel of the aft turret. It was a few minutes after noon, and the sun appeared swollen red in the blue sky.

Watching the heavyset captain pass between the ranks and awkwardly climb onto the capstan, Matyushenko waited among the others to see what he would do. Golikov was known to stare at a sailor until he withered, but this time he had an entire crew challenging his authority. He was a speck amidst the hundreds of sailors. Most quietly despised him, what he represented, or both. Each had his reason: an overzealous punishment received; a family that suffered without help because of his conscription; sleeping quarters more suited to cattle; the indignity of being forbidden to walk on a city street; a life divided into four- to eight-hour watches; the threat of dying in a war against an enemy utterly unknown to him; a lack of hope — or perhaps too much — in the future. The rotten batch of borscht merely symbolized each sailor's own particular reason. But Golikov understood none of this.

"It seems you all are dissatisfied with the soup." He addressed the crew, Gilyarovsky standing behind him like an enforcer. "Very well then, I shall seal a container of it and send it to the chief commander in Sevastopol for inspection. But I'm warning you, only bad will come out of it for you. I've repeatedly told you, and I shall not repeat myself again, of what's in store for sailors who forget discipline. You will be hanged."

He straightened his arm and pointed at the yardarm on the mast. All eyes followed his gesture; the sailors whispered among one another, some in fear, others in disbelief. Matyushenko knew the captain would follow through on his threat and, for once, realized how much they were risking.

"Turn in the instigators of this little rebellion," Golikov continued, pulling nervously at the back of his collar. "We've more than enough ropes and pulleys aboard this ship for them. And you will get through your military service, return to your villages, work the land, and feed your wives and children. Now, whoever wants to eat the borscht, step forward."

A few boatswains and petty officers, twelve in total, followed Golikov's command, but most of the sailors remained in place, looking to one another for support. As long as they stayed together, Matyushenko thought, the officers were helpless.

"Come on!" Gilyarovsky screamed at the men. "Come on! Hurry up!"

Still the sailors held fast, maintaining their lines on either side of the quarterdeck. A few shouted at Golikov, shielding their mouths with their hands so as not to be singled out. "Eat it yourself, dragon! This is the devil's ashes." Another yelled, "Whoa there," as if the captain was a galloping horse that needed to be slowed.

Golikov looked out at his sailors, giving them one last chance to obey him. They refused. "Call out the guard!" he ordered. A boatswain's whistle momentarily pierced the tension. The sailors went silent at the sound of the armed marine guard approaching, their feet ominously pounding on the deck below. They arrived in two columns of ten, each blue-jacketed guard carrying a rifle fixed with a bayonet. Stopping in front of Golikov, their backs to the sailors, the guards awaited their next command.

"Those who are willing to eat the borscht — step forward," Golikov ordered again.

Now faced with the marine guards, the first row of sailors hesitated and then advanced a step, then two. Another row followed. Along with Vakulenchuk and several other sailor revolutionaries, Matyu-shenko stood still, but it was becoming clear to him that many of the sailors would abandon the protest.

Vakulenchuk realized this as well and was the first to retreat to the protection of the twelve-inch gun turret, having no intention himself of surrendering. Matyushenko followed, as did Denisenko, then dozens of other sailors. Quickly, rank-and-file sailors broke from the starboard and port sides of the ship. Nobody wanted to be left alone in line. From the capstan, Golikov watched helplessly; his guards were not sure what to do either. Order disintegrated; sailors pushed and shoved one another pell-mell as they herded around the turret.

Life-and-death decisions were made in seconds, based on instinct, anger, confusion, or desperation. Anger drove Gilyarovsky. Trying to stop complete mayhem from overwhelming the ship, he blocked the path of the remaining sailors on the quarterdeck's port side, aided by Lieutenant Liventsev. Gilyarovsky also barked at a boatswain to take down the names of anyone else who broke rank. Yet sailors continued to retreat toward the turret. Golikov stayed on the capstan, looking on quietly as he lost control of his crew.

"Those who record names will hang today from the yardarm with Golikov," a sailor near Matyushenko warned the officers.

After directing the guards to block any other sailors from escaping via the port side, Gilyarovsky screamed in a bone-chilling cadence, "So it's mutiny, is it? . . . All right . . . we know how to deal with that. If you think there's no discipline in the navy, I'll show how wrong you are. Bosun, bring the tarpaulin."

The order sent a tremor through sailors and officers alike — those who had been in the navy long enough to understand Gilyarovsky's intent. Matyushenko knew well what the second officer had planned: the tarpaulin would be laid out on the deck; those chosen by Gilyarovsky for execution by firing squad would be ordered onto the canvas; and then they would be shot. No sense in bloodying the decks. The order far surpassed the commander's authority; by regulation, he was limited to punishing a sailor with a month's imprisonment or fifteen strokes of the lash. Nonetheless, Golikov failed to countermand the order; at this point, he would back whatever measures it took to regain control of the *Potemkin*.

While several guards collected a tarpaulin from a sixteen-oar boat,

Gilyarovsky made sure those corralled against the railing, who had hesitated in following the others toward the turret, stayed in place. That these sailors were the most innocent — or simply the most confused — of the crew appeared not to bother Gilyarovsky. An example needed to be made. One conscript was as good as another.

"Those who will eat their borscht are dismissed," Gilyarovsky said, giving his sailors one final opportunity to back down. If they refused this time, he would be forced either to follow through on his threat or face mutiny. At best it was a desperate gamble, and at worst, a deadly failure in judgment. He finished by saying, "Anyone who remains will see for himself what we do with mutineers."

For several seconds everybody was still. Then, from the starboard side, Matyushenko began to push his way through the sailors by the turret toward the two lines of guards. Their bayonet blades glinted as they caught the sun. Ahead of the guards stood Gilyarovsky, waiting for the tarpaulin so he could give the command to fire. To his side cowed the thirty sailors. Several sobbed, "Sir, don't shoot. We aren't mutineers."

The rage that had gathered within Matyushenko for years surfaced at the instant the tarpaulin appeared on the deck. Gilyarovsky was going to kill these defenseless sailors, who had done nothing. They would die for the same thing: nothing. This thought turned over in Matyushenko's head again and again as he advanced. Vakulenchuk was by his side, urging the sailors around him to follow their lead. Neither Matyushenko nor Vakulenchuk could allow their comrades to be shot. The time had come. No more patience. Revenge and revolution only.

"Brothers! What are they doing to our comrades? Enough of Golikov drinking our blood," Matyushenko roared, his heart pounding fast in his chest. This was it. Sailors began to follow him forward. "Grab rifles and ammunition! Beat these boors. Take over the ship!" Similar war cries echoed across the deck. Gilyarovsky hesitated over whether to order the guards to fire.

Matyushenko and Vakulenchuk dashed through the hatch leading down to the gun deck. Two other sailor revolutionaries followed them. They ran to the armory at the aft section of the deck, scattering the sentries at their post and rushing inside to seize several rifles stacked in a pyramid. The ammunition was locked away, but the revolutionaries had anticipated this problem. Matyushenko knocked aside an icon of St. Nicholas outside the armory, where several boxes of ammunition had been hidden in preparation. Racing back to the quarterdeck, they loaded the rifles. Other revolutionaries spread throughout the *Potemkin,* some to take control of the engine room, others to stop Sevastopol from learning of the uprising by wireless telegraph, still others to prevent the opening of the seacocks and the scuttling of the ship. Their plans to take control of the ship had been mapped out weeks before during Tsentralka meetings on the fleetwide mutiny.

When Matyushenko tried to reach the upper deck, he found a sentry positioned at the hatch. Gilyarovsky was by his side, having heard the clatter of rifles falling to the steel deck as the traitors hurried to grab them. Behind Gilyarovsky and the sentry stood the captain, who still believed his words could make a difference.

"What are you doing? Put down that rifle!" Golikov commanded.

"I'll put down the rifle when I don't have to live like a corpse," Matyushenko said. Then he drove the sentry and Gilyarovsky out of his way with the rifle butt. Vakulenchuk and several others rushed forward, following him onto the deck. They dashed around the turret to the other side of the ship. Golikov scrambled for safety behind the guards while Gilyarovsky and Artillery Lieutenant L. K. Neupokoyev attempted to assert their last shred of authority, shouting for the loyalty of the sailors and ordering them to come to their aid against those who dared to mutiny and tarnish the honor of the Russian navy.

The guards continued to aim their rifles at the sailors against the railing, unsure of what to do or whom to follow as the majority of the crew huddled by the turret. Only the officers and the revolutionaries had made it clear which side they were on. The rest waited for some turn of events that would choose their course for them. This was the decisive and terrible moment, Matyushenko thought, for the officers and the crew. Their lives hung in the balance. If the officers survived the next few minutes, they might be able to calm the crew. Then he and the other revolutionaries would be lost, as would their cause of freedom. No doubt many innocent sailors would be arrested to face the firing squad as well.

More revolutionaries streamed onto the quarterdeck with guns.

Then Gilyarovsky ordered the guards to shoot. They hesitated. Everyone on the quarterdeck was still.

"A mutiny!" Gilyarovsky yelled. "Wait! I'll teach you to mutiny."

He grabbed one of the guard's rifles.

Stoker Nikishkin, who stood armed beside Matyushenko, fired a shot in the air as a warning to Gilyarovsky.

And the red mutiny began.

# II

A man-of-war is the best ambassador.

— OLIVER CROMWELL

I'm awfully fond of forging metal. In front of you is the red formless mass, malicious, fiery. To beat the hammer on it is a joy. It spits at you with fizzing, blazing sparks, seeks to burn out your eyes, blind you. It is living, malleable, and with mighty blows from the shoulder you make of it what you need. I know I'm no hero, only an honest healthy man. And yet I say: never mind! We shall win. And with all the powers of my soul I satisfy my desire to plunge into the very depth of life, to knead it this way and that, to prevent this and help the other. This is the joy of life.

— MAXIM GORKY, *Townsfolk*

# 6

ON JUNE 14, as mutiny seized the *Potemkin,* Nicholas II was enjoying life in his bubble of splendor and routine.

For the summer months, he had moved his family from Tsarskoye Selo to their seashore dacha at Peterhof, an imperial estate eighteen miles from St. Petersburg on the Gulf of Finland. Called the Lower Palace, the dacha's central feature was a yellow and terra cotta brick tower. Four floors of living quarters stretched around the tower; barely a room lacked its own balcony or covered terrace overlooking the sea or the surrounding forests of maple and linden trees. From the tower's six-story belvedere, the family could see the Kronstadt naval base to the west and, on a clear day, the cupolas of St. Petersburg to the east. Peterhof also contained the Grand Palace (often called the "Russian Versailles"), extensive parks, several elegant summer pavilions, and, most fantastic of all, innumerable fountains — marble fancies with staircases of flowing water, soaring cascades, and jets spouting from scores of statues depicting man, fish, god, and horse alike. Of these, the most spectacular was the huge gilded figure of Samson forcing open the jaws of a lion, symbolizing Russia's triumph over Sweden in 1709. From this fountain stretched a canal wide enough to bring in sailboats from the sea. Peterhof was the kind of place where such details pertaining to the tsar's leisure were attended to with religious devotion.

Nicholas began each day at 8 A.M. He dressed, prayed, and then went down to have a simple breakfast with his daughters. At 9 A.M. sharp he went to his study on the tower's second floor, which looked out over the Gulf of Finland. The dark walnut-paneled study was filled with bookcases and black Moroccan leather sofas. Nicholas sat at a small desk by the window and began reading the newspapers, telegrams, and ministry summaries that had been prepared for him. He did not care for a personal secretary but wrote his notes by hand on the papers. Nicholas had forbidden anyone to disturb the arrangement of family portraits, writing utensils, books, and calendar on his desk. As he told visitors, he wanted to be able to come to his study in the middle of the night and find whatever he needed in the dark.

The rest of his day would proceed along its usual schedule. As it was Tuesday, his war and foreign ministers would arrive in an hour for an audience. Monday was set aside for the naval minister, Wednesday for the minister of justice, Thursday for the minister of the interior, Friday for the minister of finance, Saturday for the minister of education, and on the seventh day he had no meetings. After his ministerial audience, he would take a morning walk (anything less than an hour and a half was unsatisfactory), often with his children. At 1 P.M., he would lunch with his family for a couple of hours and then receive more visitors and attend any required formal events. If he had time before 5 P.M. tea (two cups, never more or less), he always went out for a second bout of exercise — riding, shooting crows, kayaking, bicycling, or swimming. Nicholas craved physical activity to clear his mind. Once tea concluded at 6 P.M., Nicholas would return to his study for two more hours of work, preferably alone, and then spend an hour and a half at dinner, starting at 8 P.M. He shared his evenings with his family, reading or pasting court photographs into green leather albums. At 11 P.M., he would have some tea, write in his diary, take a brief bath, pray again, and go to bed.

He rarely had trouble falling asleep, although reports in his morning newspapers and telegrams could have turned him into an insomniac. The conservative *Novoye Vremya* alone provided ample disturbing news: yet another Russian retreat from the Japanese army; a cost study on the fortune needed to care for wounded veterans; unrest in Warsaw and Odessa; rumors quoted from French newspapers that Sergei Witte, Nicholas's former minister of finance, supported peace negotiations with Japan; peasants in Kharkov asking for more land rights; and liberals meeting in Moscow to discuss a constitutional government. Then there was the editorial about the Battle of Tsushima, rehashing the disaster that had shaken Nicholas to the core, this time blaming the defeat on a navy that "stubbornly refuses to choose officers for their abilities." Nicholas preferred not to read the liberal newspaper *Russkiye Vedomosti*, but that morning its editorial page almost openly supported his regime's demise. And these were the articles that had made it past his censors.

The uncensored truth in his ministry reports and telegrams revealed much greater problems. His generals reported that the Japanese were building on their March victory at Mukden, pushing back the Russians in Manchuria as they had in Korea, though his generals sweetened their news with promises of future success. In Warsaw and Lodz, "unrest" was, in truth, outright revolution. Workers had erected street barricades, boiling tar and bombs had been thrown at the tsar's troops, and peasants armed with scythes were marching into town. The developing situation in Odessa might offer more of the same in the coming days. Thirteen other cities within his empire were also experiencing some kind of strike. As for the peasants outside Kharkov, their request for more land rights came in the indelicate form of burning their landowners' estates.

As Nicholas began his day, assaults on his reign and calls for change appeared endless. They arose from both the despised revolutionaries and from nobles who were able to gain an audience with him. In a way, the nobles' demands represented the greater betrayal — and a more plausible threat. Although the tsar tried to insulate himself from the chaos, this turmoil was enough to reaffirm his wish that he had never been born to become tsar. But that was his role, and he would be damned rather than betray his obligation to God and country. In his view, the Romanovs *were* Russia. To allow others a voice in its leadership meant nothing less than its death.

The first of the Romanovs, Michael, came to power in 1613 after nearly two decades of infighting among the princes of Moscow, which had left Russia in chaos. The country's aristocratic families decided that only a strong monarchy, like that of the past, could prevent anarchy and invasion from the Swedes or Poles. The kind of power they had in mind originated in the thirteenth century, when the Tatars overran Russia.

So they could survive and prosper under the yoke of the Tatars, the people of the Muscovite principality allowed their ruler absolute authority. The prince taxed his lands, ruled his people, and dealt with enemies, internal and foreign, as his conscience dictated, unhindered by laws or bureaucratic interference. Ivan the Terrible, the first Muscovite prince to crown himself Tsar of All Russia in 1547, revealed the limitlessness of this absolute power. With the support of the Russian Orthodox Church, the prince's authority was also endowed with a divine mandate, a mystical connection between him and the Orthodox people he ruled.

For more than 250 years of continuous Romanov rule, the tsars reigned over Russia in this same paternalistic manner. Sporadic bursts of reform — attempts to form a functioning civil service, codify legal principles, loosen censorship, and create local governing assemblies called *zemstvos* — had failed to effectively challenge the tsar's power. In 1881, when Nicholas's father, Alexander III, ascended the throne, he was determined that this kind of reform (favored most recently by his own father, Alexander II, who was nonetheless assassinated by revolutionaries) would never take hold. He repressed dissent, debilitated the civic bureaucracy, and crushed any advances toward representative government, no matter how meager. While Russia faced the encroachment of the modern world — secularism, industrialization, urban populations, and democratic ideologies — in the last decades of the nineteenth century, Alexander III raised his son to follow the Muscovite tradition of rule, believing it the one true path to maintaining the Russian Empire's greatness.

Alexander III took easily to the role of autocrat. A tall, broad-shouldered gorilla of a man who, reportedly, could tie an iron poker into knots, he was a resolute, bluntly spoken leader with tremendous energy and little patience for formality. He enjoyed power, exercising it with great enthusiasm.

His son inherited few, if any, of his father's capabilities. A timid, small boy who often fell sick, Nicholas idolized his father even as he withered in the enormous shadow that Alexander cast. Brought up in the colossal Gatchina Palace at the Romanov estate in the town of the same name south of St. Petersburg, Nicholas, his two younger brothers, and his sisters followed a Spartan lifestyle together with their parents: sleeping on army cots, rising early, taking cold baths, and, at times, barely getting enough to eat. Apparently, this was done to teach discipline, but extravagant toys, doting governesses, and the obsequiousness with which everyone they met treated them, including those charged with their education, confused the effect. Furthermore, the tsarina, Marie, tended to be overprotective.

From a young age, Nicholas had a host of tutors. His earliest ones, including an elderly English gentleman named Mr. Heath, taught him perfect manners, an impenetrable calm, a keen interest in sports, an ability to dance, and a command of French, German, and English. It was an ideal education for a courtier but not for the future leader of 135 million people. Only when Nicholas turned fifteen did his father, who still viewed him as a child and privately considered him a disappointment, arrange for an education more suited to prepare Nicholas for the many challenges he would face as tsar.

Entrusted to some of Russia's greatest minds, he began a broad range of study including mathematics, science, history, geography, literature, law, and military science. This program was overseen by Alexander III's former tutor and lay head of the Russian Orthodox Church, Konstantin Pobedonostsev. A gaunt figure, usually dressed in black and looking as if he had just climbed out of his grave, Pobedonostsev was a reactionary of the highest order. He viewed democracies as akin to rule by the devil, considered constitutions "the instruments of the unrighteous," and labeled a free press "the instrument of mass corruption." According to Pobedonostsev, God himself had chosen the tsar and guided him; if his earthly representative failed to rule as an autocrat, allowing others a hand in government, then the tsar had failed God and deserved punishment.

These lessons Pobedonostsev taught Nicholas personally. They made a deep impression, reinforced by his father's like-minded views and by the assassination of his grandfather, whose legless and bloodied body Nicholas was forced to view as a thirteen-year-old in 1881. Overall, however, Nicholas had little thirst for the knowledge imparted to him in the long, dreary lectures, which neither tested him nor allowed him to think for himself. At their conclusion in May 1890, the twenty-one-year-old tsarevich noted in his diary, "Today I finished definitely and forever my education."

Nicholas preferred his command of the Preobrazhensky Guards Regiment; he was entranced by military pomp and circumstance as well as by the leisurely life of a gentleman officer. An agreeable and courteous young man, who appeared attentive and always managed to say and do the proper thing, he would have been unremarkable in St. Petersburg's court were it not for his proximity to the throne. Yet his father was a robust forty-four-year-old in 1890, and Nicholas likely faced decades before he would become tsar, so he pursued his hobbies, idling away his time instead of learning the ponderous details of running an empire. He drank with his fellow officers, played billiards, attended grand balls, traveled the world, and had a dalliance with a ballerina before falling for Alexandra of Hesse-Darmstadt, a German princess and granddaughter of Queen Victoria.

In 1894, his father suddenly came down with kidney disease; the doctors could do nothing. Nicholas hurried to his father's side with the rest of the family at Livadia, their Crimean palace on the Black Sea. Soon after, Alexander III lost his colossal strength, and he died on November 1. That afternoon, Nicholas felt the weight of the Russian Empire crashing down upon him. After escorting his brother-in-law, Grand Duke Aleksandr, down the stairs and into his room, Nicholas embraced him and, with tears in his eyes, despaired. "Sandro, what am I going to do? What is going to happen to me, to you, to Xenia, to Alix, to Mother, to all of Russia? I'm not prepared to be tsar. I never wanted to become one. I know nothing of the business of ruling. I have no idea of even how to talk to the ministers." One of these ministers, the head of the navy, was equally troubled. On the eve of Alexander III's death, he wrote, "The heir is a mere child, without experience, training, or even an inclination to study the great problems of state. . . . The helm of state is about to fall from the hands of an experienced mariner, and I fear that no hand like his is to grasp it for many years to come. What will be the course of the ship of state under these conditions the Lord only knows."

At twenty-six years of age, Nicholas was now tsar. His official coronation in May 1896 portended the many disasters to come. Accompanied by his new wife, Alexandra, Nicholas entered the grand Uspensky Cathedral in Moscow to the chanting of the choir and climbed the fifteen steps to the throne under a purple canopy. He swore to uphold the imperial autocracy, wrapped himself in the imperial cloak, and placed the diamond-encrusted crown on his own head. The pealing of bells proclaimed his ascendancy, and Nicholas rode from the cathedral on horseback with his golden scepter in hand. For three days, Moscow and the whole of Russia celebrated the coronation.

On the fourth day, May 16, Nicholas was scheduled to present gifts to his people on Khodynskoye Field, a drill ground lined with trenches and thronged with nearly half a million peasants from every region of the empire. Early in the morning, peasants rushed to the front of the field to get their hands on the cakes and the specially engraved tin cups that were to be handed out to them later in the day. Thousands fell into the ditches, young and old alike, and they were trampled to death in the stampede of people. Into the night, wagons carted away the dead and mangled, as Nicholas, having reluctantly agreed to continue the coronation festivities at his uncles' suggestion, attended the French ambassador's ball. From that moment, he felt that his reign was cursed, while the public wondered, in outrage, how their new tsar could dance in the midst of such a tragedy.

From the beginning, the new tsar made clear how he was going to rule. A deputation of officials from numerous provinces came to pay their respects shortly after Alexander III's death. After receiving their gifts and listening to their words of support, Nicholas thanked them, but then announced, "It has come to my attention that during the past months there have been heard in some of the *zemstvos* the voices of those who have senseless dreams that they could some day be called to participate in the government of the country. I want everyone to know that I will concentrate all my strength on maintaining, for the good of the whole nation, the principle of absolute autocracy, as firmly and as strongly as did my lamented father."

But Nicholas was no equal to his father. Although personally charming and diligently devoted to the empire's affairs, he had neither his father's keen mind nor his self-assurance. "Nicholas spent the first years of his reign at his desk, listening, with a feeling best described as alarm, to avuncular advice and insinuations," recounted his brother-in-law Grand Duke Aleksandr Mikhailovich. The tsar's wife, Alix, who barely spoke Russian when they married and knew little about the country, urged her husband to lead the empire with the same forceful hand as Ivan the Terrible, ignoring the multitudes who would give him direction. Given the meddling foolishness of his four uncles and other court members, this might actually have been sound counsel.

However, Nicholas managed to create the worst of all worlds. First, he refused to delegate, personally handling the most trivial details of the empire — school budgets, provincial midwives' appointments, and peasant petitions — while neglecting to set out a cohesive plan for his vision of Russia. Second, he gave key positions within his government to family members, appointing his boorish uncle Sergei as governor-general of Moscow and his bon vivant uncle Alexis, who had little naval experience, as grand admiral of the fleet. Protective of his powers, Nicholas also favored mediocre sycophants over strong-willed, capable ministers such as Sergei Witte, his father's minister of finance, whom Nicholas eventually removed from office despite his substantial abilities and devotion to Russia. Third, Nicholas kept these ministries separated, meeting with each head individually and eliminating any chance of coordinated effort. As one official in Nicholas's administration commented, "There were as many governments as there were ministries." Finally, Nicholas relied on God for wisdom, believing completely that it was the Almighty alone who guided his hand. But, as a monarchist newspaper editor quipped in a moment of candor, "The Sovereign listens only to God, and only from God does he take advice, but because God is invisible he takes advice from everyone he meets: from his wife, from his mother, from his stomach . . . and accepts all this as an order from God."

As if his own personal failings weren't enough, Nicholas had inherited an autocratic state coming apart at the seams. Alexander III had pushed his country along the path of industrialization through the 1880s, fearing that Russia had fallen dangerously behind the rest of the world. His policies created a boom, rapidly expanding the economy and creating large urban centers, but the workers suffered in the process. Their peasant families back in the countryside fared as badly, burdened by a population explosion, low productivity, high state taxes, crippling land fees, and a useless bureaucracy. The landed nobles, who had always served as the tsar's chief supporters, continued an economic decline begun with the emancipation of serfs and exacerbated by an agricultural depression. Their attempts at bettering their position (and that of peasants) through *zemstvos,* organizations first promoted by Alexander II, were thwarted by his son, who viewed this type of localized government as a check on his authority. Progressive state bureaucrats who also came to the fore during the reforms of the 1860s, bringing with them rule of law and rational Western-minded policies, were similarly vanquished. With them, workers lost any chance at curbing the abuses of factory owners, making them ripe candidates for revolution.

The great famine of 1891 revealed the failings of Alexander III's autocratic state. The regime bungled relief efforts, deepening a crisis that eventually killed over half a million people. Alexander's belated, desperate call to the public for assistance, answered foremost by *zemstvos* leaders as well as by merchants, landless nobles, students, teachers, doctors, engineers, and other individuals in the cities, sparked a demand for change. Once the crisis subsided, however, Alexander returned to his old ways. In the aftermath, some Russians were radicalized, but many others, including *zemstvos* leaders such as Prince Georgy Lvov, campaigned for the tsar to open the government to public influence. These were the individuals whom Nicholas II addressed soon after his father's death, when he referred to their ambitions as "senseless dreams." It was a critical mistake on his part. As German chancellor Otto von Bismarck once said, "The power of revolution lies not in the extreme ideas of its leaders, but in that small portion of moderate demands unsatisfied at the right time."

By not pursuing the reforms of his grandfather, Nicholas accelerated the inevitable fall of an outdated form of government. As he mimicked his father's policies, the plight of peasants and workers worsened, as did their frustration, evidenced in sporadic countryside revolts and factory strikes. Revolutionaries increased in number. And some *zemstvos* nobles, who traditionally supported the tsar and had earlier wanted only some limited say in local affairs, now aligned themselves with liberal intellectuals such as Pyotr Struve and Pavel Milyukov. These men led the charge to replace the autocracy with a parliamentary democracy, forming the Union of Liberation and publishing their aims in illegal journals such as *Osvobozhdeniye,* which was launched in 1902.

Then Nicholas went to war with Japan, revealing how corrosive his reign had become. With each defeat in battle, his position weakened, while the voices of opposition grew louder. The state faced bankruptcy, literally and figuratively. Vyacheslav von Plehve, his reactionary interior minister, was torn apart by an assassin's bomb in July 1904, an act received warmly by almost everyone but the tsar himself.

Shaken by this death, Nicholas began a series of maneuvers that promised reform. Then he backpedaled on each, causing his opposition to press even harder for change.

For example, the tsar's selection of Prince P. D. Svyatopolk-Mirsky to fill Plehve's former post came as a welcome signal that Nicholas was moving in a new direction. A forty-seven-year-old bureaucrat known for his progressive views, Mirsky publicly called for giving the people a voice in government. With his tacit approval, 103 *zemstvos* leaders met in Moscow in November 1904 and approved an agenda of reform that included the granting of civil liberties and the election of a representative body whose leaders would participate in the State Council. This agenda was then presented to Mirsky for Nicholas's consideration. Liberals declared the assembly a historic occasion, one celebrated across the country with public banquets modeled on the ones that followed the 1848 Revolution in France. Physicians, teachers, lawyers, engineers, and the intelligentsia toasted one another, believing that universal suffrage and a constitution were just around the corner. On December 12, Nicholas's response put a stop to the festivities. He issued an edict (*ukaz*) declaring that he would grant a few concessions, including looser censorship rules and an end to the persecution of *zemstvos*. He made no mention, however, of a representative parliamentary body or a constitution. At best, the *ukaz* was a halfhearted gesture of appeasement. Afterward Mirsky lamented to a friend, "Everything has failed. Let us build jails."

A month later, a priest named Father Gapon led tens of thousands to the Winter Palace on a snowy Sunday morning to petition Nicholas to improve the conditions of the workers whom he represented. His "Most Humble and Loyal Address to the Tsar" also contained a list of political reforms inspired in part by the *zemstvos* and the liberals. His appeal was met with fixed bayonets and cavalry charges. Over one hundred died in the violence, including women and children, and many more were injured. That day, Gapon declared, "There is no God any longer. There is no tsar." Maxim Gorky, who participated in the events and was the Russian correspondent for the New York *Journal* at the time, cabled his publisher, "The Russian Revolution has begun."

In the following days, with the spread of strikes and a firestorm of condemnation directed at Nicholas for failing to sit down with Gapon and thus avoid disaster, it looked as if the tsar would have to honor some of the demands. Yet he maintained his course, albeit sadly. As he revealed to Mirsky, who resigned shortly after Bloody Sunday, "I adhere to autocracy not for my own pleasure. I act in this spirit only because I am convinced that this is necessary for Russia, but if it were for myself I would get rid of it all happily."

Nicholas replaced his interior minister with the moderate Aleksander Bulygin but appointed Dmitry Trepov as his deputy, a hardliner characterized by one noble as "a sergeant major by training and a pogrom-maker by conviction." Nicholas vacillated in a similar manner when he delivered two edicts on February 18, 1904. The first castigated those challenging his autocracy, calling them arrogant traitors, and beckoned his people to be true to their faith in God and rally around the throne. The second ordered his council of ministers to "consider the ideas and suggestions presented to us by private persons and institutions concerning improvements in the state organization." Noting the contradictions between these two edicts, Nicholas's ministers convinced him to issue a third the same day, this one announcing a commission to look into the creation of a consultative state assembly to help draft legislation. In essence, Nicholas was stalling, hoping that the discontent would run out of steam.

Over the next three months, reform petitions poured into St. Petersburg from army regiments, professional unions, factories, towns, and village assemblies. Liberal and *zemstvos* leaders were divided on how far to push the tsar. Some wanted to stop at the creation of the consultative assembly; others fought for nothing short of democracy. Both groups, however, gained in number and organizational strength. Meanwhile, socialist parties capitalized on Bloody Sunday and the call for a constituent assembly that had led to the march on the Winter Palace — neither of which they had much to do with in the first place. Although they argued about whether to push for an armed uprising, they did make significant strides in spreading propaganda and organizing workers. Sensing the tsar's weakness, border provinces such as Poland, Latvia, and Finland also launched direct challenges against their despised Russian ruler.

With the annihilation of Rozhestvensky's fleet at Tsushima in May, the forces of opposition gathered even more momentum. From every quarter, they lashed out at the current regime. "The war has been lost irretrievably," Lenin declared in the socialist journal *Proletary.* "The collapse of the entire political system of tsarism grows clearer both to Europe and to the whole Russian people. Everything is up in arms against the autocracy." Pavel Milyukov, now leader of the liberal group, the Union of Unions, took his most militant stance yet, appealing directly to the people of Russia: "We talked while there was even a shadow of hope that the authorities would listen. Now this hope has vanished. We say use all means to eliminate immediately the plundering gang that has seized power. In its place put a constituent assembly elected by the people."

Russian newspapers, from left to right, agreed the war must end and Nicholas needed to turn his attention to substantive changes at home. The liberal *Russkiye Vedomosti* quoted the Carthaginian general Hannibal after his great defeat: "Peace at all costs, even if the conditions are very severe." The popular *Slovo* announced, "For 200 years we have walked along bypaths with our eyes covered, and now we stand on the edge of an abyss. We ourselves see whither we are being led, and we have the right to say, enough." The editor of *Novoye Vremya* recommended the convocation of a national assembly: "There is no time to waste. The intelligence and sentiment of the whole of Russia are required to stem the rapidly rising waves."

Internationally, the verdict was the same. The Russian ambassador to Paris cabled Nicholas, "I don't even have the strength to describe the damaging impression that our fleet's destruction produced here." Kaiser Wilhelm, who had helped spur Nicholas to war with Japan in his letters and telegrams, now advocated peace, writing his cousin that the Tsushima defeat "ends the chances for a decided turn of the scales in your favor." On May 26, U.S. president Theodore Roosevelt, fearing the consequences of revolution in Russia, sent a note to St. Petersburg and Tokyo, offering his assistance in negotiating peace: "The time has come when in the interest of all mankind we must endeavor to see if it is not possible to bring to an end the terrible and lamentable conflict now being waged."

The day before Roosevelt's letter arrived, Nicholas convened a war council to decide if Russia should pursue peace talks with Japan, if for no other reason than to see what the enemy's demands would be. His ministers and generals argued on both sides, deciding nothing. Then on June 6, Prince Sergei Trubetskoy, representing the *zemstvos* assembly, came to Peterhof to present Nicholas with a statement. It was the first time the tsar had met with his opposition. Trubetskoy, a stately figure from one of Russia's oldest and most prominent families, spoke with deep, calm conviction about the disturbing effect of the military defeats and the need for a representative assembly. "It is essential that all your subjects, equally and without distinction, feel that they are citizens of Russia." At his speech's conclusion, tears welled in the eyes of those gathered in the chamber.

Nicholas was similarly moved: "I grieved and still grieve at the disasters this war has inflicted upon Russia, and at those yet to come, and at all our internal disorder. Cast aside your doubts. My will — the will of your tsar — to assemble representatives of the people is unchangeable. Let there be, as in days of old, unity between the tsar and all of Russia and personal communion between the *zemstvos* and myself as the foundation of an order built upon traditional Russian principles. I hope that you will cooperate in this work."

Despite his words that day and the many entreaties of peace, Nicholas was uncommitted to ending the war; nor had he changed his mind about allowing any representative body to have a decisive say in the state's affairs. He retreated to his daily Peterhof routine, fearless of, or at least oblivious to, the chance that his opposition could gather enough strength to remove him from the throne. In their hearts, he was convinced, the people loved him. If some had been misled, then they would be crushed, by all the powers of his state. The U.S. consul in St. Petersburg, Ethebert Watts, agreed that Nicholas could weather the storm surging around him, except in one situation. He cabled Washington, "I personally do not believe any strike or political uprising can succeed so long as the military remains loyal to the Government, but so soon as that falters or turns in favor of the people, then we may look for the downfall of the present dynasty."

On June 14, as Nicholas savored a beautiful day at Peterhof that included kayaking, a horseback ride with his wife, a party for his daughter Maria's sixth birthday, and a soothing dip in the warm waters of the Gulf of Finland, this was an unthinkable possibility.

# 7

O N T H E *Potemkin*, the ability of twenty officers to control 763 sailors had always relied on a fragile social construct: the officers expected discipline because that was what they had always known. The sailors were in the habit, reinforced by the threat of punishment, of obeying their commands. But that afternoon, after the guards refused to fire on the unarmed sailors by the railing, after Gilyarovsky grabbed for one of their rifles, and after Nikishkin fired a shot into the sky, this construct collapsed — irrevocably.

Gilyarovsky rushed toward the gun turret and Vakulenchuk. If he killed this leader among the sailors, he might defuse the mutiny — or so he thought. Lieutenant Neupokoyev followed the second officer. As they came around the turret, Vakulenchuk aimed at Gilyarovsky, but his shot went wide, hitting Neupokoyev in the head. His fellow officer fallen behind him, Gilyarovsky raced forward, firing on the run. His first shot hit Vakulenchuk in the chest. The sailor stumbled forward, adrenaline and momentum carrying him. He managed to grab Gilyarovsky's rifle by the muzzle and wrestle it from his hands before being shot again from behind by a petty officer. Spinning around, Vakulenchuk fell to the deck. Blood spilled from his two wounds.

Across the deck, Matyushenko threw his rifle at Golikov, hoping to spear the captain with its bayonet. He missed. Golikov stepped away, in a panic ordering one of his officers to take down the names of anyone participating in the mutiny and telling another to run and signal the *Ismail* to approach the *Potemkin* so they could escape. Sailors quickly overran these two officers, forcing them to jump overboard;

neither order was carried out. With rifles firing wildly about him, Golenko scurried off the deck toward the safety of his cabin.

Meanwhile, Matyushenko retrieved his weapon before chasing after Gilyarovsky. First, though, he had to force his way through the melee of sailors. Some were scrambling for the hatch to retrieve more guns from the armory, but most were simply stunned. On a battleship, routines and rules governed everything — except mutiny. Shocked by the sudden crack of rifles, unsure about what was happening, and confused about whom to follow or what to do, the sailors acted on instinct. They dashed off the quarterdeck; they stood rooted in place like statues; they grabbed, shoved, and screamed at one another to get out of the way of the crossfire that had already killed several of their comrades. Several revolutionaries attempted to organize these sailors as the mutiny began, but the men were too terrified to listen to direction.

Matyushenko finally cleared his way through the crush of sailors and rounded the turret where his friend had stood a second before. He arrived just in time to see Neupokoyev killed and, a few seconds later, the second officer standing over the crumpled heap of Matyushenko's friend Vakulenchuk.

A searing feeling of loss and hatred overwhelmed Matyushenko as he pulled the trigger of his rifle to kill Gilyarovsky. The rifle misfired. Gilyarovsky fired in return, narrowly missing Matyushenko. The second officer then ordered the remaining guards to kill the mutineers. In response, the guards fled. Gilyarovsky aimed at their backs, exposing himself to fire in his desire to kill these sailors for their betrayal. Seizing their chance, Matyushenko and two other sailors leveled their rifles and shot him by the railing. The second officer collapsed onto the deck. By the capstan, Lieutenant Liventsev tried to snatch a rifle from one of the guards and come to Gilyarovsky's aid. He was ripped apart by a hail of bullets.

Matyushenko strode across the deck, murder in his thoughts. As he stood over Gilyarovsky, the stricken officer hissed, "I know you, you scoundrel. You may escape from the ship now, but I'll find you."

"You won't have the chance," Matyushenko said evenly, before shooting him again. "I'm sending you to work as a ship's boy for Admiral Makarov."

Matyushenko lifted Gilyarovsky to the railing; the blood from the officer's wounds smeared his sailor's jersey. Then he tipped Gilyarovsky's body overboard to join his hero who had died at Port Arthur a year before. Matyushenko had delivered his revenge against the worst of the officers, the one who had shot down his beloved comrade. Now the revolutionary began to focus on taking over the battleship.

"Enough of this slavery!" Matyushenko yelled, rallying the sailors around him. On the quarterdeck stood thirty armed sailor revolutionaries; the officers and their loyal self-seekers had fled to every corner of the ship. Matyushenko wanted them found before they tried to re-establish control or scuttle the battleship. He also sent sailors to check that Denisenko had gained control of the engine room, that Bredikhin had cut the telegraph wires, and that the others had seized the conning tower. They had a plan to execute.

With the officers in retreat and the armory in revolutionary hands, the mass of sailors made the easy decision to support the mutiny. "Hunt them all down!" came a shout from the turret. "The ship's not ours yet." In contrast to their earlier confusion, the crew acted in unison now. They raced across the decks, plunged down hatches, and searched bow to stern for their superiors, some acting out private revenge, some caught up in the bloodlust. A few had bayonets, others revolvers and rifles, but most went on their hunt armed only with clenched fists. Fueled by their recent fear of being shot for refusing to eat, released from the bonds of discipline, and emboldened by their own superior numbers, they were little better than a mob bent on terror and murder. They shouted "Down with the tsar!" and "Freedom!" almost as afterthoughts.

In this midst of this, Vakulenchuk struggled to his feet, but his legs buckled under him. He grabbed for the railing, pulling himself up again, mortally wounded. Before anyone could get to him, Vakulenchuk lost his balance and pitched over the ship's side. A sailor leapt into the water after him. With the help of some others, they managed to haul the injured revolutionary back on board. Weakened from loss of blood, he could not stand. The sailors carried him straight to the infirmary. While he struggled in and out of consciousness, barely hanging on to life, his comrades gained control of the battleship.

· · ·

In his cabin, Lieutenant Aleksandr Kovalenko sat stiffly on his sofa, listening to screams and gunshots. Slim, with a clean-shaven, vulpine face, the twenty-three-year-old mechanical engineer, who had studied at a technological institute in Kharkov before joining the navy, treated well the sailors under his command. He sympathized with the Black Sea Fleet's revolutionary movement, though he could never have admitted it to them, for fear of discovery by his superiors. A Ukrainian nationalist, he wanted Nicholas II overthrown so that his own country could have its freedom. But he suspected the sailors would never see past his epaulettes during their rampage, even if he told them of his political views.

Kovalenko looked around his quarters. Only hours before, he had been alone in his stateroom, enjoying the scent of the field flowers that he had picked on Tendra Island and the open book on his desk before being called to lunch. Now he was shuddering at each gunshot and sitting beside three other fear-stricken officers.

He had been in the officers' wardroom when Gilyarovsky barged in to ask Smirnov if the meat was suitable for eating. With the drums sounding for roll call, Kovalenko breathed in relief that, as an engine-room officer, his presence was not required for the inevitable long speeches about discipline and the navy's strict regulations. He continued his lunch with the other officers not involved in the dressing down of the men: Lieutenant N. F. Grigoryev, Engineer Officer S. A. Zaushkevich, and the locksmith A. N. Kharkevich, along with the ship's priest and the artillery engineers from St. Petersburg who had come to watch the firing tests. Then they heard a shriek from Gilyarovsky, demanding to know if the sailors meant mutiny, and the concentrated roar indicating that they did. Faces blanched in the wardroom. Father Parmen left immediately, followed by Colonel I. A. Schultz from St. Petersburg. "Something terrible is happening," Grigoryev said, approaching Kovalenko. He agreed, and three *Potemkin* officers followed him to his quarters to decide what to do.

"This would never have happened if the captain or his second officer hadn't acted so ridiculously," muttered Grigoryev to Kovalenko, while Zaushkevich stepped outside to see what was happening.

"Are you surprised?" Kovalenko asked. "How are they capable of acting with any common sense or conscience when they follow the military traditions of Peter I?"

"So true. But what now?!"

Kovalenko felt his hands shaking and was unable to stop them. "Maybe we should go and try to calm down the crew," he said, thinking out loud.

"We're all beyond words now," Grigoryev stated firmly.

Zaushkevich returned to the cabin. "The crew have guns, and the officers ran away."

"Good Lord," Grigoryev whispered. "All of us will be killed. Can you hear what's going on out there?"

Within minutes, the crazed yells of the crew and the pounding of their footsteps on the steel gangways became louder and closer. The sailors hurled open hatches and then threw them shut upon finding nobody inside. They laughed and cackled and shouted encouragement to one another. In nearby staterooms, they shattered mirrors, splintered furniture, and shot their guns wildly. Closer and closer still — Kovalenko stood petrified, knowing they would be found. With hundreds of sailors on the hunt, there was nowhere to hide. Finally he heard someone come down the corridor. As Kovalenko was about to peer out to see if he passed, a sailor pounded on the adjacent door and lustily shouted a warning: "Every single one of you will be killed! No one will be spared!"

Another voice was heard: "There are no others. Now *we* rule the ship."

Kovalenko stepped away from the door, certain that he was going to die — and soon. It seemed so pointless and so cruelly ironic that he was to lose his life at the hands of men who shared his distaste for the tsar. He felt trapped in a hurricane, with no way to escape or find shelter. Even if his machinists supported him, they made up just a small part of the mob.

"They're going to shoot us," Kharkevich whispered.

"There's only one thing left for us to do . . . jump overboard." The thought had just occurred to Kovalenko. Although the shore was miles away, they might be able to make the swim. It was a better choice than facing a mob bent on revenge.

"It's impossible," Grigoryev scoffed.

"I'd prefer to die that way." Kovalenko began unbuttoning his jacket. The others hesitated, then stripped alongside him.

They kicked out the window in his cabin and crossed the corridor to the *Potemkin*'s starboard side. Kovalenko climbed through a port-hole, looked over the edge to the water below, and then jumped. When he surfaced, he swam out a few yards to avoid Grigoryev and Kharkevich as they plunged into the sea as well. Zaushkevich changed his mind and tried to make his way down to the engine room, only to be caught on his way.

Within seconds of their jump into the water, sailors above spotted the officers and started shooting at them. The swimmers were help-less in the water, at the mercy of luck and the sailors' aim.

Grigoryev barely even groaned as a bullet hit him. His body went limp almost instantly, blood coloring the water about him. As their dead friend slipped under the water, Kovalenko and Kharkevich swam as fast as they could along the ship's hull toward the stern, where the angle was too steep for the sailors to hit them. Then they moved as far from the battleship as their limbs would take them, hoping each stroke would not be their last.

Back on the *Potemkin,* sailors hunted down the rest of the officers and petty officers. Several had already jumped overboard, like Kovalenko, and were riddled by bullets as they paddled toward the *Ismail.* Barri-caded within one of the six-inch gun compartments, Ensign B. V. Vakhtin thought he was safe until the sailors broke inside. They pum-meled him with their fists and with a broken-off leg of a table until he lost consciousness. A group of sailors found Father Parmen stumbling down a stairwell and shattered his nose with a rifle butt. They left him crawling for safety toward a latrine. The sailors came upon Dr. Smirnov in his cabin, half-dressed and splattered with blood. He had attempted suicide but did not have the stomach to inflict more than a mild flesh wound with a razor.

"Let me die in peace," he pleaded.

"Why did you say that the meat was good?" they demanded.

"I'm not to blame. I was compelled to say that."

"You ordered us to eat maggots — now you're going to be fish bait," a sailor said. Then they took Smirnov by the arms and dragged him out of his cabin. He begged for his life while the sailors lifted him onto the railing. Then they pushed him overboard with their bayo-nets. Seeing that he could swim, they shot him for good measure.

Down in the coal-hold area, the revolutionary Denisenko had arrested the chief mechanical engineer Lieutenant N. Y. Tsvetkov, stopping him from flooding the ship's lower compartments. "Where are the rest of the officers?" Tsvetkov asked the engineer. "Killed," said Denisenko. Tsvetkov handed over his saber. "Well, whatever happens, so be it. Let them do with me whatever they want."

Torpedo officer Lieutenant Wilhelm Ton refused to surrender. At the mutiny's height, he appeared on the quarterdeck, brandishing a revolver and walking straight toward Matyushenko. "Drop your weapons, you fools," Ton shouted. "You'll all be shot for this."

Several men, their rifles aimed at Ton's chest, screamed for the officer to be thrown overboard. Matyushenko signaled with his hand for the sailors to be calm. Ton then asked to speak with him, privately. Although Matyushenko respected his supervising officer, who was a fair disciplinarian, he did not trust the gun at his side. Matyushenko demanded that Ton put the revolver away before they spoke. Ton hesitated, then put the gun in his belt. The sailors still pointed their rifles at him. The moment gave Matyushenko a chance to catch his breath after the rush of events in the mutiny's first minutes. Waving off the sailors, he followed the torpedo officer to the side of the gun turret. Matyushenko told Ton to surrender and to take off his epaulettes if he wanted to be spared.

Ton replied bitterly, "You fool. You didn't give them to me and therefore you will not remove them."

Without another word, Ton drew his revolver, and before Matyushenko could knock the barrel aside, Ton fired two shots pointblank at him. Somehow — both missed Matyushenko. One struck a sailor's arm. The other hit a sailor in the right temple, killing him. Reflexively, Matyushenko and nine other sailors turned their rifles on Ton. Their gunshots threw him backward into the turret wall. After he slid down to the deck, his chest a pulpy mess, a group of sailors tossed him over the ship's side.

"We haven't found the captain yet," Matyushenko said, so focused on what they still had to do that his hair's-breadth escape from death left him unshaken. With Golikov still on the loose, they had not yet won the battleship. "Has anyone seen him?"

"We want the captain," the men yelled together before they spread out to look for him. "We want the captain!"

Then a sailor shouted that the *Ismail* was swinging around toward them. Some began firing at the *Ismail*'s bow with their rifles, fearing it might torpedo the *Potemkin* at close range. Matyushenko rushed down to the gun deck with several revolutionaries, including Yfim Shevchenko and Sergei Guz. They knew the *Ismail* had not been stocked with torpedoes for the training exercises, but it must be prevented from getting away and alerting Sevastopol of the mutiny.

"Man the guns and put a shot across her bow," Matyushenko told the gunner, already beginning to assert command of the crew. "That'll soon stop her. They can't be allowed to escape."

Lieutenant Pyotr Klodt von Yurgensburg stood on the torpedo boat *Ismail*'s deck. With a pair of binoculars he watched sailors rush across the main and upper decks of the *Potemkin*, and he vacillated about what he should do. Officers and petty officers pitched into the water, some already dead, others swimming for their lives toward the *Ismail* as sailors picked them off from above as if they were doing target practice. In the distance, he could also hear the crew's bloodcurdling screams as they overtook the battleship. Still Klodt did nothing, too scared to even think straight.

The *Ismail* had been anchored a stone's throw from the *Potemkin* when Klodt heard Golikov order the guards to the deck. "What can we do with such commanders?" Klodt asked his second officer, dismayed at why the battleship's captain needed armed guards in order to speak with his sailors. "Does he plan on arresting or killing them?" His crew wondered too as the situation deteriorated on the battleship, sailors first shouting for mercy, then in defiance.

With the first gunshots on the *Potemkin*, Klodt had panicked. The forty-one-year-old gunnery officer was a baron of Swedish nobility. His father was a famous painter, his grandfather an even more famous sculptor whose work was prominently displayed throughout St. Petersburg. Klodt ought to have followed in their creative footsteps, as he was an indecisive, weak-kneed leader, out of his depth on this, his first voyage commanding the *Ismail*. A more experienced, willful officer would have realized that without torpedoes to sink the mutinous battleship, the *Ismail* was best served by retreating out of the *Potemkin*'s range while the sailors were focused on taking over the

ship. If the mutiny succeeded, then Klodt could steam away to notify
the Black Sea Fleet command. With a top speed of twenty-five knots
and an ability to hug the shore, the *Ismail* could easily elude the
*Potemkin* and reach Sevastopol within eight hours.

Instead Klodt watched the mutiny unfold, delivering no orders.
Supply officer Makarov was the first swimmer to arrive at the torpedo
boat's side. The crew helped him aboard, desperate to know what
had happened. Makarov removed his jacket and asked for a shirt, in
such a state of shock that he ignored their questioning and counted
the soggy bank notes stuffed in his pocket. He was brought down to
the small wardroom to dry off and settle down.

Finally, twenty minutes after the first shot was fired on the *Potemkin*,
Klodt decided that the *Ismail* should get away. He told his crew to
weigh anchor, but the mooring line accidentally twisted around the
anchor buoy. Klodt ordered his sailors to cut the line, but they were
unsuccessful. Now terrified that he might actually be captured and
killed, Klodt tried to sever the line by starting the engines and revers-
ing the ship. At this point, the *Potemkin* mutineers started shooting at
his crew with rifles. He had lingered too long.

"Your Excellency," Klodt's signalman yelled, "the *Potemkin* is aiming its guns at us."

His crew cried out that they needed to surrender. Ignoring their
protests, Klodt ordered full steam. Suddenly, one of the *Potemkin*'s
aft forty-seven-millimeter guns cracked. The shot sailed over the bow.
The *Ismail* shuddered backward, Klodt swinging the wheel around
as he tried to break free from the mooring line. A second shot
sounded. The third cut through the torpedo boat's funnel.

"Your Excellency," the signalman desperately urged, "they're ordering us to stop. Please."

Knowing the *Potemkin* could easily blow the torpedo boat to bits,
Klodt stepped out of the small wheelhouse and notified the *Potemkin*
of his surrender. Revolutionary sailor Alekseyev rowed to the *Ismail*
from the battleship with several armed sailors to arrest Klodt and take
control of the torpedo boat. They met no resistance. A few minutes
later they dragged Klodt, Makarov, and several other officers from the
*Ismail* onto the *Potemkin*, where their fate would be decided. After
Alekseyev ripped off their epaulettes, the officers began begging for
their lives. Meanwhile, several more of the battleship's revolutionary

sailors (two machinists, two stokers, and a helmsman) went over to man the torpedo boat.

The crew's thirst for blood slackened with each killing. Within a half-hour of the first shot, they completely controlled the ship and its torpedo boat escort. The sailors found officers and petty officers hidden behind oil tanks and underneath canvases; one had even crawled out to the end of the foremast. All were dragged by their heels or pushed and shoved toward the quarterdeck. They huddled along the railing, looking much like the sailors threatened with the tarpaulin before the mutiny broke out. Several crew members surrounded the officers, their rifles pointed at them, fingers poised on the triggers. Still they had yet to find Captain Golikov.

While the sailors continued their search, officers Kovalenko and Kharkevich, having escaped the first barrage of shots, floated several hundred yards away from the *Potemkin*. Their arms were wrapped over a tree trunk that had been dropped into the sea that morning for target practice. Some of the crew waved their hats at them, shouting Kovalenko's name. He heaved himself onto the trunk.

"You're an easy target now," Kharkevich said.

"They wouldn't call me if they wanted to kill me," Kovalenko reasoned, and then shouted toward the *Potemkin*, "What do you want?"

"Engineer Officer Kovalenko! Return to us! We won't harm you."

Kovalenko recognized some of his engine room machinists and decided it was safe. As he swam toward the *Potemkin*, the sailors sent a boat to retrieve him and Kharkevich. One of his machinists was on board and pulled him by the arm onto the boat, smiling. A few even apologized, explaining that they had always considered him their friend. Kovalenko was stunned that these men, who only moments before had tried to kill him, were now treating him so well. He soon learned how fortunate he was.

With the hollers of the sailors and the crack of their gunshots dying down, Captain Golikov prepared to dash out of the admiral's stateroom and make his way overboard through the port window. He was stripped down to his underwear and had a flotation vest slung over his shoulder. A young ensign named Dmitry Alekseyev was by his side, also undressed and ready to escape with his captain.

After retreating from the quarterdeck, Golikov had first gone to his cabin, with Ensign Alekseyev at his heels like a puppy the entire time. The captain decided it was too obvious a place to hide, so they slipped across to the admiral's stateroom and locked the door behind them. In a room rarely used except when dignitaries were aboard, he prayed the sailors would overlook them. They had. Now he needed to get off the *Potemkin*.

Suddenly the stateroom's door shuddered. Then again. They had been found. The sailors outside demanded they open the door, but Golikov refused, huddled at the far end of the stateroom. Finally, revolutionary Aleksei Syrov and several others broke down the door. They hauled Golikov and Alekseyev toward the quarterdeck, disregarding their screams to be let go.

Syrov, who held a particular grudge against Golikov after his recent demotion for a minor violation, threw the captain onto the deck at Matyushenko's feet. The crew circled around Golikov as he raised himself to his knees. Many eagerly waited to see him killed. Revolver in hand, Matyushenko looked down at Golikov. He felt strange, seeing the same individual who, less than an hour before, had been all powerful and ready to condemn the crew to death, now groveling for his own life, in his underwear. Matyushenko was struck that the officer, whose sagging pale flesh was exposed, simply looked silly and pathetic.

"I surrender to your command," Golikov said pitifully. "Please, brothers, spare me. I'm an old fool. Show some mercy. There has been enough killing." He spoke quickly, promising there would be no more mistreatment and that he would personally petition the tsar to pardon the sailors for the uprising. Golikov then begged the sailors to forgive him for his sins against them.

Matyushenko allowed Golikov to finish, weighing whether he should kill him. The captain represented the very system that had oppressed and exploited Matyushenko throughout his life. He had suffered under the agents of its authority many times: the police officer who beat him senseless in a prison cell as a teenager, the Kharkov factory foremen, the merchant ship officers, the railroad bosses in Vladivostok, and officer after officer in the navy. Killing Golikov would represent a strike against all of them, yet the captain was helpless now. The others killed that morning, Gilyarovsky and Ton, had threatened the sailors as they strove to take over the ship. Now the *Potemkin* was theirs. Matyushenko could easily arrest Golikov as they had the other captured officers and lock him away until they decided what to do.

"I've nothing against you, personally," Matyushenko finally said. Then he looked around at the sailors. "The crew must decide."

"Hang him!" a sailor shouted.

"He threatened us with the yardarm. Let him hang on it," another agreed.

Although some sailors were indifferent, nobody spoke in Golikov's defense. For some, the mutiny was incomplete until the captain was dead. Others simply wanted retribution or were still caught up in bloodlust. In putting the question to the crew, Matyushenko had to know their only decision would be death. But he would not deliver the coup de grâce. Perhaps he felt a tinge of guilt at killing the defenseless captain himself, or he sensed that it was better for the unified crew to choose Golikov's fate and carry it out. For whatever reason, and Matyushenko may not have known himself, he did nothing to stop the execution.

"We've waited long enough. Let's shoot him," Syrov said, pushing through the sailors with a revolver in his hand.

Golikov stood and backed away. The captain shuffled toward the railing, pleading again for mercy. Syrov raised his revolver. Behind him, several sailors raised their rifles. A moment passed. Golikov stared at his executioners, standing only a couple feet away. He said nothing else. Then Syrov pulled his trigger; his shot was followed by several rifle shots in rapid succession. Before the smoke from the guns cleared, Golikov was dead. As they had done with the other officers, the sailors lifted him onto the railing and tipped him overboard. His body splashed into the water, and the sea's current carried him toward the *Potemkin*'s stern before he slipped unseen into the anoxic waters below.

After Golikov's death, the killing ended. Ensign Alekseyev wept that he would serve the sailors if they gave him a chance. He was led away. Some sailors wanted Makarov killed for purchasing the rotten meat in the first place; others focused their remaining rage on two of the most hated petty officers, who descended to their knees and begged for their lives as well.

"Enough blood," Matyushenko ordered. He felt no remorse for

Golikov's death, but he was not about to sanction a massacre of the rest of the officers and petty officers. Nothing in the Tsentralka plan for mutiny called for the indiscriminate killing that had already been witnessed on the battleship. "Leave them alone. We'll always have time to punish them if they betray us."

The crowd of sailors backed down, and the remaining officers and petty officers were taken to their cabins and locked inside. Medics carried several wounded sailors to the infirmary. The crew brought washing soda onto the quarterdeck and began to swab away the blood and gore.

There was no celebration among the sailors over what they had done. Some milled about the decks, going over the details of the mutiny's first minutes with their comrades, relating how a particular officer faced his death or was captured underneath a pile of oily rags. There was the occasional sound of laughter, but for the most part, the sailors reflected on how easily and unexpectedly they had overthrown their officers and what this meant now. The silence was eerie. The crack of rifle shots and enraged screams had been replaced with the caw of seagulls and sounds of the sea lapping against the battleship's hull. No officers or bosuns barked orders at the crew. They could do or say what they pleased, but they did not yet know what to do with this liberty. So they stood quietly about the decks.

Many of the new recruits, totaling half of the *Potemkin*'s crew, were confused and scared. One later recounted, "I was stricken as with a thunderbolt; I didn't know what to do, which side to take. . . . I wasn't against the uprising; I wasn't for it, because I didn't understand it." They knew the tsar to be just but also swift and cruel to those who betrayed his authority. Some had witnessed, or at least heard of, how harshly his troops dealt with peasant jacqueries in the countryside. If the sailors got caught, they knew the tsar would punish their actions with nothing less than death. But at the moment, the sounds of violence having faded, nobody yet was fully aware of what they had done.

Leaning against the ship's railing, Matyushenko looked across the battleship at what he later described as a "terrible but triumphant picture" — bloodstains on the quarterdeck, the crumpled tarpaulin from the oar boat, forgotten sailor caps, a revolver, and a pair of discarded rifles. Sailors walked about the decks, rid of the tyranny of their officers — but not without cost. Vakulenchuk was absent from the deck, dying below in the infirmary, and far away in Sevastopol, the Black Sea Fleet command would want revenge once they learned of the mutiny. Many more would likely die.

Still, Matyushenko and his fellow revolutionaries had succeeded. They controlled the most powerful battleship in the Russian navy. Now they would carry their fight to the tsar himself. Before he turned to the many challenges they faced, Matyushenko surveyed the scene one last time, and a smile eased across his face. He felt free for the first time in a very long while.

# 8

W HO WILL LEAD the ship?" a sailor asked as he and
his comrades swabbed the last of the blood from the
quarterdeck. Throughout the *Potemkin,* clusters of men
raised the same question. Some spoke of blowing up the ship to de-
prive the tsar of its might; others wanted to go to Sevastopol to surrender or to flee to a foreign port and live as exiles. The core group of
revolutionaries thought only of Odessa.

After checking on the engine room and the arrest of the officers,
Matyushenko returned to the quarterdeck, knowing the crew needed
to choose the ship's leaders. He called for a drumroll to summon
a meeting of sailors. With several revolutionaries at his side, Matyushenko climbed onto the same capstan that Golikov had used that
very afternoon when he threatened to hang the traitors on the
yardarm. Hundreds of men surrounded Matyushenko, looking not
only for direction but also for validation that they had signed their
own death warrants for more than a refusal to eat bad meat.

"All of Russia is waiting to rise and throw off the chains of slavery.
The great day is near," Matyushenko began, pumping his fist for em-
phasis. "And it's on *this* ship that the revolution has started. Soon the
other vessels of the Black Sea Fleet will join us, and then we shall link
up with our brothers on shore — the workers in the factories and
those who slave on the land. We have the most powerful ship with the
most modern guns in the navy. The *Potemkin* can fight whole armies
and defeat them. But we'll be helpless if we don't work together.
That's why there must be discipline. There will never again be tyranny on the *Potemkin,* but there must be some to give orders and

some to carry them out if we're to win. So there must be a people's committee."

Aside from the occasional shout of agreement, the sailors listened to Matyushenko in rapt silence; his conviction was revealed in every word. Above everything else, he understood his fellow sailors: what they needed to hear and how they needed to be led. As one who participated in the mutiny later wrote, "Matyushenko had a rare intuition, and instinctively felt not only the ruling temper of the crowd, but also what was brooding within it. . . . He knew the people, knew their psychology, and therein lay his power and his influence. He was the foremost of them."

When Matyushenko stood down from the capstan, the slightly built stoker Nikishkin took his place. Known as "the Preacher" by many sailors for his philosophical ruminations and tendency to weave Gospel tales into revolutionary discussions, he spoke eloquently of how everyone needed to come together in this great struggle. For the first time they would choose their own leaders rather than have leaders imposed on them. The battleship would be ruled by a people's democracy.

As Nikishkin and several other revolutionaries explained, the crew would elect members to a committee that would have complete authority over the *Potemkin*. This sailor committee would hold open meetings that everyone could witness. It would control the ship's funds, uphold order, elect individuals for key positions in the day-to-day running of the ship, decide on a course of action against the tsar, negotiate with his government, and communicate with revolutionary groups in the ports. Choosing a committee to run the ship was based on the organization of the revolutionary sailor circles, which in part mirrored the communal leadership of the peasant villages, known well by most of the sailors.

Readily agreeing to the plan, the sailors called out potential candidates for election to the committee. Shouts of yes or no decided the matter. Within a half-hour, they had chosen twenty-five members and had elected Matyushenko as chairman. The committee included Pyotr Alekseyev, Stefan Denisenko, Ivan Dymchenko, Aleksandr Makarov, Fyodor Nikishkin, Yvtikhiya Reznichenko, Yfim Bredikhin, Ivan Lychev, Iosif Martyanov, and Frederick Vedenmeyer, among others. Whether they were Bolsheviks or Mensheviks, anarchists or Socialist Revolutionaries, was almost impossible to decipher. As committee member Nikolai Ryzhy recalled, "Not all of us were clear about the differences." Although drawn from every quarter of the ship, the majority were technical specialists — machinists, gunners, telegraph operators — who had been recruited from cities, were already skilled, and were to some degree sympathetic to revolution when they entered the navy, just as Matyushenko had been.

The committee members left for the admiral's stateroom to hold their first meeting. Much had to be discussed. The twenty-five sat around a long boardroom table covered with green felt. Their chairs were intricately carved and as solid as thrones. Most had never before set foot in the room. A bovine portrait of Grigory Potemkin, the battleship's namesake, hung on one bulkhead. Opposite to it could be seen a rectangular outline of dust where Tsar Nicholas's oversized portrait had hung before the sailors tossed it into the Black Sea.

Over one hundred crew members crowded into the room to watch the proceedings, standing against the walls or huddled on the leather divans. A cloud of cigarette smoke soon rose to the ceiling. At the meeting's onset, the mood was light. A stoker turned to his neighbor and joked, "And you, Your Excellency, would you like to have a smoke of Makhorka? This tobacco is too strong for a general's nose, especially nowadays." Laughter echoed throughout the room. Soon enough, the sailors turned to the serious decisions at hand.

First they settled the issue of where to take the *Potemkin*. The battleship required a steady supply of coal and provisions, and they needed a base from which to lead the revolution on land after the other ships in the Black Sea Fleet mutinied, as Tsentralka had planned. Whether or not these mutinies would happen before Vice Admiral Chukhnin sent a squadron of battleships after them, they could not know. Most certainly, however, Chukhnin would eventually send such a squadron. The sailors chose Odessa over Batum, Nikolayev, or the well-defended port of Sevastopol. Given the strikes in Odessa, they hoped to find support among its revolutionary organizations. With the *Potemkin*'s guns backing the struggle, the people would be sure to overthrow the local government there.

Then came the question of who would captain the battleship, set course for Odessa, and lead the sailors in the event of a confrontation, whether from land or on sea. Obviously the committee would make the strategic decisions, but they needed someone with the authority and experience of commanding a battleship to address tactical issues. Some pitched Matyushenko for this role, but he openly acknowledged that as a torpedo quartermaster, he lacked the skills for the position. Nor did any of the sailors on the committee.

As much as Matyushenko hated the thought, he suggested using one or two of the officers to run the battleship under the committee's direction.

"What do we need of officers?" Bredikhin asked. "*We* can navigate the battleship."

Senior signalman Vedenmeyer, a skinny, redheaded sailor, countered that the officers were harmless as long as they were always under the committee's control. Among those in the stateroom, he was most adamant on this position.

Matyushenko also raised the point that the crew, half of whom were raw recruits, were trained to take orders only from officers. They might look skeptically at — or rebel outright against — obeying someone beside whom they had slept and eaten for months. The committee knew that support for the revolutionary fight was not unanimous. They had overheard conversations indicating that some wanted to surrender and repent; others wished to flee to safety. No, the sailors needed an authority figure, an officer, to lead them and maintain discipline. Again, this person would be subject to the elected committee's direction.

"It's impossible to rely blindly on any of the officers," Reznichenko said, sensing the majority leaning toward this option. "Don't forget: they're the sons of noblemen. If they aren't controlled, they'll turn on us."

The committee took a vote of hands, deciding in favor of selecting an officer. They chose Ensign Alekseyev as captain and Senior Boatswain F. V. Murzak as his second in command. A couple of hours before, this ensign, who had curly blond hair, had pleaded for his life next to Golikov, lamenting that he was no less a sailor than any of them. He was spared then and now elevated to a new position by the committee because he had shown himself even-handed in his treatment of sailors (given the crew's estimation of his fellow officers, this was high praise). Before the war, Alekseyev had been in the navy reserves, serving on a merchant ship as a captain's assistant; therefore, he was not viewed as the typical career officer. His education at a navigation school would also prove useful. Murzak had been drafted into the navy over a decade before as a second-class sailor and had climbed the ranks from there. As committee member Lychev later described him, "Murzak was a typical sea wolf. He loved the sea and his job . . . and he knew the ins and outs of the battleship and what needed to be done."

Two hours into the meeting, the committee disbanded so they could ready the ship for departure. "But what of the flag?" a sailor asked. "How can we go to Odessa flying the tsar's colors?"

"True," Matyushenko said. "We should decide."

The stateroom erupted. "Destroy the tsarist flag! Down with it!"

"We're now in a state of revolution," Matyushenko agreed.

"I know!" another committee member said abruptly. "Vakulenchuk brought a flag. He hid it somewhere."

Fifteen minutes later the committee gathered on the main deck with the rest of the crew. They had spoken with Vakulenchuk, who lay dying in the infirmary, and found out where he had concealed the flag. In a solemn moment, a sailor stripped the St. Andrew's flag from the mast. While he slowly raised a simple red flag in its place, the sailors sang the "Marseillaise": "Arise, children of the fatherland / The day of glory has arrived!" The words drifted across the deck and over the open sea.

Soon thereafter, with the steam raised in the engine room, Ensign Alekseyev ordered the sailors to weigh anchor. Matyushenko stood at his side in the conning tower, keeping a watchful eye on him. The young officer had agreed to serve as captain only after hearing that the alternative was to join Golikov in the sea. Saving his own skin seemed to be his motive in helping the sailors.

As the *Potemkin* began to cut across the water, Matyushenko watched the sailors move about their tasks as they always had done, but now they were men acting on their own behalf. Nonetheless, he worried whether the sailor committee could maintain the crew's loyalty, given the awesome responsibility they had taken on. Betrayal was possible from many quarters, particularly from the petty officers, whose allegiance to the tsar had been cemented by long naval service (and better pay and privileges). After the meeting in the stateroom, Matyushenko had even given a revolver to Denisenko, who was charged with running the engine room. "You might need this if it's hard to control your men," Matyushenko warned, knowing well that they had chosen a course, as had others throughout history, from which there was no return. "Don't surrender."

The French coined the word *mutinerie* in the sixteenth century to describe a revolt of troops against lawful authority, but its origin dates back to the earliest known wars. The Roman historian Tacitus wrote of a widespread military revolt that occurred after Augustus Caesar's death. Three legions in Rome, many of whose soldiers were gray-haired and wrecked after years of campaigning, staged a mutiny and pillaged the countryside. "You'd do better to dip your hands in my blood," their commander threatened at the mutiny's beginning. "It is less of a sacrilege to kill me than to fail your emperor." Although mollified temporarily by this speech, the soldiers continued to resist for several weeks until Caesar's successor, Tiberius, stepped in. He had Praetorian soldiers assassinate the leaders of the mutiny in their camp.

The new emperor understood that mutiny challenged one critical foundation of the state: the legitimate control of military power. By contesting the state's command of the military, a mutiny contested its very survival. Therefore, no effort was too swift or too forceful when it came to suppressing a rebellion and treating its participants to the harshest of consequences, both on land and, especially, at sea. When sailors overthrow their officers and take over a ship, they become, in effect, a state unto themselves.

In the sixteenth century, during Ferdinand Magellan's circumnavigation of the globe, several of his officers attempted to mutiny off the coast of Brazil. Magellan crushed the revolt. One officer was stabbed to death, a second beheaded, a third left to die on an uninhabited island. In 1790 the Royal Navy sent a twenty-four-gun frigate halfway round the world to scour Tahiti's shores in order to capture the mutineers of the famous HMS *Bounty*. The ones they found were brought back to Portsmouth, England, and condemned to hang in the port for everyone to witness, as a warning. In 1852, on the U.S. brig-of-war *Somers*, the captain skipped an official court-martial and hanged three young sailors at sea. They had merely conspired to act against their officers. Short of a death sentence — and sometimes worse — other punishments for mutinous sailors included receiving 500 lashes from a cat-o'-nine-tails in weekly sessions of 125 each, so the convicted would suffer every stroke rather than die; being keelhauled, by which a sailor was dragged underwater from one end of the ship to the other against the sharp barnacles on the bottom of the ship's hull; or having MUTINY scored across the forehead and then being passed from ship to ship across the entire fleet to be flogged on each.

Some mutinies ended peacefully and redressed the sailors' complaints, but these were rare exceptions. In 1910, Afro-Brazilian sailors led the "Revolt of the Lash," seizing several Brazilian battleships and demanding that use of the whip be ended. They won their ban, though hundreds of sailors were later executed in revenge for their insubordination. Over a century before, in 1797, at the height of British naval prowess, sailors on sixteen of His Royal Majesty George III's ships refused an order to sail. They sent ashore their officers with a petition to Lord Richard Howe, demanding better pay and food and less harsh disciplinary measures. Howe avoided bloodshed with a mass pardon of the sailors and an agreement to improve their conditions. Only a few months later, however, a British admiral hanged a mutineer and gleefully announced, "Discipline is preserved!"

The law was clear. The British navy's Articles of War, the standard at the time, promised a court-martial and death to anyone participating in "any mutinous assembly upon any pretence whatsoever" or merely by "uttering words of sedition or mutiny." Striking an officer or failing to report traitorous words could lead to the same punishment. Russia's code of military discipline mirrored these articles but added a higher level of mutiny labeled "manifest insurrection." The minister of war defined this as an uprising of eight or more sailors that used or threatened to use force against an officer. The Russian military deemed this the most heinous crime, and though they could not improve on capital punishment, the tsarist government would likely suppress this kind of mutiny with particular relish and ferocity.

The sailors of the battleship *Potemkin* had already committed manifest insurrection and had killed seven naval officers. By flying the red flag of revolution, they added treason to their crimes.

As the *Potemkin* steamed westward toward Odessa, Matyushenko and Nikishkin went down to the infirmary to check on Vakulenchuk.

They found several sailors huddled around their comrade, holding vigil. With eyes closed and every breath labored, Vakulenchuk lay on a cot at the brink of death. Next to him, Ensign Vakhtin groaned miserably, suffering from the beating he had taken. Dr. A. S. Golenko, the assistant ship's surgeon, had been assigned to care for them, but he could do little for Vakulenchuk but bandage his wounds and hope that the sailors did not blame him for the inevitable.

Aware of his approaching death, Vakulenchuk asked a friend since his first days in the navy to promise to take the eighty rubles he had saved and send half to his father. The other half was to be distributed among the poorest sailors.

With despair in his eyes, Matyushenko looked at Vakulenchuk and then came to his side. "Grisha," he said softly.

"Who's that?" Vakulenchuk muttered, confused.

"Nikishkin and Matyushenko."

"Where are they?"

"Grisha, we're with you," Matyushenko said.

Vakulenchuk finally recognized his voice. His eyes fluttered open for a moment. "How's it with the ship?"

"On the mast there is a red flag, Grisha. We control the ship."

Vakulenchuk managed a thin smile.

"We shot Golikov," Nikishkin added.

"And Gilyarovsky?" he asked.

"We finished off the dog," Matyushenko answered, hovering over Vakulenchuk.

"Good, good." He tired with each word. "Brothers, I want to ask you something: don't quit."

"We won't," the sailors promised.

Matyushenko leaned closer to Vakulenchuk, whose voice faded to a whisper. "Don't throw it away, Afanasy."

These were the last words he spoke to Matyushenko. A couple of hours later, Vakulenchuk died. The sailors brought his body to the ship's church and lit candles around him. They swore to give him a hero's burial once they arrived in Odessa.

Afterward, Matyushenko wandered the *Potemkin* almost in a trance. The closer they came to Odessa, the more excited the crew grew — having lived so long with each day resembling the next, the unknown electrified them. Matyushenko, however, thought mostly of Vakulenchuk.

They had first met when Vakulenchuk was assigned to the *Potemkin* as an artillery quartermaster two years before. At the time, Matyushenko was already a crew member and looked to as the leader of the battleship's revolutionaries. But Tsentralka wanted a more seasoned, less impetuous sailor to take charge of their activities and prepare the crew for future uprisings. When they first met at a garden in Sevastopol popular with sailors on leave, the two were skeptical of each other, not even mentioning politics. Once Vakulenchuk had a better sense of the crew and Matyushenko's role in its revolutionary activities, he spoke to him again. Each won the other over in this second meeting. It was obvious to Matyushenko that Vakulenchuk was better suited to lead the sailors. He was a great organizer, and the men admired his temperate, even-handed personality. He was more cautious than Matyushenko, but no less ambitious in his desire to overthrow the tsar.

Likewise, Vakulenchuk respected Matyushenko for the work he had already accomplished and his unyielding courage in fighting for the cause. Matyushenko also had a keen sense of how to motivate the sailors. The two drew closer as Matyushenko shared this insight and introduced him to the crew. Over the next two years, they struggled together: spreading literature, organizing meetings, hiding their revolutionary activities from their officers, and developing plans for mutiny. Vakulenchuk would never see the fruits of their struggle, nor be there to provide counsel to the rest of the sailors — or to Matyushenko, as he so often had. In a way, though they were only a few years apart in age, Matyushenko had lost a father figure in Vakulenchuk.

"Don't throw it away," Vakulenchuk had said to him, no doubt believing they had taken over the ship too early and that his friend might be too tempestuous to lead the sailors well. Much as Matyushenko yearned to fight, he had never coveted the role of leader.

After roaming the ship awhile, he went to speak with Lieutenant Kovalenko, as he had earlier promised. But Matyushenko was still too lost in his own thoughts to discuss what lay ahead. He simply told

Kovalenko that he was free to move about the ship and then went off to be on his own again.

Kovalenko had paced about the wardroom impatiently with the other officers ever since the sailors had weighed anchor and directed the battleship toward Odessa. A few times he had caught himself wondering if he were trapped in a dream. But he had only to look at the armed guard outside the door, and his menacing glance, to dispel any hope that he might wake up to discover Captain Golikov still in charge of the battleship.

Once Matyushenko had told this guard to allow Kovalenko to pass, the officer left the wardroom and went down to the engine room. There the sailors told him how the mutiny had unfolded just a few hours before. They spoke as if they could not wait to explain their actions. They talked mostly of the rotten meat that had sparked the violence, but Kovalenko knew there was much more to the frenzy that had swept over the *Potemkin*. Sailors had *always* grumbled over the food served to them. Although their daily life was difficult, the roots of unrest ran much deeper. While the sailors recounted the first shots fired, Kovalenko tried to put himself in their shoes and understand their actions. He later wrote down his thoughts:

> Can a sailor or a soldier be satisfied with the fact that he's well fed, if he can't get away from the idea that at the same time his family sits at home without any bread on their table? Can he go to bed at night without worrying that the next morning will bring news that his brother or father had been killed on the street? Can he calmly and effectively perform his duties when every time he takes a gun in his hands, he involuntarily thinks that he could be sent with the same gun to kill his brothers in spirit and even in flesh? Can he be respectful or thankful towards the officers when he sees in them — with few exceptions — the faithful servants of a dying regime so hated by the people?

Kovalenko knew he had to choose whether to help the sailors in their mutiny, if given the opportunity. The crew had yet to confirm what they would do with the officers and petty officers. They had spoken of sending them ashore to Odessa but had yet to deliver their decision. Kovalenko believed they had made a mistake in selecting

Alekseyev to captain the ship. Even though a figurehead, he had never shown a leaning toward progressive ideas that would align him with the sailors. He had surely taken the position only because he feared the alternative.

When Kovalenko finally returned to the other officers, he found them equally anxious as to what would happen next. Most sat on the edge of the sofas, including Colonel Schultz, looking as if they had just been told to walk the plank. Kovalenko was not scared for his life because of his relationship with the sailors. Rather, he debated with himself whether he should track down Matyushenko and ask to join the cause.

On the evening of June 14, as the *Potemkin* steamed westward, the Odessan revolutionary Kirill led forty quarry workers across the steppe toward a peasant village that lay eight miles outside the city. Stars shined bright as diamonds overhead in the clear night sky. The crops beside the road rustled slightly in the wind as the workers marched forward. They carried a pair of banners: one was red, with the words BREAD, LAND, AND FREEDOM, and the other was black, promising DEATH TO TYRANTS. In the village, they hoped to rally more men to join the strikes in Odessa.

That morning, workers throughout the city walked off their jobs and poured into the streets. There was little organization to these strikes. They began in different sections of the city, small conflagrations that steadily expanded as factories emptied and workers called on their neighbors to join them in the streets. As the situation worsened, some factory owners tried to negotiate with their people — offering shorter working days and the elimination of general searches — but it was too late for compromise.

By late afternoon, the strikes of the previous day looked minor in comparison. Thousands gathered on Preobrazhenskaya Street, the city's finest thoroughfare. Every shop, merchant office, and bank along the wide street had shuttered its doors. The crowd, armed only with rocks and their rage, surged forward against the police. This scene played out throughout Odessa; tens of thousands took part.

Children and teenagers joined the workers behind barricades of upended carriages, wooden planks, and telegraph poles. At the corner of Kanatnaya and Yvreiskaya Streets, a handful of girls employed at a tea factory joined an advancing line of workers; they were met head-on by a company of policemen. Sabers flashed and rifles cracked, leaving what one witness described as "bloody hills of flesh where people had been only minutes ago." Workers ambushed isolated police and soldier patrols, administering a similar brand of street justice. Soldiers marched into the city in the hundreds to protect city hall and other government buildings.

At 10 P.M., a policeman chased a man in Sobornaya Square; he tossed a bomb at his pursuer. The explosion rocked the city, decapitating the policeman and mortally wounding the man who threw the bomb. The tension between the workers and the police escalated. Into the night, sirens blared throughout Odessa.

A couple of hours before dawn on June 15, Kirill and his party of workers reached the village and rang the bell in the square. Unfortunately, Kirill found the peasants were more interested in cutting their landowner's crops than in joining a struggle within the city. They even threatened to arrest him for stirring up trouble. Disheartened, he left the village with only ten peasants joining his countryside army. Halfway to the city, the spirits of his followers waned. Many had walked all night, and they knew that their hundred rounds of ammunition and three revolvers were a pathetic arsenal to bring against the well-armed mounted soldiers. When they stopped to discuss their next move, the majority curled up to sleep. Finally, Kirill abandoned them all to return to the city alone. He left instructions on where to meet if some decided to join him later. Reaching Odessa's outskirts after dawn, he walked, half passing out from exhaustion, across the cobblestone streets, feeling that he had failed. Cheerless and defeated, he could think only of finding a bed and sleeping for days.

In the city he stopped at a fellow Menshevik's apartment. Before he had a chance to knock, his comrade swung open the door, beside himself with excitement. He reported that a battleship had entered the harbor during the night. Some suspected that General Kakhanov had called for the navy to support his troops and to frighten the workers, but rumors abounded that its sailors had actually mutinied and had come to spread revolution.

Kirill hurried to the port to see for himself. As news of the battleship's arrival spread through the city, a crowd started to swell. Reaching the embankment above the harbor, Kirill spotted the

*Potemkin* outside the breakwater. Charged by the thought that the battleship might be in the hands of sailors who would support the strikes, Kirill rapidly descended the embankment.

From Primorsky Boulevard another revolutionary, Konstantin Feldmann, stared down at battleship. A tall, dark-bearded student, Feldmann had joined the fight against the tsarist system in large part because of its treatment of his fellow Jews. He had spent the night in Peresyp, participating in the strikes and narrowly escaping being trampled by Cossacks. As disheartened as Kirill at having no way to resist the soldiers, he was dumbstruck at the sight of the colossal battleship floating in the harbor and flying the red flag. At first he thought it simply an apparition but then realized his eyes were not deceiving him; he ran down to the harbor as well. In the moment of their retreat from the government's forces and their superior weapons, he thought, the workers had received reinforcements of overwhelming strength. He meant to get on board and lead the battleship to the people's triumph.

# 9

A MILE OUT in the harbor, on the *Potemkin*, the boatswain's whistle roused the crew. "Get up! Make the beds! Wash!" came the command at 5 A.M. on June 15. Feet pounded on the decks; Father Parmen came out to deliver the morning prayer, and then the crew assembled for tea and breakfast. Half an hour later, the pumps ran and hoses splashed water across the decks as the sailors began to clean the ship. In the officers' wardroom, Lieutenant Kovalenko awakened to the familiar sounds, thinking that everything was as it always had been at sea. But a glance around him at the sleeping officers scattered about the room on sofas and on the floor, still in their uniforms, reminded him otherwise.

Stepping over the sleeping guard in the doorway, who had a rifle across his knees, Kovalenko, still half asleep, went to the ship's side and looked toward Odessa. A light morning fog covered the waters. Fishermen sailed their small boats out of the harbor while seagulls floated overhead. In the distance the rising sun struck the gold crosses atop the churches. For a moment, Kovalenko lost himself in the view. When his attention returned to the *Potemkin,* he suddenly wondered what the sailor committee had resolved during the night that had prompted the crew to bustle about with so much purpose that morning. He soon learned what he had missed while under guard in the wardroom.

Shortly after the *Potemkin* and the torpedo boat *Ismail* had arrived outside Odessa's harbor at 10 P.M. the evening before and dropped anchor, the committee had gathered in the admiral's stateroom. Few on board slept. Many sailors packed into the room to listen to the debate chaired by Matyushenko. Others manned the guns and search-lights, in case the Black Sea Fleet command had somehow already discovered the mutiny and sent a surprise attack. The majority of sailors were simply too agitated to do anything but smoke cigarettes feverishly, pace the battleship, and stare out at the distant lights of Odessa. Now that the *Potemkin* had come to port, they knew the tsar would know of their mutiny by the morning, and the consequences of their actions would turn suddenly real. The sailors now looked to the ship's leaders for their survival, knowing that the tsar would throw all his force against sailors who killed their own officers and raised the revolutionary flag.

By 4 A.M., the committee had settled on a number of plans: to load the ship with as much coal as possible; to buy more provisions with money from the ship's safe; to create a record of the events that had instigated the mutiny, for the officers to sign; to release the petty officers so that they might help run the battleship; and to prepare for the Black Sea Fleet's arrival, whether in the form of an attacking squadron led by Admiral Chukhnin or a revolutionary fleet commanded by fellow sailors who had successfully overthrown their officers. Finally, the committee agreed to celebrate Vakulenchuk as a revolutionary martyr, making his death and funeral a rallying point for Odessans to join with the *Potemkin* in their battle against the tsar.

Immediately after the meeting had broken up, sailors Alekseyev and Bredikhin, both of whom knew the city well, sneaked into port. They found the streets quiet and deserted, showing few signs of the previous night's violence, except for some overturned trams. Their task was to connect with Odessa's revolutionary groups, seek their guidance on taking over the city, and request their help in notifying Tsentralka members in Sevastopol to hurry and launch the fleetwide uprising and join the *Potemkin*. While in Odessa, Alekseyev and Bredikhin were also to distribute the committee's proclamation appealing to the soldiers and Cossacks stationed in the city to surrender their weapons. If their commanders attempted to attack the *Potemkin* or thwart their plans, the proclamation warned, "we will raze Odessa to the ground."

Now that the day had dawned, the sailors on board moved quickly to carry out the committee's other plans. Time was of the essence.

The longer the battleship stood in the harbor, the more opportunities they gave the tsar and his naval command to crush the rebellion before it had a chance to gather strength. On the side of the ship opposite of where Kovalenko stood, the men prepared to bring Vakulenchuk into the port. They had carefully dressed him in a fresh uniform, laid him on a stretcher, and draped a military flag over his body. They had also pinned a note to his chest, written by Nikishkin:

Citizens of Odessa!

Before you lies the body of the Battleship *Potemkin* sailor Vakulenchuk who was savagely slain by the first officer because he refused to eat borscht that was inedible. Comrades! Workers! Rally under our banner and we shall stand up for ourselves! Death to the oppressors! Death to the vampires! Long live freedom!

The crew of the Battleship *Potemkin*. One for all and all for one.

The sailors lowered Vakulenchuk's body into a launch; his hands lay across his chest, and his stoic face remained uncovered. The *Ismail* escorted two launches with forty sailors and their martyred leader to one of the harbor's piers. Matyushenko headed the detachment. Roughly two hundred people stood on the pier, mostly dockworkers curious about the battleship's mysterious appearance in their harbor. The sailors brought Vakulenchuk ashore and erected over him a tent of sailcloth and spars. First, the dockworkers came forward to look at his body. Over the course of the next hour, more and more people arrived at the pier. Matyushenko and the other sailors told the Odessans of the mutiny and how they needed their help in bringing down a government that had the very men who protected Russia eat maggot-infested meat.

The crowd was stunned and moved by their story, punctuated most forcefully by the presence of Vakulenchuk's body. Some offered assistance, promising to bring the *Potemkin* food and supplies. Others simply pledged their allegiance, gripping the sailors by the hand or taking off their hats and yelling, "Down with the tsar!" Watching the tremendous outpouring of support, Matyushenko felt that there was little the sailors could not accomplish: they would first sweep away the tsar's minions in Odessa, then spread the fight from city to city around the Black Sea, and finally bring liberty to all of the Russian people. The sight of crew members embracing the dockworkers in solidarity struck him as nothing less than beautiful.

An honor guard of sailors was left to watch over Vakulenchuk to ensure nobody disturbed his body. Then Matyushenko boarded the launch. A worker had told him that a collier docked at a nearby pier contained more than enough coal to satisfy their needs. When Matyushenko arrived at the collier *Emerans,* the men unloading the coal onto the pier stopped their work and cheered the sailors. Matyushenko offered to buy the coal from the *Emerans*'s captain. He had no choice but to relinquish his supply.

While the dockworkers hitched the collier to the torpedo boat to tow it to the *Potemkin,* a sailor next to Matyushenko noticed a boat approaching their battleship. Several port officials and a host of gendarmes were aboard. Matyushenko directed his launch to speed back to the *Potemkin.* With a rifle in one hand and a revolver in the other, he stood at the bow as the boat cut across the water. The gendarmes did not have their guns drawn, but they were almost certainly armed. Under no circumstances did Matyushenko want them to board the *Potemkin* and influence the crew.

The launch neared the battleship. The sailors on the decks above yelled at the port officials to go away, refusing to answer their questions about who was in charge and why the *Potemkin* had come to Odessa. Everyone turned toward Matyushenko as he approached.

"What do you want on our battleship?" Matyushenko asked, aiming his rifle at the three officials, whose faces were now drawn and pale.

"We want to investigate and report on what has happened here," the port official, Gerasimov, said, as much confused as scared. As the port's second-highest-ranking official, he was unaccustomed to being addressed by a lowly sailor, let alone one pointing the barrel of a gun at him.

"Throw your revolvers into the water," Matyushenko ordered the gendarmes. "We dropped your superiors overboard and we don't need new ones."

The gendarmes looked at the revolutionary sailor, then at the port officials, and finally at one another. Slowly, they stood and dropped their revolvers into the water.

"Same goes for your sabers, you cowards," Matyushenko added.

Following Matyushenko, several sailors on the *Potemkin* now aimed their guns at the officials. The gendarmes removed their sabers. Gerasimov stood helplessly by as his men followed Matyushenko's orders without the slightest resistance.

"Now off you go, you tsar's slaves. Turn around and get lost," Matyushenko barked.

The boat pushed off from the *Potemkin* and retreated toward the shore. The sailors cheered Matyushenko for his boldness in chasing the officials away.

A flotilla of fishing and rowboats gathered around the *Potemkin* to greet the sailors, some bringing gifts of tea, sugar, tobacco, and fruit. On his way back toward the *Emerans*, Matyushenko stopped one of these boats, which happened to be carrying Konstantin Feldmann, who had convinced some workers to row him out to the *Potemkin*.

"Where are you going?" Matyushenko asked, worried that visitors, some of whom might be spies for Odessa's authorities, were overrunning the *Potemkin*.

"To the free revolutionist ship," Feldmann told the sailor, unaware he was speaking to the battleship's leader.

"And who are you? A Social Democrat?"

Feldmann nodded but was then asked to verify it. "I haven't got proof," he replied caustically. "They don't ask for proof when they send us to rot in prison or to Siberia."

"Come on then, get in here with us." Matyushenko beckoned, smiling at Feldmann's answer.

At the same time, on the pier where Vakulenchuk's bier had been erected, Kirill stood in a swarm of people. Thousands of Odessans had come down to the port after the arrival of the dead sailor. No police or troops were in sight. The whole city appeared to be emptying into the port; everyone was curious to see this funeral bier and to find out what the sailors were doing in their city.

A long line on the pier led to the sailor's corpse under the tent, sheltered from the June morning sun. Men and women, young and old alike, shuffled forward to have a look, stooping to read the message written by the *Potemkin*'s crew. The faces of those who emerged from the tent a few moments later expressed a range of emotions: inspiration, horror, rage, sadness. Many crossed themselves or sobbed uncontrollably. Some laid flowers alongside the bier or dropped a coin into the little bucket that someone had left to collect money for a monument to the sailor. Few left unaffected. Turning back toward the port, they paused to stare at the *Potemkin*. In their eyes Kirill saw suffering and the desperate hope that the battleship would take revenge on the tsar's forces and help lead the strikers to victory.

Standing on top of a woodpile, one speaker gestured toward the *Potemkin* and declared, "We may have lacked firearms in the past, but *now* we have them." His words were met with a chorus of agreement. Another speaker railed, "Enough of this enduring! Death to tyrants! Let's die for freedom!" Thunders of applause punctuated his tirade. On several merchant ships in the harbor, sailors blew steam whistles and raised red shirts on their masts (lacking flags of the same color) in solidarity with the *Potemkin* sailors.

Kirill grew more and more excited as the crowd's emotions rose. After one speaker stepped down from the barrel he was using as a platform, Kirill dashed forward and climbed onto it himself, eager to speak to those around him. "Comrades!" he started, his voice like a lion's roar. "There are thousands of us here, and none of us will stand for the slavery and oppression of the tsar any longer. Everyone, let's march to the city center. With rifles and the protection of the *Potemkin*'s guns, we'll gain our freedom and a better —" He tried to finish, but his voice was drowned out by the boisterous crowd.

Minutes later, fifty mounted Cossacks and a phalanx of policemen descended into the port. They charged toward the pier to break up the huge assembly. As the Cossacks rode forward to clear the way, they were slowed by the crush of people. Still, they forced their horses down the pier, threatening the crowd with sabers if they failed to open a path. Some had to jump into the water to escape being trampled.

A worker who had seen the government forces arrive had rushed out on a boat to alert the *Potemkin*. When the Cossacks neared Vakulenchuk, a battle flag was suddenly seen rising on the battleship's mast. A member of the honor guard posted at the bier screamed out, "Comrades, run away! They'll fire at the Cossacks from the guns." A mad scramble ensued on the pier. The Cossacks hastened back toward the port, scattered by the threat; Kirill even saw a police lieutenant jump into a pile of coal, begging his officers to cover him with the pieces and hide him.

As the Cossacks and the police hurried off the pier, the ship's guns remained silent. After the *Potemkin*'s battle flag was lowered, the crowd reassembled, more confident than ever that their victory was at hand. Kirill left to board a rowboat heading out to the battleship. He needed to convince the sailors that an attack on the city must begin straight away.

On his approach, he noticed the collier *Emerans* anchored at the *Potemkin*'s side. Three hundred dockworkers joined with the sailors in loading the coal, a vision that struck Kirill as a true sign that the revolution had begun. On the collier, the workers shoveled coal into huge canvas sacks that weighed over one hundred pounds each when full. These were carried to the edge of the *Emerans* and then hoisted by crane onto the *Potemkin*'s decks. Sailors then emptied the sacks into chutes leading to the coal bunkers. A black cloud of dust hung over the area, and many covered their mouths and nostrils with cloth or stuck oakum between their teeth to avoid inhaling the contaminated air. Yet everyone labored enthusiastically. Time and again, a sailor and a worker embraced and shouted together, "Long live democracy!"

A rope ladder was lowered to allow Kirill to climb onto the battleship. Once aboard, he declared himself a Social Democrat who represented some of the dockworkers. The sailors warmly shook his hand. They invited him to walk through the guarded gun deck to reach the forecastle, where some of the crew had gathered to meet with other Odessans. Along the way, several sailors asked him about the situation in the city. He described the strikes that had taken place over the past few days and how the police and soldiers had met each one with butchery.

As he had the chance, Kirill asked different sailors how and why the mutiny had started. Dymchenko, the committee member who had greeted Kirill at the ladder, believed wholeheartedly that it was right to get rid of their officers. His sunburnt face and expressive eyes lit up as he told Kirill of his hope that the *Potemkin* would lead Russia to revolution. But other sailors that Kirill spoke to lacked this confidence, undercutting the impression of unity that had inspired Kirill as he watched the coaling. Several looked at him with distrust, thinking him a rabble-rouser who would get the sailors in more trouble than they already faced. One sailor told Kirill how afraid he was of the crew's revolutionaries, who had so swiftly and cruelly dispensed with their officers and how he failed to understand their cause. Another reported a conversation he had shared with a petty officer a few hours before; this traitor told him that the tsar would only punish those who continued to support the mutiny, and therefore, if he wanted to keep his head, he should act against its leaders. By the time Kirill reached the upper deck, he realized the sailors would need constant attention to keep them informed and faithful to revolution. Otherwise, they might easily lose the battleship to apathy and traitorous actions from within their ranks.

At the forecastle, Kirill found his comrade Feldmann surrounded by sailors, delivering the kind of speech the crew needed:

> You might at any moment be carried off into warfare . . . For whose benefit? The autocracy's. So you had to struggle against it. But how could this be done? Could you hope to triumph over the tsar's forces alone? No! On whom then could you depend? On the people, and on the people alone. . . . *You* were the first who dared to bridge the separation between the people and the military. Let us pass boldly along that bridge, and, united with the people in the great conflict, achieve liberty for all of us.

In response to Feldmann's words, the crew chanted with enthusiasm, "Death or freedom! Death or freedom!" Another Odessan revolutionary, a Jewish Bundist, echoed Feldmann's words. Then Kirill stood to speak, but a whistle blew, signaling lunch. The sailors asked the Odessan Social Democrats to join them in the mess deck for lunch. Seated at a long bench there, Kirill tipped back a dram of vodka and ate cabbage soup with the others. He shared a look with Feldmann, as if to say, "Can it be that this is not a dream? Can the freedom of Russia be so near?"

After eating, Kirill returned to the forecastle. The coaling had been completed. More boats bearing gifts docked at the battleship's side. Some teenagers had come aboard and were touching the guns and climbing through the hatches as if the *Potemkin* was a playground, a situation that troubled the sailors, who felt possessive about their battleship. Kirill looked back to the port, where people continued to arrive in droves. At that moment, Dymchenko approached and invited him to a special meeting that had just been called.

At noon, Matyushenko stood at the head of the long table in the admiral's stateroom, surrounded by the sailor committee. He introduced each member to the leaders of Odessa's revolutionary parties, who were seated on stools and chairs about the room.

A couple of hours before, when sailor Alekseyev had alerted the Odessans to the mutiny, the revolutionary joint commission (a body of Bolsheviks, Mensheviks, Bundists, and Socialist Revolutionaries formed during the May strikes) met to decide how best to persuade the mutinous sailors to take over the city. Once they finished arguing over this, they commandeered some fishing boats and went to inform the *Potemkin* leaders of their plan.

"Will the workers follow you?" Matyushenko asked at the meeting's start, before the Odessan revolutionaries had so much as a chance to speak.

Sailor Reznichenko added, "Are they making political demands? Do they want the autocracy overthrown?"

"Yes," one of the Odessans, a Bolshevik, answered. "But they've no weapons."

Another jumped in with the joint commission's plan. "We propose to launch an assault with four hundred armed sailors as the spearhead, backed by workers and soldiers. The *Potemkin* will support the attack by firing from the sea. First, we'll take over the railroads, preventing more government forces from coming into the city. Then we'll move on the rest of Odessa."

Matyushenko listened to the plan, unconvinced. Kirill, who had slipped into the meeting during the introductions, sensed his skepticism. Although junior to those on the commission, Kirill interrupted. "There's panic in the city. The authorities have lost their heads. They have no artillery, few troops, and the situation is favorable to a sudden attack. If we miss this opportunity, we allow our enemy to organize and strengthen themselves."

Swayed by his argument, a few sailors echoed Kirill, saying, "We mustn't lose this moment."

By instinct, Matyushenko wanted to act against the tsar's forces quickly and decisively, but the words of their former leader tempered his reaction now. Vakulenchuk had always told Matyushenko that the sailors could achieve their victory only by acting with the other battle-ships in the fleet, as Tsentralka had originally planned. Alone, they were lost. They needed to wait for the planned mutiny and then act together as one. If Vice Admiral Chukhnin sent a squadron after the *Potemkin* before this occurred, they had to be prepared for battle; the four hundred sailors (over half the crew) who were on land would be sorely missed. What's more, the ship's crew, who knew little about making a land assault, would not stand a chance against infantry troops trained for exactly that type of action. It was too big a risk.

Matyushenko explained this to the Odessans and pointedly con-cluded, "We must look toward the sea right now, not toward the shore."

The members of the joint commission sat back, stunned. How could the sailors refuse *them,* the revolution's rightful leaders? With the workers and the battleship's guns behind them, their victory would be assured. Could the sailors not see? At the very least they should send arms to the workers and begin bombing government buildings. That was their duty to the cause.

Despite protests, most of the sailor committee agreed with Matyushenko that they must await the Black Sea Fleet's arrival before they took any action. One member also explained to the Odessan revolutionaries that the only reliable force of sailors that could ad-vance on the city were those committed to the mutiny. "If we go our-selves," he said, "then those left on the *Potemkin* may take the ship to Sevastopol instead of supporting us. The only option is to wait for the rest of the fleet. When it's joined us, we can take over the whole Black Sea."

As the committee got set to take a vote, a sailor entered the state-room and approached Matyushenko. The crew wanted to know, he said, what fate was being decided for them. There was talk of abandoning the battleship to escape punishment, and many were nervous about the presence of so many civilians on deck. Were they relinquishing control to people who had risked nothing in the taking over of the *Potemkin*?

"Gather everyone together," Matyushenko ordered. Then he told the Odessan revolutionaries to leave the ship before the situation worsened.

When the clock struck noon in his office, General Kakhanov, the military governor of Odessa, knew he had a decision to make. Few options were available to him, together with a haunting multitude of risks.

The sight of the *Potemkin* in the harbor had mystified him as much as it had the rest of the city. By protocol, the navy was to alert the port before a battleship's arrival, but no word had been received. Rumors of a mutiny on the battleship reached him at daybreak. The very thought was outlandish, yet at 8 A.M., Odessa's police chief informed him that it was true. A sailor, part of the detachment sent to deposit a crewmate's body on the pier, slipped away and notified a gendarme of the mutiny. Less than an hour later, Mayor Dmitry Neidhardt hurried into Kakhanov's office. A former officer of the Preobrazhensky Guards Regiment, the spineless Neidhardt had neither the experience nor education for his position, but he had the tsar's favor, and his brother-in-law Pyotr Stolypin was the governor of Saratov (and future interior minister). Neidhardt told Kakhanov that he was leaving for St. Petersburg by express train to inform Tsar Nicholas of the situation — apparently, the telegraph system would not appropriately convey the news. The mayor asked the general to take command of the city and declare a state of martial law — though only the tsar could grant Kakhanov the power to do so. Nevertheless, Kakhanov took preliminary steps along that course, calling for more troops from garrisons within his military district, including an artillery brigade. His attempt to short-circuit the flow of Odessans to the port by sending fifty Cossacks to remove the dead sailor's body had proved Kakhanov's worst fears: the sailors were prepared to bombard the city.

At 10:30 A.M. the head of the commercial port, Brigadier General Pereleshin, stormed into his office, demanding that a larger force of troops be sent to disband the thousands gathering on his piers. His senior assistant, Gerasimov, had gone to the *Potemkin*, demanding to know who was in charge, only to be humiliated and turned away by Matyushenko. Before dismissing Pereleshin, Kakhanov asked him whether he had considered that the battleship might let loose a barrage of destruction on the city.

Even before the *Potemkin* arrived, Odessa had been descending into chaos. Two days of strikes had crippled the city. Kakhanov's troops were at siege with tens of thousands of workers; both sides had suffered losses and many more would die. Shops were shuttered. Factories were closed. People jammed the railway stations, fighting over tickets to get out of the city. Outright chaos was just a misstep away.

Now a mutinous battleship threatened Odessa with ruin. Revolutionaries had been spotted approaching the *Potemkin* — to plan a coordinated attack, Kakhanov suspected. From his window, he watched as more people descended the Richelieu Steps to the port where, he had been informed, propagandists were inciting the crowds to attack his troops and to start a citywide uprising. Kakhanov had been warned that other mutinies in the Black Sea Fleet could be expected.

Whether these mutinies ever occurred, the Sevastopol naval base was a day's journey away, and a squadron to combat the *Potemkin* would need time to assemble. In the meantime, the city could be bombarded by almost fifty tons of high explosives within the space of one hour, half from the ship's main battery, the other half from its assortment of secondary guns. One hour. Fifty tons. The *Potemkin* could launch this firestorm from more than five miles out, far surpassing the accuracy of the field artillery that Kakhanov had only just ordered. Furthermore, if the sailors somehow managed to lead a concerted assault on the city by land, he had too few troops to repel them.

Kakhanov felt trapped in a terrible corner. Responsible for one of the Russian Empire's most important and populous cities, he was at the mercy of sailors whom he believed to be scarcely better than beasts. As he saw it, he had two choices: first, quell the developing uprising in the port, thereby inviting an attack that would ruin the city; second, close off access to, or exit from, the port, corralling the unrest away from Odessa's center, and then wait for the sailors to leave or for the navy squadron to arrive. There was no question — he had to choose the latter. Kakhanov sent the order to his officers:

cut off the port from the rest of the city; any attempts to break through the line in either direction should be resisted with whatever force necessary.

At 12:30 P.M., Kakhanov telegrammed the tsar, informing him of the mutiny and outlining the measures he was taking to protect Odessa. He had set the stage for slaughter.

# 10

NICHOLAS BEGAN his day as usual on June 15. He prayed, ate breakfast, and arrived in his study by 9 A.M. The morning papers offered little welcome news. *Novoye Vremya* editorialized that his government had lost its moral bearing and was clearly resorting to violent suppression to stay in power. He put aside the newspaper to read the latest reports from his ministries and telegrams from the war's front in Manchuria: typical fare on a typically hot, quiet June day at Peterhof. An hour into his routine, an aide brought an urgent message from General Trepov, the deputy minister of the interior:

> Your Imperial Majesty, I have received a ciphered report from Odessa that the battleship *Potemkin* has arrived there from Sevastopol and put ashore, at 4 A.M. [*sic*], a sailor's body bearing a message on his chest that the sailor was an innocent victim of his captain. In revenge, the sailors killed every officer. At the same time, the sailors state they will support the uprising in Odessa with their guns.

The report originated from an Okhrana agent in the city. In his message to the tsar, Trepov, who was one of the autocracy's most vigorous defenders and widely known for his strong-arm tactics, urged Nicholas to declare martial law in Odessa.

At first, Nicholas simply refused to accept the report's accuracy. A mutiny in his navy? Every officer killed? One of his battleships supporting the revolutionaries? The thought itself was beyond imagination.

The Romanovs had always considered the military their most

prized institution, owing the greatness of their empire to its many conquests. But for Nicholas, the military was also an object of personal affection. As a child, he had attended countless parades and reviews, always wearing a miniature uniform of one of the regiments in attendance. He watched in awe as the soldiers snapped to attention and raised their swords and bayonets when his father passed down their lines. Later, as a young man, he served as a colonel in the Preobrazhensky Guards Regiment, savoring the camaraderie with the other officers and the many ritualized traditions. At the time, he wrote to his mother that he was as happy as he had ever been. As the tsar, one of his ministers once declared, Nicholas "regarded himself as a soldier — the first soldier in the Empire." He even took it upon himself, when a new infantry uniform and kit were commissioned, to go on a forty-kilometer hike and personally test it. He further showed his affection for the military by choosing former generals, such as Trepov, for many of his government's highest positions.

Therefore, a mutiny within his beloved military was a bitter, personal betrayal. Over the past two years, a handful of minor incidents had flared up — a few soldiers or sailors refusing commands — but nothing of the magnitude Trepov would have him believe had occurred on the Black Sea.

Beyond his own romance with the military, Nicholas was well aware that his soldiers formed the bulwark of his state, especially against insurrection within its borders. Although the War Ministry occasionally complained, he had little choice but to use soldiers to put down revolts, since the police were incapable of managing them alone. If Nicholas lost the military's allegiance, he was doomed. He could hardly bear to contemplate that this had happened.

Alone in his study, Nicholas received more distressing telegrams every hour. There was no escaping the truth. His disbelief soon turned to anger. He approved an *ukaz* declaring martial law in Odessa, as Trepov had suggested. The tsar also instructed Trepov to strictly censor any information related to the mutiny or the uprisings in Odessa. Until the situation was in hand, the Russian people were not to know of the *Potemkin*. To General Kakhanov, he responded, "Immediately take the most severe, resolute measures to suppress the revolts both on the *Potemkin* and among the population of the port. Each hour of delay may cost rivers of blood in the future." In a telegram from the naval minister, Admiral Avelan, which came last and offered the same information provided by Trepov and Kakhanov, Nicholas handwrote on the page, "Where is the chief commander? I am *sure* he could deal with the mutiny and *severely* punish the rebellious crew." Nicholas expected Vice Admiral Chukhnin to deal quickly with the disgrace and have its instigators killed. Indeed, he was depending on him.

On the banks of the Neva River, adjacent to the Winter Palace, stood the Admiralty Building. A colossal structure running almost a quarter-mile in length and crowned by a soaring gold spire, this "maritime acropolis" — as its architect boasted — spoke of the navy's prominent place within the empire. Behind its walls, the commander of the Black Sea Fleet was meeting with a host of other admirals in a week-long conference to deliberate on the navy's future expansion.

At 1 P.M., a telegram about the *Potemkin* from General Kakhanov made its way to the office of Admiral Fyodor Avelan. He then forwarded the news to the tsar and ordered an aide to bring Chukhnin to him. Leaving his meeting in another part of the building, Chukhnin hurried through the corridors and entered the minister's office. A huge chamber overlooking the Alexander Garden, the office was decorated with paintings depicting epic sea battles of Russian history and portraits of tsars and famous admirals. Under their gaze, Chukhnin crossed the thick Persian carpet to sit by Avelan. The somber expression on his usually good-humored face boded ill.

The two men were a study in contrasts. Avelan, the privileged son of a noble Finnish family that had long served the tsars, was accustomed to the riches that surrounded him. A bon vivant, he had risen through the Admiralty by virtue of his family name and his charm. Although a skilled seafarer, the naval minister lacked the range of intelligence and the work ethic essential to running a modern navy — evidenced by his plan to send Rozhestvensky's squadron around the world to challenge the Japanese navy. From the moment of its conception, the mission was plagued by delays, indecision, and perhaps most dangerous of all, overconfidence. After the Tsushima disaster, Avelan had tendered his resignation and would have happily retired that previous May, but Nicholas had yet to choose a successor.

Grigory Chukhnin, who had served in a squadron commanded by

Avelan in 1893, was still eager for advancement, perhaps to naval minister. Born in the Russian port Nikolayev, he was the youngest of
twelve children. His father and several brothers also served in the
navy. Although a noble family, the Chukhnins were of minor rank and
were, for all intents and purposes, penniless. When Grigory turned
five years old, his mother died, and he was sent to the Alexander Cadet Corps school located at Tsarskoye Selo outside St. Petersburg.
Essentially an orphanage for sons of military men, the school prepared its charges to follow in their fathers' footsteps. Instructors
meted out punishments with birch rods and hair shirts. At age ten,
Chukhnin was transferred to the Naval Cadet Corps, only a few years
before the Alexander Cadet Corps school was forced to close because
of its inhumane treatment of students.

The strict regimen of each school shaped Chukhnin. Unlike most
of his classmates, he did not have relatives in St. Petersburg to provide
Sundays away from school, nor enough money to return home during the summer break. He never experienced an alternative to rigid
military life. Self-discipline became his trademark. He studied more,
practiced harder, and pushed himself to succeed in every endeavor.
To learn English and French, he memorized one hundred words a
day from the dictionary. When he was diagnosed with potential tuberculosis at age fifteen, he instituted for himself a Spartan regimen of
vigorous swimming and gymnastics, cold showers, sleeping without
sheets, and a promise to abstain from drinking and smoking for his
entire life. He emerged the specimen of good health, with the lean,
muscular build of a wrestler and a face flushed with color.

At age seventeen, Chukhnin graduated at the top of his class and
took his iron will and strident devotion to the state (which had, in
effect, raised him) to a career in the navy. He excelled in a range of
posts aboard corvettes and monitors and participated in a secret ex-
pedition to the United States in 1877, during the Russo-Turkish War,
to collect merchant ships refitted with guns. With each promotion he
won, his reputation as a tough and supremely capable leader grew. He
learned every aspect of the ships under his command and expected
his subordinates to do the same. Such was his attention to detail that
while on voyages he personally inspected the boilers, climbing into
them to make sure they had been properly cleaned. The Admiralty elevated him to rear admiral in 1896, charging him with the revitaliza-

tion of the naval port in Vladivostok. His success there led first to his return to the Naval Cadet Corps in the position of superintendent, then his selection to head the Black Sea Fleet as vice admiral in 1903.

Chukhnin devoted nearly every hour, seven days a week, to his naval career; this single-mindedness ruined his ten-year first marriage (he had it annulled, citing his wife's infidelity) and estranged his daughter and son. His one hobby was painting in watercolor, landscapes usually, which he found relaxing.

Although he deserved his reputation as a martinet, Chukhnin was also reform-minded and far from a sycophant of the status quo, as were many of his fellow officers. At the cadet corps he pushed the Admiralty to modernize the curriculum to include more technical and practical lessons. As leader of the Black Sea Fleet, he risked his career by publicly questioning the quality of the navy's officers and promotion policies that rewarded length of service rather than merit. He was devoted to excellent service to the tsar, not politics.

Given his efforts, the news that Avelan delivered about the *Potemkin* came as a severe blow to Chukhnin. He suspected right away that revolutionaries had driven the crew to mutiny; the rest of the sailors had merely followed their lead, too foolish to realize the gravity of their sin. Since he took command in the Black Sea, Chukhnin had tried to root out this revolutionary disease within his fleet, bearing down with the same fierceness and discipline he had used to defeat his suspected tuberculosis — but his failure was now obvious. Not only would the event blemish his record, but also, more distressing to Chukhnin, it was an affront to the tsar.

"I must leave for Sevastopol immediately," Chukhnin said. He had little confidence in Vice Admiral Aleksandr Krieger, the officer in charge of the fleet in his absence. Krieger was a "palace admiral" if there ever was one.

Avelan agreed, informing the Black Sea Fleet commander that the tsar also wanted Chukhnin to personally handle the situation. While Chukhnin explained to the naval minister his theory of how the mutiny started and what steps needed to be taken, an aide brought two telegrams from Sevastopol. In the first, Krieger detailed his plan to dispatch two battleships, a destroyer, and a torpedo boat, led by Rear Admiral Fyodor Vishnevetsky, to pursue the *Potemkin*. The second telegram, also from Krieger, detailed the addition of a third battleship to the task force.

The telegrams exasperated Chukhnin, confirming his lack of faith in his senior flagman. Did Krieger underestimate the severity of the crisis? Three battleships, a destroyer, and a torpedo boat? Moreover, Krieger did not feel it necessary to lead the squadron himself, sending an underling instead — was this cowardice, incompetence, or both? The *Potemkin* could outgun every battleship in the fleet. The mutinous sailors had removed the St. Andrew's flag and had raised the red flag of revolution; they threatened to bombard Odessa at the slightest sign of resistance. And if Krieger failed to squash the mutiny soon, it might spawn similar uprisings throughout the Black Sea. Chukhnin knew quite well that there were instigators aboard every ship in his fleet.

While sitting with Avelan, Chukhnin devised a new set of orders for Krieger to implement. That afternoon, Avelan sent them in his name from the Naval Ministry:

> Proceed to Odessa with the entire squadron and every torpedo boat. Propose to the crew that they surrender. If they refuse, immediately sink the battleship by firing two torpedoes at close range. Prepare these torpedoes before confronting the battleship, so as not to give the *Potemkin* the chance to fire on the city or other ships. Shoot any rescued crew member who resists. Hand over the rest to Odessa's military commander for arrest.

They also sent a telegram to General Kakhanov, alerting him of their plans to deal with the crisis and save Odessa from the *Potemkin*'s guns.

Afterward, Chukhnin left for the Grand Hotel to gather his belongings so he could take an express train to Sevastopol that evening. He avoided the handful of foreign journalists who, having learned of the mutiny over the wires from Odessa, had descended on the Admiralty Building. A French reporter cornered Avelan's chief of staff on his exit a few hours after Chukhnin left. His response to the torrent of questions reflected the entire naval staff's mood: "For God's sake, don't speak of this."

# 11

AT THE FORECASTLE, Matyushenko stood before the crew. It was 2:30 P.M. All but three of the Odessan revolutionaries had been removed from the battleship after their meeting broke up. Kirill, Feldmann, and a Bolshevik who went by the alias Boris stayed aboard, having earned enough of the crew's trust to remain, at least for the time being. They were to keep the *Potemkin* connected to the city's workers and help rally the sailors to the revolutionary cause.

Still, Matyushenko knew he was ultimately responsible for unifying the sailors. One of the greatest risks was dissension within their own ranks, particularly at this early stage of the uprising. Only after other ships within the Black Sea Fleet had come to their side would the majority of the crew, who now felt alone against the whole empire, have enough faith to commit fully to their fight. Until then, the leaders must inspire them to do so. If Matyushenko showed any hint of wavering now, the sailors would succumb to their fears.

"There are about one hundred of us on the *Potemkin* who are absolutely committed to revolution," Matyushenko stated. "We've taken the side of the people's fight, and, if need be, we'll sacrifice our lives in the effort. We call you, brothers, to join us in this glorious cause. If you don't want to listen to our call, if you want to go to Sevastopol and surrender, then we don't wish to live to see that shame. We'll line up, and you can take our guns and kill us now."

Nobody doubted his sincerity. He capably forged his words like a blacksmith shaping a piece of hot metal.

"Take the *Potemkin* and report back to Sevastopol. Surely, you'll

be met with music and great celebrations. The tsar will honor your
actions and shower you with rewards for selling out the sacred cause
of the people's freedom. Choose, then." He paused. "With us to the
fight — or without us to Sevastopol!"

Silence followed his stirring speech. Then one called out, "We
don't want to ask the tsar for forgiveness." Another shouted, "We'll
fight together until the last drop of blood." Soon the crew cried out
together, "Fight for victory or die trying!" Those still skeptical dared
not openly challenge Matyushenko, nor would they have been heard
over the rousing chants.

Matyushenko left the deck, and a boatswain ordered the crew
to return to their posts. The sailors went enthusiastically, clear in
their purpose again — for now. Kirill and Feldmann walked along the
length of the battleship, amazed at the crew's discipline. Kirill had reluctantly seen his comrades off the *Potemkin,* believing the sailors
were making a mistake by turning their backs on the Odessan strikers
while waiting for the Black Sea Fleet's arrival. By staying aboard, he
hoped to convince the ship's leaders to reconsider and, if not that, at
least to raise the crew's political consciousness.

From the port, fishing vessels and a jumble of skiffs, rowboats, and
small steamers continued to approach and circle the *Potemkin.* The
crew accepted those bringing gifts, except one carrying crates of
vodka, a delivery the sailor committee suspected was sent by a port
official to get the crew drunk so they would forget their purpose.
They also turned away several revolutionary agitators who tried to
board, drawing up the rope ladders and cutting the ship off from any
more visitors. Kirill could only stand back and watch. In his view, the
battleship was abandoning the Odessan workers when they needed
them most.

Feldmann, who was at his side, pointed out a pair of soldiers rowing briskly toward the battleship in a small skiff, waves lapping over
its side.

"What have you come here for?" Feldmann yelled out.

"We're delegates from our regiments," they replied.

Feldmann ran to the admiral's stateroom, where the committee
was drafting a communication to the Odessan authorities that threatened bombardment if they interfered with the gatherings in the port
or prevented the workers from assisting the *Potemkin* in any way. In-

terrupting the meeting, Feldmann told them about the soldiers. The stateroom emptied.

"Comrades," one of the soldiers said after being allowed on board. "Our two regiments — the Ismailovsky and the Dunaisky — have sent us to tell you that we're with you. As soon as you step on shore, we'll come to your side."

Matyushenko and the other ship leaders circled around the soldiers, greeting them as brothers. If the army joined their fight, Odessa would easily fall into their hands. The danger the pair of soldiers had faced by rowing out to the battleship in their uniforms proved how earnest they were. They then addressed the crew, repeating their pledge of allegiance. The sailors cheered. This was almost too good to be true.

As the soldiers returned to their skiff, Matyushenko advised them to prepare to join an assault on the city once the rest of the fleet arrived. Until then, they must refuse to fire on the people if their commanders ordered them to. This discipline was critical.

After the soldiers had rowed away, Kirill and Feldmann vowed to each other to get the *Potemkin* to act against the city. They retreated to a stateroom with Boris to plan their propaganda campaign. Exhausted from nearly two days without rest, Kirill eased into a low chair and closed his eyes. Sleep was irresistible. But suddenly he was jarred awake by two words repeated over and over again: "The squadron!" When he rushed out of the stateroom, sailors already lined the railings, everyone looking toward the southeast. It was approaching 6 P.M., and the sun had lost most of its strength — a single trail of smoke could be seen on the horizon. Finally a ship appeared, alone in its approach toward Odessa.

Baron P. P. Eikhen, the colonel in command of the military transport ship *Vekha*, had left Nikolayev early that morning. When he neared Odessa, his signalman spotted the *Potemkin* in the harbor; a torpedo boat was moored to its side. He saluted the *Potemkin* with flags and then signaled that he had supplies to unload on shore.

The battleship responded by semaphore: "Do not go into the harbor. . . . Stop the engine and stand at anchor. . . . Captain to come aboard the *Potemkin*."

Surprised by the *Potemkin*'s presence, but aware that it might have something to do with the reported strikes in the city, Eikhen complied. He dropped anchor 160 yards off the *Potemkin*'s stern and then went by boat to report to its captain. A few minutes later he climbed onto the battleship's deck in his full dress uniform, expecting to be greeted by an officer. There was none in sight. He thought some emergency situation had occurred until fifteen sailors surrounded him with rifles. Confusion and then horror seized him.

"You're under arrest." Matyushenko stepped forward.

Eikhen was speechless. Two sailors grabbed him by the shoulders, and he finally stammered, "My men are always very comfortable."

"Hand over your saber," Matyushenko said, brandishing a revolver. Reznichenko was by his side, holding a rifle.

"Let me go to my ship, brothers," Eikhen said, struggling against the sailors. "I won't try to run away, you know. I have a woman with a baby on board."

"Your wife?" Reznichenko asked.

"No, someone's else's."

The crew roared with laughter.

"It's the wife and child of your second officer, Gilyarovsky," Eikhen explained. The sailors grew sober at the news. "Brothers, let me go to her. She must be protected from insult."

"Are we criminals? Have no fear . . . we're not like you. She will not be touched," Matyushenko said. He and Reznichenko pointed their guns at the colonel. "Now you'd better go along with us, or —"

Eikhen dropped his saber to the deck with a clang. In disgrace, he was led to the wardroom where the other officers were being held. Along the way, Ensign Alekseyev sidled up to him and whispered the obvious: "There are troubles on the battleship."

When the colonel had disappeared, Matyushenko asked his signalman to send another message to the transport ship: "Commander of the *Vekha* requests the officers to come on board the *Potemkin*."

Minutes later, two officers and the ship's doctor approached the *Potemkin* in another boat. Also surprised by the sailors, they were promptly arrested. Another signal instructed the *Vekha* to position itself close to the *Potemkin*'s port side. Then Matyushenko led a host of armed guards onto the transport ship. Devoid of officers, the *Vekha* easily fell into their hands. Their deception had worked: the *Potemkin* took control without firing a shot.

The *Vekha*'s sailors told Matyushenko that Eikhen and the other officers treated them decently and asked him to spare their lives. Considering their words, he went back to the *Potemkin* to see the officers. Perched on stools, they looked pitiful and scared as Kirill and Feldmann preached to them about the revolution's inevitability and how they would be "judged for all their crimes." Matyushenko told Kirill, who, he had realized, was a gifted speaker, to go to the *Vekha* and convince its sixty sailors to join their fight. The ship's leaders would decide what to do with these officers — as well as, finally, their own — that night. As for Gilyarovsky's wife and young daughter, they would be brought into Odessa as soon as possible. Fearing the woman might go into shock or become hysterical, the sailors decided not to tell her about her husband's death until she was safely on shore and no longer afraid for her or her daughter's life.

When the committee reassembled, the sailors were buoyant. Their revolutionary squadron now numbered three ships. The *Potemkin* was stocked with coal and provisions and the crew was more unified in purpose than ever before. Matyushenko led the discussion on the fate of the officers. Except for the declaration they had sent to the French consul, stating that nobody would be harmed if the city's authorities did not interfere with the *Potemkin*'s activities, Odessa was largely forgotten for the moment. As Matyushenko had told the city's revolutionaries, the sailors first needed to look to the sea before turning to an assault on land.

But events in Odessa, set in motion by the ship's arrival and the impact of Vakulenchuk's bier, had taken on a life of their own.

By late afternoon, more than ten thousand Odessans had filled the port and jammed the piers before Kakhanov's cordon was in place. They came from nearly every sector of the population: workers from the poor outlying districts of Peresyp and Moldovanka — many accompanied by their families as if they were on an outing, secondary-school and university students, dockworkers, merchant sailors, shopkeepers, a scattering of liberal professionals, and the *bosyaki* ("barefoot ones") — a ragtag collection of day laborers, the homeless, and vagrants. Throughout the morning and most of afternoon, a celebratory, peaceful air had prevailed, as if everyone were savoring a day of freedom filled with raucous speeches, courtesy of the *Potemkin*'s protection. But as the day wore on, a scattering of individuals, drunk on either alcohol or a feeling of invincibility, sometimes both, began to stir up trouble: a few fights, some petty thefts at the warehouses. Mostly, however, all was well.

Then, a few minutes after 5 P.M., a merchant sailor, Nikita Glotov, made the mistake of jeering at a speaker who had jumped up on a barrel to better address the crowd as he called for the tsar's downfall.

"And just who then will be our overlords?" Glotov taunted. "Ah, you Jews! You're all Jews, I say."

Several women struck Glotov with their parasols, but his ranting continued. Someone yelled that the sailor was actually a spy sent by the police to incite a pogrom. Then suddenly a shot rang out, followed by three more. Glotov collapsed, and a mob threw his lifeless body into the water. At the port entrances, the police and Cossacks held back and did not respond, seemingly oblivious to the first blush of violence.

As the crowd at the scene of Glotov's murder scattered, the collier *Emerans* returned to the port and docked. After helping load coal onto the *Potemkin,* the stevedores had celebrated with some vodka and become rowdy. Their presence added to the mood of lawlessness. Meanwhile, some vagrants looted a bonded warehouse and opened crates filled with bottles of spirits. Several workers and sailors tried to stop them from passing out the bottles, shouting, "It's freedom we need, not vodka," but few listened. A speaker standing atop a coal pile declared, "Comrades, there are heaps of clothing made by your hands in this port. They belong to you!" Some cheered his words. "Now. Are you feeling hungry?" He then pointed to a row of warehouses, inviting them to start the plunder.

The first curls of smoke from a burning warehouse rose at about the same time the *Potemkin* captured the *Vekha,* at 7 P.M. When a fire crew tried to enter the port, they were beaten back by stones. Hundreds started breaking into warehouses to steal silks, jewelry, sacks of sugar, vodka — anything they could get their hands on and carry away. Mostly, the *bosyaki* carried out the theft and vandalism, but others participated as well. With each passing hour, the crowd became more unruly. Some were getting wildly drunk, feeling increasingly empowered by the police's absence.

More and more warehouses were ransacked, and by 10 P.M. several buildings were on fire. Panic began to spread throughout the port. Many had already tried to leave the area but found their escape routes, including the Richelieu Steps, blocked by Cossacks and police. Some returned to the quays; others tried to force their way through and were met with blows to their chests and heads from rifle butts. Those who persisted were shot. Trapped in the port, the crowd became desperate to get away, pushing against the soldiers and calling them bloody monsters. Tempers mounted and raced out of control. Those who managed to slip through the cordon brought news of the port's desperate situation. Workers and revolutionaries on the city side of the blockade confronted the police on the streets and attempted to break through. The city was spiraling out of control.

General Kakhanov resisted every request from the police and from the port commander to move on the docks and quell what was nothing short of a riot. He even refused to push for more fire crews to extinguish the mounting blazes. Having received an official statement from St. Petersburg that Odessa was in a "state of war," Kakhanov, the city's senior military commander, had the authority to do as he pleased to retain control of the city. He had settled on his course of action. Since the Black Sea Fleet would not arrive until the next day, as he learned by telegram from Sevastopol, he had to buy more time, even if the price was death and mayhem in the port. Kakhanov was certain that if he suppressed the hostilities there, the *Potemkin* would launch an attack on Odessa. His primary purpose was to save the city and protect his troops. If the crowds wanted to loot warehouses and kill themselves in an orgy of destruction, so be it. The fact that many innocents were caught behind the port's cordon did not color his thoughts. As his assistant, General K. A. Karangozov, had coldly explained to a staff member earlier that day, "Let them gather in the port. We won't let them out. Then we'll shoot everyone."

But over the next two hours, the riotous tempest escalated to a level that Kakhanov had never anticipated. The city streets became the site of pitched battles. When some Cossacks tried to disperse striking workers, a homemade bomb was thrown at their feet, severely wounding six in the patrol. The police were taking gunfire from the rooftops, and more and more people flowed from the city center toward Primorsky Boulevard, breaking into fights with soldiers and police who had shut off access the port. Yet this disorder could not compare to the nightmare — obscured by billowing clouds of black smoke — now raging below, at the bottom of the steps.

An inferno ravaged the port. A wall of flame ran a half-mile alongside the water and expanded every minute. Fires leapt from warehouse to lodging quarter to warehouse to port office to storefront. The supports of the elevated railway were being consumed, as were the wagons on the tracks above. Goods stacked in crates on the quays served as fuel for bonfires, and the decks of several barges and steamships docked in the harbor also burned. Even the surface of the water became a blaze after explosions of fuel dumps on the quays released flammable liquid into the harbor itself.

The thousands trapped in the port faced confusion, panic, and death. Smoke enveloped the entire area, searing the lungs and blinding the eyes. The fires sent shock waves of heat that stopped people in their tracks. Some had already passed out from drink when the flames overcame them, but many died after escaping one fire, only to find themselves encircled by another. Their terrible screams cut through the smoke and darkness. Others were caught on ship decks, in warehouses, or under falling debris. Smoke and stampedes killed many more. Attempts to escape from the port by the Richelieu Steps and other exits were met with police resistance, but thanks to luck, cunning, or a merciful soldier, many did manage to get away. These fortunate ones looked as if they had emerged from hell: eyes filled with terror, faces blackened with soot, bodies wracked by fits of coughing. While they tried to recover, the police arrested them and led them away.

At midnight, Kakhanov finally decided that he could not allow the fires to rage unchecked. He needed to move with force into the port, clear away the crowds, and send in the fire crews. His troops also had to ruthlessly crush the rebellions blossoming in the streets. Let the *Potemkin* fire its guns; it was out of his control. As of yet, the sailors had taken no belligerent actions; the battleship remained far out in the harbor. If he did nothing, the inferno might raze the entire city. Kakhanov remained unsympathetic to the hundreds dying and injured in the port. In his view, they had brought this on themselves — and many more would die, once he got started. But the economic and physical damage had to be contained. From the reports he received from his men, the port railway station and the great warehouses of the

Russian Company were in ruins, and thieves had already stolen or torched millions of rubles in goods.

Kakhanov gave the order: attack.

From every port entrance, soldiers and Cossacks advanced on those pushing to get through the cordon. On the Richelieu Steps, fifty Cossacks urged their horses down the long flight of steps jammed with people. They cut down anyone in their way, slashing men and women, young and old alike, with their sabers and whips; their ferocity was spiked by the deaths of several of their own comrades over the past three days. The sheer mass of people on the narrow steps at the staircase's top slowed their charge, as did those who resisted by throwing stones. Another party of Cossacks dismounted and formed a line at the edge of the steps. Then they began to discharge their rifles, at close range.

Hysteria gripped the crowd on the steps. Stumbling over those wounded or killed by the first shots, people surged down the steps; at the same time those below, trying to flee the inferno, surged up. Many were unable to move; even if they could, they were not sure which way to go. The Cossacks drove down the steps, taking advantage of the confusion to send round after round of gunfire into the muddled mass of bodies. Shrieks of the terrified and the dying filled the night. Every three steps, the dismounted troops dropped to one knee, chambered another round in their rifles, and then fired together on command. Those hit often tumbled down the cobbled steps until they reached the next landing. Gaining momentum, the Cossacks fixed bayonets and stormed downward in their polished black boots, stabbing those who had yet to flee, their sabers jangling at their sides. At the base of the steps, the soldiers reassembled and then headed toward the piers, slashing and shooting at will.

The same scene was played out in other parts of the port. Gunfire sounded from every direction. In the city streets, soldiers positioned snipers on rooftops to kill any protestors who attacked their positions. People watching the massacre from their balconies were at risk of being mistaken for armed revolutionaries and were told to stay away from their windows. Many crouched in the back of their apartments, praying that the madness would soon end. They were to have a long wait.

Russian and international correspondents scrambled about the city, dodging patrols and wading through the smoke-filled streets to report on the slaughter. Foreign consuls bolted their doors and cabled their embassies in St. Petersburg that a mutinous battleship had taken Odessa hostage and that the city was descending into chaos. General Kakhanov stared out at the harbor, fearing the *Potemkin* would let loose its guns at any moment. The billows of smoke passing across his window allowed him only the occasional chance to catch its searchlights.

As the first fires began to spread in the port, at 10 P.M., Lieutenant Kovalenko stood on the battleship's gun deck, the still night air sending a chill through him. He was lost in thought. The sailor committee had decided to send the *Vekha*'s officers, as well as Gilyarovsky's wife and baby daughter, ashore in an outlying district. Now they were deliberating on what to do with Kovalenko and the rest of the *Potemkin*'s officers. The day's events had inspired Kovalenko: workers embracing the sailors as comrades, Odessan officials trembling in the battleship's presence, the taking of another ship, a feeling among the crew that they were participating in historic events. He wondered if this was the beginning of the revolution that he and other students in Kharkov had once conceived of in only distant terms. Should he cross the Rubicon and ask to join the sailors now?

Kovalenko considered the question. With the isolated fires in the port and the faint but unmistakable sound of sporadic gunshots, he imagined workers fighting the government's troops and breaking into their arsenal. Then a sailor interrupted this daydream, telling Kovalenko to return to the quarters where the officers had been held over the past day and a half.

The room felt like a morgue. His fellow officers leaned against the bulkheads, listless and fearful about their fate. Several minutes later, Matyushenko stepped in, with two committee members at his side. He looked around, making sure everyone was there, before he spoke. "Officers, the crew has decided to send you ashore. But before this is done, would any of you like to stand alongside us?"

Astonishment and confusion met this offer. Kovalenko felt his heart leap in his chest. This was the moment to choose. He could leave the *Potemkin* and be safe. But would he then be able to face the knowledge that he had forsaken the chance to fight against the regime that had subjugated the Ukrainian people for so long? This battleship might indeed be the spark that would light the revolution. Kovalenko nearly rose to accept the offer when fresh doubts overcame him. Did Matyushenko speak for the entire crew? What if the next day the committee retracted their offer? Then Kovalenko would have risked everything, only to be sent ashore, where he would face charges of treason.

"Listen, Matyushenko," he finally said; the other officers turned to him in surprise. "I'm on your side and would consider it an honor to share the crew's fate. But I'm tortured by doubt. Can I be sure that among seven hundred sailors, there aren't some who would want me gone?"

"Let's step aside." Matyushenko took Kovalenko by the arm to the corner of the room. Quietly he said, "I have to tell you there are very few officers we'd like to see left on the ship. There are some who, even if they wanted to join us, the crew can't accept. As for you, I give you my word the crew will gladly take you as one of our own. If you want, I'll bring you a statement —"

"No." Kovalenko interrupted. "I trust you and I want to stay."

"I knew you'd do this!" Matyushenko grinned, obviously pleased. He turned to the rest of the room. "What have you decided?"

An officer glared at Kovalenko and whispered, "Why are you doing this?"

"I'm doing what my conscience tells me," he replied.

Then Dr. Golenko stood. "As a doctor, I consider it my duty not to leave the sick and wounded that I'm responsible for on the ship. I'll stay as well."

The others remained silent, and Matyushenko invited Kovalenko and the doctor to participate in a committee meeting. As they left, Ensign P. V. Kaluzhny came to Kovalenko's side. Twenty-one years old and chronically nervous, he appeared more a child than a Russian naval officer.

"I'll stay with you, too," he said, fearing that Odessa was already in the hands of revolutionaries who would have him killed once he went ashore.

"Are you sure?" Kovalenko asked. "If you stay, you can't go back to your old life."

"And still, I'd like to stay."

"Then I'll tell Matyushenko."

When Kovalenko entered the admiral's stateroom, he pledged his solidarity with the sailors, telling them that he had long held a desire to fight the tsar's regime. Golenko followed, saying that he was the son of a simple farmer and wanted to help the sailors. A few questioned the doctor's sincerity, asking where he was when the captain ordered them to eat foul meat. Needing a doctor aboard the battleship, however, the committee voted that he could stay as well. Afterward the two officers were asked to leave.

For the next hour, the committee debated what to do when the squadron arrived and how to prevent a potential counter-mutiny. They decided to pass out revolvers to those among them who were the most committed to the cause. As the conversation turned to Vakulenchuk's burial, a watchman burst through the door in a panic. "Fire! The city's on fire! The city's on fire!"

Matyushenko led the rush through the door. He had seen a few conflagrations in the port when they convened the meeting but dismissed their importance. Looking out at Odessa now, he was horrified. Fires devoured nearly every building in the port. Feldmann, who was by his side, later described what they saw: "A terrible spectacle unfolded before our eyes. A vast glow of red lit up the whole bay. Wherever one turned his gaze, it met gigantic tongues of flame. They leapt ever higher and higher, and spread ever wider and wider, like beacons flashing the tiding of the all-devouring vengeance of the old regime."

Then they heard a distant but unmistakable series of gunshots. A sailor turned the ship's powerful searchlights toward the shore to see where the shots were coming from, but the light failed to penetrate the columns of smoke.

"They're firing on the people!" a sailor screeched.

Ensign Alekseyev, who always seemed to be lurking at the opportune moment, offered a different opinion. "What nonsense are you talking! That firing? It's simply the roofs cracking in the heat."

Not sure what to think, Matyushenko ran to board a launch, to see for himself. Kirill, hoarse after two hours of speeches aboard the *Vekha,* followed him. Minutes later, they cast off from the battleship.

As they approached the port, buildings buckled and collapsed. Oil drums exploded. The closer they came, the sharper the rifle fire sounded, and they saw people stumbling about in the flames.

The horror was too great for words. Matyushenko felt a shiver run down his body. He had come to free the people of Odessa, and instead, they were facing wholesale slaughter. Matyushenko and Kirill attempted to get close to the piers to help some escape, but waves of heat and smoke forced them away before they could catch sight of the Richelieu Steps, where the Cossacks had launched their attack. They directed the launch to a beach at the port's edge, where some people had gathered to avoid the inferno. These people told Matyushenko of the cordon around the port and how the troops were shooting at anyone who tried to break through. For Matyushenko, no amount of curses, hand wringing, or pounding on the launch's side could relieve the furies that seethed inside him. He had seen countless injustices served up by the tsar's men, but nothing on this scale of cruelty.

He directed the launch back to the *Potemkin*. Returning to the other leaders of the ship, Matyushenko demanded, without explanation, that they shell the city. The crew looked toward Kirill, who told the sailors what they had seen. It was agreed, and a battle alarm soon rang on the *Potemkin*.

As the crew ran to their positions, Ensign Alekseyev asked how they were planning to aim the guns. The city was hidden in smoke. They lacked firing coordinates. He insisted the leadership on the bridge reconsider this idea. Several terrible moments of indecision passed. Reluctantly, one by one the sailors realized Alekseyev was right. Shooting blind, they were as likely to hit workers as government troops.

"Whom will we be killing?" one sailor, Kuzma Perelygin, reasoned. "There are many poor people who can't leave, and for this we'll be cursed. That's why we can't bombard the city."

Matyushenko felt sick to think that they commanded a battleship able to decimate Odessa's forces, yet they were relegated to watching the fire and listening to the *rat-tat-tat* of gunfire. Having to accept this fact, he left the quarterdeck, escaping from the sights and sounds of the massacre before they drove him mad.

# 12

FELDMANN AND SEVERAL *Potemkin* sailors took a launch into the harbor at first light on June 16, the mutiny's third day. The waters were eerily absent of boats, and in the distance, a haze of smoke still covered the port. As they neared one of the piers, the extent of the fire's destruction became sickeningly clear. The launch passed several bloated corpses floating in the water. Barges and steamers anchored by the piers were burned-out skeletons. Scores of buildings had been gutted in the inferno, and small fires were consuming any that had survived the night. The elevated railway had partly collapsed, and tens of wagons that it had supported were now piles of smoking timber. The entire port, from one end to the other, had been leveled to ashes.

Dressed in a sailor's tunic, breeches, and a cap with the ship's name embroidered on it, Feldmann stepped ashore, to make the arrangements to bury Vakulenchuk. Before dawn, some workers had rowed to the *Potemkin* to tell how the presence of the sailor's body had started the terrible violence. Speaking to the ship's leaders, Dr. Golenko insisted, "We can't let people go on being killed for the sake of a dead man. We must bury him and make an end of it. If no one will go with me, I am going alone." The assistant surgeon, who had chosen to stay on the battleship to tend the wounded, seemed only to care about saving lives, if he could. Though the sailors agreed with him, they refused to simply cast their hero anonymously into the sea. They wanted a martyr's ceremony, both to honor Vakulenchuk for his sacrifice and bring together the workers and the sailors.

In an effort to avoid another massacre, Feldmann planned to request permission from General Kakhanov to hold the funeral. Although he might be arrested — or shot — on sight, Feldmann had volunteered for the mission to show the sailors that he too was willing to risk his life. The machinist Vasili Kulik, two other committee members, and Father Parmen accompanied him. None were armed. They hoped the general would not dare seize them or prevent the funeral, since the *Potemkin*'s guns threatened even more ruin if Kakhanov took such action.

On the pier, they found that some people had stacked sandbags around the bier to protect Vakulenchuk's body from the fire. Still, the heat and the smoke had blackened his face, which had begun to decompose. The stench from the body almost made Feldmann gag. Parmen prayed over the sailor, and then the deputation walked toward the Richelieu Steps.

Everywhere lay corpses, many burned beyond recognition. A lone cart pulled by two horses rocked and creaked on the cobblestones. Its driver stopped now and again to allow two men walking behind to pick up a body and heave it onto the cart. Climbing the steps, Feldmann tripped over a young worker, his face frozen in horror, bloodstains on his shirtfront. Feldmann turned to Kulik, who was also looking down at the dead man. They shared a glance, silently asking how this could have happened. Then they climbed upward.

On the plaza, near the statue of Richelieu, a large detachment of soldiers, with bayonets raised, suddenly encircled the party from the *Potemkin*. One officer took Father Parmen by the arm and led him away, promising that he would be treated well. Feldmann and the others were pushed along after him, toward the commander's headquarters. Feldmann explained their purpose, but the soldiers were uninterested.

The scene on the city streets made it difficult for Feldmann to disguise his increasing panic. Soldiers occupied corner after corner, and notices of a military occupation were posted everywhere. Every shop was closed, and no trams were running. Patrols marched past Feldmann, eyeing him and the other sailors with murderous looks. The few groups of people in the street talked in whispers, their faces weary and distraught, no doubt expecting more violence. Every few minutes a gunshot rang out, occasionally accompanied by a cry of pain. In Sobornaya Plaza, soldiers were building a military camp, some raising tents, others huddling around a makeshift kitchen while their horses nosed a pile of hay.

Feldmann and the others were ushered into the courtyard of the military headquarters, sure they were going to be shot. Cossacks stood around the perimeter, glaring at them. Kulik, a descendant of Cossacks, tried to speak with them, but they turned away from him. Fear of what was in store for the sailors finally overwhelmed him.

"Look here, I'm going to be hanged, maybe, any minute," Kulik fumed, "and you shun me like a leper. For whose sake do you think we're going to our death? Is it for our own? Is it — ?"

He stopped his tirade when he heard a nearby rifle report. His words had clearly had some effect on the Cossacks, who now assuaged him. "Don't worry about that," one of them said to Kulik. "They're just firing in the air to scare people."

Soon the Cossacks had warmed to Kulik enough to tell him that thousands of troops were on their way to Odessa from the surrounding regions; some were bringing heavy artillery. Feldmann eavesdropped, becoming more convinced every minute that the *Potemkin* could not simply wait for the arrival of Black Sea Fleet squadron before moving on the city. They needed to act before the government strengthened its forces. But now he might never get the chance to alert the battleship. An hour had passed since their arrival at military headquarters, and still there was no word about what the soldiers meant to do with them. Feldmann cursed his foolishness. He might soon die over a funeral that could have easily been arranged at sea.

Then, amazingly, Father Parmen stepped out of the building.

The colonel at the priest's side approached them. "Permission is given to bury the sailor. . . . Now you can go."

For the first time since they cast off from the battleship, Feldmann and the sailors breathed easily. Kakhanov must have been cowed by the threat of their guns. Before they left, Feldmann gave Father Parmen some rubles to prepare for the ceremony later that day. They would never see him again.

While Feldmann and the sailors made their way back to the battleship, the surviving *Potemkin* officers and Colonel Schultz from St. Petersburg climbed down the rope ladder into a fishing boat. Some sailors jeered at the "dragons," now stripped of their epaulettes and sabers, as they huddled in the boat before it cast off. For their part, the *Potemkin* officers stayed silent, glad to at least escape with their lives, unlike their captain. In hand, they had a decree written by the sailor committee to deliver to General Kakhanov, reinforcing their warning of the consequences the city would face if he acted against the battleship. "Our final hour of suffering has come," the decree read. "We ask all Cossacks and soldiers to take up arms and to rally together under one banner in the struggle for freedom."

The fishing boat pushed away, and the *Potemkin* crew were completely free of their former oppressors. They did not celebrate, however. Only forty-eight hours had passed since Nikishkin had shot his rifle in the air, sparking the mutiny, and the crew were deeply afflicted with doubt. Most had gone without sleep again; the fires and echoes of rifle shots had been too disturbing to ignore. Then they had to face the sight of the port's devastation at daybreak. Were they the cause of such a nightmare? How many hundreds, if not thousands, had lost their lives? Would the tsar place blame for these deaths at their feet as well?

Whether on watch, resting in hammocks, sitting in the mess decks, or merely pacing the foredeck to pass a few quiet moments, the sailors contemplated these questions with a sense of anxiety. They had mutinied, an act warranting the firing squad, and yet they were standing at anchor outside Odessa as the tsar's forces undoubtedly were being amassed against them. The crew wanted to know what was next. Was the revolution as near as the Odessan agitators had promised? Would other battleships in the Black Sea Fleet come to their aid, as the ship's leaders hoped? Should they return to Sevastopol and surrender, begging for mercy? Should they make a run to some foreign shore?

The crew talked constantly about these possibilities, and the absence of firm answers made rumors spread like a contagion. Before noon, when Kirill sat down for some bread, a sailor by his side turned to him and said, "Is it true that we're going to Romania?"

Kirill stared at the sailor, speechless for a moment. Then he coldly asked, "Who told you that?"

"All the crew is saying it," he said apologetically.

Leaving his bread uneaten, Kirill left to tell the sailor committee what he had heard. On his way, he ran into Kovalenko.

"The crew is troubled," Kirill said. "Out of nowhere, there's an idea to go to Romania, and I'm afraid it will confuse the sailors."

"I doubt this idea would be popular among the crew," Kovalenko said, though he was far from certain.

Then he recounted to Kirill a troubling conversation he had just had with Ensign Alekseyev. The young officer had cornered him to ask if there was a chance he could be sent ashore like the other officers. Clearly, Alekseyev had agreed to serve as a figurehead captain because he feared being shot if he refused; he was doing everything he could *not* to help the sailors, obviously knowing that if the mutiny was suppressed, the naval command would accuse him of aiding the mutineers. Kovalenko pitied Alekseyev but told him he could not help him. Then the ensign attempted to convince him that the crew's only chance of survival was to go to Romania — as he said some of the departed officers had suggested — and abandon the *Potemkin*. That the officer from whom the crew expected leadership was spreading this kind of talk was definitely inexcusable; Kovalenko was rushing to alert the sailor committee.

The two left to find Matyushenko, sure that Ensign Alekseyev needed to be removed from command; defeatist thoughts such as going to Romania had to be dispelled before they inspired a countermutiny. But after hearing their concerns, Matyushenko dismissed the suggestion that Alekseyev be dismissed from the battleship, believing this action would only further confuse the crew. Nonetheless he called a committee meeting to discuss this and other matters, including the rampant spread of rumors. A drumroll sounded on the quarterdeck, and the ship's leaders gathered in the admiral's stateroom a few minutes before noon.

Matyushenko had been busy dealing with the officers as well as sending sailors into port to find accurate maps of Odessa, to use in case they needed to shell the city. Although he was still convinced that they should not launch an attack until the Black Sea Fleet joined them, the night's events had made him reconsider this unwillingness to act. Although neither he nor his fellow revolutionaries had uttered the words, they sensed an unspoken agreement that they would fol-

low through on their threat to destroy Odessa if General Kakhanov
took one wrong step — whether it was interfering with their martyr's
funeral or causing further bloodshed among the city's populace.

Once everyone had assembled at the table, Matyushenko broached
the question of keeping Alekseyev as captain. Some sailors complained that he had forestalled their resolution to bombard Odessa;
others pointed out that the ensign spent most of his time wallowing in
self-pity. And now he was speaking of Romania.

"He doesn't do what he is told. He's not with us," one committee
member said.

Another retorted, "He's still new in his role."

Alekseyev was not their only problem, Kirill interjected. The petty
officers did not support the mutiny and should be sent away. "They're
the most rotten people on the ship," he said.

"If we remove them," a sailor countered, "the crew will lose confidence in our ability to control the ship. Their spirit might collapse,
and we won't be able to do anything at all. We'll be better off if we let
them stay, but watch over them closely."

Despite the dissension, the committee voted to keep Alekseyev
and the petty officers on the *Potemkin,* primarily because of this latter
argument: the officers helped maintain the crew's confidence. But the
committee needed to silence malicious rumors and involve the crew
more in their plans, so the men understood the reasoning behind the
committee's resolutions — particularly the need to wait for the squadron. Matyushenko moved to conduct future meetings in a large wardroom, where more sailors could attend, as well as to announce each
decision on the quarterdeck for their approval. That way, everyone
would feel they had a say in the ship's efforts, solidifying their commitment. If the sailor committee wanted to maintain a hold on the
crew, they could not act like their former officers, issuing orders and
expecting blind obedience.

Into the early afternoon, the mutiny's leaders remained in the
stateroom, in an effort to make decisions democratically. They argued
over how best to prepare the *Potemkin*'s crew for a battle against the
Black Sea Fleet if their fellow sailors on other ships had not yet mutinied, or, if provoked, how to convince their own crew to fire on
Odessa. Feldmann returned with welcome news about the funeral but

then instigated a whole new debate about the wisdom of sitting idly while Kakhanov reinforced the city with more troops and artillery.

Matyushenko left before the meeting's end to bring food to the sailors guarding Vakulenchuk and to check on the progress of another group who had been sent to find provisions. On the pier, he met with a military deputation carrying a message from General Kakhanov, guaranteeing the safety of the honor guard of sailors who would accompany Vakulenchuk's cortege to his burial. The procession, Kakhanov said, could begin at 4 P.M.

Before the deputation departed, a soldier unexpectedly drew Matyushenko aside. "There's a big military conference taking place this evening," he said. "It's a council meeting to decide what they're going to do about you. Why don't you drop a few shells on them?"

"Where's it being held?" Matyushenko asked, electrified by the information.

"In the theater. All the senior officers will be there. As soon as you've killed them off, we'll join you. You can be sure of that."

After this conversation, Matyushenko rushed back to the battleship, eager to tell the sailors that they would not have to wait any longer to act. This was their great chance to revenge the previous night's massacre, and, in one barrage, eliminate the military's high command. Once this was accomplished, the workers would rise up, hopefully with the assistance of the soldiers, and the city would fall into their hands. Finally, the sailors had the opportunity to use the *Potemkin*'s destructive force in the name of the revolution. Matyushenko could almost taste victory.

That very morning, Naval Minister Avelan and Vice Admiral Chukhnin boarded the first train from Baltic Station in St. Petersburg to Peterhof. The forty-minute ride out of the city, past birch forests and fields of oats, offered much time for reflection. Before midnight on June 15, Chukhnin had received a telegram from Tsar Nicholas at his hotel, instructing him not to leave for Sevastopol until they had a private meeting. Reports of mayhem and a huge fire provoked by the *Potemkin*'s arrival in Odessa had made a grave situation worse. Apparently, the tsar felt he needed to express this face-to-face.

Chukhnin had alarming news to deliver himself. First, the transport ship *Vekha* appeared to have joined the *Potemkin*. Second, the squadron he had ordered to intercept the mutinous battleship was still a day away from reaching it. Delayed by preparations to assemble crews and arm the battleships, Vishnevetsky had only just left Sevastopol at 2 A.M. that morning, and Krieger was not scheduled to leave until that evening to meet up with his rear admiral off Tendra Island. They were taking too much time. Third, two battleships, the *Chesma* and *Ekaterina II,* had to remain behind in Sevastopol because their crews were unreliable; in fact, their captains had disabled each ship's engine room in case of mutiny or any effort to join the *Potemkin*. Finally, reports had reached the Admiralty that another mutiny had broken out among sailors stationed in the Baltic navy base of Libau. The sailors had seized rifles and attacked the officer quarters, requiring a call to local Cossack and infantry regiments to put down the revolt. The event seemed unconnected to the *Potemkin,* but the Admiralty could not know for sure. Taken together, Avelan and Chukhnin had much to explain to their tsar, none of it good.

When they arrived at the station, a footman with a cocked hat and dark green uniform led them to an open carriage. The two admirals had taken the long drive through the grounds often enough to be no longer awed by its splendor. In fact, Chukhnin had last visited only five days before, for a social call with the tsar and his mother. But this morning was different. When they reached the Lower Palace, they did not face the usual interminable wait in the cream-colored antechamber outside the tsar's office. Instead, a tall servant in a long black and scarlet coat immediately led Avelan and Chukhnin to one of the terraces overlooking the sea. The tsar was waiting for them. The meeting was brief; Nicholas was direct and uncharacteristically upset.

"Go to Sevastopol today," he told Chukhnin. "Direct the squadron to quickly crush the uprisings, even if it means sinking the battleship. I'm depending on you."

When Chukhnin returned to St. Petersburg, he telegrammed Krieger and Vishnevetsky that the tsar had granted him unlimited powers to put down the mutiny. Therefore, he advised no hesitation in executing his previous order to sink the *Potemkin* if the sailors refused to surrender. No half measures were to be taken, Chukhnin explained, even at the cost of Russia's premier battleship. He also sent a message to Nikolayev, instructing the commander of the *Eriklik,* Captain Second Rank Boisman, to begin preparations for a firing squad and a burial site for the mutineers.

Once these orders were delivered, Chukhnin boarded a special express train to Nikolayev, from whence he would travel by boat to Sevastopol. He was anxious to be back in command there, as he doubted Krieger could handle the situation effectively. That the squadron had delayed its departure enraged Chukhnin, and he wondered if the moment to deal expeditiously with this mutiny (and to limit the embarrassment caused by it) had already passed.

After his admirals left Peterhof, Nicholas returned to his office and notified the deputy minister of the interior, Trepov, to expand the previous *ukaz* of martial law to include Nikolayev and Sevastopol and the surrounding countryside. With the *Potemkin* on the loose, revolution threatened to spread throughout the Black Sea region. The disaster in Odessa proved the stakes involved. Over the past sixteen hours, Nicholas and his ministers had received frantic messages from the city, pleading for help. The reports spoke of three hundred dead and the burning of a portion of the port. The only precise details available were recorded in a callous note from an army officer, which noted that his troops "expended 1,510 bullets and broke several rifle butts" during the night. In truth, the violence on June 15 took 1,260 lives, and the damage to the port totaled over fifteen million rubles, but the estimates were enough for Nicholas to fear that this was only the beginning, if the *Potemkin* continued its revolt.

The tsar had other concerns as well. His war minister, Vladimir Sakharov, had announced the mobilization of reserves in St. Petersburg and Moscow in order to reinforce troops in the Far East; this act had spurred threats of mass strikes in Russia's two largest cities. Riots in Lodz and Warsaw continued to rage unchecked as well. Trepov was cracking down harshly on strikes in the industrial town of Ivanovo-Voznesensk. "Negotiate less, and act more energetically," Trepov had recently instructed the police, believing the unrest would spread throughout the empire if he were unsuccessful. Furthermore, a conference of city council representatives met in St. Petersburg that week, apparently blaming Nicholas for the continuing defeats at the hands of the Japanese and for Russia's deteriorating internal situation, particularly the rising number of agrarian revolts. Other liberal leaders continued to prod him on political changes that he felt would betray the state. And, finally, rumors had reached Nicholas that some army regiments based in the capital as well as in the Far East were at the brink of mutiny themselves.

Given these troubles, punctuated most forcefully by the *Potemkin,* Nicholas had to reconsider pursuing peace with Japan. Prior to the Battle of Tsushima, talk of a truce had arisen, but the words were mostly empty. In the days after the defeat, Nicholas considered the real possibility of negotiations to end the war, convening with his ministers over the prospect, but he made no decisions, favoring the opinion of his war minister that Russia needed at least one significant victory over Japan before seeking peace. Otherwise, his minister argued, the Japanese would have too much leverage at the bargaining table. Subsequent discussions with his ministers edged him closer to seeking peace, as he came to fear that his enemy would soon attack Russian soil at Sakhalin Island. But still he hesitated.

On May 25, in a private audience with Nicholas, the new American ambassador in St. Petersburg, George von Lengerke Meyer, informed him of President Theodore Roosevelt's proposal to broker a peace conference between Russia and Japan. Finally, Nicholas assented to opening talks. However, agreeing to a conference was a long way from committing to peace, particularly considering the notorious double-speak of the tsar's regime. One day, his ministers spoke of a desire for a deal; the next, they spoke of fighting the war indefinitely, a promise backed by the calling up of more reserves. This vacillation reflected Nicholas's own indecisiveness. Roosevelt expressed his frustration to his close friend Henry Cabot Lodge: "Russia is so corrupt, so treacherous and shifty, and so incompetent, that I'm utterly unable to say whether or not it will make peace, or break off the negotiations at any moment."

In the two weeks before the *Potemkin* mutiny, Nicholas debated where the meeting should be held and who should represent his government as plenipotentiary; his choice of the latter would reveal how seriously he took the talks. From the outset, he refused Sergei Witte, who would have been the best person to send to the table. Towering in height, with a booming, rough voice and grating manners, Witte had a presence similar to that of Alexander III. During his tenure, Witte had orchestrated the empire's rapid economic development and was considered by many at home and abroad to be Russia's only hope at navigating away from ruin. His vehement opposition to war with Japan had led Nicholas to force him aside as minister of finance, and his vocal call for peace had alienated him even more from the tsar. When his name was suggested by the Russian foreign minister, Nicholas sighed, "Only not Witte!" Instead the tsar chose the ambassador to France, A. I. Nelidov, who was a diplomatic antique, ill of health, and frightfully incapable of managing the complexities of the negotiations with Japan. It was clear that Nicholas had not yet set his sights on peace.

That afternoon, June 16, after his meeting with Avelan and Chukhnin, Nicholas wrote letters to each of his ministers, requesting their opinion again on the war. The developing situation at home demanded resolution.

Nicholas received a quicker, blunter response from the international community, which was only just learning about the mutiny and the Odessan massacre. Not only a personal embarrassment for and political threat to Nicholas, the *Potemkin* could potentially have global repercussions. The tsar had a stranglehold on his own press, but he was helpless to keep news of the mutiny from the rest of world; their awareness of the crisis only deepened it.

Around the globe, newspaper front pages and editorials sensationalized the *Potemkin* story. "Fate of the Empire Depends on the Loyalty of the Black Sea Fleet," wrote John Callan O'Laughlin, a *Chicago Daily Tribune* reporter and a confidant of President Roosevelt. "Czar's Warship in Rebels' Hands — Revolution Now Feared" headlined the *New York Times.* London's *Daily Telegraph,* whose star reporter, E. J. White, was an ally of Sergei Witte, cut to the quick: "There is always in every despotism one weak spot. . . . It is, of course, the discipline of the troops. So long as authority can rely on the fidelity of its bayonets, it is safe against popular assault. But when monarchy loses its right arm, then, indeed, its hour of tribulation is near." The *Times* of London, an unapologetic supporter of the Russian liberals, was breathless in its coverage as well, stating that the tsarist government had brought this situation on itself and that reform must be the consequence. Paris's *Petit Journal* believed it was too late for this course: "It had been hoped that the concessions which the tsar seemed inclined to make might avert a catastrophe. It is now perceived that the situation is desperate, that the evil has gone too far to be remedied, and that Russia is from end to end, in a state of revolution." Berlin's *Tageblatt* called the mutiny "a flashlight revealing to the dullest eye the true situation in the interior of that wide empire and the dangerous disintegration of political order." Tokyo's *Nichi Nichi Shimbun* was equally pessimistic: "What is left for the autocracy to stand upon? If the tsar is wise he will now, when it is still possible, by a bold and steadfast policy of reform, save his state from a tremendous upheaval. It looks as if he, like Louis XVI of France, will not be wise."

Much as ill-fed, mistreated sailors shooting their officers and instigating a massive riot in one of Russia's biggest cities made for exciting copy and provided fodder for editorial writers, world political leaders took the *Potemkin* uprising very seriously. In the realm of finance, a mutinous battleship on the Black Sea threatened the region's substantial commercial trade, and the fire in Odessa's port damaged more than just Russian business. Stock markets nose-dived as soon as reports of the mutiny broke. Grain prices skyrocketed. The events provoked a sharp exchange in the British Parliament on June 16. Some raised the possibility of the *Potemkin*'s bombarding Odessa and questioned whether the British government was taking precautionary measures to protect its citizens and shipping interests. Revealing a sentiment shared by other leaders, Prime Minister A. J. Balfour succinctly responded, "It seems difficult to see what precautions can be taken in regard to disorders taking place in a town not under British jurisdiction."

The potential consequences in the sphere of international relations were even greater, given Russia's prominent role. France depended on its alliance with Russia to stave off Germany's bullying. Great Britain, which had a long history of troubled relations with Russia, most recently over the tsar's territorial ambitions in the Far East, was bound to friendly relations with Japan. Yet Balfour's government had recently brokered the Entente Cordiale with its long-time adversary France, to check Germany's dominance in Europe. Kaiser Wilhelm II wanted Nicholas focused on — and weakened by — his war with Japan, thereby reducing Russian influence in Europe, particularly in the Balkans and Austria-Hungary, where Wilhelm was seeking a stronger hand. However, given the new relationship between France and Britain, the kaiser was also interested in securing his ties with his cousin Nicholas. The sultan of the Ottoman Empire, Abdul Hamid II, the last of the true autocrats alongside the tsar, was split between his fear of Russian power and concern that his country's own revolutionaries would sweep him from his throne if this were to be Nicholas's fate. As for the United States, Roosevelt was sympathetic to the plight of the 150 million Russians whose ruler, as he had recently written to Secretary of State John Hay, was a "preposterous little creature" who "has been unable to make war, and now he is unable to make peace." Yet Roosevelt was a realist, understanding that without the tsar's interest in the Far East, Japan might become too powerful in the region. If Nicholas lost control of his empire, this fragile balance of power and web of alliances might unravel. The status quo was preferable to the alternative of new Russian leadership, socialist or otherwise, with its own unpredictable interests.

That was why a mutinous battleship flying a revolutionary flag on the Black Sea sowed trepidation at the highest levels. The French ambassador to Russia, Maurice Paleologue, was terrified of the "revolutionary tornado" storming across the country. He relayed to Paris that the *Potemkin* was another serious sign that Nicholas was lost if he neglected to pursue peace with Japan, followed by a stiff prescription of reform. Government circles in Berlin mirrored this sentiment, watching developments closely. Wilhelm II persistently urged Nicholas toward a deal with Japan. British ambassador Charles Hardinge predicted that more repression — not reform — would follow in the mutiny's wake. American ambassador Meyer drafted a letter to Roosevelt about the navy rebellion, believing the army might follow suit. Despite this danger, Meyer wrote that Nicholas and his ministers held to form, equivocating and delaying over the peace talks, trying the very "patience of Job." Meyer promised to press the regime nonetheless. Sultan Abdul Hamid II took rapid steps to reinforce his defenses along the Bosphorus Strait and heightened the watch on his own armed forces. As for the Japanese, the Black Sea crisis only strengthened their position, a fact that even the Russian ambassador to the United States admitted to a reporter: "Japan has had the luck of the devil. We are in the position of a man in a poker game who has had fortune against him in every hand." Others would see opportunity as well in the mutiny.

From his small Geneva apartment, Lenin fought his revolution against the Tsar of All the Russias. On the morning of June 16, he finished his daily exercises (forward bends and chest presses), shared a pot of hot tea with his wife, Krupskaya, and then cleared off his desk after another long night of writing. Afterward, dressed in a coat and slacks, he headed out of his tenement building to go to the library and read the morning newspapers.

With his bald, egglike head, copper-red beard, and dark slanted eyes, Lenin cut an easily recognizable figure in the neighborhood where many exiled Russian intellectuals lived in 1905. Often they congregated at night in the Café Landolt, Mensheviks in one back room, Bolsheviks in another, fighting their doctrinal wars far from the frontlines of the workers they claimed to represent.

Born in 1870 in a small town alongside the Volga River, Lenin came from a family whose high position was earned by the dogged efforts of his father. Although a brooding introvert, Lenin enjoyed an easy childhood and won good marks in school. He might never have turned to revolution were it not for his older brother, the family favorite, who was hanged while still a student in St. Petersburg for plotting to kill Alexander III with a homemade bomb. Lenin was seventeen; the family name was smeared. He was expelled from the University of Kazan for participating in a minor student demonstration. While in jail, a fellow student asked him what he thought he was going to do with his life. Lenin responded, "What is there for me to think? My path has been blazed by my brother."

Seeking solitude, Lenin moved with his mother to Samara, studied law on his own, and read constantly. His first influences were the writings of Russia's early revolutionaries. Of particular impact was Nikolai Chernyshevsky's *What Is to Be Done?*, a novel in which the hero, Rakhmetov, finds redemption through revolution, devoting himself to a life absent of pleasure, clear in purpose, and immune to human suffering, all in the name of progress. Lenin also fell under the spell of Pyotr Tkachev, who believed in capturing power violently, establishing a dictatorship run by an elite revolutionary vanguard, and then advancing socialism. These writings had crystallized in his mind long before he took to reading and interpreting the works of Karl Marx.

In 1893, Lenin passed the bar exam and left for St. Petersburg, joining a revolutionary study group almost before unpacking his bags. He met his future wife, Krupskaya, there and embraced Marx's teachings. In his earliest writings and activities, Lenin revealed himself to be fiercely analytical, a brilliant broad-ranging thinker, politically agile, and supremely determined to dominate every argument. This fire intensified after his arrest in 1895, a year in a St. Petersburg jail, and then three more in Siberian exile, where he spent his time studying and writing. On his release, many considered him one of the leading Social Democrat intellectuals. Shortly afterward he left Russia for Europe to join others in exile.

There he followed a road that led away from Julius Martov, one of his closest friends, as well as away from the father of Russian Marxism, Georgy Plekhanov. All of them wanted revolution, believed in a centralized organization, and despised the soft stance of liberals. But Lenin, hearkening back to his earliest influences, battled for a tightly controlled, militaristic command structure. In July 1903, at a formal party meeting in Brussels, the Social Democrats split into two parties, taking the names Bolsheviks ("Majoritarians") and Mensheviks ("Minoritarians") after Lenin won a floor vote on the definition of party membership. Lenin wanted only those who actively participated in the organization to be included, while Martov preferred to admit anyone who endorsed their efforts.

Having witnessed Lenin's ruthless moves to dictate the party's direction, Plekhanov commented prophetically, "Of such dough, Robespierres are made." After the meeting, Lenin was forced off the editorial board of *Iskra*, the revolutionary paper he had helped create to focus the mission of the Social Democrats. For the next eighteen months he struggled almost alone to build his new party, an effort that brought him close to mental collapse and deepened his rift with Martov and the other Mensheviks.

At the start of 1905, Lenin published a new revolutionary organ, *Vperyod (Forward)*, and his spirits lifted. In the first issue, Lenin wrote, "A military collapse is now inevitable, and with it there will

inevitably come a tenfold increase of unrest, discontent and rebellion. For that moment we must prepare with all our energy." Lenin
espoused the street-fighting techniques of Paris Commune leader
Gustave Cluseret: "Squads must arm themselves, each man with
what he can get: a rifle, revolver, bomb, knife, stick, a rag dipped in
kerosene."

Lenin labored night and day, feverishly committed to freeing Russia of the tsar. Yet he spent most of his effort in battles with the
Mensheviks, delivering invectives against the tsar and liberal bourgeoisie and sending letters to his Bolshevik representatives in Russia.
He begged them for news and complained that they weren't doing
enough for the cause. His organization was poorly funded and limited
in number. Bloody Sunday, and the outbreak of strikes in its aftermath, took him by surprise. Throughout, he remained in Geneva, as
did Martov and the great majority of other exiles, reacting to and interpreting events, rather than participating in them.

However, on the morning of June 16, when Lenin ran his eyes
across the front page of the *La Tribune de Genève* and spotted the sur-
prising news about the *Potemkin* mutiny below the underwhelming
headline "The Situation in Russia," he could barely contain his excitement. This was the beginning of a revolutionary army, he thought.
He rushed to find Mikhail Vasilyev-Yuzhin, a fellow Bolshevik who
had once lived in Odessa. That afternoon, they met in the apartment
of another revolutionary off the rue de Carouge. Rumors about the
mutiny had shot through Geneva's exile community.

"You'll leave for Odessa tomorrow," Lenin told Vasilyev-Yuzhin,
whose neat suit, tight-collared shirt, and air of propriety made him
look like a clergyman.

"I'm ready today if you want. What's the job?"

"It's of the most serious nature. I fear our comrades in Odessa
won't succeed in making use of the revolt. You must try, at all costs, to
get on board the battleship, to convince the sailors they must act decisively. If need be, don't hesitate to shell the government institutions.
We *must* seize the town. Then arm the workers at once."

Vasilyev-Yuzhin, who had known Lenin for several years, had
never seen him so eager to take action. He remained silent.

"Further, it's essential to get the rest of the fleet in our hands."

"You can't seriously think that's possible, Vladimir Ilyich?"

"Obviously I think it's perfectly possible. It's merely necessary to act boldly."

Vasilyev-Yuzhin left with his orders, wondering whether Lenin was not too carried away to think that the sailors would simply relinquish their leadership over the battleship to him — if he somehow managed to arrive in time. It was more than likely that most of the sailors had never even heard of Lenin.

# 13

AN ORTHODOX PRIEST led the funeral procession slowly down Preobrazhenskaya Street at 4 P.M. on the afternoon of June 16. Matyushenko and eleven other *Potemkin* sailors followed behind the horse-drawn carriage bearing Vakulenchuk in his wooden coffin. Thousands of Odessans lined the street and stood on their balconies overhead. Many held candles. Some tossed flowers as the carriage passed on its way to Uspensky Cathedral. It was so quiet that one could hear little else than the *clop-clop* of horse hooves on the cobblestones. Save the escort of two mounted Cossacks, General Kakhanov's forces held back in the side streets.

Matyushenko looked at the tear-strewn faces in the crowd to his left and to his right. These people had already suffered so much, but here they were now, risking their lives again to pay their respects to a man they had never known. The funeral was helping align the Odessans with the sailors, so they could act as one. Given the sailors' plan to bombard the military meeting that night, they would soon need the citizens' help to take over the city. But still, for Matyushenko, this funeral was about more than its contribution to the struggle. He did not need to serve in the honor guard — it put him within grasp of the soldiers if Kakhanov betrayed them and kept him away from the battleship, where the crew was dangerously unsettled. But he did so anyway.

Matyushenko had come to honor his friend, who had thought only of helping free his enslaved fellow sailors. For his efforts, he had died before ever seeing the revolutionary flag fly over the *Potemkin*.

Still, he was not forgotten, and the sight of so many people in the streets, risking their own blood to honor his friend, struck Matyushenko deeply. Vakulenchuk had been born one of the many millions of nameless peasants who lived out their days under the yoke of oppression. But now, Matyushenko thought, his friend was being celebrated in a way that a king or tsar could only hope to match.

After the simple funeral service at Uspensky Cathedral, the procession moved toward the cemetery. As they approached Chumka Hill, a company of soldiers cut off the thousands of Odessans following the carriage. When the crowd pushed against their line, a soldier shot his rifle into the air. Matyushenko approached the company's sergeant to complain.

"Keep moving, or we will open fire!" the sergeant screamed.

Matyushenko turned away though he was tempted to strike the officer; for once he held back his temper, which could surge with such speed and ferocity that he easily became a prisoner to it. Instead he continued to the cemetery. Several minutes later, hundreds of Odessans circumvented the blockade and emptied out of side streets behind them once again. Outmaneuvering the soldiers had charged up the crowd, and the procession took on a celebratory mood. People called out, "Long live freedom! Long live equality! Long live solidarity!" On Chumka Hill, many more had gathered in advance to attend the burial. A few held banners proclaiming, DOWN WITH AUTOCRACY! As they filed into the cemetery, the crowd voiced their solidarity with the sailors.

"We'll never forget this," Matyushenko told a worker.

Before the ceremony took place, a Cossack officer dismounted and walked up to Matyushenko, saying that the sailor and his men would have to leave immediately; their presence was stirring up the crowd too much. Unarmed and unwilling to cause trouble for the Odessans, Matyushenko agreed to leave. He and the other sailors climbed into some carriages waiting outside the cemetery, and they left before Vakulenchuk was lowered into the ground. Halfway back to the port, on Preobrazhenskaya Street, a company of soldiers blocked their path. "You'll have to walk," the officer in charge commanded. Matyushenko suspected nothing, as they had been allowed to hold the funeral peacefully. The sailors stepped out of the carriages.

But as they walked forward, a second company of soldiers appeared down a side street, rifles drawn, blocking their escape to the right. The moment Matyushenko realized they had stepped into an ambush, a trumpet blasted. It was the signal to fire. The twelve sailors spun around, looking for cover and finding none. The line of rifles cracked. The first barrage missed Matyushenko. He sprinted down the block with several others at his side.

Another round of fire thundered.

Matyushenko scrambled around the corner, narrowly escaping the first volleys. He did not have a chance to see who had survived along with him as he heard footsteps beat behind him — the soldiers gave chase. The *Potemkin* sailors dashed down several side streets, one after the other, getting lost. Nonetheless, they kept running, not sure where to go but with instinct telling them to rush until their lungs burned and legs deadened. At every corner they stopped and peered around the building's edge, expecting to face a line of rifles. Finding none, they kept running. Finally, they managed to shake loose their pursuers. When Matyushenko slowed his pace, he realized that three of his shipmates were missing — killed or arrested in the ambush. He would never know.

Matyushenko led the surviving sailors to the port and commandeered a fishing boat to return them to the *Potemkin*. On their way out, he discovered a bullet hole in his pant leg, proving how narrow and lucky his escape had been. He was certain, however, that they all would have died, had several soldiers not purposely aimed astray — the other sailors agreed that they had seen this.

When Matyushenko stepped back onto the battleship, he had one thought: they must bombard Odessa now. They would have their revenge on Kakhanov, and the battle to take the city would finally begin. It was time.

When an officer reported that all but three of the sailors had escaped the ambush, Kakhanov set off to meet with his commanders at the city theater to decide on further steps to pacify the workers and defend themselves against the *Potemkin*. With thousands of troops pouring into the city from the surrounding region, Odessa was in a state of lockdown. A curfew had been set for dusk; the streets were under heavy patrol; and the approaches to the city and its major government buildings and foreign consuls were all under guard. Except for a few confrontations in the city's outskirts, everything was calm. But now matters had changed.

When Kakhanov had authorized the ambush, a plan he had developed after the sailors petitioned him about the funeral, he was working with little information and few options. He had expected the squadron's arrival before the funeral procession even began. A morning telegram from the Admiralty had informed him that Vishnevetsky would near Odessa by 3 P.M., but that was the last he had heard from either St. Petersburg or Sevastopol. Therefore, arresting the sailors who came ashore to bury Vakulenchuk, particularly if this group contained some of the battleship's mutinous leaders, made strategic sense, as it would decapitate the *Potemkin*'s leadership before the naval confrontation. But as the day passed, with the squadron yet to appear, Kakhanov had to decide what to do himself.

Although in a desperate position, at least he had known more about the sailors' plans than he had the night before. After leaving the ship, the *Potemkin*'s deposed officers had informed him that the crew was already committed to bombing the city and arming the workers. If so, then ambushing the sailors was not going to put the city in more peril than it already was threatened with. Kakhanov could not simply let mutinous sailors come and go as they pleased within his city. Perhaps he would capture one of their leaders — perhaps even this Matyushenko himself; the officers had said that he controlled the crew. By making a move on the sailors after the funeral, Kakhanov would avoid inciting another riot.

But now the ambush had failed and Vice Admiral Chukhnin's squadron was still nowhere in sight. Now, Kakhanov despaired, the *Potemkin* would begin its bombardment long before the squadron appeared.

At 5:20 P.M., the battleship *Three Saints,* commanded by Rear Admiral Vishnevetsky, dropped anchor off Tendra Island. The rest of his squadron — the battleships *St. George* and *Twelve Apostles,* the light cruiser *Kazarsky,* and four torpedo boats — followed its lead. Ten minutes later, Vishnevetsky called a meeting of commanders aboard his battleship.

Although he had orders to engage the *Potemkin,* he clearly told his officers that he would do no such thing, at least until Krieger came with reinforcements. They would approach Odessa, but if the *Potemkin* refused to capitulate and remove the red flag from its mast, Vishnevetsky's squadron would not fire on it, inciting a sea battle. Instead they would surround the harbor entrance and lay siege to the battleship, until it ran out of food or coal.

He explained to his officers that, given the unreliability of the squadron's crews, this was a better tactic than engagement, echoing the advice he had received from the former Black Sea commander, Admiral Nikolai Skrydlov, before setting to sea. Vishnevetsky planned to send a note to Odessa, ordering city officials to prevent the *Potemkin* from accessing supplies. Eventually, the sailors would be forced to surrender.

The squadron would attack only if the *Potemkin* fired first, and in this case, their strategy would be to send torpedo boats into the harbor, while the battleships stayed at sea and kept the *Potemkin* from escaping. Vishnevetsky reminded his officers that this option would be only the last resort. Early the next morning, he said, they would advance toward Odessa, but before they did, two torpedo boats would reconnoiter the area. The crews should prepare for a night attack against the squadron by laying out anti-torpedo nets around each battleship and keeping a close watch. Before dismissing his officers, he handed out copies of a proclamation for them to read to their crews. Gently and without creating alarm, they were to inform their men of what to expect in the coming hours.

But Vishnevetsky was too late. A couple of hours into the journey, on board the *Twelve Apostles,* sailor Mikhail Volgin had learned the reason for the rushed departure from Sevastopol. The officers were obviously nervous, smoking more than usual and trying to fraternize with the sailors as if they wanted a favor.

Then a comrade approached him, winked, and said, "What's wrong? Either you've lost everything gambling or something very bad happened." The coded greeting meant there was a meeting of sailor revolutionaries in the machine room.

After Volgin and the others arrived, one of the battleship's senior mechanics, Gerasimov, a dedicated Social Democrat, confirmed that their mission was against the *Potemkin*. Then he said, "The question's whether we take over the *Twelve Apostles* ourselves, or go to the bottom of the sea instead."

Those gathered gave the mechanic a questioning look.

"All the other captains said they can't rely on their crews," he continued. "But our Captain Kolands, the old fool, has given his word to Krieger that he'll destroy the *Potemkin*. If his crew hesitates to fire, he promised to ram the *Potemkin* and blow up both ships."

The sailors left the machine room with troubled looks. Few slept more than a couple of hours during the early morning voyage to Tendra. Instead, Volgin and the others plotted how they could stop their officers and considered the consequences if they failed. Throughout the squadron, similar conversations played out. A few sailors had told their officers, even before they arrived at Tendra Island, that the crew would refuse to fire on the *Potemkin* if directed to.

This being the case, Vishnevetsky was right to be cautious in preparing his proclamation. At 7 P.M., the captains gathered their crews at the forecastle of each ship and read Vishnevetsky's words straight from the page, beginning, "Brothers, an incident unprecedented in the Russian fleet's history has taken place on the battleship *Potemkin*. The crew has revolted, and, it's rumored, murdered the commander and raised the revolutionary flag."

The officers then explained their plan to fight a war of attrition against the *Potemkin,* whose supplies of food and coal would last for no more than seven days, turning the ship eventually from a "fortress to a trap." There was a lesson here for any sailor who attempted a similar crime. This squadron had been sent to "tame" the *Potemkin* and "to end the scandal." Its size guaranteed that the mutinous battleship's crew would understand the threat and capitulate.

The captains read the conclusion of the proclamation:

> I have no intention of attacking the *Potemkin,* thereby only exacerbating this shameful situation. I'll take every action to bring about a peaceful resolution. In this, I'm relying on your cooperation, my brothers, and ask you to heed the voice of reason, which tells us to act just as I've described. Nothing, however, prevents us from being attacked. In this case, God forbid, our blood will spill, or we'll spill the blood of our comrades. We will have to respond to the attack with force.

Remember, brothers, and believe me when I say that every word written in this proclamation proceeds directly from my heart and is dictated by the love for the Russian sailor, which I bear.

Rear Admiral Vishnevetsky.

On the *St. George,* Captain Ilya Guzevich finished and dropped his hand, holding the paper to his side. Looking out at his crew, he demanded they do their duty. With a faint reply, less than one in every ten sailors of the 616-man crew said, "We'll try." The rest remained silent. Just as on the *Twelve Apostles,* a band of sailor revolutionaries, organized by Tsentralka leader Dorofey Koshuba, were on board the *St. George,* plotting to stop their officers from firing on the *Potemkin.* Despite what Vishnevetsky might like them to believe, he and the rest of the officers were no brothers of theirs.

The sun was setting over the city when Matyushenko and the others returned to the battleship, having survived the ambush. They found a crew that had grown even more anxious as another day ended with the ship anchored outside of Odessa.

The boatswains had kept the sailors occupied. Even at idle, the crew maintained their watches and duties. Gunners scoured the barrels to prevent deterioration from humidity and sea air. The cooks peeled potatoes and scrubbed dishes. The telegraphists hovered over their machines, waiting for any intercepts. The mechanics and stokers below cleaned the boilers, lubricated the engines, and swept away the coal ash. Guards stood watch over the quarterdeck. Medics bandaged the injured, and the cobbler mended shoes. The bakers baked, and the launderers laundered. The *Potemkin* was like a small city, and there was always work to do.

But as much as they kept to their routine, the sailors knew they were on a rogue battleship that the tsar would blow out of the water, if need be. Sitting outside the harbor, the battleship made an inviting target, and the ship's leaders still had not indicated what they planned to do next. Doubts about these leaders were heightened by the petty officers, who whispered to the crew that surrender was their best — and only — option. Otherwise, they promised, the sailors were signing their own death warrants. Then, late that afternoon, a ship had been sighted on the horizon, instigating cries of "The squadron is coming!" It turned out to be the training ship *Prut,* which never approached the harbor; but the panic it caused revealed the crew's raw nerves.

When Matyushenko came aboard, the sailors were gathering for a general assembly. Although the sailor committee had earlier agreed to shell the military council meeting and had procured a few city maps for this purpose, they had hesitated in revealing this decision to the crew, precisely because of the uneasy mood. Nonetheless, they needed the men's approval before turning the guns on the city.

The sailors formed an impromptu amphitheater around the capstan, where the committee leaders spoke. In the front rows, sailors sat cross-legged on the deck. Behind them, several rows of sailors stood, arms akimbo or held tightly across the chest. Above them, sailors dangled their legs over the sides of the upper decks or sat atop the twelve-inch guns, looking down on Kirill, who was the first to speak. They listened skeptically as the Odessan revolutionary told of the enslaved Russian masses and the heroic struggle in which they were joined.

Then sailor Dymchenko stood and introduced Feldmann, saying simply, "Here, lads, a good man wants to say a word to you."

In the sharp, fluid speech of a veteran debater looking to score point after point, Feldmann told the sailors that the line had been crossed and their chances of pardon were lost. Their struggle now was to the end.

"True. Very true," some sailors called out, bolstering Feldmann.

"We must deal the enemy a deadly blow," he urged. "The troops in Odessa are ready to come over to us. They're only waiting for the first step. This step *you* must take. Every moment of delay strengthens the enemy and weakens us. Ahead of you is the glory and honor that are granted to fighters for the people. Behind you is the yoke of your former torturers. You choose which one you want. What we must do is to open fire on the city, now — without wasting any more time."

Caught up in the revolutionary fervor, the crew shouted, "Hurrah!" But this excitement dissolved into protests against firing on the town. One sailor pushed forward, saying that bombing Odessa would hurt the people, not the tsar or his government. Such arguments splintered the crew. Perhaps they were better off leaving the city behind in their wake, some felt.

Kirill sidled up to Feldmann after he stepped off the podium.

"You went to work too abruptly. It can't be done like that." Only one man, Kirill admonished, one of the sailors, could demand that kind of action.

"Away with the landsmen!" the crew chanted. Then they looked to Ensign Alekseyev, calling for him to speak. The officer meekly retreated from the deck.

Mingling among the crew on the quarterdeck, Matyushenko watched the sailors quarrel; a few almost came to blows. Unable to remain silent another second, he jumped onto the capstan. The shouting faded into murmurs. Then silence. Then he began, channeling all his inner resources: his sadness over Vakulenchuk's death, his desire for revenge for what Kakhanov had done over the past twenty-four hours, his hatred of the tsar. The words came almost as a release, and they gushed forth.

"Stay, brothers! We must have unity! Our rulers have done enough in setting us against each other, and now you want to fall to killing yourselves. All the people are looking to you now. Listen, we were beaten and harassed by our officers, treated worse than dogs. We couldn't stand to live like that any longer, and we killed our dragons. Now we rule ourselves, yet will the Russian people have a better life because we dropped our officers into the sea? Will a peasant or worker be better off because of that? Don't forget, I'm not talking about strangers — our brothers and fathers are among them. The people are broke, many of them are being killed in the war, and the whole Pacific fleet has been sunk."

The sailors were enthralled, as much with Matyushenko's delivery as with what he had to say. On the capstan, he spoke with the urgency of a commander in the midst of battle. But more than anything, his power over the men came from the intensity of his movements. He threw his whole body, slight and lost as it was in his uniform, into his speech. He swayed and twisted and rocked back and forth. He thrust his arms up and down and left and right with a conductor's frenzy. And the sailors followed where he led.

"Now they want to hang us all, because we stand up for what's right. No, we won't let them finish us without a fight. If we want a better life for the people, not only for ourselves, we must fight. We're here with an entire fortress loaded with huge guns, but we're just watching indifferently while our brothers get killed. Shame on us!

The Russian people will damn us in the future. We can't let it happen! We'll achieve freedom or die today, together with our brothers!"

"We stand for the same cause!" the crew roared — almost involuntarily, they were so galvanized by his speech — "We will die all together!"

"Okay, then. Let's start the bombardment of the city today," Matyushenko returned. "We can't wait any longer. They should pay for the blood of the workers they spilled. Do you agree?"

"We agree!" the crew answered.

"Well, brothers, now stand steady. Go to your places."

When Matyushenko stepped down, sailors slapped his back and shook his hand. In that moment, and for the moment, his words had unified the crew again, and they set off to prepare to fire on the city. Matyushenko, too, was swept away by his own words and by the feeling that had overcome him as he spoke. Afterward, he embraced Kirill and, holding him by the arms, said, "We will die together." His tone was that of one who had chosen and accepted his own fate.

"Weigh anchor and get up steam!" came the order across the quarterdeck. A bugle sounded across the *Potemkin,* hurrying the sailors to their stations. Black smoke coughed out of the funnels. The decks were cleared, the iron hatches battened down. Gunners brought up shells from the magazines and removed the tompions from the gun muzzles. A first-aid team led by Dr. Golenko prepared bandages and stretchers as if they were going into battle. Matyushenko strode toward the bridge while sailors drenched the wooden decks with cold seawater to prevent fires catching from the shells. Within ten minutes, every gun, from the quick firers to the twelve-inchers, was loaded. Spare dark-gray shells coated with greasy lubricant were stacked on the decks. At 6:35 P.M., the *Potemkin* moved out half a mile to take up a better firing position.

Dusk had fallen over the city, the silhouettes of its buildings fading with each passing minute. In the port, a scattering of unattended warehouse fires still burned; a slight breeze drew the smoke across the harbor's waters. As the *Potemkin* turned its starboard side toward Odessa, the sailors stood silently at their posts, most of them feeling a strange blend of nervous excitement and somberness. On the bridge, Matyushenko waited beside Dymchenko, Nikishkin, Kovalenko, and Ensign Alekseyev, all looking out toward the city. Their three targets, identified on a map without any scale, included the city theater where the council meeting was taking place and Odessa's military and city government headquarters. Kirill and Feldmann watched from the bridge as well, standing well back and out of the way.

The sailor committee had voted to fire three blank shots in succession from the thirty-seven-millimeter guns to warn the city's residents to take cover. That these shots also gave the military council the chance to do the same was a risk they accepted. A trumpet blasted a few staccato notes, signaling the gunners to fire. The sailors cringed, waiting for the concussion, though they would be startled by its ear-splitting blast nonetheless.

Boom.

The trumpet blared again.

Boom.

The trumpet.

Boom.

The acrid smoke from the first three shots drifted away as a sailor hoisted a red battle flag on the foremast. Using a range finder, senior signalman Frederick Vedenmeyer, a redheaded sailor who was also a committee member, relayed the range and bearing to the six-inch-gun crew. The gun mount turned slowly into position. A trumpet sounded again. Silence. Then a thunderous clap followed a flash of white and green light from the gun's muzzle. The *Potemkin* quaked. The crew looked toward Odessa, the concussion echoing in their ears.

With the firing of the shell, Matyushenko felt that he was sending a message personally to the tsar. He should free the land to the peasants. He should give up the factories to the workers. He should open his palaces to the people. Otherwise, the sailors would force him from the throne.

"Overshot!" Vedenmeyer called out to the bridge.

A horrified hush fell on the *Potemkin* as everybody realized that the errant high-explosive shell likely meant innocent deaths. Matyushenko harshly instructed Vedenmeyer, "Get it right this time. We must hit the theater and nothing else, do you understand?"

Vedenmeyer relayed new coordinates to the battery. The bridge signaled fire. The crew covered their ears. The gun flashed. Kovalenko heard the shell whine and, with his binoculars, spotted people on the

Primorsky Boulevard dashing for cover. Along with everyone on the bridge, he prayed this shell would find its mark.

In Odessa's streets, panic reigned. After the warning shots, many hurried to their basements or simply dropped to the floor. Off Preobrazhenskaya Street, soldiers who were camped in the square scattered to the nearest buildings, yelling to one another that the *Potemkin* had finally launched its campaign of destruction. The American consul foolishly stood at his window to watch the barrage, swearing later to his superiors in Washington that he saw the first shell arc into the sky.

That first shell crashed into a corner building in the city center. A cloud of dust and smoke consumed the house. The walls groaned, then fell in on themselves. A three-yard section of an adjoining roof teetered for a moment before shearing off and shattering on the street below. Hysterical screams filled the area. A pair of startled carriage horses bolted down the street, throwing off their driver. A resident next to the destroyed house came out on his balcony, pushing aside hunks of stone and wood, in complete shock. He looked down to the street, asking a tailor who worked in a neighboring shop why someone would want to blow up his house.

As the dust cleared, people came out of their houses to inspect the damage. The roof of 71 Nezhinskaya Street was split in two, its timber supports frayed like rope. Nobody emerged from the house. A giant hole gaped in the wall of a nearby building. Telegraph wires had fallen, and the streets were strewn with rubble. Underneath a nearby acacia tree, a janitor discovered a fragment of the six-inch shell. In a daze, people surrounded it and pointed at the smoking fragment as if they didn't know from where it came.

Then came a second roar from the harbor and the shrill whine of another shell descending into the city. The street emptied.

"Overshot. Overshot!" announced several spotters on the *Potemkin* after the second shell disappeared over the rooftops.

Sailors pounded their fists against the bulkheads and swore at the gunners. They had meant to strike the military council, not rain terror on the city. If they opened up a broadside with all their guns, they would no doubt eventually find their mark, but many innocent civilians would die in the process.

"A white flag! They're waving the white flag!" Vedenmeyer cried out, shortly before the sailors could blame him for the inaccuracy of the six-inch battery.

The misfirings had undermined the crew's resolve to fire on the military council, and now the sighting of a white flag gave them reason to cease the barrage altogether, though Vedenmeyer was the only one who spotted the flag in the encroaching darkness.

Soon after, the sailor committee met and agreed on a new ultimatum to send to General Kakhanov, demanding that the police and troops withdraw from the city. While the crew unloaded the shells from the batteries, Matyushenko and Feldmann boarded a launch to deliver the ultimatum. In case they were arrested or attacked, Matyushenko brought two signal flares to alert the *Potemkin*. He stashed one under his shirt. He left the other on the boat for the sailors to use.

When the launch landed ashore, the port was as still and empty as a cemetery. On the way to the Richelieu Steps, the men passed several charred corpses that had yet to be carted away after the previous night's violence. The ominous silence was broken only once, by the hooves of a pair of galloping horses hauling an ambulance carriage. At the top of the steps stood General Karangozov, a dwarf of a man, towered over by the host of officers at his side. He asked why they had come.

"We've fired two shells today as a demonstration that we may take decisive action at any moment," Feldmann said. "But we don't desire unnecessary bloodshed. We invite the commander of the troops to come out to us on the ship or to send some fully authorized person to hear our demands."

"And if we don't accede to this request?" Karangozov asked crisply.

"Then we consider ourselves free to take action," Matyushenko said, deadpan.

"Very well. I'll report your request to General Kakhanov."

"If we don't return to the ship by ten o'clock," Feldmann warned, "they'll open fire from all the guns."

While the sailors waited at the top of the Richelieu Steps, Karangozov departed to military headquarters. He found Kakhanov in a foul temper. The city's elite were fleeing Odessa, taking freight trains where necessary, and all the factories remained shut down. Civilian officials had wired the minister of the interior, begging for help and insisting that the military had "no means to appease the population." Kakhanov had still not received an update from the squadron, and even though his troops had finally set up artillery positions on the hillsides, they would be useless if the *Potemkin* maneuvered out of range. No, he told Karangozov, he refused to meet with these mutinous sailors who had dared fire on the city — and, what was worse, without any accuracy. They were mad, Kakhanov finished, if they believed he would discuss terms.

Fifteen minutes later, Karangozov returned to the sailors. He relayed this response to Matyushenko in a contemptuous tone: "The commander in chief doesn't desire to enter into any negotiations with mutineers. If you want to fire more shells at the houses of peaceful citizens, then God and the tsar will be your judges. I can only suggest you give yourselves up and ask for forgiveness. Now you can go."

Matyushenko was stunned by the response: would Kakhanov truly rather let them destroy the city than accept their demands? If he would not listen to reason, then the sailors had no other choice. The delegation returned to the *Potemkin*. One committee member hissed, "We'll show him whether we are mutineers. If he won't talk to us, then let him answer to our twelve-inch guns." Another sailor voiced what others were hoping: "*If only* the squadron would come, Kakhanov wouldn't talk to us like that."

They resolved that if the squadron failed to show up the next day, they would launch another assault on Odessa, concentrating their guns on the main boulevards and city parks where the soldiers were stationed. This time they would sustain their bombardment until Kakhanov surrendered. When two representatives from the city's united revolutionary commission pulled their boat alongside the *Potemkin* later that night, the sailors told them of their plan and asked that they be ready to join this battle against the government.

The sailors settled in for another night. Those on watch panned the harbor's waters with projector lights, fearful that the Black Sea Fleet command might launch a torpedo attack on them in the dark.

They were blind to the fact that an attack had already been perpetrated — from on board the *Potemkin* itself. The signalman Vedenmeyer, a trusted committee member, had double-crossed them.

Even before the battleship left Sevastopol, Vedenmeyer had been one of Golikov's informants. He reported on the *Potemkin*'s revolutionary activities and was paid generously for his efforts. In the hours immediately after the mutiny, he had secured the fleet's secret codebooks from the captain's stateroom to prevent the sailors from using them.

Although Vedenmeyer blamed the overshots of the six-inch guns on their lack of a scaled and detailed map of Odessa, he had purposely given the battery crew the wrong range. And the "white flag" that he had seen was actually soldiers in the port signaling by semaphore: "Keep up the bombardment. In the morning, we will join you." His sabotage that evening would later earn him the tsar's thanks. He was the first of two traitors to act decisively against the *Potemkin*.

Nicholas II

*Historical Photo Foundation,*
*St. Petersburg, Russia*

Vice Admiral
Grigory P. Chukhnin

Admiral
Fyodor K. Avelan

Vice Admiral
Aleksandr Krieger

*All photos are from the Central Naval Museum,*
*St. Petersburg, Russia, unless otherwise noted.*

Tsentralka meeting

Afanasy Nikolayevich
Matyushenko

Grigory N. Vakulenchuk

The *Potemkin* mutiny (torpedo boat *Ismail* in the background)

Sailor Vakulenchuk's funeral bier in Odessa

The silent battle — the *Potemkin* against the Black Sea Fleet

The crew of the battleship *Potemkin*

The battleship *Potemkin*

The battleship *Rostislav*

The battleship *St. George*

The destroyer *Stremitelny*

Anatoly P. Berezovsky
("Kirill")

Konstantin I. Feldmann

General Semyon Kakhanov,
military governor of Odessa

*Niva Magazine, 1905*

Lieutenant
Aleksandr Kovalenko

Officers and petty officers of the battleship *Potemkin*
(Captain Yevgeny Golikov, center; Lieutenant Ippolit Gilyarovsky, to his right)

The *Potemkin* sailors disembark in Constanza.

# 14

A FEW HOURS after midnight, the start of the mutiny's fourth day, a sailor committee member overheard a petty officer mention how easy it would be to sink the battleship by blowing up one of the magazines stocked with shells. He was arrested, and Matyushenko demanded the traitor be shot. Instead, the committee ruled to lock him in a cabin and send him ashore the next day.

Looking pale and haggard after the confrontation, Matyushenko retired to one of the staterooms to catch a few hours' rest. He had barely slept in three days, and his voice could manage little more than a whisper. He knew they had reached something of a standstill. Alone in their mutiny, they were, as Vakulenchuk had warned him, not as much of a threat to overthrowing the tsar as Matyushenko had hoped. Without other battleships at their side, their rebellion might be doomed — either to be sunk by the tsar's loyal ships or lost to a counter-revolt staged by the crew. They needed allies.

Into the early hours, Kirill roamed the battleship, exhausted but reluctant to lie down and risk being overwhelmed by his steady parade of fears and thoughts about what still needed to be done. He encountered sailors on the decks with the same problem, anxious either that the crew's support for the mutiny was waning, particularly among the youngest sailors, or that they had not made enough progress in bringing revolution to Odessa. The slaughter in the port still weighed heavily on their minds, as did the errant six-inch shots. Mostly, however, the sailors spoke of the Black Sea Fleet. They wondered when it would arrive and what they should do if the crews aboard had not revolted, forcing the *Potemkin* to engage them. Then sailor would have to fire on sailor, a thought they hated to contemplate. Finally, an hour before dawn, Kirill had heard enough, returned to a stateroom, and sank into a sofa. He had been asleep for barely a few minutes when a sailor banged on the door before bursting inside.

"We intercepted a telegram," he said breathlessly. "The squadron's coming!"

Kirill hastened to the small wireless telegraph room. It was already crowded with fifteen committee members standing over the machine, anticipating another message from the battleship *Three Saints*. All they had intercepted was a question: "Why don't you answer?" The intended recipient was unknown. Hoping to draw out more information, the *Potemkin* sailors sent a message, without identifying their ship: "Where is the rest of the squadron?" Finally, after it seemed they might not receive a reply, the telegraph machine shook and clicked out: "For *Twelve Apostles:* Why don't you answer? *Potemkin* remains off the harbor of Odessa — *Three Saints.*"

The message excited the sailors. The wireless telegraph had a limited range, so the squadron had to be a few hours away, at most. The ship's leaders hurried to the wardroom, deliberating quickly about what they should do.

"What if the squadron still hasn't mutinied?" Matyushenko asked.

The committee agreed that it was likely the other ships had yet to overthrow their officers. Otherwise, they would have informed the *Potemkin* of their success by telegraph and come straight to Odessa to join them.

"We ought to remain here and try to stop the squadron on the horizon," Feldmann suggested. "If the commanders refuse to negotiate, we open fire from a distance." The *Potemkin*'s guns outranged those of the rest of the fleet.

"No. We have to go out to meet them," Kovalenko argued. Matyushenko backed this course. If their revolutionary comrades were still planning to take control of their ships, the *Potemkin* could not very well fire on them before they had a chance to do so.

This reasoning swayed the committee. Over the next few minutes, they hashed out a plan: they would steam toward the squadron as soon as they spotted its smoke on the horizon; the *Potemkin* would move at full speed, battle-ready, but it would not fire first; if the squadron attacked, the *Potemkin* would respond, with devastating force. There would be no surrender. They would scuttle their own battleship themselves as a last resort.

Matyushenko ended the meeting, and the order rang out: "Prepare for action."

The sailors cleared and hosed down the decks, filled the oar boats with water in case of fire, stacked coal sacks around exposed quickfiring gun positions, and jerry-rigged shields, using ropes and soaked tarpaulins to protect against shell splinters. The religious among them sprinkled holy water onto the guns while the gun crews loaded them with shells. Down in the engine room, the stokers fired eighteen of the twenty-two boilers. The battleship's searchlights were directed out to sea. The *Vekha* was prepared as a hospital ship (a red cross had been painted on its funnel), and the *Ismail* was sent out to scout the surrounding waters. Everyone had been ordered to try to sleep once they finished, at their stations, dressed and ready. But most remained awake. They chain-smoked and guessed what would happen when the squadron arrived.

As dawn lightened the sky, the *Potemkin* intercepted broken portions of two more telegraphs. The first was directed to the *Rostislav* with the message "Distinctly visible." The second was cut off: "We are wiring you at a distance of five —" Matyushenko was certain the squadron was drawing closer, but they needed to know exactly how close and how many ships it numbered. Kirill suggested commandeering a steamer to spy on the squadron's movements. The idea was welcomed. Sailors Dymchenko and Reznichenko left for the port. They found a fast steamer called the *Smely,* whose captain agreed to the mission at gunpoint.

After the *Smely* cut out of the harbor, the *Potemkin* crew kept staring out to sea, expecting to see the squadron take shape on the horizon at any moment. Kovalenko descended a series of iron ladders to the engine room to make sure everyone was prepared. As he walked across the gangways, they vibrated with the rhythmic hum of the engines. The air smelled of hot oil, and steam hissed through the web of pipes surrounding him. Through a hatch, he watched the stokers shovel coal into the furnaces, their faces glistening with sweat, illuminated by the fire's orange glow. The spirit of the sailors inspired him with confidence. He told the men who had once taken commands from him that he was now their comrade, and he hoped they would perform at their best in the hours ahead.

Then he left to check on the ship's hospital. He found several medics rolling bandages on the operation table, but Dr. Golenko was missing.

"Where's the doctor?" Kovalenko asked.

"Aboard the *Vekha*," a medic answered.

"He hasn't returned yet?"

"No. He said he was setting up a hospital there in case of a battle."

"But that's insane," Kovalenko said. "If there's a fight, the wounded will be on the *Potemkin,* not the *Vekha*."

The medic shrugged, obviously not in the habit of questioning his former superior. "He took almost all the medical supplies with him," he finally added.

Kovalenko went to the quarterdeck and told a sailor to go to the *Vekha* and bring the doctor and the supplies back to the battleship. A few minutes later, the sailor returned with the supplies only. Disgusted, the lieutenant almost went to the *Vekha* himself to drag the doctor back when, at 8 A.M., he was sidetracked by the *Smely*'s return.

Dymchenko told the sailor committee that they had spotted three battleships twenty minutes after steaming out of Odessa. They were traveling at a slow six knots, and the flags above the *Three Saints* indicated that Rear Admiral Vishnevetsky was leading them. When the *Smely* ventured farther out to sea in order to check for additional battleships, a torpedo boat chased after them, firing several warning shots. Reznichenko ordered the captain to increase speed. "Cut steam. Will sink you," the torpedo boat signaled to them. "No steam here," Reznichenko taunted. The *Smely* reached its top speed of twenty knots, outrunning the torpedo boat, and then veered back to the *Potemkin.*

The squadron would appear soon, Dymchencko warned his comrades. Very soon.

Ten minutes later, a lookout using a telescope sighted the first smudge of smoke from the squadron and yelled, "On the horizon! The squadron's coming!"

Matyushenko rushed to the bridge. This was what he had been waiting for since they had arrived in Odessa. He believed so much in their cause that it was beyond his imagination to think that the revolutionary sailors on other ships would not risk their lives to join the *Potemkin*. When they did, the advance of the revolution would be unstoppable, he thought.

After looking through the telescope himself, Matyushenko turned to Ensign Alekseyev. "Give the order to raise anchor. We'll sail immediately. We don't want to be trapped in the bay."

Trumpets and drums sounded the battle alert. Everyone rushed to their positions as the anchor was raised, knowing this was not a drill. Through the wireless telegraph came a message from the *Three Saints*: "The Black Sea crews are saddened by your actions. Enough scandal. Surrender. The sword spares the penitent head. Explain your demands. Be reasonable. Rear Admiral Vishnevetsky."

Matyushenko told the telegraphist to respond: "Unclear. Please repeat."

The *Potemkin* began to accelerate, passing between the harbor breakwaters. As the battleship gained speed, the red flag snapped in the wind on the foremast. The twelve-inch turrets rotated on their mounts, steel grinding against steel, until the big barrels pointed forward. The smoke from the squadron finally could be seen with the naked eye. Several minutes later, the *Potemkin* sailors could distinguish the lines of three battleships and a flotilla of torpedo boats.

"What do you want, madmen?" Vishnevetsky telegraphed. The *Potemkin* traveled on a direct course toward his squadron, five miles distant.

Matyushenko answered, "If you want to know our demands, come aboard the *Potemkin*. We guarantee your safety." He hoped that if he could get the admiral on the battleship, the crews would sense weakness among their commanders and mutiny.

The *Three Saints* did not answer. Four miles away, the three battleships shifted into a line-abreast formation. "Now they're forming up for battle. They'll be opening fire soon," a sailor in the conning tower predicted. With no hesitation, Matyushenko told Alekseyev to maintain their course. The sailors braced for battle.

The *Potemkin* closed on the squadron. Suddenly, the *Three Saints* turned hard to port, followed by the *St. George* and the *Twelve Apostles*. The battleships increased speed through the maneuver until they had turned almost 180 degrees. Cheers echoed throughout the

*Potemkin* when the crew realized what was happening: the squadron was fleeing. "Apparently, it's no fun to taste our guns," a sailor joked.

Kirill and Feldmann demanded that they pursue the squadron and fire on its battleships while in retreat, but Matyushenko ordered the engine room to slow down. They had to give the sailors on those vessels more time to mutiny.

The *Potemkin* returned to Odessa while the squadron disappeared out to sea. Matyushenko knew they would see the Black Sea Fleet again soon enough. If his fellow revolutionaries aboard the squadron's battleships failed to wrest control from their officers, the next confrontation would likely end in a hail of steel.

"*Three Saints*, what is keeping you?" Admiral Krieger telegraphed to Vishnevetsky at 10:10 A.M., spotting his second in command's squadron heading toward Tendra Harbor without the *Potemkin* at its side. "Why are you not on your way to Odessa?"

The *Rostislav*, Krieger's flagship, had dropped anchor off the sliver of an island an hour before, accompanied by the battleship *Sinop* and four torpedo boats. When he discovered his senior officer absent from the rendezvous point, he suspected that Vishnevetsky had already departed to win the *Potemkin*'s capitulation and that he would soon return with the *Potemkin*, now once again flying the St. Andrew's flag. An inevitable result, Krieger believed. The mutinous crew would never dare resist the gathered strength of the Black Sea Fleet. But now Vishnevetsky was returning, and the *Potemkin* was nowhere in sight.

Steaming at full speed toward the island, Vishnevetsky made no reply to Krieger, sure that an abbreviated telegraph message was an ill-advised way to explain the past couple of hours. He had never expected the *Potemkin* to race out of Odessa, guns trained on the *Three Saints*. His ships were unprepared for battle, and he was definitely against engaging the *Potemkin*, of all battleships. He had come only to negotiate the mutiny's surrender.

When Vishnevetsky neared Tendra, Krieger signaled by semaphore that every commander was to report to his flagship at once. As a launch from the *St. George* carried Captain Guzevich to the meeting, sailor Koshuba met with the other revolutionaries on his battleship, certain they had to act if the squadron was sent after the *Potemkin* again. Krieger, now in command, would undoubtedly order the sailors to fire on their brothers. As usual, Koshuba — whose gaunt, uncomely face and sallow skin belied his tremendous passion — was adamant they follow through on Tsentralka's plan to launch a fleet-wide mutiny, even if the *Potemkin's* actions had changed the timetable. They had witnessed the cowardice of their officers when the *Potemkin* approached the squadron: they dashed about the ship like frightened children, and some begged the engine room to increase speed as they fled toward Tendra Island. Koshuba was sure these same officers lacked the courage to resist an uprising among their men. His task was to persuade and lead the crew to mutiny, and this was exactly what he meant to do.

Meanwhile, on the *Rostislav,* Krieger berated his senior officer for his retreat that morning. He told his commanders he would never allow the same, regardless of their concerns about the loyalty of their crew if given the order to fire. Yes, Krieger hoped to avoid a sea battle, but every preparation, including armed boarding parties, was to be made in the event that such a fight transpired.

Then he laid out his strategy against the *Potemkin.* The squadron would travel toward Odessa in two columns, his flagship directing the first, the *Three Saints* the second. The light cruiser *Kazarsky* would run ahead of the squadron to reconnoiter, while the torpedo boats trailed behind the two columns in line-abreast formation. He reminded his officers that they outnumbered the *Potemkin* by five battleships to one; they also boasted a surfeit of torpedo boats.

"The tsar himself has ordered the elimination of this shameful blot on the honor of his fighting forces," Krieger concluded. "There must be no failure."

After the meeting ended, Captain M. N. Kolands of the *Twelve Apostles* stepped down into his steam launch. Since the squadron had left Sevastopol, his mood had darkened with every hour, a change noticed by his crew. Returning to his battleship, Kolands stared absently toward Odessa, speaking to himself in disjointed sentences: "This is the shame we've lived to see . . . There's no more respect for the tsar and Russia . . . They've been dishonored . . . The crew aboard the *Potemkin* is worthless garbage . . . There's no place for them in this world . . . Not a single commander is confident in his crew besides Rear Admiral Vishnevetsky and myself."

Then he turned to the sailors in the launch. "You, brothers, must serve our emperor with faith and honesty."

Once back on the *Twelve Apostles,* Kolands hurried to his stateroom. Fifteen minutes later, he came out wearing his finest dress uniform, pinned with a line of medals. Given his promise to ram the *Potemkin,* some of his sailors had to suspect that their captain was outfitted for his funeral. Then the signal came to raise anchor.

Gathered on rooftops and the embankment overlooking the harbor, the people of Odessa stared out to sea, wondering what was to happen next. Would the squadron return? Would the *Potemkin* go out to sea after them, as it had before? Even the city's revolutionaries, who had interrupted their heated debates about the next steps they should take when the squadron was first sighted, maintained their seaward watch.

Using field binoculars, General Kakhanov also looked out to the horizon from his military headquarters, praying the squadron would soon return. After sending away the *Potemkin* delegation the previous night, he had telegrammed Vice Admiral Chukhnin and the Admiralty in St. Petersburg, desperately pleading for their battleships to hurry. Finally, at 11 P.M., he was comforted by a message from Vishnevetsky that the squadron was near. That morning, on the war minister's orders, Kakhanov stationed troops along the coast to arrest those who survived the attack on the *Potemkin* and attempted to come ashore.

When Vishnevetsky's squadron finally appeared on the horizon, Kakhanov had turned to one of his officers and confidently said, "What can the *Potemkin* do against such a force? Finally these mutineers will get what they deserve." But then the commander had turned around his battleships and disappeared, leaving the general at a loss. He had received no further communications from the Admiralty or Vishnevetsky, and there was still no sign of Krieger's ships.

Now Kakhanov waited like everybody else, his fate in the hands of a navy that had proved sluggish to respond to Odessa's crisis and that had fled at the first confrontation with the *Potemkin.* Still, he was optimistic the squadron would prevail.

• • •

When the *Potemkin* dropped anchor back in the harbor, the sailors ate some cabbage soup and bread on the forecastle. It was eighty degrees and humid, with only a slight breeze coming across the water. Eating in the open air provided some relief from the stifling heat on the decks below, and, despite the anticipation of the squadron's return, the crew was buoyant after their first showdown.

"We knew they would be back and that this time we should have to face the guns of the whole fleet," a sailor later explained. "But this didn't worry us. We were all-powerful. We had nothing to fear." The sailors sang and cracked jokes about the "courage" of the Black Sea Fleet's admirals, but this false bravado would last only as long as the lookouts scanning the horizon remained quiet.

From the *Vekha,* Dr. Golenko came aboard with a smile on his face. "Ah, how glad I am, friends, you've come back. I was afraid you had gone off without me," he said, rubbing his hands together. "I'm on your side, you know." Kovalenko upbraided him for leaving the *Potemkin* when they needed him most. Then he instructed the doctor to stay on the battleship, no matter what needed to be done on the *Vekha.*

In the wardroom, each ship department reported its battle-readiness to the sailor committee. Everything was in order, although the engineers requested a few items, such as sulfuric acid, from shore. The committee sent a sailor wearing street clothes into the city to obtain these items. The Odessan revolutionary Boris, who, short of a few speeches, had proved less useful to the crew than Kirill or Feldmann, accompanied him. The committee wanted him to get detailed, scaled maps of Odessa so that they could realize their plan to take the city — if the *Potemkin* survived the afternoon.

Matyushenko reaffirmed the intention to go straight at the squadron, provoking Krieger and Vishnevetsky to fire on them, a move, he believed, that would spark the other crews to mutiny. It was a gamble. If the sailors stayed loyal to their officers, the *Potemkin* would be facing more battleships than Japanese admiral Togo had required to defeat Rozhestvensky's fleet at Tsushima. What's more, all the battleships and torpedo boats were commanded by experienced officers, some battle-tested. There would be a fight, and the *Potemkin* would likely be sunk, many of them with it. Nonetheless, the ship's leaders held to the plan.

After they disbanded, Kirill went to check on the crew to make
sure they were equally committed. On a lower deck, he ran into a
young medic named Morozov, who was carrying supplies to the hospital. Stopping him, Kirill asked for some medicine for his splitting
headache.

"I'll fix a powder for you," Morozov said, leading him into the
pharmacy with the eagerness of someone who liked to please. As he
measured out medicine onto a small scale, he said, "You seem to understand what's going on, right?"

Kirill nodded.

"Please tell me what we're fighting for? I asked some others," he
said innocently. "But they don't see it clearly either."

Kirill stared at the sailor for a moment, touched by his earnestness.
The medic, who looked no older than sixteen, was about to risk his
life, and he had no idea why. In language stripped of his usual revolutionary rhetoric, Kirill explained they were fighting against a ruler
who had always taken from his people yet had never given anything in
return. If the sailor wanted a better life for himself and his family, then
they needed to fight.

"This is certainly worth a battle," Morozov said after he had asked
a few more questions. "Now I understand."

The two shook hands and Morozov gave Kirill the packet of powder. "Please come again to speak with me," he said as Kirill walked
away. "I'll fix you more powder." Years later, Kirill would remember
every detail of this conversation and of the young man himself, right
down to his hazel eyes, as if for the first time the Odessan revolutionary had discovered these sailors to be more than instruments useful to
his cause.

At 11 A.M., the *Potemkin* received a message from the squadron:
"Send representatives to the *Three Saints* for peace talks. We guarantee their safety. We are on our way to Odessa."

The jokes and songs ended. The squadron would soon arrive.
For the next hour, sailors paced around their battle stations, waiting
for the confrontation to begin. Some scribbled their addresses and
gave them to friends, asking them to write to their families if they died
in the upcoming battle. Others embraced in farewell or stood alone,
keeping their thoughts or prayers to themselves.

At 12:05 P.M., a lookout spotted the squadron. The battle alarm rang, and the battle flag was hoisted, once again, over the *Potemkin*. On his way to the conning tower, Matyushenko whispered to himself, "This will decide things." Either the *Potemkin* and the squadron would meet in battle or the rest of the Black Sea Fleet would join in their mutiny. The waiting was over.

# 15

S EE OVER THERE? *That* is honor and glory," a *St. George* sailor said to a comrade, as they watched the *Potemkin* advancing alone against the squadron of battleships and torpedo boats and flying the flag of revolution. "They will go down in Russian history for this day."

In the conning tower, Matyushenko stood still, his face impassive. "This will decide things," he repeated. The *Potemkin* steamed at twelve knots away from the harbor; the coastline was getting more distant with every minute while the squadron, at first just a dark smudge on the cloudless blue horizon, took shape. Matyushenko knew they were inviting death. The squadron had twenty twelve-inch guns to the *Potemkin*'s four, plus a six-to-one advantage on smaller-caliber guns. Further, Krieger could simply forward his flotilla of torpedo boats to attack. If the *Potemkin* was to have a chance against such overwhelming numbers, naval strategy dictated that they keep at a distance, trying to score hits with their twelve-inch guns. If they advanced within close range of the squadron, Krieger could devastate them with his superior arms.

Yet that was exactly the course Quartermaster M. M. Kostenko at the *Potemkin*'s helm had been directed to set. In effect, the sailors were walking defenselessly toward a firing squad, hoping that those whose eyes were sighted down the guns refused to execute their orders. Otherwise, the battle would be over before the smoke cleared from the first barrage. No wonder, then, that Ensign Alekseyev, who was supposed to be leading the ship into the engagement, had come down with a sudden bout of faintness when they weighed anchor.

The sailors refused his request to be sent ashore, but he was useless to them.

Seven miles distant from the squadron, the *Potemkin* received a telegraph message from the flagship *Rostislav:* "Black Sea sailors. I am appalled at your conduct. Surrender."

"Respond," Matyushenko told the telegraphist, who sent this reply: "The crew of the *Potemkin* asks the commander of the fleet to come aboard for parley. Promise security."

Krieger did not reply. At four miles out, Matyushenko looked through the telescope to get a better look at the squadron's battleships. They were arranged in two columns, with the *Rostislav* and the *Three Saints* in the lead. The flagship commanded by Krieger was a sleek, fast twin-funneled battleship that lacked the *Potemkin's* firepower. The *Three Saints,* named after the 120-gun sailing ship that participated in defeating the Turkish navy at Sinop in 1853, had once boasted the world's strongest armor, but it had been surpassed since its launch in 1893. Individually, none of the battleships equaled the *Potemkin;* but together, with the line of torpedo boats spread behind them, the squadron looked to be an imposing force.

Finally, a few minutes later, Krieger telegraphed, "You do not understand what you are doing. Surrender immediately. Only by immediate capitulation will you be spared."

"Wonderful. Now we know what the admiral wants," Matyushenko said acidly. He turned to the telegraphist again. "Respond: The squadron should drop anchor."

On the *Rostislav,* Krieger signaled the other captains to full battle alert. The *Potemkin* was refusing to back down, and he had orders to engage and sink these scoundrels if it were necessary. When Captain Guzevich sounded the alert on the *St. George,* a handful of sailors warned their officers, "We won't fire! We won't man the guns! We refuse to battle the *Potemkin!*" Besides this outcry, however, no sign of a rebellion broke out as the squadron closed on the lone battleship.

"Five thousand meters!" a sailor reported to the *Potemkin's* conning tower. At this range, Matyushenko could now see that the squadron was prepared for battle, its decks cleared and its guns trained on the *Potemkin.* The crews remained loyal, which might mean his revolutionary comrades had been arrested or had abandoned the cause. If this were not the case, they needed to act soon — very soon — or the *Potemkin* was doomed.

"Three thousand meters!"

Matyushenko expected the squadron to fire at any moment. The *Potemkin*'s gunners nervously awaited the same, prepared to answer with their own salvos. To keep in check their strong instinct for self-preservation, they had to repeat to one another and to themselves that their orders were not to fire first. Down in the engine room, unaware of developments above, Kovalenko watched over the stokers and machinists, making sure they kept to their duties as expectations of a battle mounted.

"Two thousand meters."

Matyushenko directed Kostenko to maintain the *Potemkin*'s course, which would take it directly between the two columns of battleships. The forward twelve-inch turret was turned starboard at the *Three Saints;* the aft turret was directed to port at the *Rostislav.* The other seventy-four guns on the *Potemkin* were also loaded and ready, their crews adjusting their aim as the battleship cut quickly through the water. The tension aboard the battleship was too much for one sailor charged with watering down the upper deck in case of fire — "Guns to the left! Guns to the right!" he screamed with mad glee, spraying his hose from side to side before some sailors wrestled him down.

"One thousand meters."

Krieger signaled to the *Potemkin* by semaphore, "Drop anchor."

"*Rostislav* and *Three Saints:* cut your engines," Matyushenko answered.

Krieger repeated his command. Neither party intended on backing down.

Matyushenko responded, "Cut your engines or we will fire."

Despite this threat, Matyushenko reminded the *Potemkin*'s sailors that the committee's decision was to fire only if fired upon first. He still believed the crews of the squadron would revolt if the choice fell between killing their fellow sailors or overthrowing their officers. It was his only hope.

With the squadron less than a half-mile away from the *Potemkin*, Kirill remained on the bridge with Feldmann, staring at the dull luster of the *Rostislav*'s guns. Kirill found himself surprisingly calm, even as he envisioned the blood of dying men on the *Potemkin*'s decks, their cries, maybe even his own among them, lost in the thunderous roar of the guns.

On the *Rostislav*, a sailor watched, mesmerized, as the lone battleship bore down toward him. He later recounted, "It was the kind of scene one sees only once in a lifetime. The *Potemkin*, powerful, frightening, massive, and strong, advanced at full speed at the squadron of five battleships. This was a scene suitable for an artist's brush." The squadron sailors felt a mix of terror and rapture, as the *Potemkin* came closer and closer. Only a few sailors were visible on the *Potemkin*'s decks, giving the battleship the appearance of a ghost ship.

On the *Rostislav*'s bridge, Vice Admiral Krieger was similarly stunned at the *Potemkin*'s suicidal approach. His orders were clear: sink the battleship if the mutinous sailors refused to yield. Yet he hesitated to give the command to fire to his crew or to the other captains in his squadron. It was an order that Captain Kolands of the *Twelve Apostles,* for one, awaited impatiently.

"Two hundred meters."

Kostenko held course. The *Potemkin* was about to cleave the squadron in two, running a gauntlet of five armor-plated battleships with scores of guns, all within point-blank range. The possibility of retreat had passed long ago.

"One hundred meters."

Desperate to get the squadron to fire on the *Potemkin,* thereby instigating a mutiny, Matyushenko ordered Kostenko to veer toward the *Rostislav,* threatening to ram her. But the squadron and battleship, moving in opposite directions, both nearly at full steam, closed on one another before the command could be executed.

The *Potemkin* crossed into the five-hundred-meter channel between the *Rostislav* and the *Three Saints.* An unnatural silence fell on the sea. No explosions of smoke and steel. No shrieks of panic and death. Hundreds of guns were aimed at the *Potemkin,* yet the only sounds were the deep, reverberating bass of the engines and the slow whine of the turrets as they tracked their quickly passing target. The *Potemkin* passed between the squadron's two columns. Many felt time slow down; seconds passed like days. A single gun or rifle shot, accidental or otherwise, from any ship would have precipitated a catastrophic chain reaction, sending hundreds of men to their deaths.

But there was only silence. Krieger lost his nerve, never giving the order to fire. When one of the *Potemkin*'s six-inch guns pointed at his position on the bridge, he fell prostrate on the deck, along with several other officers. Resolved not to fire first, Matyushenko remained in the conning tower, watching the squadron pass harmlessly on either side. He felt little relief at escaping death. Instead, he was crestfallen that the other battleship crews had not mutinied.

Then, at that darkest moment on the *Potemkin,* when Matyushenko and the others felt they had been completely abandoned, several sailors on the battleships *St. George* and *Sinop* streamed onto their battle-cleared decks, waving their caps and shouting, "Hurray! Long live freedom!" On the *Potemkin,* sailors left their stations and poured out of hatches onto the upper decks to greet their comrades, urging them to commandeer their ships. Kovalenko, who had come up from the engine room, tried to rein in the sailors. "Gun crews!" he barked. "Back to your posts. The squadron still has its guns aimed at us."

The brief celebration ended as the *Potemkin* steamed past the *St. George* and the *Sinop;* the torpedo boats at the squadron's rear scattered to clear a path for the battleship to the open sea. Matyushenko told Kostenko to turn the battleship around so they could advance against the squadron once again. He was exultant at the first sign of support from the other crews, later writing, "This was the moment we had been waiting for. . . . The end of tyranny was near. The tsar's puppets had ordered us a welcome of shellfire. Instead, there were cheers."

But, as Kovalenko warned the celebrating sailors, the engagement was far from over. Krieger and the other captains still had command of their battleships and crews. The squadron moved toward Odessa, perhaps to wait out the *Potemkin* or strategize a new battle plan. Then a signal from its flagship ordered a hard turn to port. They were coming back.

Krieger sent a message by semaphore to the *Potemkin:* "Drop your anchors."

Matyushenko had his signalman answer, "Officers of the squadron are to leave their ships and go ashore."

Neither paid any attention to the other, and, once again, the *Potemkin* and the squadron sped toward each other across the sea.

From the shores of Odessa, an epic sea battle looked imminent. Krieger hoped the mutineers would capitulate on the second pass, but he quickly realized how wrong he was. The *Potemkin* kept coming toward him, the double-headed eagles on its bow getting clearer and clearer. As the battleship reached the squadron, apparently about to pass through again, one sailor, then two, then wave after wave of sailors poured onto the decks of *St. George*, the *Sinop*, and the *Twelve Apostles*, greeting the *Potemkin* as a victor. Krieger was dumbfounded. Only his and Vishnevetsky's decks were still cleared for action.

As the *Potemkin* passed between the *St. George* and the *Sinop*, Matyushenko burst out of the conning tower. He yelled at the *Sinop*'s sailors, lined three deep at the railings, "Arrest your officers and join us." Matyushenko was so excited that Kirill had to hold him by the waist to keep him from pitching overboard. In response, the sailors threw their caps into the air and shouted in unison, "Long live the *Potemkin!*"

Then Krieger signaled the *Twelve Apostles* to attack the *Potemkin*, knowing Captain Kolands would do whatever he could to maintain control of his crew and sink the mutineers. Krieger was right. Not yet past the *Potemkin*, Captain Kolands ordered his helmsman to steer a direct course at the battleship. He would ram it and then detonate his magazines. It was worth his life, he thought, to end this shameful affair. Returning to the bridge, he ordered his officers to regain control of their sailors and clear the decks. They were going into battle.

The *Potemkin*'s signalman intercepted the order from Krieger. As the *Twelve Apostles* turned its bow, he flashed by semaphore: "*Twelve Apostles:* stop." But Kolands was committed. The distance between the battleships closed. The revolutionaries aboard the *Twelve Apostles* had prepared for this moment, however. With several others, Volgin rushed down to the machine area, forcing aside the lieutenant in charge of the engines. "Full speed reverse," Volgin screamed at the sailors. Moments later, the *Twelve Apostles* shuddered to a halt, less than ten meters from the *Potemkin*, which steamed safely past.

Realizing that his orders had been countermanded, Captain Kolands scrambled to the conning tower and pressed the switch to detonate the magazines, an act of suicide and outright murder on his part. Fortunately for the crew, the revolutionaries had cut the wires between the tower and the magazines that had been rigged in order to sabotage the battleship before the squadron left Tendra Island. Kolands bitterly proclaimed, "Shame! It's shameful not to die for the tsar and the motherland."

Unaware of how close they had come to destruction, the *Potemkin*'s crew watched the squadron proceed out to sea, their officers apparently still in command. When the squadron returned to formation, retreating in the direction of Sevastopol, the *Potemkin* sailors were stunned, wondering how it was that none of the ships had joined them. To have shown down the Black Sea Fleet was certainly impressive, but what they really needed was more crews to mutiny, adding strength to their rebellion.

Just when they were convinced that their cause was lost, a lookout spotted the *St. George* falling from the squadron's line.

When the squadron turned out to sea after its second advance on the *Potemkin,* Captain Guzevich, on the *St. George*'s bridge, received an angry message from the *Rostislav.*

"Why are there so many lower ranks on the decks and not at their battle stations?" Krieger demanded to know.

Guzevich looked across his battleship. The riotous mass of sailors was growing every minute, and his officers seemed powerless to stop the flow of men. "Our time has come!" the sailors yelled. "Off with the officers. We don't need them. Cast them into the sea." Calls to mutiny paralyzed Guzevich with fear.

"The crew is rebelling," he finally replied to the flagship. "They are threatening to throw the officers overboard."

"Go to Sevastopol," Krieger insisted. "Go to Sevastopol."

In the midst of these exchanges, Koshuba and several other revolutionaries stormed onto the bridge, rifles in hand, demanding that the captain stop the battleship.

From the moment the squadron had first set its course from Tendra Island to Odessa, Koshuba had worked to convince the *St. George*'s crew to dismiss any orders to fire on their brothers. During the *Potemkin*'s advance against the squadron, with its guns leveled at the two columns of battleships but silent, Koshuba ran through the lower decks, a shovel in hand, urging sailors to mutiny. His fellow revolutionaries, including Zakhary Borodin and Simon Deinega, summoned the crew to leave their stations and go to the decks to show their allegiance to the *Potemkin*. Those who tried to thwart these efforts were knocked aside; to push through, the revolutionaries used whatever they could find — mops, steel pipes, even a fishing pole. For many sailors, shouts of "We've no need for the tsar, only freedom!" and "Enough of our commanders spilling our blood!" were enough to motivate them to back the uprising.

By the time the *Potemkin* made its second pass, the revolutionaries on the *St. George* had chased hundreds onto the decks. Their officers did not fire one shot in resistance. While Captain Guzevich turned the battleship toward Sevastopol with the squadron, Koshuba broke into the armory and dispensed rifles to the sailors. Then he hurried to the bridge to take command.

"Stop the engines," Koshuba ordered the captain.

Guzevich refused. Koshuba knocked him out of the way and sent a message down to the engine room to come to a full stop. A revolutionary comrade left to take over the helm. A few minutes later, the *St. George* slowed down, leaving the formation.

"Why is the *St. George* not moving?" Krieger asked by semaphore.

Koshuba allowed the captain to give this answer: "The crew wishes to land the officers and join the *Potemkin*."

"Use all your power and follow the squadron," Krieger demanded.

"I can't. I can't. I can't," Captain Guzevich desperately responded, in his final communication with the squadron. Stalling for time, hoping Krieger would turn around to help him, Guzevich tried to negotiate with the crew. He called out to the sailors below, asking those who wished to go to Sevastopol to stand to the battleship's starboard side and those who wanted to join the *Potemkin* to stand to port.

When some stepped to the battleship's port side, he begged, "Brothers, what do you want? I'll do anything you want. Let's just go to Sevastopol." Standing by his side, Lieutenant K. K. Grigorkov, the only officer on the bridge armed with a revolver, felt shamed by his captain's words. This shame was deepened by Guzevich's offer to send to the *Potemkin* any sailor who so wished and his promise not to report the mutiny.

"I'm captain now," Koshuba said harshly, interrupting Guzevich. He then put the officers under guard and directed the battleship toward the *Potemkin*. Before they moved, he had the signalman relay their intentions by semaphore.

Then Koshuba and his fellow revolutionaries left the bridge to secure their command. They were surprised to find that the crew was
more willing to refuse their captain's orders than they were to take the
irrevocable next step of aligning themselves with the *Potemkin.* At
most, Koshuba could depend on seventy sailors from the crew. On
the spar deck, some even demanded outright that the *St. George* return to Sevastopol.

On the *Potemkin,* Matyushenko waited for his signalman to interpret
the semaphore message. "The . . . crew . . . of . . . the . . . *St. George,*"
the signalman announced, watching his counterpart moving his flags
back and forth through the telescope, "wants . . . to . . . join . . . you.
. . . We . . . ask . . . the . . . *Potemkin* . . . to . . . approach . . . us."

A wave of joy and relief broke over the crew. The *Potemkin* finally
had won an ally. A true revolutionary squadron had been born. While
Matyushenko and Kirill formed a team to approach their sister ship,
Ensign Alekseyev, who had finally emerged from the stateroom where
he retired during the confrontation, preached caution. He advised
that even though the rest of Krieger's battleships were retreating,
Captain Guzevich might be trying to get close enough to torpedo or
ram them.

To avoid a trap, Matyushenko had his signalman order the *St.
George* to cut its engines. Yet the *St. George* continued to approach,
now less than one thousand meters away. Alekseyev pressed the sail-
ors to fire if the battleship came any closer. Then they saw the *St.
George*'s signalman rapidly flag the *Potemkin.* "The crew of the *St.
George* is asking comrades from the *Potemkin* to come to their ship."

The *St. George* slowed down and dropped anchor. Through the
telescope, Matyushenko saw Captain Guzevich still standing on the
bridge. "Arrest your officers," Matyushenko relayed, "and bring them
to us."

"The situation is bad. Not everybody agrees. We can't manage.
Send help as soon as you can," the *St. George* signaled.

Stirred to action by the plea and disregarding Alekseyev's further
cautions, Matyushenko called the torpedo boat *Ismail* to the
*Potemkin*'s side and boarded it with Kirill and several committee
members, including Dymchenko and Kulik. They sped toward the *St.*

*George.* Some sailors waved their caps enthusiastically at the torpedo boat; others eyed them suspiciously from the lower decks.

When they arrived at the *St. George,* a rope ladder was sent down, and Matyushenko climbed aboard with the others. Then the torpedo boat moved to the *St. George's* stern, its firing tubes aimed at the battleship's side in case the invitation to board was an ambush. Matyushenko warmly greeted Koshuba and his revolutionary comrades on the quarterdeck, but their reunion was cut short when Matyushenko recognized the dangerous situation on the battleship.

Half the crew welcomed them with shouts of triumph, and Koshuba obviously had control of the battleship's key stations. But others on the *St. George* treated them like intruders. They wanted the *Potemkin* sailors cast off, so they could reconnect with the squadron. Equally troubling, the ship's officers looked down on them from the bridge. Though they were under guard and looked scared, their presence alone signified that the mutiny had yet to be secured. Suspecting the sailors could turn against them, Matyushenko sent one of his shipmates back to the *Potemkin.* He wanted an armed guard sent as soon as possible.

Then Matyushenko stepped up on a capstan on the forecastle to attempt to inspire the sailors to join them. He knew exactly what he wanted to say, but he found that from overuse and lack of sleep, his voice was strained and robbed of its strength. Turning to Kirill, he asked him to take his place.

The Odessan revolutionary mounted the capstan and looked across the sea of faces. Those sailors close to him eagerly awaited his words, but others, near the hatches at the back, frowned and watched with hostility. Believing his words might decide the fate of the *St. George* mutiny, Kirill spoke with thunder in his voice. "Our exhausted people, stripped of the most basic of rights, can no longer bear their humiliation and powerlessness. They're coming out on the streets of the cities and villages, fighting the tsar who's torn apart Mother Russia. Will our sons and brothers, dressed in soldier's clothes, be the tyrant's butchers, punishing our very own who only seek a better life? We, proud men of the *Potemkin,* refuse to murder our own people, and won't allow anybody else to either."

He paused, turning his gaze to the officers on the bridge. "You gentlemen . . . You're rotten servants of the tsar. You're responsible for rivers of innocent blood. They lie on your conscience. But the day of judgment has come. . . . Now there's no place for you here. This ship, built by workers, has now passed into the hands of men who will serve and *protect* these workers, not enslave or oppress them."

His words provoked an outcry from the crew: "Up for the people's freedom! Off with the tyrants!"

Kirill pointed at the officers. "In the name of the people, you're under arrest and will be taken to shore."

When a handful of armed *St. George* sailors attempted to usher the officers from the bridge, Lieutenant Grigorkov suddenly shrugged off his captors. Disgusted by the thought of being taken captive and shamed by his captain, he stepped to the end of the bridge. Without hesitation, he raised his pistol, put the barrel to his temple, and fired. His body fell over a railing and into the sea. Everyone stood, astonished, for a moment. Then Kirill told the sailors to take the other officers to the admiral's stateroom.

After Guzevich's removal and another stirring speech by Kirill, most of the crew committed to siding with the *Potemkin* — or at least they raised their voices to that effect. By the time the armed party led by Feldmann had arrived, the crew had already assembled to elect a committee of sailors to lead the battleship. Meanwhile, the officers packed their belongings. Once ready, Matyushenko led Guzevich and his subordinates down into the steam launch. Sitting between the sailors, the officers, eyes downcast and uniforms stripped of epaulettes, looked pathetic. One kept muttering wretchedly, "That I should live to see such things." Revolver in hand, Matyushenko guarded them on the way toward the *Potemkin*.

When they drew up to the battleship's side, Kovalenko came down to see the officers, several of whom he knew well. Yet he no longer felt a bond with them, and they traded glances like complete strangers.

A half-hour later, the two battleships weighed anchor and steamed together toward Odessa, the *Ismail* following behind. As before, Kirill and Feldmann wanted to chase after the squadron, but the *Potemkin*'s leaders thought they had tempted fate enough that day.

Once back on the *Potemkin*, Matyushenko was flushed with success. The sailors had won their revolutionary squadron, and the rest of the Black Sea Fleet was shamed into retreat, its captains weakened by crews obviously sympathetic to the rebels' cause. The days without sleep, the constant concern about betrayal, the false starts in Odessa — all were worth the victory they had now won. Many shared his elation. Kovalenko imagined the great steps they would make the next day. Nothing seemed impossible now. Kirill also looked to the future with optimism, later describing the crew's mood that afternoon on their return to the harbor:

> Looking at the sailors, sensing their eagerness, we felt good in our hearts. The nightmare of fear that our efforts would fail was replaced with confidence in our success and victory over our age-old enemy. . . . Tomorrow we would take over Odessa, establish a free government, create a people's army, march on Kiev, Kharkov, and other cities, join with the peasants in the villages. After that, we would march on the Caucasus, along the shores of the Black Sea. Everywhere we would bring freedom and independence from slavery. Then on to Moscow and finally St. Petersburg.

Sixteen miles southeast of Odessa, the Black Sea Fleet squadron hove to and anchored. For the final time that day, Krieger called a meeting of his captains to decide their next move. Shaken by the *St. George*'s defection, Krieger wanted to know if they believed their crews could be relied on to reengage the *Potemkin*. Their response was unanimous: no.

The captains of the *Sinop* and *Twelve Apostles* had narrowly escaped outright mutiny on their battleships; they did not want to test their good fortune by going after the *Potemkin* again. If given the order to fire, their crews would assuredly revolt. Vishnevetsky agreed that this outcome seemed likely on his battleship as well. Krieger then suggested a surprise night attack undertaken by their torpedo boats, but this idea was rejected because even the small, more easily managed crews on these ships could not be trusted. He felt they were all in an intractable situation. He could return to Sevastopol in disgrace or risk the entire fleet to mutiny. With reluctance he chose the former, but he made one last attempt to negotiate with the *Potemkin* before the squadron left.

At 7:15 P.M., torpedo boat No. 272 steamed toward Odessa, captained by I. N. Psiol, the second officer of the *Three Saints*. On its approach, Psiol signaled the *Potemkin* to surrender. "Never!" was the response. Still, the *Ismail* left the side of the battleship to open talks. Fearing that the *Ismail* would attack, Psiol reversed direction and sped back to the squadron.

Since even this meager attempt ended in failure, Krieger telegraphed Admiral Avelan, informing him of the *St. George* mutiny and Krieger's planned retreat to Sevastopol. Before returning, the squadron discharged its six- and twelve-inch guns. The shells fell harmlessly into the open sea.

# 16

APART FROM a horseback ride through Peterhof, Nicholas spent the gray, drizzly day of June 17 in a series of long meetings while waiting to hear of the outcome of Krieger's confrontation with the *Potemkin*. Finally, in the early evening, his deputy minister of the interior, Trepov, telephoned his office, forwarding a message from General Kakhanov. The information it conveyed was, however, mistaken. Kakhanov stated that the squadron had surrounded the *Potemkin* that afternoon and that the mutinous sailors had lowered their battle flags, apparently surrendering without a shot being fired. The relief that Nicholas felt was tempered by a demand for vengeance. He wrote an order to Chukhnin directly onto the transcribed note: "After a most prompt investigation and court-martial, the execution of the sailors must be carried out in front of the whole squadron and the city of Odessa."

Nicholas felt that the embarrassment and trouble the sailors had stirred up over the past few days warranted this public reckoning. In St. Petersburg, the *Potemkin* story had spread despite his censors. At a city concert hall, some workers had interrupted the performance and demanded a song be played in honor of the sailors. Russian aristocrats feared the mutiny might precipitate revolution, and many had even left the city for the countryside. The *Potemkin* mutiny disturbed some of them more profoundly than the Battle of Tsushima or the repeated defeats in Manchuria because mutiny revealed that the tsar's regime was rotting from within. Reports of simultaneous, though short-lived, uprisings at the naval bases of Libau and Kronstadt — thousands of sailors at each place refused to work, wrecked their barracks, and broke into the armory before being brutally suppressed by infantry troops — reinforced doubts that the tsar's government could hold out much longer.

Revolutionary groups quickly took advantage of the *Potemkin*'s feat in their propaganda war within Russia. One Social Democrat leaflet called on the people to unite, promising that the sailor revolt showed that "the last support of autocracy is falling. The feelings of solidarity with working masses, long locked beneath the bark of discipline, is bursting forth . . . and how!" They also distributed leaflets to army regiments, encouraging more rebellion:

> Soldiers! Follow the example of the Black Sea sailors. Stand on the right side of the people! Let each of you take an oath: "I'd rather chop off my own right hand than raise it against my brother!"
>
> Soldiers of the Russian army! Follow the example of the heroes of the *Potemkin*! Go to battle for the truth and the people's freedom!

Inspired by the mutiny, workers at several major St. Petersburg factories went on strike on June 16, announcing their solidarity with the sailors while also pushing for better conditions for themselves. Similar scenes occurred in Moscow and other cities within the empire. Of course, a series of strikes had erupted throughout Russia since Bloody Sunday, but so hopeful were the revolutionaries that the *Potemkin* marked the launch of an armed uprising that the Social Democrats and Socialist Revolutionaries in the Russian capital formed an inter-party committee to coordinate efforts with workers for the first time.

Among the liberal opposition, the drive to institute a constituent assembly gained further momentum. In Moscow, representatives from eighty-seven towns and cities were meeting to put together a reform program. The recent events on the Black Sea had convinced some liberal leaders, such as Milyukov and Struve, that they had taken the wrong path after Tsushima, when they called for allying with the revolutionaries and fighting the tsar's power in the streets. Sailors killing their officers and the destruction in Odessa were examples enough that Russia risked outright ruin if they continued their militant stance. In part, the *Potemkin* mutiny renewed their commitment to using peaceful efforts to achieve reforms.

In the foreign press, Nicholas faced a parade of bad publicity. Regardless of how often Russian ambassadors assured reporters that the Black Sea revolt was an isolated situation perpetrated by drunks who would soon quit their mad scheme, Nicholas felt hounded by a spate of news stories and editorials arguing that his regime was in serious jeopardy. Although most journalists doubted that the entire Russian military was a honeycomb of sedition, they predicted that disloyalty could easily spread if the tsar was seen as vulnerable. "Insurrection follows mutiny," the *New York Herald Tribune* editorialized. "Its ominous gravity can scarcely be exaggerated." The Parisian *Temps* reported that even Russian officers had been caught spreading seditious literature.

The intense violence incited by the *Potemkin* in Odessa and expectations of a massive strike in St. Petersburg to protest mobilization orders only reinforced the opinion that Nicholas was in an intractable situation. His only hope was to end the war with Japan and summon a representative assembly. The Associated Press forecast, "Not since the insurrection in December 1825, when a portion of the Guard regiments joined in an attempt to set up a republic in Russia, has the situation of the Romanov dynasty been so serious. Nevertheless, the crisis may be passed in a few days. Either the open revolt will by that time be stamped out or the flames will have spread, possibly beyond the hope of control."

The *Potemkin* had especially driven fear into the Romanov family. At the mutiny's onset, Nicholas's sister Xenia frantically wrote in her diary: "God knows what's happening and there is nothing to be done! It's terrible, terrible. . . . This news has simply killed us. We have been wandering around in a daze all day — what a nightmare, it's too awful." A few days later she added, "Why, why are we being punished so by God?!" Their cousin, Grand Duke Konstantin Konstantinovich, who had been a close friend of Captain Golikov, lamented, "What is happening to Russia? What disorganization, what disintegration. Just like a piece of clothing that is beginning to rip and tear along the seams, and fall open . . . There is an actual mutiny on the Black Sea Fleet warship *Potemkin*. . . . It's complete revolution."

Yet even as the pressure mounted on Nicholas from all sides, he resisted pursuing peace vigorously with Japan or changing his mind about liberal reforms. Nelidov, his first choice for plenipotentiary at the proposed peace negotiations, had backed out, citing illness, and the tsar again avoided choosing Witte, the foreign minister's recommendation, to be his representative. Instead, he selected one of Witte's rivals, Nikolai V. Muravyev, the ambassador to Rome and a favorite of the late hardliner Grand Duke Sergei. More concerned with being adequately recompensed for his travel expenses to the peace talks than with their substance, Muravyev was another weak choice as emissary to represent Russia in negotiations with Japan. Nicholas held to the belief that his empire would survive a prolonged war and that, with more time, he could bleed concessions out of the Japanese.

Meanwhile, he stalled any progress on the proposal for a duma — holding committees on the matter, promising that he was considering the possibility, but deciding nothing. Sending a distressing signal to reformers, he had also invited a delegation of staunch monarchist nobles to an audience at Peterhof.

On the evening of June 17, news of the mutiny's end from Kakhanov came as a great comfort. Nicholas could once again dispel the rash of nervous proclamations that revolution was at hand. The mutineers would be punished, and that was the end of it. Then, only a few hours later, he learned from the Naval Ministry that not only had the *Potemkin* not surrendered but also another battleship had gone to its side. Further, Krieger had retreated to Sevastopol with the squadron, frightened about additional mutinies.

The whole Black Sea Fleet appeared lost, Nicholas thought; his nightmare only worsened. Each day that the mutiny dragged on was another blow against his reign. In his secluded idyll on the Gulf of Finland, try as he might to ignore the thought, it was impossible to know whether these unfolding events might be the first stages of his own downfall. Only God knew what was to be the tsar's fate.

That same evening, at a railway station deep in the Ukraine, Vice Admiral Chukhnin was handed two secret telegrams from the naval minister before he reboarded his special train from St. Petersburg. The comforts of the private railcar — its curtained bedroom and salon fitted with mahogany tables and velvet-covered chairs — did little to ease his strain. He was impatient to get to Nikolayev, still twelve hours away, and personally take control of the disaster revealed in the telegrams clutched in his hand.

The first one repeated the mistaken report of the mutiny's end but also included a note from Avelan, complaining about how much time Krieger and Vishnevetsky had taken to confront the *Potemkin.* Chukhnin was well aware of his officers' embarrassing timidity, an issue that he had often raised with his superiors at the Admiralty in St. Petersburg. At least the squadron had somehow managed to win the *Potemkin*'s surrender. The second telegram, explaining the true course of events, sent Chukhnin reeling. The day before, helpless to do anything but worry while on the train, he had written to Avelan, telling him that if Krieger and the other captains faced revolts by their own crews, the officers would surrender without resistance rather than risk being killed. Now that he had been proved right, he planned to see Krieger removed from his post after this debacle ended.

Chukhnin was most troubled over losing the chance to end this mutiny within seventy-two hours. If Krieger had shown more initiative and decisiveness, he was certain the sailors in the squadron would have remained loyal. But delays had given traitors within the crews time to seed dissent. Obviously, Krieger and the other captains had neglected to arrest such men before they confronted the *Potemkin.* Now the mutineers had the momentum, and every battleship in the Black Sea Fleet was suspect.

As the train hurtled across the dark countryside, Chukhnin sat at a table and devised a plan to deal with the evolving crisis. Foremost, he had to prevent the *Potemkin,* or any other battleship, from taking the Sevastopol naval base. He drafted orders that were stricter than the measures taken by the Russians to protect Port Arthur from the Japanese: first, the fortress should have its troops and guns ready to fire on any ship, day or night; second, torpedo boats must stop any ship five miles from the base and determine the loyalty of the crew; third, another set of torpedo boats should inspect these same ships two miles from the base for the same purpose; and fourth, if any ship was suspect, the fortress was to fire on it immediately.

Having decided this defensive plan, Chukhnin still needed to come up with a way to defeat the *Potemkin* and the *St. George* if the mutinous battleships did *not* attack Sevastopol. Their prolonged presence in Odessa was unacceptable, and they posed a grave danger to the entire Black Sea region. Through the night, Chukhnin deliberated on the problem. Because the fleet's crews had clearly shown sympathy with the mutineers, he could hardly send the squadron back after the *Potemkin,* even if he commanded it himself. There had to be another way to end this treason. Until Chukhnin figured out how, General Kakhanov would have to do what he could to defend Odessa.

Once again, Kakhanov found himself alone, trying to protect the city — but now against two battleships instead of one and without the hope of the Black Sea Fleet's aid. Odessans fled on whatever transport they could find. "The train station is a veritable Armageddon. There are no tickets to be had," a witness recounted. Those who did manage to get out packed the hotels and lodging houses in surrounding towns. Troops flowed into Odessa, camping in parks and courtyards throughout the city. The streets, usually bustling with commerce, were busy only with soldiers on patrol. They posted signs threatening that they would fire on gatherings of more than twenty people. Throughout the day, most of the population had been too captivated by the action out at sea to muster any strikes. Even with the squadron's retreat and the *Potemkin*'s victorious return alongside the *St. George,* the Peresyp and Moldovanka worker districts remained calm. Everyone was waiting for the next move of the mutinous sailors.

Despite the futility of his previous efforts, Kakhanov prepared for an attack. He sent reinforcements to the artillery brigade stationed at Langeron Point. He ordered the assembly of a battery of nine-inch guns that had recently arrived. He requisitioned more high-caliber bombs from Ochakov and torpedoes from Sevastopol, though they were unlikely to be delivered in time. Finally, he told his officers to strengthen their guard along the shoreline to prevent the sailors from mounting a land assault or coming into the city for provisions.

While he delivered his orders, foreign consuls, city officials, and journalists pestered his office, asking what would happen next. His earlier statement that the *Potemkin* sailors had surrendered when the squadron approached had already been proved wrong — a black mark for Kakhanov with the tsar and an embarrassment sure to be headlined worldwide. Enough of pronouncements, he thought. Everyone would have to wait, including himself, for what the sailors had planned next.

After arriving at Odessa's harbor, the *St. George* approached and saluted the *Potemkin,* the revolutionary squadron's flagship. Sailors congregated on the *St. George*'s forecastle, full of confidence and eager for the next step in their struggle. The sight lifted the hearts of the *Potemkin*'s crew, who had fought alone for three days, desperate to know if others in the fleet would join them. "We're not afraid of anybody — any longer," a crew member said, capturing the mood. "And tomorrow we'll take Odessa." Even the most timid sailors walked the decks, recounting the confrontation with the squadron as if it had already entered legend. The success of their fight for freedom seemed assured.

Matyushenko left this revelry to deliver the *St. George*'s officers ashore. Moments after he had dropped them off and turned back toward the battleship, he saw a band of dragoons rush at the officers, who were scrambling up the steep shore. "Get down on the ground!" one of them yelled; rifles drawn, the dragoons had mistaken the officers for *Potemkin* rebels. Matyushenko looked back to see Captain Guzevich and the others retreat into the water. A few dived under in an attempt to escape; others even tried to swim back to the launch. "Another act of heroism on the part of the tsar's officers," Matyushenko joked to his fellow sailors. Leaving the officers to fend for themselves, they returned to the *Potemkin*.

On the *St. George*, the crew elected Koshuba and nine other sailors to the ship's committee. Senior Boatswain A. O. Kuzmenko was nominated to command the battleship, a role parallel to that of Ensign Alekseyev on the *Potemkin*. Then, the roll call sounded, and the sailors came together for the evening prayer. Feldmann, who had stayed on the *St. George* to educate the sailors on the revolution, listened to the crew chant in unison. He found it strange to listen to the sailors, who were now on a free ship, utter words that honored the tsar. The scene revealed to him how difficult it would be to break the sailors from their instincts and traditions. "It was strange to hear the patriotic words of this prayer, here now, on a free ship, in the midst of the sea," he remembered. "They were a reminder that, though the old bogeys were thrown down, their power was still unbroken."

After the prayer, the committee headed to the admiral's stateroom, where they found a sailor haphazardly banging on the piano, enjoying his newfound liberty. Once he was ushered out of the room, the sailors sat around the table. With smoke and a feeling of serious consequence heavy in the air, they made their first decisions as the *St.*

*George*'s leaders. Suspecting that the petty officers might spread dissent, they resolved to send them ashore the very next day. Koshuba and Deinega were also worried about their crew's loyalty. Many sailors had been slow to help take over the ship.

While the committee met, a government cutter approached the *St. George*. It was commanded by port official Nikolai Romanenko. "I've been sent by Brigadier General Pereleshin to inquire whether the new ironclad needs anything," he said, clearly hoping to spy out the situation.

"Go to our flagship," the sailors advised.

When Romanenko came to the *Potemkin*'s side, Matyushenko allowed him aboard in order to learn more about the situation in Odessa. The port official was elusive, though, steering the conversation to why the sailors had fired on the unarmed city the day before and what they wanted now.

"Tomorrow we want coal and provisions delivered to the *Potemkin*," Matyushenko said harshly, tiring of the game. "And tell General Kakhanov that he should disband his troops and let the people rule the city."

Romanenko made his exit. Soon after, Koshuba and several other *St. George* committee members arrived with boatswain Kuzmenko to coordinate their actions with the *Potemkin*. As the new commander, Kuzmenko made a poor first impression. His ruddy, flat-nosed face had a "dull, feral, and aloof expression," Kovalenko recalled. "His little eyes moved back and forth constantly, like he had stolen something, and his movements and gestures were unnaturally free and loose." Putting aside his initial disgust, Kovalenko introduced himself and asked Kuzmenko about the battleship's operations. As they shuffled toward the wardroom, Kovalenko concluded that much needed to be done on the *St. George*, especially in terms of making it battle ready.

Over two hundred sailors crowded into the wardroom, anxious to hear about their sister battleship's mutiny and the revolutionary squadron's next course of action. The hubbub of conversation had to be quieted before the committee could begin. Koshuba recounted their journey from Sevastopol and Vishnevetsky's morning retreat. He then explained how they had overtaken the *St. George*.

"With a single shot," one sailor interrupted, referring coldly to the lieutenant who had killed himself on the bridge. The wardroom erupted in laughter.

When Koshuba finished, he requested the exchange of three hundred sailors between the two battleships to solidify support for the mutiny, but the *Potemkin*'s leaders thought this too extreme. Instead, they agreed to send fifty sailors to the *St. George*. Then they settled on a list of demands for Kakhanov to fulfill: the delivery of necessary provisions (coal, drinking water, and other supplies), the release of all political prisoners, the removal of troops from the city, and, finally, the transfer of political and military control to the people. If the general failed to comply within twenty-four hours, the joint committee agreed that they would bombard Odessa. With cheers, the sailors welcomed the plan to take the city by force.

After the meeting disbanded, Kirill drafted the ultimatum in the name of the "Crew of the Revolutionary Squadron." The ultimatum concluded with the statement that the loss of innocent life during any bombardment would be Kakhanov's responsibility. He had been given proper warning.

As the crews retired to sleep after this momentous day, the *Ismail* patrolled the surrounding seas on the distant chance that the squadron might return for a surprise attack. The cloudy night was illuminated only by the sweep of searchlights from the *Potemkin* and the *St. George,* their yellow beams scanning the waters for floating mines. At one point, a shout rang out on the *Potemkin*'s spar deck that a mine had been spotted, but when some sailors took a rowboat to investigate, they discovered only a bale of straw bobbing on the waves. Apart from this incident, the decks remained silent.

In the peaceful night, Kovalenko walked the *Potemkin*. Most of the crew was already asleep. Only the late watch remained awake, speaking among themselves of the day's events and their newfound hopes for the future. Kovalenko was carried away by the thought that their success that day would prompt a revolution throughout the empire. It was a couple of hours after midnight before he relaxed and drifted to sleep in one of the staterooms.

For the first time since the mutiny began, the committee was not to be found debating into the early morning hours. Matyushenko rested, finally giving in to exhaustion. Like the rest of the crew, he looked forward to the next day, when the fight would finally be taken onto land, where it would spread like wildfire. He could not imagine who could oppose them now. Kirill and Feldmann were spending the night on the *St. George*, revolvers at their side, after hearing subversive talk against the mutiny among the crew; but they were equally confident of realizing their plan to launch an insurrection in Odessa the next day.

None of them knew that while they slept peacefully, a band of petty officers was meeting in the *St. George*'s galley, plotting to wrest the battleship from the mutineers.

# 17

T 8 A.M., Matyushenko took a launch across the unusually calm harbor waters and struck out alone across the barren port. He had one thousand rubles stashed in his pocket — charity for Gilyarovsky's wife and a ploy to survey the city for the attack. Other sailors could have gone, but Matyushenko rarely delegated dangerous assignments, and he wanted to see the positions of the troops himself. It was June 18, the mutiny's fifth day, and the *Potemkin* now had allies to help force General Kakhanov into submission and carry the revolution to land.

Confidently, he ascended the Richelieu Steps. Bloodstains were still clear on the cobblestones from the slaughter two nights before. A company of soldiers stationed at the top of the steps watched with curiosity as this lone unarmed sailor headed toward them as if he ruled the city. Their officers made the first move, stepping forward to see who he was and why he had come. Matyushenko explained he wanted permission to send some money to his former commander's family as a gesture of goodwill.

Uncertain if this was possible, they sent a soldier to ask General Kakhanov. Taking a seat against the Richelieu statue to await an answer, Matyushenko brusquely asked for a light of his cigarette from the regiment's colonel, a request whose impudence he knew would have normally landed him in jail. Instead, the colonel obliged him. While he waited, Matyushenko observed Primorsky Boulevard and the adjacent streets, noting troop positions and the location of the commander's palace. He also managed to speak to a few soldiers, discreetly inquiring whether they were behind the sailors. The soldiers told him that their regiment and several others would come to their side once the bombardment began.

Several minutes later, a staff general approached and agreed to deliver the money. He looked none too pleased to be speaking to, let alone taking requests from, this ordinary sailor.

"May I have a receipt?" Matyushenko asked. The insult was obvious.

The general bristled at the suggestion that he might take the money himself, but then dashed off a note that he had accepted the rubles and would send them according to the sailor's request. Matyushenko suspected that the two battleships standing in the harbor were enough of a reason for the general to swallow his pride. Then Matyushenko returned to the port and stepped aboard the launch that was waiting for him. On his way to the *Potemkin,* he carefully sketched out what he had seen on Primorsky Boulevard. The sailors would need to know troop positions for the attack on Odessa that night.

By 10 A.M., the sun disappeared behind the slate-gray clouds of an approaching storm. In his cabin, Lieutenant Kovalenko was jotting down in a diary the events of the past few days when Dymchenko entered, with a worried look on his face.

"What's happened?" Kovalenko asked.

"Several people just came from the *St. George,*" Dymchenko said, perched on the sofa's edge. "The crew's divided. Some insist on sailing to Sevastopol to start talks with Chukhnin. They say the *Potemkin* can do as it pleases."

"This is the work of the petty officers," Kovalenko said.

"Without a doubt."

"We have to go there straight away."

They left Kovalenko's cabin to discover that Matyushenko and Kirill had already prepared a launch to go to the *St. George.* Matyushenko, who chastised himself for not dealing with this problem earlier, wanted the petty officers arrested, but Koshuba believed that if they tried this now, the battleship would surely erupt into further division. Instead, he wanted speakers from the *Potemkin* to convince the crew to stay the course in Odessa. Skeptical, Matyushenko agreed to this line of action.

Along with several sailors, Kirill and Kovalenko volunteered to go. As the launch was prepared to cast off, Dr. Golenko rushed to Matyushenko, who now planned to stay on the *Potemkin,* asking what was happening. Before Matyushenko finished explaining the unrest on the *St. George,* Golenko asked to go to that ship as well, saying he could attend to any sick sailors on the battleship since their doctor had gone ashore. Although Golenko had not previously involved himself much in political actions, he had proved helpful to the mutineers as a doctor, and this kind of gesture would further the solidarity between the two battleships. Matyushenko waved him aboard.

When the launch arrived, boatswain Kuzmenko blocked their path to the *St. George*'s quarterdeck, to keep them from further influencing the crew. "Our crew no longer wishes to remain with the *Potemkin,*" he said. "They want to leave for Sevastopol."

"Allow us to speak to the crew," Kovalenko said, forcing him aside.

On the quarterdeck, he found the situation much more perilous than he had suspected. The crew argued among one another as to what they should do; some nearly came to blows. Kirill jumped onto a pile of lumber, an impromptu podium from which to address the sailors. His voice, weakened as it was, was easily drowned by shouts of "No more words from the *Potemkin!*" and "We won't listen. Enough. We're going to Sevastopol."

"We'll stay with the *Potemkin,*" Koshuba yelled, trying to rally the sailors. "We won't leave them alone. Any cowards who want to go to Sevastopol can step ashore and walk."

A cacophony of voices erupted on the quarterdeck. No particular side sounded as if it was winning, and the sailors looked for someone to lead them. They noticed Kovalenko and Golenko. Soon the uproar shifted to a call for the officers to speak.

"Comrades . . . comrades . . . comrades," Kovalenko yelled, replacing Kirill on the lumber pile and motioning with his hands for the crew to settle down. They calmed down as he spoke. "Yesterday was the most remarkable day since the beginning of the *Potemkin* uprising. Yesterday we gained a powerful ally in the *St. George.* We welcomed your decision to join us, hand in hand, to fight the tsar. . . . But now, barely a night has passed, and you're wavering. Some among you want to go to Sevastopol, but aside from your surrender, what outcome do you expect from Chukhnin? Did you voluntarily join us yesterday only to betray us the next day? What kind of evil spirit has spread the seeds of doubt in your soul? What confuses you? Is our fight not righteous?"

The crew remained silent as Kovalenko embraced the words of revolution in a way he had never done before. "Comrades, our cause is righteous because we fight against a government that started a pointless, destructive, and shameful war for its own pleasure. We fight a government that answered the humble requests of the St. Petersburg workers with a shower of bullets and a government that leads to the gallows the defenders of the people's rights. So, comrades, power and truth are on our side. Let us be strong, and with our battleships, rush to the help of the people. Long live the rule of the people! Long live freedom and justice!"

For a few moments, the crew was unanimous, calling out, "We won't go to Sevastopol. We won't leave the *Potemkin*." Kovalenko stepped down, eyeing Kuzmenko, who was obviously shocked by hearing these words come from an officer.

Then a *St. George* sailor stood forward, breaking the temporary spell cast by Kovalenko. "If the *Potemkin* doesn't want to join us, we can find our own way to Sevastopol. If they want, they can follow."

Kirill shouted, "Why go to Sevastopol?"

"We'll anchor out at sea and start negotiations with Chukhnin!"

"Are you going to negotiate how to bring Golikov and Gilyarovsky back from the sea?" a *Potemkin* sailor retorted.

"No," Kirill answered for them. "They're going to ask forgiveness and crawl before Chukhnin in surrender."

The *St. George* sailor retreated into the clusters of men. Still there was no consensus. Surprisingly, Golenko then clambered onto the pile of lumber. Kovalenko urged the doctor to come down, fearful of what he would say.

"I'm the son of a peasant," Golenko began, undeterred by Kovalenko. "I care about what happens to every one of you. But if you go to Sevastopol, what will you demand? That the borscht be cooked better or that you be allowed ashore more often?"

The crew had no response.

"Comrades, there's too much injustice in Russia. I joined you to demand that everyone be equal. You can see for yourselves the kind of injustice that exists. We must eradicate it."

The doctor's short but pointed speech brought numerous nods of agreement from the crew. After he stepped down, a petty officer renewed the call to surrender the battleship, but the enthusiasm for this course of action had waned, now that the crew questioned what was to be gained by pleading with Vice Admiral Chukhnin. Koshuba then promised the sailors they would take no further action until they convened again with the *Potemkin.* This placated them further.

Golenko slipped off to speak with boatswain Kuzmenko and several petty officers. "I can't stay on the *Potemkin* anymore," he told Kuzmenko. "They'll shoot me, one way or another." Knowing that Ensign Alekseyev's passive resistance had proved useless and that the *Potemkin* would soon shell Odessa, Golenko had resolved to launch a counter-mutiny. His speech to the crew had won their trust, which he would need later, in order to act against them. Kuzmenko and the petty officers accepted the doctor's offer of help, and they plotted how to take back the battleship.

With the dissent on the *St. George* settled, at least temporarily, all those from the *Potemkin* returned to the launch. Nobody had noticed Golenko's brief absence. As they climbed down the ladder into the boat, Kuzmenko leaned over the railing and said, "Our committee shouldn't go to the *Potemkin* again. There's nothing for them to do there. By noon, we will weigh anchor."

"Watch yourself," Kirill said, pointing to the anchor chain, "or you'll find yourself at the bottom of the sea along with that anchor."

The launch cast off. Koshuba and several other *St. George* leaders followed in another boat to the *Potemkin,* to report on the heightened dissent among the crew. Matyushenko listened impatiently. They had come too far to be delayed by a few petty officers on the *St. George* who were more loyal to the tsar than to the ranks of sailors from which they themselves had risen. The joint committee agreed to send another group to the battleship, this time with an armed guard. They would arrest the traitors and bring them to the *Potemkin.* No more half measures.

It was clear that the *St. George*'s crew also needed some inspiration, but the problem was whom to send. Days of speaking on behalf of the revolution, often over the clamor of engines or in smoke-filled rooms, had ravaged Matyushenko's voice. Kirill and Feldmann, both compelling speakers, were hoarse as well, incapable of shouting down a boisterous crew. Furthermore, several other good agitators had gone to meet with Kakhanov and obtain provisions and coal. This left Koshuba and his fellow *St. George* revolutionaries to rally their own crew.

Then, for the second time that day, Dr. Golenko volunteered, this time to lead the armed guard and speak to the sailors again. The committee hastily deliberated. Those favoring him, the majority, said the doctor had chosen to stay aboard when he could have left with the other officers; he had presented himself well earlier on the *St. George;* and the sailors would respect his authority as an officer. Only Kovalenko, who could not go again because he needed to prepare the battleship for the potential bombardment of the city, voiced serious concerns. He argued that the doctor was the one who had first approved the rotten meat bought in Odessa and that he had abandoned the *Potemkin* for the *Vekha* during their first confrontation with the squadron. Could he be trusted now? But Kovalenko's concerns did not sway the ship's leaders. They had little choice but to send Golenko now; he would be accompanied by two *Potemkin* committee members who would guarantee that he would do as told. The doctor would go, it was decided.

After they left, the delegation that brought the ultimatum to Kakhanov returned to the *Potemkin.* General Kakhanov had refused them. Despite the threat of two battleships in the harbor, he agreed to send only a package of medical supplies. With Cossacks patrolling the shorelines, preventing any further deliveries to the *Potemkin,* Kakhanov was obviously spoiling for a fight. The sailors agreed to give him exactly that if he failed to change his mind by evening. They would no longer wait twenty-four hours.

A crew led by Kirill commandeered a coal barge in the port, and the *Ismail* towed it alongside the battleship. After two sojourns out to sea during the confrontation with the squadron, they needed to replenish their supplies. Unaware of the strife on the *St. George,* most of the *Potemkin* crew cheerfully loaded the coal into the hold, the sailors' white jerseys turning black from the dust. They appeared united as never before. The sight heartened Matyushenko and his fellow leaders. Once they were finished and the armed party had been sent to the *St. George* rid their sister battleship of its petty officers, the combined might of the two battleships could be turned on Odessa to free the people. Lulled into overconfidence after success against the squadron, they were blind to how tenuous were the ties that bound their revolutionary squadron.

In the late afternoon, a light rain began to fall when port official Romanenko, "a red-nosed man with the typical Bourbon profile," as Feldmann described him, pulled alongside the *Potemkin* in a cutter flying a white flag. Romanenko came aboard to inform the sailors that he had brought some provisions. He also offered to facilitate negotiations between the sailors and General Kakhanov. Something about his manner and convoluted descriptions of the state of the city gave the sailors the impression that he was stalling for time, but they neglected to confront him on it.

By 4 P.M., with Romanenko still on board and an hour after the armed guard had left with Golenko, Matyushenko began to get nervous about the *St. George*. The *Potemkin* delegation had yet to signal once with an update. Nonetheless, when the *St. George*'s decks cleared, he and everybody else thought it was because of the worsening downpour. At first.

When Dr. Golenko revisited the *St. George*, he called the crew together on the quarterdeck to inform them of the *Potemkin*'s decisions: first, every petty officer on the *St. George* was to be arrested; second, the two battleships would shell Odessa into oblivion that evening. Golenko offered no explanations, as if the decisions had come as fiat from the *Potemkin* superiors. As he suspected, the sailors reacted angrily to his remarks. Some insisted they would not shell the city nor turn over any of their crew because the *Potemkin* had so ordered it. Boatswain Kuzmenko and his co-conspirators had obviously succeeded in stirring up resentment against the *Potemkin* on the *St. George*.

Then Golenko made his move. "Most of the *Potemkin* crew wants to end the mutiny. . . . But they're afraid of the revolutionaries. The *St. George* must serve as an example, weighing anchor and sailing to Sevastopol."

Koshuba and the armed guard could barely believe the doctor's words. For a few seconds, they were too dumbstruck to stop him.

"I'll personally defend, before the Black Sea Fleet command, anyone who helps end this mutiny," the doctor promised.

Finally, Koshuba and the two *Potemkin* committee members tried to grab Golenko, but he escaped into the crowd of sailors. Confusion reigned on the quarterdeck; nobody was quite sure what was the truth or whom to follow, exactly as Kuzmenko had planned. While Golenko spoke, a petty officer raised the anchor until it was only several feet below the water, still hidden from the *Potemkin*'s sight. Several others took command of the engine room and disabled the rifles in the armory. Kuzmenko headed to the bridge, where he ordered a battle alert. The decks cleared.

Koshuba screamed, "Kill the traitors!" He and other revolutionary sailors moved to stop the counter-mutiny, threatening to throw overboard anyone who helped the petty officers. The sailors ignored their threats, and the revolutionaries found that the weapons in the armory had been rendered useless. Their hold over the crew had always been tenuous at best, and the sudden confusion caused by Golenko and the organized resistance of the petty officers gave the counter-mutiny the upper hand. A pair of *Potemkin* sailors tried to escape to get help, but they were arrested and thrown into a cabin.

Kuzmenko received a message that the anchor was raised. He gave his orders to the engine room: full speed ahead.

A sailor ran into the *Potemkin*'s wardroom, nearly knocking Matyushenko over in his rush to report that the *St. George* had weighed anchor. Romanenko explained that the battleship was probably taking up the slack on its anchor chain. Matyushenko pushed him away from the door, and the rest of the committee followed him onto the deck to find the *St. George* steaming past the *Potemkin*'s starboard side, out to sea. Then they received a signal from the escaping battleship: "Going to Sevastopol. We invite the crew of the *Potemkin* to follow."

Matyushenko could not believe what he was seeing; he was at a loss for what to do. By his side, Nikishkin yelled, "Action stations! To the guns, comrades!"

Hundreds of sailors ran to their positions. "Hurry up! Raise the anchor!" some cried out. Others yelled, "There's no time. Stay the anchor and fire! We'll teach these cursed cowards!" Gathering his senses, Matyushenko sprinted to the bridge and, to buy some time while they cast off the coal barge, signaled the *St. George:* "I see you clearly. Wait fifteen minutes. We will go to Sevastopol together." Meanwhile, Romanenko, who had been sent by Kuzmenko to distract the *Potemkin*'s crew, slipped off the battleship. He had more yet to do.

Kuzmenko ignored the *Potemkin*'s message, leading the battleship out of the harbor. Koshuba and his comrades tried again to gain access to the engine room and bridge, but they were pushed back with rifles, hopelessly outnumbered.

"Heave to and anchor at the same location," Matyushenko then signaled. Still the *St. George* drove forward, faster with each minute. An alarm rang throughout the *Potemkin*. The sailors cleared the decks, finally untied the coal barge, and raised the battle flag over the bridge. Their twelve-inch guns turned slowly on their mounts. A sailor by Matyushenko urged, "We can't let them give up the ship like this. We've got to teach the cowards a lesson." His words were superfluous: Matyushenko intended to destroy the ship if it did not stop. He signaled again. "I shall fire." Several seconds passed. The gun crews held their breath, waiting for the order.

On the *St. George,* the sailors spotted the battle flag and balked at the sight of the gun turrets aimed at them. They demanded Kuzmenko turn around the battleship before they were sunk. Knowing they could not escape to Sevastopol without a fight, the boatswain gave the order to slow the battleship. Then he sent a message to the *Potemkin:* "I am going back to place." Dr. Golenko, terrified that Kuzmenko was about to return to the *Potemkin*'s side, rushed the bridge himself, shrieking, "Brothers! This is treason. Push that boatswain overboard." But the terrified petty officers refused to listen.

As the *St. George* swung back into the harbor, the *Potemkin*'s crew yelled at their gunners, "Don't shoot, comrades. It's coming back. It turned back." The crew left their positions, crowding the quarterdeck and shaking their fists at their fellow sailors their betrayal.

Then the *St. George* veered directly toward the *Potemkin.* On its decks, sailors scrambled back and forth, confused about what was happening. Suddenly Kuzmenko shifted course again, heading now toward the port. He followed the small cutter that Romanenko commanded. The *St. George* moved at full steam once again.

"Look, they're turning toward the port," sailors hollered on the *Potemkin*. The had no idea what the *St. George* had planned next. "Order them to stop! Order them to stop!"

Havoc overcame the *Potemkin;* sailors were crying for action but were unsure what to do. The *St. George* maintained its course straight into Odessa's port; its enormous screws were churning the ever-shallower water. Some on the *Potemkin* thought the battleship was out of control, but Kuzmenko knew exactly what he was doing. Romanenko was guiding him. A minute later, the *St. George* shuddered. Sailors were thrown from their feet as the battleship's bow ran aground on the shoals near Platonovsky Wharf. It turned almost ninety degrees to port before stopping.

On the *Potemkin*'s bridge, total chaos reigned. Matyushenko ordered the signalman to send a message to the *St. George* to heave to or they would fire. Hearing these instructions, Ensign Alekseyev fell to his knees, hysterically muttering, "More blood. I can't take it anymore. Free us, dear God, to the shore." The signalman informed the bridge that the *St. George* was permanently beached on the shoals.

While the *Potemkin* leaders wavered as to whether they would destroy the battleship, Dr. Golenko and the counter-mutineers escaped onto Romanenko's cutter. Afraid that the Odessan military would soon converge on the *St. George,* Koshuba and his revolutionary comrades released an oar boat into the water and jumped aboard. The armed guard from the *Potemkin* followed on another boat.

The *Ismail* was sent to meet the launches halfway back to the *Potemkin*. "The doctor's a traitor," Koshuba yelled as the *Ismail* neared. "He betrayed the *St. George!*"

News of this treason devastated the *Potemkin*'s crew and fueled even more panic. Their mightiest ally against the tsar had abandoned them. "What do we do now?" yelled one sailor. "Sink the *St. George!* Send them a package of bombs," some furiously demanded. "We should go to sea," said others. "To Sevastopol to surrender," a petty officer suggested. But drowning out the many divergent cries came the shout, "To Romania! To Romania!"

Standing on the bridge, Matyushenko cursed the *St. George.* At the moment the crew of the *Potemkin* should have been planning the assault on the city, they had been betrayed. Their days of waiting for the squadron, their triumph in winning another battleship to their side — all were for nothing now. Several boats carrying soldiers were already cutting toward the *St. George,* whose guns could now be turned to defend Odessa against the *Potemkin.* As Matyushenko considered their next move, he heard increasingly loud and impassioned demands to head for Romania, an idea that he knew had been spread by those opposed to the mutiny. The hope of the squadron coming to their side, then the alliance with the *St. George,* had decreased the attractiveness of that option. But now, with their spirits crushed, the sailors were easily swept away by the desire for an easy surrender rather than a continuing fight.

The crew began to chant, "Romania! Romania!"

Kirill and Feldmann attempted to silence them. "Brothers, comrades," they pleaded, "what are you on about? You're turning against the cause —"

"What are you leading us into?" A sailor interrupted them. "Do you want to see us drowned like sheep?"

Although fear gripped the crew, Matyushenko refused to listen to any call for surrender. Even so, chances of success in Odessa were limited. The sailors could attack the *St. George* with their guns. They could fire on Odessa again to try to force General Kakhanov to accept their demands. Either action meant that many, many would die. Moreover, given that the *Potemkin* now found itself without another battleship at its side, nor much of a connection with the city's revolutionaries, their actions might be for nothing.

Vakulenchuk had always cautioned Matyushenko not to be at the mercy of his tempestuous urge to strike out in hatred against the tsar. He must think first. "Don't throw it away," his friend had said, in his final words to Matyushenko. He had always pushed him to do whatever was necessary to realize his revolutionary ambitions. But the cost of using the full force of the *Potemkin*'s guns was too great, Matyushenko reasoned, for a revolution that was supposed to be in the name of the people. He could not lead the sailors to commit this kind of bloodshed.

Although he hated retreating to Romania, Matyushenko agreed to head to its port city, Constanza. There they could obtain more provisions and fuel and then focus on a new plan to serve their cause. Once the crew settled down, he and his fellow revolutionaries could convince them that capitulation was the wrong path. But for now they needed to follow the call to leave Odessa. The committee agreed, and Murzak gave the order to prepare the battleship to leave. The *Potemkin* signaled the *Vekha* to take on as much coal as possible from the barge and then follow.

As the battleship cleared the harbor, with the *Ismail* by its side, Kirill and Feldmann pulled Matyushenko aside. "How come you want to go to Romania?" Kirill shouted. "Don't you see the shame of it?"

Burdened with a decision he never wanted to make, Matyushenko spat out, "If you're frightened for your own skin, I can send you ashore." Then he walked away.

The shores of Odessa soon disappeared. Night fell a few hours later, and the sailors were alone again on the Black Sea. The stars overhead and the pale moonlight cast across the water were the only signs that they had not abandoned the harbor for some black oblivion. While heading southwest toward Constanza, steaming slowly to conserve coal, each crew member contemplated the events of the past few days and the grim future.

In the wardroom, Koshuba made a frantic appeal to change direction toward Sevastopol. "This is what we'll do, brothers. We'll get close to Sevastopol and land one hundred determined fellows. We'll stuff their shirts full of cartridges, and by night they will fall upon the sentry and enter the town. Then we can make our way into the fortress, disguised as government troops. There, we'll arrest the officers and proclaim an insurrection." The foolhardy, though bold plan was dismissed. The crew was set on Constanza.

The *Vekha* struck a further blow to their morale when it ignored the *Potemkin*'s repeated wireless telegraph messages. After a few hours, it became clear that its crew had betrayed the battleship as well. The dramatic turn of events within the past twenty-four hours left the sailors exhausted and dispirited, particularly in contrast to their frame of mind the night before, when they had returned to Odessa, painting in their minds beautiful pictures of the revolutionary squadron bringing the tsar's regime to its knees.

Looking out into the emptiness of the sea, Kirill and Feldmann despaired together. "It appears that we're lost," Feldmann sighed.

"There's nothing else for us," Kirill agreed. "But until we see that all is utterly lost, we must fight on. And it's not clear yet that all is lost."

With nothing left to say, they each thought about the fact that they might never see their hometown of Odessa again. It was likely they would die in the coming days.

Kovalenko could barely stand the terrible flight from Odessa, either. The crew's hopes had been upended so swiftly, and he was also worried about the men's low morale, fearing that the "dark forces" that had taken over the *St. George* might also find similar success on the *Potemkin*. Bearing the weight of the revolution without another battleship at their side might prove too great a responsibility for the crew.

A disheartened silence fell across the battleship. Some sailors thought they had fled Odessa like cowards. Others believed they had been helpless to do anything else, but now that they were alone, they were more helpless still. "What now?" was the question on everyone's mind. The journey to Romania, one sailor felt, reminded him of a dying man barely hanging on to life.

The only voice heard on the *Potemkin* that rang hopeful, strained though it was by overuse, came from Matyushenko. He walked about the battleship, reassuring the crew that there was no reason to be discouraged. Late that night, he entered the wardroom, where some of the committee members had assembled to avoid being alone. With a bold mien, Matyushenko told his comrades, "All was not lost, even now." He promised they would revive the crew's spirit and that their journey to Romania was merely a way station in their struggle for freedom.

Heartened by his conviction, the ship's leaders left for the open air of the spar deck. They looked out to the sea, almost as if in the darkness they might see a vision of the future confirming what Matyushenko had said.

In Odessa that evening, Kakhanov negotiated the *St. George*'s surrender. The nightmare that had begun with the *Potemkin*'s arrival four days before was almost over, and he felt triumphant in *his* saving of the city.

At first, he had thought the *St. George*'s mad dash into the harbor signaled the beginning of the bombardment. While bracing his troops for the attack, he learned that the battleship had run ashore, aided by the courageous effort of the port official Romanenko. Soon after, the counter-mutiny's leaders delivered the *St. George*'s flag to Kakhanov. However, the battleship's complete surrender was stalled by the crew's demand for an official pardon before they disembarked. Kakhanov sent General Karangozov to the battleship and was awaiting his response. In case the sailors refused to leave peacefully, Kakhanov repositioned his artillery batteries for a clear shot at the battleship.

The citizens of Odessa waited impatiently as well. The past twenty-four hours had been a tumultuous experience. The night before, Kakhanov had announced that the squadron had defeated the *Potemkin* and won its submission. But then Krieger's battleships disappeared from the horizon and the *Potemkin* returned to the harbor with the *St. George* at its side. Troops still occupied the streets, and the city was shut down for yet another day. The foreign consuls, expecting the worst, instructed their expatriate citizens to leave the city by any means possible. Now the *Potemkin* had left without firing a shot. In a letter to St. Petersburg, the American consul praised the *Potemkin* sailors for their restraint in not bombarding Odessa in retribution before leaving. But with the *St. George* still under its crew's control, the city faced the possibility of a devastating assault.

At 11 P.M., General Karangozov returned to the military headquarters with three sailors from the battleship who wanted to express their regret and plead for Nicholas II's mercy. The *St. George* crew finally allowed Kakhanov's troops to take over the battleship. The boarding soldiers arrested those suspected of participating in the mutiny. Everyone was led to shore peacefully, except for machinist quartermaster Pavel Gulyayev, one of the mutiny's leaders. While being transferred by ferry, he jumped into the harbor and drowned. Three hours later, General Kakhanov telegrammed Nicholas II, detailing how successful he had been in ending the *St. George* mutiny. He also told him that the *Potemkin* was likely on its way to Sevastopol.

That same night, Lenin's representative, Mikhail Vasilyev-Yuzhin, arrived by train at Odessa. He had traveled from Vienna with a fake passport and residence permit (using the name of a famous general's son), passing through border patrols, once even receiving a salute from the guards. He was excited to return to Russia, although his chances of getting on board the *Potemkin* were limited. All hope was lost when he looked out at the harbor and realized that the battleship was no longer there. He contacted the Odessa Bolsheviks to find out what had occurred and where the *Potemkin* was heading. They could only guess at its destination. Distraught that he had come too late, Vasilyev-Yuzhin made preparations to take a steamer to the Caucasus port city of Batumi. Given the inroads made by the Social Democrats among its people, it was the obvious base for the sailors. This decision guaranteed that he would never meet up with the *Potemkin*. The battleship's crew was alone, without help from its fellow Black Sea sailors or any revolutionary political leadership on land.

# III

We must dare, and dare again, and go on daring.

— GEORGES JACQUES DANTON,
French revolutionary

What tragic poetry lies in the fate of this exile, condemned to wander far at sea night and day, alone, cut off from friends, pursued by enemies. Its fatal cannons gaze wrathfully toward the horizon, the watchman stands his guard without rest, every moment may prove decisive for the crew — though the enemy does not dare approach the floating fortress — and no harbor is safe for the brave souls; the menacing shore compels them onward, and only the sea that knows not the meaning of shackles and servitude, embraces the freedom fighters.

— *Proletary,* on the *Potemkin* mutiny

# 18

ON THE AFTERNOON of June 19, the *Potemkin* traveled slowly across the Black Sea. On the forecastle, the crew congregated in small groups. One sailor played a Russian folk song on his accordion and those around him sang along. In another group, a sailor wearing an army private's tunic mimicked a marching soldier. His crewmates laughed uproariously at his mock stiffness and at the badly sewn patches on his sleeves. Many lounged on the decks, enjoying the sun or watching the school of dolphins that followed the battleship at a distance. Now that only open waters surrounded them, their gloom over events in Odessa was dispelled by a renewed sense of freedom.

As the battleship steamed toward Constanza, the sailor committee convened to determine a plan of action. Before the meeting started, the crew presented an impromptu fund they had collected in a sailor's cap — many sailors donated their meager savings for the entire battleship's benefit. The sum of money was insignificant compared to the amount in the ship's safe, but the gesture reassured the ship's revolutionary leaders that they still had the crew's allegiance.

Matyushenko refused to consider using Romania as anything more than a stopping point on the journey — never a surrender — but even the sheer force of his personality had yet to win everyone over to his position. Furthermore, the sailors questioned how Constanza's officials would receive them. One thing was certain: the shock over the *St. George*'s actions had inspired a determination not to follow in its path. The committee believed that Romania was their best option for help because of its independent stance against the tsar. Romania's lands had long been caught between the shifting domination of the Ottoman and Russian Empires — as well as the interests of Austria-Hungary and western Europe. In 1878, the Treaty of Berlin had formalized its true sovereignty, a long and hard-fought victory that its constitutional monarch, King Carol I, was eager to protect, particularly from his country's former occupier, Russia. Given his respect for civil liberties, the sailors suspected the Romanian government would sympathize with their struggle. On the other hand, King Carol would not want to inflame relations with Russia, and therefore he might reject the *Potemkin*'s requests for aid, or, worse, try to win favor from Nicholas by capturing the battleship.

In the midst of this discussion, a sailor standing against the wall voiced a desire that many crew members secretly held: "Maybe they'll let us stay in Romania." Another sailor seconded this idea: "That's right. Their tsar will allow us to live there."

Having anticipated this thinking, Kirill opened an old naval-regulations handbook he had fortuitously found in Golikov's library. He read from an earmarked page stating that foreign governments under international law were required to return mutineers to their country of origin.

Sailor Lychev then pushed for resolution. "After we get fuel and supplies in Constanza, we'll return to Russia to fight. Yes?"

Matyushenko looked around the table, sensing agreement. "Are there any other opinions?"

The wardroom was silent. It was unanimous: the *Potemkin* would stop in Constanza to obtain coal, drinking water, and food. The sailors would also plumb for any word on the squadron's movement and news on other uprisings in Russia, hoping Odessa was the start of many. Then they would decide where the *Potemkin* could best advance the revolution back in Russia. Perhaps, some hoped, their Tsentralka brothers in Sevastopol would lead a revolt to take over the naval base or manage, at least, to win control of another battleship to join the *Potemkin*. But since they no longer had the element of surprise, this would not be easy.

While most of the crew relaxed outside, the sailor committee continued meeting until early afternoon, discussing the reasons for the *St. George*'s counter-mutiny and for their own failure in Odessa.

Feldmann stridently argued that they must avoid falling prey to further dissension or indecision.

Then Kirill interrupted. "Comrades, there's a significant reason for our failures. You all know that, don't you? It's the petty officers and Ensign Alekseyev. They've shown us time after time that they're just waiting for a critical moment to throw the whole crew into confusion . . . to hurt us and to interfere in our plans. We should've gotten rid of them long ago."

Some agreed that the petty officers should be cast off in a boat from the *Potemkin*. Others disputed this. "They already know our plans and intentions and about the conflict among the crew. On reaching Sevastopol, they'll tell Chukhnin everything. They'll even advise him on how to act against us." Unable to reach a consensus, committee members tabled the issue for later discussion.

Finally, they turned their attention to the best way to present themselves in Constanza. Reznichenko spoke up: "We need to let the workers of *all* countries find out about the campaign of the Russian people against the tsar. Once we get the word out in Germany, Italy, France, and elsewhere about our uprising, we'll have the support not only of Russia but abroad as well."

"True . . . We must let everyone know," Matyushenko said. They then decided to draft a declaration to issue to the international community.

The meeting concluded. Some of the sailors stayed in the wardroom as the *Potemkin* cut through the choppy waves of the Black Sea. They spoke of the great revolution that would sweep Russia by virtue of their actions — how the people would embrace their newfound freedom and equality, how the sailors could return to their families and pursue the lives they wanted. For a brief time, they forgot the many challenges ahead, such as what to do if the Romanians rejected their request for help, how to survive with enough coal for only a few hundred miles of travel and enough food and water to last three days, whether dissent among the crew would spark a counter-mutiny, and how the tsar and the Admiralty were planning to crush their rebellion. They would face these realities in the days ahead, but for now, they dreamed of what could be.

●　●　●

In Nikolayev, a port at the mouth of the river Bug where the *Potemkin* had been launched in 1900 with much celebration (the presence of dignitaries, the sprinkling of holy water, the stirring sounds of a full orchestra, and the boom of gunfire), Vice Admiral Chukhnin now prayed for that ship's demise. At naval headquarters, a host of aides and telegraph operators sent out his orders in a flurry, giving wings to those prayers.

Chukhnin had arrived in Nikolayev the day before, June 18. The fights that broke out there between sailors and Cossacks, simultaneous with the first reports of the *Potemkin* mutiny, had already been quelled, but Chukhnin wanted to judge the fleet's morale for himself. From the train station, he went straight to the port to speak to his sailors. In his usual fervent manner, he explained to them their moral obligation to serve the tsar faithfully and told them that "shameful acts of treason" wrought tremendous harm to Russia. In conclusion, he asked the sailors to take an oath that they would perform their duties without hesitation, even if sent against the *Potemkin*. Without exception, the sailors gave their oath, but Chukhnin heard listless hesitation in their voices. He knew that, given the chance, they would rebel against their officers; moreover, he was convinced that the sailors would refuse to fight against their own.

Later that same afternoon, Chukhnin learned from Krieger, who had since arrived back at Sevastopol, that a similar spirit plagued the rest of the fleet and that rumors were spreading about a planned uprising on the *Ekaterina II*. The battleship's senior doctor had learned of the potential mutiny, became drunk from worry, and blurted out to his captain, "Your Highness will soon be Our Highness, and you'll be chasing crabs in the sea. . . . We're having a revolution. Taking off to see the *Potemkin* in the evening. Everyone's going. I'm going."

Given such reports from Sevastopol, it was doubtful Chukhnin would have been soothed by the knowledge that the *Potemkin*'s leaders felt alone and in desperate need of help. From his perspective, he felt as if only his steadfast leadership and forceful measures prevented his entire command from falling into revolutionary hands and joining the *Potemkin*. That night, before learning of the *St. George*'s surrender to Kakhanov, Chukhnin wrote to Tsar Nicholas that more trouble should be expected within the Black Sea Fleet. He painfully concluded, "I am afraid the sea is in the hands of mutineers."

Reports about the *St. George* and the *Vekha* brought some measure of relief. Chukhnin ordered Captain Guzevich to return to his command and obtain complete confessions from every crew member. These "criminals" were to state their participation in a "military mutiny" with a priest present, and if they declined to do so, Guzevich was to guarantee that they would never see their families or home-towns again. Chukhnin would brook no mercy in dealing with these men.

The *Potemkin*'s departure from Odessa created even more problems for the vice admiral. Nobody knew where the crew planned on going next. All sea traffic had ceased days before, but a mutinous ship of its strength was a threat to every city on the Black Sea, Russian or otherwise, and there was nobody to stop them. As a prosecutor in the region remarked to the Russian minister of justice, "The squadron has returned to Sevastopol. The mood among the naval units is disloyal. Chukhnin is in Nikolayev. Krieger and the naval leaders refuse to take energetic measures. The population is nervously awaiting events. Otherwise, everything is in order."

The governor-general of the Caucasus instructed his troops to stockpile twenty oxen and sacks of flour and bread on Sukhumi's wharf in case the *Potemkin* demanded provisions. In other seaside cities, officials organized militias and instructed their citizens to leave the streets if the battleship arrived in their harbor. It was widely accepted that the *Potemkin* would bombard to ruins any city that resisted the mutinous sailors.

Chukhnin was scheduled to leave by express train to Sevastopol that evening so that he could ensure that his commands were followed to the letter. It would have been faster to go by sea, but given his fleet's rebellious state and the unknown location of the *Potemkin*, he feared being caught — not so much out of concern for his own well-being as, rather, the knowledge that his subordinate officers were inept. As he bluntly telegraphed Avelan, "It would not suit me to be captured." The pressure from above to end the mutiny was intensifying, and the fact that he could not travel safely on the Black Sea made him tremble with anger. It was yet another black mark on his once-sterling reputation.

Throughout the day, Chukhnin had made exhaustive efforts to capture or sink the *Potemkin* and save the Black Sea Fleet from ruin.

First, he sent the plans drawn up on his journey from St. Petersburg to his staff to secure Sevastopol against any sea approach. Second, given the dangerous inroads revolutionaries had made at the naval base, he instructed Krieger to detain any disloyal lower ranks, no matter the number. Third, he told Krieger to disable the machinery and weapons systems on battleships known to have untrustworthy crews, to forestall further mutinies. Fourth, Chukhnin alerted the lighthouses dotted along the Black Sea coast to maintain a close watch for the *Potemkin*. Fifth, he asked the War Ministry to amass troops at coastal batteries outside every major Russian port in the region and order them to fire on the *Potemkin* if it came within range. Sixth, he won the foreign minister's commitment to open diplomatic negotiations with neighboring countries such as Turkey and Romania about how to deal with the *Potemkin* if it was sighted along their coasts; Russia requested that supplies be withheld from the battleship and that, if possible, its surrender be secured.

But Chukhnin placed his faith mainly in his seventh and final measure, one known only to Avelan and a handful of others. The six other orders were defensive in nature, but the Black Sea Fleet commander detested simply playing a waiting game. He preferred to be on the offense, but until he brought his sailors into line, he dared not risk another mutiny or the loss of more officers by sending additional battleships after the *Potemkin*. This reduced his offensive options to using destroyers or a squadron of torpedo boats, but even their smaller, more easily supervised crews were impossible to trust. Avelan had suggested recruiting men from St. Petersburg's Imperial Guard, whose devotion to duty was inviolate, to staff these ships, but they would take too much time to assemble and train.

Then, while in Nikolayev, Chukhnin had received an unexpected but welcome offer from Lieutenant Andrei Yanovich. The thirty-two-year-old officer served under Rear Admiral Sergei Pisarevsky, the head of the Black Sea Training Unit and the most reliable, battle-tested commander that Chukhnin had in the fleet. Eager to restore the tsar's honor and avenge the murders of Golikov and the others, Yanovich informed Chukhnin that he had assembled a score of like-minded, hard-line monarchist officers willing to take a destroyer and hunt down the *Potemkin*. Although known to have a penchant for gambling and too quick a temper, Yanovich was a daring young lieutenant (later, he would be one of the first volunteers for the Russian air force). He had already participated in a perilous Arctic Ocean hydrographical survey and had been rewarded with the St. Stanislaw Medal for his Baltic Fleet service under then Captain First Rank Rozhestvensky. A senior gunnery specialist, he now lectured at the Sevastopol training fleet in electrical and mechanical engineering, proving his knowledge of every aspect of running a ship. In short, he was perfect for the mission.

Chukhnin readily accepted the offer, arranging for Yanovich to take command of the *Stremitelny* ("swift"), the fleet's fastest destroyer, which could travel at twenty-six knots and was armed with torpedo launchers and two rapid-firing guns. Every effort was made to keep the mission secret so that the destroyer could take the *Potemkin* by surprise.

At 1:30 P.M., on June 19, while Chukhnin delivered some remaining orders before leaving Nikolayev, the "suicide squad," as Yanovich and the other officers referred to themselves with an air of braggadocio, slipped out of Sevastopol's harbor. They steered a course northwest toward Odessa. Chukhnin may well have wished he were on board with them, seeking revenge for himself.

While the vice admiral focused on chasing the *Potemkin,* another crew within his fleet was on the precipice of mutiny. Anchored off Tendra Island, the training ship *Prut* was prepared to leave for Sevastopol once its Sunday Orthodox service was over. At 9:30 A.M. on June 19, over six hundred sailors gathered on the deck, two-thirds of them machinist trainees. A priest chanted a prayer in front of several large icons. The ship's commander, Captain Second Class Aleksandr Baranovsky, was eager for the service's end so the ship could return to the safety of the fleet's base. Since awakening that morning, he had sensed something was wrong about the crew. They seemed unusually tense and excited, and he had already received a telegram from Krieger, warning him to be particularly vigilant of his men.

Unknown to Baranovsky and his twenty-two officers, sailor Aleksandr Petrov, one of Tsentralka's leaders who had recently been removed from the *Ekaterina II* because he was a suspected agitator, was ready to seize the ship. On the foredeck, he cautioned patience to several other revolutionary sailors, including machinist D. Titov and firemen I. Adamenko and I. Atamasov. They awaited word that their comrades were in place to break into the arms room. Behind Petrov, a sailor passed around a flask of vodka, saying, "Come on, boys, take a drink to brace yourselves!" Atamasov snatched away the bottle and warned the sailor to be quiet. They could not be caught now.

Early on June 15, the *Prut* had left Sevastopol to survey Tendra Island's training fortifications. After Baranovsky dropped anchor off the island, he received a telegram from the Black Sea Fleet command, alerting him of the *Potemkin* mutiny and instructing him to take the training ship to Nikolayev for caution's sake. Offering no explanation to his crew, Baranovsky took the *Prut* to the port city, arriving the next morning. He restricted his crew from going ashore, citing the recent fights between sailors and Cossacks as the reason. The crew first learned of the *Potemkin* mutiny that night when a teenager swam out to the ship and tossed a military cap onto the deck. It was stuffed with Social Democrat proclamations about the battleship. The next day, fifty sailors went to the port to load military cargo and confirmed this news. Excited, Petrov and the other revolutionary sailors insisted they mutiny themselves.

Later that afternoon, the *Prut* left Nikolayev for Sevastopol to deliver the cargo. En route, Baranovsky received instructions from Krieger to wait off Tendra Island until further notice. The training ship arrived early on June 18. The crew spent the day idle, waiting for the squadron and speculating about what had happened to the *Potemkin*. That night, Petrov met with over fifty sailors in the passageway that ran alongside the propeller shaft. He confirmed they would overthrow the ship the next morning and then go to Odessa to join the *Potemkin*'s revolutionary squadron (which, they were unaware, had broken apart only hours before their meeting). Titov would signal when to launch the mutiny.

Several minutes into the Sunday service on June 19, Titov learned that the other sailors were in position and ready. With a voice strong enough to carry across the ship, he yelled, "Hurrah! Hurrah!" Petrov and Titov led the charge from the foredeck down to the arms room, where another comrade had already broken the locks with an iron bar. While they handed out rifles, a young lieutenant rushed to stop them and was stabbed in the chest with a bayonet. On the quarterdeck, a boatswain also tried to quell the mutiny, but, moments after calling for the guard, he was shot and fell wounded to the deck. As planned, the sailors ran with their loaded rifles to key sections of the ship. The watch officer, who refused to step off the bridge, was killed with a bullet to the head, but otherwise, the mutineers met no resistance from the officers and petty officers. Most of the crew rallied to their side or stood by passively while they took over the ship.

Titov captured Baranovsky while the captain was trying to escape to his stateroom. "Where do you think you're going? Do you want to be shot?" Titov asked, shoving him toward the quarterdeck. Baranovsky found himself surrounded by sailors whom he had once threatened with death if they merely attended a socialist meeting. Adamenko told the captain he was under arrest and to drop his saber. When Baranovsky hesitated, the fireman struck him several times in the face. Then he was thrown down onto the deck. The sailors screamed, "Cast him overboard!" Baranovsky pleaded for his life. Finally, Petrov stepped in to prevent his death. On the other side of the ship, the priest held forth his crucifix, trying to mollify the crew. A sailor cut the priest's hand with a bayonet and said, "The devil himself wouldn't have allowed what you've allowed to go on here."

A short time later, the sailors corralled the rest of the officers into their wardroom and stripped them of their epaulettes. Little bloodlust, which had for a time overwhelmed the *Potemkin,* was evident during the first hour of the mutiny on the *Prut* (except in the case of two sailors, who dragged a wounded lieutenant by his arm to the infirmary, taunting him the whole while as to when he planned on dying). Once the ship was secured, Petrov and Titov cheered from the bridge: "We are free! Now — on to Odessa!" Then they instructed one of the navigation officers to chart a course to the city. They warned him, "If you try to deceive us, we'll never forgive you."

During the journey, the crew elected a sailor committee, with Petrov as its leader. Afterward, he gave a rousing speech, telling the men that they were participants not in a mutiny but rather in a revolution to win their freedom. However, at 4 P.M., when they steamed into Odessa, they were crushed to discover that the *Potemkin* was gone from the harbor. With no shells for the guns, the *Prut* was helpless against attack and desperate for the protection of the powerful battleship whose cause it had come to join. Less than an hour later, the training ship left Odessa, short on coal. Petrov paced the decks, wondering where the *Potemkin* had gone and what they were to do now.

Onshore in Odessa, General Kakhanov alerted Sevastopol that the *Prut* had entered the port and that no officers could be seen on the bridge.

Many miles away on the Black Sea, the *Potemkin* proceeded toward Constanza, its crew unaware of the *Prut* mutiny. Petty Officer M. Zubchenko stood by a railing on the battleship's starboard side. In his hand he held a bottle into which he had slipped a note, which he prayed would be found ashore. A couple of hours before, the sailor committee had told the petty officers they would be shot if they were caught spreading propaganda against the mutiny. Scared for his life, Zubchenko had written a message he hoped would reach his family: "Orthodox fellow believers! I ask you to inform my dear wife and children that I'm dying not by my enemy's hand but rather by the hand of my brother. . . . Every minute I expect death, only I don't know what it will be. Dear Marusya, I beg you, forgive me. I am dying for Faith, Tsar, and Fatherland. I strongly embrace you in my dying arms. . . . Bury me in the Sevastopol cemetery. June 19, 1905."

After securing the cork stopper, he tossed the bottle overboard, watching it bob to the surface and then slip astern. Overhead, on the stern mast, fluttered the proof that, for Zubchenko, meant the revolutionary sailors were not planning to surrender in Constanza. They had raised a large red flag with the words LIBERTY, EQUALITY, FRATERNITY sewn onto one side and LONG LIVE POPULAR RULE! on the other. They had also returned the St. Andrew's flag to the foremast to reinforce that they were not lawless marauders.

In a stateroom, Kirill made the last revisions to one of two declarations that the sailor committee had mandated. Feldmann worked on the other. When finished, the two Odessans returned to the wardroom where the ship's leaders had spent the day. Kirill read his handwritten pages:

To the Whole Civilized World — Citizens of all lands and of all nationalities.

The grand spectacle of a great war for freedom is taking place before your eyes; the oppressed and enslaved Russian people have thrown off the yoke of despotic autocracy. The ruin, poverty, and anarchy, which the Government has brought long-suffering Russia, have exhausted the patience of the working people. In every town and hamlet, the fire of the people's fury and indignation has flamed up.

The mighty cry from millions of Russian breasts, "AWAY WITH THE SHACKLES OF DESPOTISM AND LONG LIVE LIB-ERTY!" rolls like thunder over the boundless plains of Russia. But the Tsar's Government has decreed it better to drown the country in the people's blood than to grant the people's freedom.

But the Government has forgotten one thing — that the Army — the powerful weapon the Tsar uses for his bloody designs — is made up of the same people, the sons of the very same workers, who have sworn to win their freedom.

Thus do we, the crew of the battleship *Prince Potemkin-Tavrichesky,* resolutely and unanimously take this first great step. May all those peasants and workers, our brothers, who have fallen in the fields of our fatherland by the bullets and bayonets of the sol-diers, release us from their curse now! We are not their murderers. We are not the butchers of our own people. We are their defenders, and our common cry is — "Death or Liberty to the People!" We demand the immediate end to bloodshed in faraway Manchuria. We demand the immediate convocation of a constituent assembly through direct elections. For these demands we are all prepared to fight, and to perish with our ship, or to attain victory.

We are certain that honest citizens of all nations and countries will sympathize with our great struggle for freedom. Down with autocracy! Long live the constituent assembly.

The sailors applauded his words. As committee member Kulik said, the declaration showed that "We are not pirates." Feldmann then stood, delivering his address to "All European Monarchs," a short statement that guaranteed the security of foreign vessels on the Black Sea. The committee approved both declarations, and a sailor was sent to type a number of leaflets of each. Then, finally, the meeting broke up.

At 4 P.M., the *Potemkin* passed Serpent Island, twenty miles from the coast. The small, rocky island looked fit only for a grave-yard. Soon after, the sailors saw Romanian shores. When they neared Constanza, Matyushenko and Kovalenko joined several others on the bridge. Constructed on a low promontory jutting a half-mile into the Black Sea, the city was Romania's main seaport. Named after his sister by the Roman emperor Constantine the Great in the fourth century, the town, originally called Tomi, was first founded, so legend had it, by King Aeetes of Colchis, as a burial place for his son Absyrtus. Aeetes' daughter Medea had hacked her young brother to death and scattered the pieces on the road, to slow the king in his pursuit of her, Jason, and the Golden Fleece. She had known that he would stop to gather up the pieces.

As the *Potemkin* came closer, the sailors spotted an old lighthouse on the cape, and then a cathedral tower farther inland. Constanza took shape when, seemingly from nowhere, a fog rolled across the sea, completely obscuring the city. "A bad sign," a sailor said, half joking, on the bridge. A few minutes later, the wind swept away the fog, and the city appeared again. Respecting international custom for arrivals to a foreign shore, Matyushenko ordered a twenty-one-gun salute. The guns boomed. When the echo faded away, the crew looked to starboard, waiting to see how they would be welcomed. Their mutiny's fate depended on it.

# 19

WITHIN MINUTES of dropping anchor, the *Potemkin* attracted a throng of gawkers on Constanza's seafront. The presence of a colossal battleship on their waters was intriguing — "was it that mutinous Russian battleship?" While the city's residents wondered about this, a cutter flying the Romanian flag left the port. It headed straight toward the *Potemkin*.

"Guard, attention!" Kovalenko yelled as the boat neared the battleship. On the quarterdeck, an honor guard of thirty sailors dressed in fresh uniforms formed two lines to welcome the Romanian officers. Aiming to earn their support and esteem, the crew planned on showing the Romanians every courtesy.

When Captain Nikolai Negru, Constanza's port commander, and a lieutenant from the Romanian cruiser *Elizaveta* ascended to the deck, the honor guard saluted. Negru returned the salute, and the rest of the sailors waved their caps in welcome. Kovalenko and Matyushenko then stepped forward to greet the officers.

"Where's your watch officer?" Negru asked stiffly, in French, observing that neither of the two men bore any indication of their rank.

"We have none," Kovalenko responded.

"Please take me to your commander then."

"We've no commander either."

"Why not?" Negru asked, with a look of surprise.

"Are you aware of the events in Odessa?" Kovalenko asked.

Negru shook his head, even though he knew about the mutiny

from the Romanian newspapers and had been notified earlier that day
by the Russian captain N. N. Banov, whose transport ship *Psezuape*
was docked in the harbor, that the *Potemkin* had left Odessa. (The
Russian ambassador in Bucharest had warned Banov that the
*Potemkin* might sail for Romania.) Negru feigned ignorance to stall
the *Potemkin* while he waited to hear from his superiors as to what he
should do.

Kovalenko and Matyushenko led the captain and lieutenant into
the admiral's stateroom, where ten other committee members had
assembled, as well as a sailor who spoke Romanian. After briefly
recounting their mutiny and their revolutionary ambitions, Matyushenko handed Negru a list of requisitions: four hundred tons of
coal, two hundred kilograms of machine oil, two hundred liters of
wine, a head of cattle, three days' supply of bread and fresh water for
eight hundred men, forty kilograms of tobacco, and fifteen kilograms
of cigarette rolling paper. "Most of all," he said, "the crew needs food
and water."

"I have to ask Bucharest for permission," Negru said. "I can't
allow it until I hear otherwise. Perhaps in a day I'll have your answer."

Another sailor asked the interpreter to tell Negru why they had
come to Romania: "Yours is a liberal country that wouldn't let them
starve if they observed international law and restricted using military
force." A note of desperation colored his voice, a feeling shared by the
others.

"What will you do if you're refused?" Negru then asked.

"We don't know what we'll do," Matyushenko said — honestly.
"But no matter what, we'll return to Russia to launch the revolution.
Other battleships will follow our example."

Negru looked at the sailors around him, impressed by their resolve, especially given their situation. The Russian government would
not stop until they found the *Potemkin* and punished its sailors. Still,
Negru's job was to make sure the battleship did not attack the port to
get what it wanted, which he knew it could easily do. He had limited
artillery on shore, and the *Elizaveta* was the only Romanian warship
in the area. It could provide little resistance against a battleship like
the *Potemkin*.

The captain told Matyushenko he would forward their request. In the meantime, a small deputation could enter Constanza and order the provisions they needed in case his superiors allowed their delivery. "But," he said earnestly, "the best thing for you to do is to come ashore. Surrender the battleship. Then you'll be free and able to go where you wish."

The sailors dismissed this suggestion, and Negru left the battleship. As his cutter returned to the port, the *Potemkin* fired another salute from its guns.

The ship's leaders appreciated the respect that Negru had shown the sailors, and they conveyed this to the crew. But his refusal to allow them to purchase provisions without Bucharest's approval distressed the sailors. "They want to conspire with the tsar over telegraph," some warned. "They want to starve us to surrender," others predicted.

While a handful of sailors prepared to go ashore to meet with the city's merchants, a military sloop from the *Psezuape* approached the *Potemkin*. "Officer coming!" a lookout yelled. "A Russian officer's coming!"

"Don't make any noise, comrades," Matyushenko cautioned, knowing the transport ship was under Romanian protection while in their waters. "Let him come. We'll see if he's worthy."

"Put him under arrest!" a sailor recommended. "Pluck his epaulettes from his shoulders."

Minutes later, Captain Banov, a short, corpulent officer in full dress uniform, came aboard. He assumed that the mutinous battleship had come to surrender, since the St. Andrew's Cross flew from the foremast and the sailors had fired a salute on entering the port. Feldmann approached him, asking what he wanted.

"How dare you speak to me like that!" Banov hissed. "Where's your commander?"

"This is the ship of the people, not of the Russian government," Kovalenko interjected. "You may have heard about us from the Romanian papers."

"I can't read Romanian." Banov backed away, realizing the mutineers had not surrendered.

"Our commander is at the bottom of the sea," Matyushenko pointed out.

"So . . . now . . . *brothers*," Banov stuttered, almost incapacitated with fear. "What are you going to do with me?"

"You can go," Kovalenko said. Banov hurried from the deck, wishing the sailors luck as they jeered at him.

After Banov skittered off the battleship, Matyushenko and several others took a launch to the port. Since Captain Negru had given them only an hour to arrange for provisions, they divided into several groups. While taking a horse-drawn carriage alone to one of the markets, Matyushenko suddenly found himself heading away from the city center. Suspecting an ambush like the one in Odessa, he told the driver to return to the port. When the driver refused, Matyushenko drew a revolver and threatened to shoot him. The cab stopped. Matyushenko stepped out, his revolver trained on the driver as he backed away. He then returned on foot toward the port, uncertain as to whether the driver had simply been confused or if he was part of a plot to capture him. Days of constant danger had put him on edge.

In the port, Matyushenko and the others waited a half-hour for Grigory Rakitin, one of the sailors in their group, to show up, but he never did. They suspected he had abandoned the *Potemkin*. Dusk had fallen over Constanza by the time they pushed away from the quay. The dark void to the east, on the Black Sea, threatened many dangers, including a rumor the sailors had heard in the city: a torpedo boat manned solely by officers, sent by Vice Admiral Chukhnin to sink the *Potemkin*.

On their return to the battleship, Matyushenko had the launch stop alongside the Romanian cruiser to ask its captain's permission to use the battleship's searchlights during the night. The *Elizaveta*'s officers invited Matyushenko to come aboard alone. The Romanians permitted the searchlights but then urged him to surrender the *Potemkin*, guaranteeing the crew's safety. Matyushenko declined. Then the captain made an unexpected offer to *buy* the battleship from the sailors. When the interpreter relayed his offer, Matyushenko drew back, insulted at the suggestion that he sell the people's battleship for a few rubles.

"We didn't come here to save our skins. They're worth only three kopecks at the bazaar," he answered, his tone laced with acid. "Before I sell you our ship, tell me, how much do you want for your

*Elizaveta?*" This response ended the conversation, and Matyushenko left the cruiser.

On the *Potemkin* later that night, as the searchlights panned for torpedo boats, the gunners rested beside their weapons while most of the crew sought shelter below. An approaching storm sent gusts of wind across the decks, and the sea grew rougher by the hour. Kovalenko walked the rolling quarterdeck, looking at the silhouettes of Constanza's houses and churches. Faintly, he heard music playing. He imagined the local people under the twinkling lights of their terraces, talking about the *Potemkin*. He wondered what they really thought of the sailors who had come to their shore in the name of revolution.

Throughout the ship, crew members talked worriedly about whether or not the Romanians would provide supplies. For several days now, they had subsisted on soup made from cabbage and potatoes. The bread was almost gone too, and in a couple of days, only tea and sugar would be left. They were also desperate for more coal — always more coal. Before midnight, Matyushenko received a note from the port commander: he would have a response from Bucharest by 8 A.M. the next day.

In Constanza, Captain Negru waited nervously for a telegraph from his foreign minister. The *Potemkin* sailor Rakitin, who had jumped ship, had reported to Negru that the crew was divided, and two to three hundred men were ready to abandon the battleship as soon as they had the chance. Despite this information, the captain had seen for himself the conviction of the mutiny's leaders and their hold over the sailors; he doubted they would abandon their cause. Therefore, he had to anticipate the worst for his already panicked city. Although he planned to tow the Russian *Psezuape* to a secluded section of the port, prepare the *Elizaveta* for attack, and conceal artillery units along the coastline, these efforts amounted to mere gestures if the *Potemkin* sailors chose to take the supplies they wanted by force — or punish Constanza for not providing them.

Out in the darkness of the Black Sea, hundreds of miles from the Romanian coast, the destroyer *Stremitelny* sped across the water at eighteen knots. Lieutenant Yanovich had directed the destroyer toward

Odessa, hoping to pick up the *Potemkin*'s trail from its last known location. With his sharp features and narrow head, the young officer on the foredeck had the look of a hatchet, an impression reinforced by his fanatical personality.

The day before, he had received approval for his plan to hunt down the mutinous battleship, and he had wasted no time in relieving Captain Second Class Konstantinov from his command of the destroyer. An hour later, the twenty officers, mostly lieutenants and ensigns Yanovich had recruited for the mission, came aboard, along with thirteen sailors (primarily stokers and machinists to operate the engines). Under typical circumstances, four officers would have overseen fifty-two sailors on the destroyer. But this was far from a typical voyage. To maintain secrecy, the *Stremitelny* steamed out of Sevastopol without the customary signaling to the flagship. Since then, the destroyer had stopped only once to take on a few more crew members from a torpedo boat.

At 2 A.M. on June 20, Yanovich observed the lights of a ship through his binoculars. The destroyer slowly approached, battle ready, but discovered only the training ship *Prut* heading back toward Sevastopol. Yanovich directed his searchlights across the *Prut*'s bridge and saw an officer, presumably the one on duty.

"Have you seen the *Potemkin*?" he signaled by semaphore, ignorant of the *Prut* mutiny and the fact that the officer on its bridge was following the orders of the mutineers. If he had, Yanovich would have no doubt already sent a pair of torpedoes into its waterline.

"No," the *Prut* answered. "Is everything all right?"

"Everything's fine," Yanovich returned, fooled by the officer's presence. He then resumed course to Odessa. An hour later, the *Prut* was less fortunate; the torpedo boat *Zhutky* came across the training ship, this time with a captain informed of the mutiny. He took the *Prut* under guard and led it to Nikolayev, depriving Yanovich of his first capture.

At first light outside Odessa, the *Stremitelny* came across the British steamer *Cranby,* which had been charged by the British consulate to remove English expatriates from the city after the recent violence. Yanovich ordered the steamer to return to the port so he could see if any revolutionary refugees were hidden on board. When the *Cranby*'s captain hesitated, Yanovich ordered his gunners to fire a shot across the steamer's bow, showing his willingness to attack if resisted (as well as his disdain for niceties of international relations). The *Cranby* wisely turned toward the harbor, with the *Stremitelny*'s guns trained on it. Nobody suspicious was found aboard.

In Odessa, Yanovich soon learned from Captain Boisman, who had been sent there by Chukhnin to arrange for the mutineers' punishment, that the *Potemkin* had gone to Constanza. News of its arrival in a foreign port had spread around the Black Sea as quickly as the telegraph wires could carry it.

While Yanovich prepared to leave Odessa for the next stage of the chase, his second officer informed him that the valves on the torpedoes had been bent, an obvious act of sabotage. Enraged at this discovery, Yanovich discharged torpedo quartermaster I. Babenko and several other sailors, even though he had no proof of their involvement. Despite having officers stationed throughout the ship, outnumbering the few sailors by two to one, the crew *still* could not be trusted. While repairs were carried out, the *Stremitelny* was obliged to anchor in Odessa. Yanovich prodded his engineers to hurry. He planned to reach Constanza and engage the *Potemkin* within half a day.

In the throne room of the Grand Palace at Peterhof, Count V. F. Dorrer and six other nobles from the Kursk province were led across the intricately patterned parquet floor to an audience with Nicholas II. The hall, with a high, lily-white ceiling decorated with stucco reliefs of garlands and roses and a row of gold and crystal chandeliers, bespoke the tsar's power, an autocracy to which these nobles now came to pledge their devotion. Along with other monarchists who had created the Union of Russian Men to oppose the liberal nobles who sought a constitutional government, Dorrer recognized that many problems afflicted the empire. But he believed strongly that placing any limits on the autocracy guaranteed Russia's ruin. Instead, as the count politely advised Nicholas that morning, he felt that an election of landed nobles (of which he was one) to form a consultative assembly would help restore the connection between the tsar and his people.

Sitting in a gilded oak throne raised on a small dais, Nicholas was touched by the delegation's sentiments of loyalty. But he likely paid little attention to their words: as tsar, his role was to remain above partisan bickering and self-interest. He alone should decide what Russia needed, uninfluenced by others, no matter how fervently they might make their case. Anyway, his thoughts were elsewhere; he was too distracted by the mutiny on the Black Sea.

The *Potemkin*'s arrival in Constanza the night before had heightened his distress. Having failed to control the situation while they had the chance, his admirals deserved to be punished alongside the sailors. On the telegram informing Nicholas of the situation aboard *Prut,* he handwrote, "Krieger must be sternly reprimanded in my name for the intolerable discipline within his division."

For nearly a week, Nicholas's representatives had downplayed the *Potemkin* uprising to foreign governments, calling it an insignificant aberration incited by the crew's wanton drunkenness. These spokesmen promised that the mutiny would be easily suppressed. Yet almost a week later, the battleship was still on the loose, and other ships had rebelled as well. With the *Potemkin* imperiling Romania, Turkey reinforcing its batteries on the Bosphorus Strait, and Britain contemplating abrogating the Treaty of Paris in order to send warships to the Black Sea to end the threat, Nicholas knew he looked weak. Talk that the army might join the mutiny, unrealistic though he believed it to be, only debilitated him further.

Privately, his closest advisers mirrored the same concern. The Russian ambassador in London, Count Aleksandr Beckendorf, wrote the following to his foreign minister, Vladimir Lambsdorf:

> The *Potemkin* uprising has delivered a significant moral strike against the prestige of the autocracy. About recent sad events in Russia, I have to point out that none of them, even our military failures, have made more distressing an impression on public opinion, and I believe, on the British government, than events in Odessa and the uprising on the *Potemkin*. For the first time, I clearly see that a question has arisen seriously here, whether the revolution that broke out in Russia threatens the stability of the government's existence.

With the Japanese poised to invade Russian territory for the first time in the war, at Sakhalin Island, and with the fragility of his rule at home revealed by the mutiny, Nicholas reconsidered pursuing peace.

His war minister, Sakharov, responding by letter to the tsar's recent request for opinions from his inner circle on whether to proceed with the war, advised, "Under the present conditions to conclude peace is impossible, because one cannot admit that Russia should confess herself beaten by Japan." His other generals agreed. Yet the minister of finance, Vladimir Kokovtsov, braved a contrary view: "I feel compelled to admit the continuation of the campaign — things being in the condition they are in the war theater and more particularly in the interior of the country — appears extremely difficult, and conclusion of peace is, from the financial point of view, extremely desirable."

Nicholas was finally leaning toward this view as well. On June 19, he had informed the American ambassador, Meyer, that his plenipotentiaries, led by Muravyev, would be invested with full powers to negotiate peace, and that he had also decided to dismiss Sakharov. Nonetheless, Nicholas had yet to settle the issue definitively. Privately he still considered backing away from the talks altogether; but if the Black Sea mutiny dragged on and the Japanese took Sakhalin, he might have no choice but to end the war.

Oppressed by these troubles, Nicholas could be excused for the spare attention he paid to Dorrer and the other Kursk nobles. As with most audiences, he had received his guests as a courtesy, merely to alleviate their concerns. Before the meeting ended, Nicholas indicated that he agreed with their proposal, though he did so in vague terms and absent any commitments. He then concluded, "A state is only powerful and sound that keeps sacred the precepts of the past. We ourselves have sinned against this and God may be punishing us for that. . . . I am convinced that you all, and each in his sphere, will help *me* restore peace and quiet in our land and thereby will render *me* the service that I expect from all *my* loyal subjects."

Nicholas's apparent calm in the midst of the storm was typical of him. In public he rarely showed his emotions or revealed the true nature of his thinking. But in his diary entry later that day, he expressed how troubled he was. "The devil only knows what is happening in the Black Sea Fleet. Three days ago, the crew of the *St. George* joined the *Potemkin* but soon came to its senses and asked the commander and officers to come back, and, after confessing, surrendered fifty-seven mutineers. The *Potemkin* appeared at Constanza in Romania. Aboard the *Prut* there was some unrest that stopped upon arrival in

Sevastopol. If only the rest of the crews of the squadron would stay loyal!"

The longer the *Potemkin* sailors endured, the deeper Nicholas would feel this despair.

At 7:30 A.M. on June 20 in Constanza, the winds and restless seas forced the *Ismail* to take refuge in the harbor. As the torpedo boat entered the calmer waters, the Romanian cruiser fired two shots, one a blank, the other with explosive charge, ahead of the *Ismail,* to warn it off. It turned back and anchored next to the *Potemkin* again, a grim omen for the sailors waiting for Bucharest's answer.

Two hours later, Matyushenko and four committee members boarded a launch to receive their promised answer. Captain Negru had visited the battleship at dawn, once again trying to convince the crew to leave the *Potemkin,* even though he had yet to hear from his superiors. The sailors refused, holding out for the possibility that King Carol would allow them to resupply their battleship.

In the port, Matyushenko stepped onto the quay, where Negru was waiting with a translator by his side. "I've received instructions from Bucharest. Very favorable ones for you — if you surrender," Negru said. Then he explained that he could not, however, by his foreign minister's order, allow them to buy any coal or provisions.

Matyushenko demanded to see the original telegram, too astonished to believe the rejection. They had followed every protocol. They had not shown any belligerence toward the Romanians. They had rubles to pay for the goods. And still they were denied.

Negru handed over the document and then read for Matyushenko the surrender terms the port commander was instructed to offer: "Try to persuade the Russian sailors our government will recognize them as foreign deserters and consequently they will be allowed to go free if they leave the ship. As soon as they accept these conditions, they will have permission to go to Bulgaria or any destination by passenger steamship. After this, I ask you to post a military guard on the *Potemkin* and to assist the sailors to buy provisions for themselves."

Matyushenko coldly asked the translator to write out the telegram in Russian. Then he told Negru that he would return with an answer once he had presented the proposal to the crew. Before Matyushenko's delegation left, Negru pressed the sailors to quit the battleship, arguing that it was their sole chance at survival. Matyushenko walked away.

On the *Potemkin,* Koshuba interrupted Matyushenko halfway into his reading of the telegram. "Are we really being asked to accept this?"

"We need bread and meat," a sailor yelled, unseen among the crew.

Matyushenko silenced the men and finished the proposal. Few believed the Romanians would honor their terms. "This is a fraud. They'll seize us and turn us over to the tsar," a crew member predicted, to a rousing chorus of agreement.

"So, you don't want to surrender, do you?" Matyushenko asked.

"To Russia!" the crew cried out. "To Russia!"

As these shouts died down, the ship's leaders left for the wardroom to plan where to take the *Potemkin* next. They would not seize provisions by force in a foreign land whose safety they had guaranteed in their proclamations. Nonetheless, they were desperate for coal, fresh water, and food. They urgently needed to find a place that had these supplies in ample amounts. A sailor brought in a Black Sea chart and spread it across the table. At first, Kirill suggested they return to Odessa, given its many coal barges, but Feldmann countered that Kakhanov would now have the city completely defended.

"How about Poti?" Kirill then offered. "We could seize a Turkish coal ship en route to Constantinople."

Again he was rebutted. The sailors would not resort to piracy. Then Denisenko proposed Batumi in southwest Georgia, where revolutionaries, including a young Iosif Dzhugashvili (later known as Josef Stalin), had launched several uprisings in the past few months, but this idea was dismissed because the city's fortress was armed with enough artillery to destroy the *Potemkin.*

Then Feldmann drew his finger across the map, stopping on Theodosia, a port on the Crimean coast. Theodosia was a railroad hub, unprotected by a fortress and close to the Caucasus, where they might want to go afterward to spread revolution. This, he believed, was where they stood the best chance of obtaining supplies so they could continue their revolt. Further, its proximity to Sevastopol improved their chances of getting information about the squadron's movement. The sailors began to favor this suggestion when Ensign Alekseyev broke into the conversation.

"You don't know anything, but still you interfere," he spat at

Feldmann. "My advice is to go to Evpatoriia. . . . It's the only place where we can get coal."

"You want to go there *only* because it's close to Sevastopol. Am I right?" Feldmann asked, knowing that Evpatoria was a small town with little trade apart from sheep.

"We're going to Theodosia," the committee concluded.

Kirill and two sailors went to the port to tell Negru of their decision to leave. He also delivered copies of the two proclamations they had written. When Negru asked where they planned to go, Kirill lied. "Turkey," he said, to throw pursuers off their trail. "We hope the Ottoman sultan will welcome us more cordially than the European king." Negru promised to send their proclamations to the city's foreign consuls.

On the *Potemkin,* Matyushenko mustered the crew to win their approval to travel to Theodosia. Over the past two hours, the sailors had grown less sure about leaving Romania. Most knew about the desperate state of their supplies, and many had wearied of the struggle. Resisting this sentiment, Matyushenko rallied the sailors, his speech punctuated by the electrifying movements of his body, as if he felt every word he spoke. Then he concluded his speech: "Every country has its laws, its customs, but there's one feeling that all nations hold sacred — the feeling of responsibility to one's own country. Now, brothers, think a little about how the Romanian people will feel toward you if they see you betray your country — that when you might have saved your homeland from tyrants, you basely surrendered to save your skins."

Once again, he won over the crew. While the sailors readied the battleship for the journey to Theodosia, Captain Negru came aboard to convince them of the futility of their plans. "The cause you fight for is impossible to win with only a single ironclad," he reasoned. "The rest of the Black Sea Fleet hasn't joined you, so what can you hope for in Russian waters?"

"What we mustn't do is to lose hope in our success," Kovalenko said plainly. Then he ushered Negru off the battleship.

When he returned to the port, Captain Negru sealed in an envelope the sailor proclamations that he had promised to deliver to the consuls. He planned to forward them directly to his superiors in Bucharest. Although he admired the sailors for their bravery and for

their noble restraint in not attacking his city — telling the foreign minister as much — he dared not embroil Romania in a conflict with the
tsar of Russia by distributing the proclamations.

At 1:20 P.M., the *Potemkin* steamed away from Constanza, charting
first a course toward Constantinople, knowing well that Captain Banov
would telegraph their direction to Sevastopol. Even before the crew
lost sight of land, however, their initial excitement at returning to Russia was replaced by a feeling of isolation. Nothing but empty miles of
sea lay ahead, except for the promise of meager rations and little rest
under the blistering sun. All for the dim hope that they might find in
Theodosia the help they needed. The freedom they once enjoyed on
the open waters felt now more like a curse.

# 20

ESPITE THE OFFER of political protection, the sailors refused to surrender their weapons and hand over the battleship to authorities. . . . The *Potemkin* has left the port, heading southeast."

Chukhnin read the secret telegram from Romania only a few hours after his train arrived at Sevastopol on the morning of June 20. The news ruled out any chance of the *Stremitelny* making a quick capture of the battleship in Constanza. But with the *Potemkin* on the run, low on coal and food, and with Bulgaria, Romania, and Turkey all having agreed not to aid the sailors, the rebels' ability to sustain their mutiny was growing weaker by the hour. Soon they would be seized or sunk — whether at sea or in a Russian port. Chukhnin's preparations for the mutineers' trial and punishment, in accordance with the tsar's orders, no longer looked so premature. He had already selected a pier in Odessa for their execution — to be conducted, on his orders, in front of the squadron. A hangman and coffins were being arranged. Only the issue of where they would be buried remained unanswered, but state property around Peresyp was likely the best option.

Equally pressing on the vice admiral's mind was the state of insurrection among Sevastopol's sailors. His spies had already learned of a revolutionary plan to break into the base's armory, man the rest of the fleet, and join the *Potemkin*. Chukhnin struck preemptively that very morning. Over two thousand sailors were brought to the fleet's main yard for, they were told, a parade to celebrate Chukhnin's return from St. Petersburg. While the sailors waited, gendarmes locked the gates to the yard. Meanwhile, the officers removed every weapon from the armory and secured them outside the base.

That afternoon, Chukhnin resolved to speak to the battleship crews that had returned from Odessa. As in Nikolayev, he believed if he reasoned with the sailors, they would see the evils of mutiny and resist the "deceptions" cast by the revolutionaries. Before he departed for the *Rostislav*, his staff attempted to dissuade him from going.

"The crews despise you," one of his officers dared say. "You're putting yourself in danger."

"I'm performing my duty," Chukhnin replied. "I have to see in person the fleet's condition. Whether something happens to me today rather than tomorrow is all the same to me."

On the deck of each ship, surrounded by guards, the vice admiral spoke as though he had nothing to fear. He delivered his patriotic defense of autocracy, and the crews responded with pledges of obedience. During one speech, some sailors were even moved to tears by Chucknin's call to honor duty and country. Nevertheless, Chukhnin had seen enough of mutiny to reinforce his words with action.

He brought in additional troops from Odessa to guard the fortress against rebellion. Nearly one thousand sailors were arrested, many with only tenuous ties to revolutionary groups — or none at all — and imprisoned in the fortress. After quickly running out of cells there, Chukhnin established a floating prison aboard the *Prut* — a symbolic move that was not lost on many. He also ordered that a couple of thousand reservists be sent away from Sevastopol on leave.

The next morning, June 21, when the *Sinop*'s crew was on the verge of revolt following the arrest of a number of sailors, Chukhnin had the ship surrounded with several battleships and sent an infantry unit aboard with orders to randomly execute every tenth man unless the crew gave up the instigators. They named sixteen men straight away, and the revolt died down.

If Lieutenant Yanovich showed the same kind of decisiveness when he met the *Potemkin*, the ship, the threat it posed, and its role as the last rallying point for rebellious sailors in Sevastopol would be eliminated. Delayed by repairs in Odessa, the *Stremitelny* reached Constanza long after the *Potemkin* had left. The destroyer's entry in the harbor prompted a Romanian cruiser to fire a warning shot across its bow, not to mention a maelstrom of diplomatic complaints from Bucharest at the surprise presence of another Russian ship in Romanian waters. Undeterred, Chukhnin redirected the *Stremitelny* toward the large Bulgarian port of Varna where the mutineers might travel to resupply — they had to be running low on coal. The naval command dismissed the report that the battleship was destined for Constantinople; they suspected this was a ploy to deceive their pursuers. Until the *Potemkin* was sighted, however, Chukhnin could only guess at its destination and hope the destroyer would soon be near enough to stop it. After two fruitless days at sea, Yanovich was also eager for this opportunity.

While naval officials in Sevastopol and St. Petersburg speculated on the *Potemkin*'s next move, the Ministry of the Interior finally released news to the public about the mutiny through its mouthpiece, *The Official Messenger*. "A regrettably shameful event, and one without parallel in the annals of the Russian navy" was the author's preface to the government account, before describing the mutiny in a dry, matter-of-fact way. According to this source, the sailors took over the battleship because of some bad meat and then mercilessly killed their officers before traveling to Odessa. Thirty individuals in civilian clothing were in charge of the *Potemkin,* and they had ordered a barrage on the city without provocation. Brief mention was made of the *St. George* and *Prut* mutinies, merely in terms of how expeditiously the rebellions were suppressed. The thousand-word chronicle, published to minimize the *Potemkin*'s effect on the populace, was extraordinary for what it did not mention: the fires, the riots, and the many dead in Odessa; the revolutionary declarations made by the sailors; the absolute disarray of Chukhnin's fleet; and the fact that the battleship now roamed the Black Sea at will. No Russian newspaper had yet been allowed to publish a story on the *Potemkin,* and government censors promised to remain strict and vigilant on how these details — and their significance — would be revealed in the days that followed.

The foreign press offered no such hesitancy, and Black Sea events dominated front pages and editorial sections around the world, featuring dramatic reading for the seventh straight day. On June 21 the headlines proclaimed: "Rebels Defiant: *Knyaz Potemkin* Sails Once More" (*Manchester Guardian*); "Mutiny Rules in Russia" (*Chicago*

*Daily Tribune*); "The Tsar Without a Fleet" (*Vorwärts*), "Will Try to Torpedo Rebel Battleship" (*Los Angeles Times*). European and American newspapers provided exhaustive reports, detailing how a revolutionary committee ran the *Potemkin,* the cowardly manner in which Krieger retreated to Sevastopol, the mutinous battleship's refusal to surrender in Constanza, the *Stremitelny*'s hunt, fears in Odessa that the *Potemkin* would circle back to wreak more damage on the city, and how, according to the London *Times,* "the government of the Tsar is stooping to beg the Sultan of Turkey and the King of Romania to be good enough to do for him the police work which he is no longer able to do for himself."

Running side by side with these articles were stories about the Japanese threat to Sakhalin Island, the thousands of workers who had gone on strike in St. Petersburg, and Nicholas II's hastening approach to the negotiating table. To the average newspaper reader, Russia appeared on the brink of collapse and the *Potemkin* looked to be pushing it over the edge.

On the other hand, international public opinion had made a notable turn against the sailors. In the first reports of the uprising, the sailors' actions were framed in relation to their atrocious treatment and living conditions, and, more important, the necessity for substantive political reform to prevent revolution. Over the past few days, however, except in socialist journals such as *L'Humanité,* which viewed the sailors as heroes, the *Potemkin* crew suffered many scathing attacks. "They are practically pirates, and their predicament only offers limited avenues for escape," the *Chicago Daily Tribune* opined. "Their situation being desperate, a desperate course may well be expected of them." The editorial page was similarly harsh, impugning everything from the crew's intelligence to their navigational abilities. It concluded, "They ran their necks into the halter for no particular purpose, unless it was to kill some harsh officers and have a few days of unbounded freedom and vodka."

This was one of many newspapers that replaced the term *mutineers* with *pirates* and *criminals* to denote the sailors. The *New York Times* argued that the sailors should be hanged for their dearth of patriotism. Its competitor, the *New York Herald Tribune,* warned of what could happen if a mutinous fleet was to prey on the civilized world. The London *Times* ran an article on the Russian navy dominated by an interview with a tsarist officer, who likened commanding one of its battleships to "coming into a cage of wild beasts." In *Le Figaro,* an editorial pilloried the sailors: "They were willing to do anything, except to do their duty! It is not good either for Russia or for civilization that the question be put — like an absurd and brutal dilemma — between absolutism and anarchy."

International political leaders shared this disdain for the sailors. Although the *Potemkin*'s crew opposed a regime these leaders thought corrupt, the tsar was considered the lesser evil when compared to a battleship whose very presence in Odessa had wrought the chaos and destruction they feared most from revolutionaries. In addition, mutiny, by its very nature, was anathema to any government. A successful mutiny would only prove to be a dangerous example. The Romanians had already tried to win the battleship's surrender by refusing aid to the sailors — putting Constanza at tremendous risk. The Bulgarians promised to do the same, and the Turkish sultan was prepared to use his navy and land-based artillery against the *Potemkin* if it came into the Bosphorus Strait. Worried that his military might follow suit, he had instituted strict censorship on the mutiny in Turkish newspapers.

Notwithstanding the British Parliament's debate over sending warships into the Black Sea, powers outside the region could not interfere directly to stop the *Potemkin.* Instead they endeavored to eliminate what they believed was the cause of not only the mutiny but also Russia's surge of unrest: the war with Japan. Almost daily, President Roosevelt cabled Paris, Vienna, Berlin, and London, requesting assistance in convincing the tsar to pursue peace vigorously so he could better deal with his domestic crisis. George Meyer, the American ambassador in St. Petersburg, alerted Roosevelt of the urgency in a letter written on June 20: "Heretofore, I have thought Revolution improbable, but the events of last week (the increasing strikes, the disturbances at Lodz, the Marines revolting at Libau, the successful mutiny at Odessa, which resulted in the officers being killed and the vessel, *Potemkin,* captured) have entirely changed the aspect of affairs."

Even the Japanese, who had the most to gain from a tsar hobbled by mutiny, sympathized with Nicholas rather than with the sailors. A Japanese official told the newspaper *Jiji Shimpo,* "We have lately heard that a mutinous spirit was rife among the Russian troops. This, combined with the disgrace of the Black Sea, makes us fear that the

Russian government might be overthrown. . . . Then we should have nobody with whom to negotiate. It is sincerely to be hoped, both for the sake of Russia and Japan, that the trouble will end soon."

With worldwide political and public opinion leveled against the *Potemkin* sailors, with Russian liberals disavowing their actions, with additional Black Sea Fleet mutinies disbanded, and with Chukhnin marshaling resistance against the battleship throughout the region, the crew had only their exiled revolutionary leaders — men such as Lenin and Martov — to look to for assistance. These leaders were found wanting. Their representatives in major Russian cities printed leaflets referencing the mutiny, but they merely used the *Potemkin* to further their own propaganda. "The ironclad *Knyaz Potemkin* has raised our red revolutionary flag. . . . Comrades, now it's our turn. We must, we have to perform our duty in support of our Lodz, Warsaw and Odessa comrades. After Bloody Sunday, all of Russia pays careful attention to what is happening here," the Social Democrat's St. Petersburg committee proclaimed, in its effort to recruit workers to strike against mobilization.

In Geneva, the revolution's intellectual leaders busied themselves interpreting the *Potemkin*'s significance to their larger struggle against the tsar. But beyond Vasilyev-Yuzhin's improbable mission, which was arranged by Lenin, they were incapable of coordinating any help for the sailors in the various Russian ports to which the battleship might next travel.

Lenin did write a letter to the International Socialist Bureau, urging it to appeal to workers everywhere to protest against sending any European warships into the Black Sea to sink the *Potemkin*. Apart from that, he devoted his time and prodigious work ethic to the internecine conflict within the Social Democratic Party. Specifically, he issued a vindictive attack on a recent Menshevik conference for its lack of organization. Later that same day, Lenin ran across an editorial in the Paris newspaper *Le Matin* that chastised all Social Democrats for the same problem: "One cannot overstate the lack of organization of the revolution. The revolution gains possession of a battleship, an event unique in history, but it does not know what to do with it."

On the afternoon of June 21, the *Potemkin* and the *Ismail* steamed sluggishly across the Black Sea, their crews worn down by the heat and the lack of food. Nowhere was the situation worse than down in the *Potemkin*'s engine room. Day and night, the machinists and stokers were at the mercy of the humid, slack-choked air and constant noise while they kept the battleship running on its 370-mile journey to Theodosia, though at half its normal speed. Because of the lack of fresh water (the onboard distillery provided only enough for drinking), they used saltwater for the boilers, which corroded and clogged the pipes. Only a few boilers could be used at a time, so the sailors could clean the others. The walls were searing to the touch as the men crawled inside with rags and scouring brushes; their work merely delayed the inevitable ruin of the boilers.

When these sailors ascended from the engine room to the open decks, they could barely stand or speak. "We haven't the strength," one machinist gasped, in a report to the ship's leaders. "Our arms are weak. Every moment we feel we will drop." Still, they managed to keep the engines going, using their two- to three-day supply of coal sparingly.

The machinists and stokers found little cheer among the other sailors. A few sang songs or played cards to entertain themselves between watches, but the lightheartedness they had enjoyed on the voyage to Constanza was now gone. Eight days had passed since the men had eaten a proper meal, and the cooks were left with only four bags of dried bread and some porridge to feed them. Some sailors deserted their duties, and ensigns Alekseyev and Kaluzhny holed up in a stateroom; idleness allowed their fears to fester as they imagined dying in a squadron attack. The battleship's slow progress to Theodosia also cut at the crew's spirit. Many were terrorized by the thought of being caught on the open sea by their pursuers, namely, the rumored torpedo boat manned by officers. The previous night had been spent in complete darkness; the ship's searchlights were turned off so as not to give away the *Potemkin*'s position.

Alone on the Black Sea, with nothing but rolling waves in every direction, the sailors experienced a deep sense of isolation. On their first day in Odessa, they had been greeted like heroes by the workers, but since then, they had no contact with the people for whom they might sacrifice their lives to help. The flush of success they had felt when the *St. George* came to their side had been dashed by betrayal. This disappointment deepened as the sailors realized that a fleetwide mutiny was unlikely to occur. The flight to Romania had provided a glimmer of hope, but now it too had been extinguished.

While in Constanza, the crew still had two choices, as Feldmann later described it: "To surrender under the protection of the Romanian authorities or to enter on a war to the death with tsarism. We chose the latter." This irrevocable decision weighed heavily on every crew member during the two-day journey to Theodosia.

Preying on this collective feeling of doom, the petty officers quietly turned some sailors against the revolutionaries. They sowed doubts, telling the crew that the battleship needed repair or it would soon lose its fighting ability, making it an easy target to capture or — worse — to send to the bottom of the sea. At every opportunity and about every issue, whether cleaning the boilers or raising festive banners along the yardarm, they bitterly complained about Matyushenko and the ship's other leaders. When Kirill overheard two petty officers discussing how the tsar would show no mercy to the sailors, he threatened to have them thrown overboard, knowing how poisonous their talk had become. If the majority of the crew lost faith, the mutiny was finished.

Standing on the bridge, Matyushenko discounted the crew's troubled mood. In Constanza, they had clearly expressed that they would rather starve than relinquish the *Potemkin*, and the sailor committee had chosen their new course of action after an open debate. In the morning, the sailors had shown continuing resolve when they came across a Turkish coal ship. Although the *Potemkin*'s coal stock was dangerously depleted, they held true to their promise not to attack foreign vessels, letting the ship pass. Like Kovalenko, who often joined Matyushenko to observe the men, he was less inclined to see the crew's increasingly beleaguered appearance than he was to recall how eagerly they had congregated to hear the discussion at committee meetings or speakers such as Nikishkin discussing the revolution's goals.

That afternoon, machinist Denisenko, who had been laboring mightily to keep the engines running, came to the bridge to speak with his friend.

"What do you think of our chances?" Matyushenko asked, keen as always to talk about the fight ahead.

"When we arrive in Theodosia, it'll be clear enough," Denisenko said.

"I think we should go to Batumi next," Matyushenko replied. "We can land along the coast, and other comrade-revolutionaries will join us. There are lots of Armenians in the city, and many of them are socialist. We'll really go to it against the tsar, taking towns, one by one, until we reach St. Petersburg."

Denisenko protested that this plan was premature, but Matyushenko cut him off mid-argument, his face reddened and jaw clenched. It was obvious that he did not want to hear any doubts. In his view, their single battleship could still triumph over the tsar. He could not stand to believe otherwise.

Before the sun set that evening, the snowcapped mountains of the Caucasus came into view on the horizon. At a great distance, they seemed almost to float in the sky. The sailors stood mesmerized by the sight. Soon, however, the peaks vanished in the encroaching darkness, and feelings of isolation returned.

# 21

A T 8 A.M. on June 22, the *Potemkin* steamed toward the crescent-shaped Gulf of Theodosia, the red revolutionary flag flying stiffly in the wind. The gunners had removed the covers from the twelve-inch guns and had polished the long black barrels. Decorative flags hung from the fore and stern masts, and the decks and brasswork glistened. The sailors briskly attended to their duties, wearing their newest (or least soiled) uniforms. The ship's leaders wanted to present the best possible image to Theodosia: they were freedom fighters, not wayward rogues, as the tsar would have others believe. A mile out from the port's breakwater, the sailors dropped anchor.

Located on the southern Crimean coast, between Sevastopol and the Kerch Strait, the small trading town of Theodosia was a relic of former greatness. Set at the juncture of the Crimean mountains and the steppes, Theodosia ("gift of the gods") was founded by Greek traders in the sixth century B.C. to export grain. Over the next fifteen hundred years, the city shifted hands as often as the wind changed, controlled at one time or another by the Persians, the Romans, the Goths, the Huns, the Tatars, and the Byzantines. In the thirteenth century, the Genoese took over the port, constructing a stone fortress with tall defensive towers and renaming the city Kaffa. At its zenith as the seat of Genoese power in the Black Sea, hundreds of trading vessels, feluccas, and warships cruised in and out of Kaffa's harbor daily; dozens of languages were spoken in the streets; and merchants traded gold, silk, spices, pearls, caviar, Russian furs, and, most lucratively, slaves (over fifteen hundred a year). It was through Kaffa that the bubonic plague likely entered Europe from Asia in 1347. The Turks replaced the Genoese in 1475, and then, in the late eighteenth century, General Potemkin conquered the Crimea for Russia. The city's heyday came to an end when Catherine the Great focused on building Odessa, shifting the region's locus of power. She restored the port's former name but otherwise left Theodosia alone. It withered away. The *Potemkin* sailors saw the ruins of its once great fortress on their approach.

The crew lowered a launch, and Kirill, Koshuba, and Reznichenko went into the port, shadowed by the *Ismail,* to negotiate with city officials about purchasing coal and other provisions. Protected by a garrison of only five hundred soldiers without artillery, Theodosia could never withstand an attack from the battleship, but the crew wanted to use their guns only as a last resort. By the time the launch reached the port, hundreds of people had gathered on the quays. There had been rumors that the mutinous battleship might come there. Mounted police, with rifles at their side, directed their horses through the crowd but made no effort to disperse it. The three revolutionaries came ashore armed with revolvers — eager to make a show of strength.

Kirill walked straight to the nearest policeman and asked to speak with his commander. Moments later, a police captain came forward.

"We represent the crew of the revolutionary battleship *Potemkin,*" Kirill said, in a low voice. "We would like for city representatives to come to our ship immediately. In addition, we need a doctor. Finally, I must warn you, if you deny our demands or delay us in any way, we're quite prepared to destroy the city. We'll wait here for the representatives."

The police captain told Kirill he would inform the mayor. Then he disappeared into the crowd. An hour passed before Mayor L. A. Durante approached, accompanied by a clerk and a doctor. The mayor was as round and amiable as the clerk was reed-thin and stern. Kirill invited them out to the *Potemkin.*

"We're at your service," Durante said, politely, making his way toward the launch.

Kirill and the two sailors stayed ashore to speak to those on the quay. In his usual fervent manner, Kirill told the crowd of the mutiny: "We, sailors of the *Potemkin,* offer you our brothers' hands and are

willing, with the Russian people at our side, to battle the monarchy."
On hearing these treasonous words, the police attempted to scatter
the crowds. Kirill unholstered his revolver and threatened to signal for
the battleship's guns. The police retreated.

On the *Potemkin*, Matyushenko greeted Mayor Durante and his
companions on the quarterdeck before leading them to the admiral's stateroom, where the committee had convened. The doctor was
taken to the infirmary, where several sailors were suffering from a
stomach illness. In the stateroom Kovalenko spoke first, informing
the Theodosian officials that the *Potemkin* was fighting for Russia's
liberty and that it was "the duty of every citizen, of every public institution, to support us, by attracting the people's sympathy to our
side." Then Matyushenko stood. Everyone in the room was tense: the
mayor waited to hear what was expected of him, and the sailors wondered if these expectations would be met.

Matyushenko assured Durante that the sailors had no intention of
harming the city as long as he helped them. First, they needed to
purchase supplies — Matyushenko handed the mayor a list similar to
the one given to Captain Negru in Constanza. Second, he explained,
they wanted the mayor to convene a city council meeting attended
by the general public to inform Theodosia of the *Potemkin*'s aims.
Matyushenko then passed the mayor the proclamation "To All the
Civilized World," which Kirill had written.

Durante surprisingly said he would have their requests fulfilled
by 4 P.M. that same afternoon. The mood in the stateroom eased immediately; the sailors did not even question why their demands had
been agreed to so easily — unlike their experience in Odessa and
Constanza. Apparently, they so desperately needed and wanted this
answer that they refused to suspect that the mayor's promise would
not be fulfilled. Minutes later, Matyushenko led the city officials back
to the launch. Before boarding, the mayor turned back to the crew.
"Gentlemen, please have mercy on the city. I'm begging you."

Several sailors assured him they would. As the launch cast off, the
crew waved their caps goodbye and then broke for a lunch of bread
and a dram of vodka. With the promise of meat borscht for dinner
and replenished stores of coal and water, they felt hopeful for the first
time in days. Their long journey to Theodosia seemed worth the

effort, and, once they had their supplies on board, they would be free
to fight their revolution — though how to accomplish this, without
the rest of the Black Sea Fleet at their side, they had yet to resolve.

On his return to the port, Durante called an emergency city council
meeting to decide what to do about the *Potemkin*. Theodosians packed
the hall, spilling out into the streets, desperate to know what the
*Potemkin* sailors wanted and how the city's residents would be protected. The wealthy were already at the train station, arranging an escape to the countryside.

"Don't disgrace Theodosia," General F. Pleshkov, the garrison
commander, beseeched the council almost at once. "Do not accept
the demands of these rebels. You'll only raise their morale!"

As soon as the battleship was spotted on its way into the harbor,
Pleshkov had sent a stream of telegrams to Vice Admiral Chukhnin as
well as the provincial governor in Simferopol, Major General E. N.
Volkov. Volkov ordered the garrison commander to protect Theodosia's
government buildings and to use military force "energetically" to
crush any disorder. Yet he said nothing about whether to supply
the battleship with key provisions, such as coal and water. As for the
Black Sea Fleet commander, he had already sent orders around the
region to deny the *Potemkin* supplies, but he had not informed
Pleshkov how he would protect the city if they stuck to this course.
Volkov believed that supplying a mutinous battleship would go
against the vice admiral's order. Mayor Durante, on the other hand,
stated that the Black Sea Fleet commander had not yet informed either Pleshkov or the mayor as to how he intended to save their city.
Until he did so, the mayor had to act in the interest of the city in whatever way he thought best.

"Having just returned from the ironclad," Durante said, "I can
only give my vote in support of satisfying their demands." He recounted to the council how well he and the other visitors to the ship
had been treated and how the crew was far from the disorderly, riotous mob that they had been told to expect. Finally, he insisted that
bombardment was a grave danger, and he did not dare deny the sailors' requests. Applause followed his remarks.

"We've no moral duty to satisfy their demands. They're traitors," a
council member countered. Several workers whistled him down.

Although Pleshkov and the police chief, Colonel M. Zagoskin, suspected that Durante simply wanted to protect his vast real-estate holdings in the city, they failed to dissuade the council and, absent a specific order from the provincial governor to the contrary, the mayor had the votes to meet the *Potemkin*'s demands. Knowing this, Pleshkov pleaded with the council to deliver only food and medicine to the sailors. Until they heard back from Simferopol, he argued, they should not send coal or water. Reluctantly, the council approved this compromise.

Once the meeting disbanded, Durante returned to his office. As a barge was loaded with supplies, Durante telegrammed the provincial governor: "I was summoned to the battleship *Potemkin*. They demanded provisions and coal in a very modest amount. The city was threatened with bombardment if they were refused. They have been entreated by me not to come ashore, and promised they would not, if they received their supplies. The public wants their demands fulfilled. The city is in panic. The situation is dangerous. Request instructions. Because of the extreme situation and insistent public demands, need to send provisions."

At his headquarters, General Pleshkov impatiently waited for additional orders from Major General Volkov that would clarify that he was to reject *all* of the *Potemkin*'s demands, despite the consequences. With a limited garrison, a couple thousand workers who had already gone on strike in recent days, and several hundred court-martialed Russian soldiers held in the city's prison, the risks were substantial. The *Potemkin* could easily capture Theodosia — or, at the least, it could instigate the kind of uprising that Odessa had suffered. Nonetheless, Pleshkov despised the mayor's meekness and expected that his superiors would direct him to restrict any further assistance to the battleship, even under threat of attack.

Under the glare of the hot afternoon sun, the sailors congregated on the *Potemkin*'s forecastle after their tasteless lunch, for another round of speeches. Matyushenko mounted the capstan first to raise the crew's spirits after their turn of good fortune in Theodosia. In his hand he held a proclamation from St. Petersburg that Kirill had found while in the port. It promised that the tsar was using the sternest measures to crush their rebellion. Noting the proclamation, Matyushenko implored the crew to resist any attempts to end what was nothing less than a fight for all the Russian people. His words encouraged the crew, and Kirill and Koshuba followed with speeches of their own. Yet despite their efforts, they sensed fear and doubt among the sailors at a level nonexistent even in the mutiny's early days. It could not be dispelled by a few inspiring words.

At 3 P.M., a barge dropped anchor at the *Potemkin*'s side, finally bringing the provisions they had requested. The crew sprang into action, throwing open the hatchways, to take on board the much-needed supplies. A sailor hitched a rope to the windlass and lowered the noosed end under the front legs of one of the four oxen lowing on the barge. A signal was given, and the ox rose toward the main deck. Other crew members unloaded medicine, machine oil, and sacks of flour, bread, and potatoes as well as eggs, tea, sugar, a cage of ducks, and a barrel of wine. The men could almost taste their next meal. But coal and water were conspicuously absent.

Before they could ask whether these other supplies would arrive on a second barge, a sloop approached the *Potemkin*, carrying the tall clerk who had accompanied the mayor during his visit to the battleship. Beside him was a French photographer, who asked if he could take some pictures for his newspaper's readers. As the Frenchman toured the decks, snapping photographs of the men in bold poses at their stations, the clerk met with Matyushenko and Feldmann on the bridge. He explained that the garrison commander had argued against delivering coal and water — despite the mayor's best efforts. This arrangement was unacceptable, Matyushenko warned him. The clerk then explained that the provincial governor was expected to arrive in Theodosia before the day's end. He might possibly overrule General Pleshkov. Matyushenko dismissed the clerk from the battleship.

The sailor committee met briefly, electing to send Kirill and Reznichenko back to the port to convince the garrison commander of the danger of stonewalling. Before they left, a steamer entered the harbor. The *Potemkin* signaled it to come alongside.

"Have you heard anything from Russia?" a sailor asked the steamer's crew members. They were desperate for news from Sevastopol.

"Didn't you read the newspapers?" one answered.

"Not for a long time!"

A few minutes later a sailor on the steamer tossed across a bundle of international and Russian newspapers. A knife was quickly brought forward to cut the cord around the pile. The *Potemkin* crew devoured the news. The rumor they had heard in Constanza was confirmed: a destroyer, staffed completely by officers, was hunting them down. With false bravado, the sailors laughed off this desperate move by Chukhnin, despite having searched the horizon for the past several days, guns at the ready, for their pursuers. Also, the newspapers briefly mentioned a failed mutiny aboard the transport ship *Prut* and rumors of uprisings on the *Ekaterina II* and the *Sinop* as well. The possibility of further mutinies enlivened the crew, but only briefly. They then read a report about the *St. George*'s fate, detailing how sixty-seven men had been arrested after their fellow sailors had turned them in. Each faced a court-martial and likely a death sentence. This news, coming directly after the disappointing hedging from Theodosia's authorities, blackened the crew's mood even more.

Disturbed by these events, Kirill accompanied Reznichenko on an oar boat towed by a launch into the port. The small boat's bow occasionally dipped into a wave, soaking the sailors' pants and shoes. As they neared one of the quays, they released their boat from the launch so it could return to the *Potemkin,* in case the crew needed the launch for supply deliveries. Then Kirill and Reznichenko rowed to shore. More workers had crowded into the port since the morning, and this time a company of soldiers cut off the sailors as they stepped onto the quay.

"Don't let them pass," their officer ordered.

Stirred with anger, Kirill marched forward, stopping only when his chest touched the tip of a young soldier's bayonet. "Stab me!" he taunted.

The soldier stepped back, casting glances from Kirill to his commanding officer and back again, not sure what to do.

"Stab!" Kirill repeated, pushing against the blade point again, this time feeling the tip sharp against his chest. "I'm a mutineer! We believe the government and your superiors are evil. They rob us and they spill our blood. If you think this false, stab me now. I won't move."

The soldier finally lowered his rifle.

"If you really understand," Kirill said, "then stab your officer, who sends you like a dog to kill people that fight for a just cause."

A few moments passed. Nobody moved. Then the company commander ordered his soldiers to turn and march away, avoiding further confrontation.

Inspired by this success but still fuming, Kirill mounted the deck of a nearby ship and shouted to the stevedores unloading its cargo: "We're now fighting under the revolutionary flag. We will continue until our last breath. Let the people join us. Whoever is against us, let them go to the side of our enemies. It's the people who will share our victory. It's the people we will die to save.

The workers hollered their approval. But when Kirill and Reznichenko traveled into the town, General Pleshkov rebuffed their attempts to speak with him, turning them away from his headquarters. When they returned to the *Potemkin,* just before dusk, the sailor committee met. Everyone in the wardroom knew they were lost without coal and water. They would have to bombard the town if the provincial governor failed to bow to their demands. Kirill argued strenuously for taking this action. Matyushenko assented. Senior boatswain Murzak drafted an ultimatum to be delivered after midnight, giving Theodosia's authorities until 10 A.M. the following morning to send the supplies — or the *Potemkin* would open fire.

Once the ultimatum was typed, there was little to do but prepare the ship for the attack and wait. As the hours ticked past, the *Stremitelny* drew ever nearer to Theodosia.

Across the Black Sea, one hundred miles east of the Bulgarian coast, the destroyer was on the move again. Lieutenant Yanovich had started the day in Varna, where he had taken on more coal and had repairs made to the torpedo-launching mechanisms, which had been suspiciously damaged for the second time. At 4:45 A.M. he received a telegram from Vice Admiral Chukhnin, pressing him to find and sink the mutinous battleship. Before the *Stremitelny* left Varna an hour later, Yanovich learned from a Bulgarian merchant ship captain that the *Potemkin* was suspected to have been seen near Sevastopol. With this new information, Yanovich charted a course for the Crimea.

On the way, the destroyer stopped a British steamer and learned from its captain that the *Potemkin* was harbored in Theodosia. Finally Yanovich had a definite location. He and the other officers aboard the destroyer were grimly determined to accomplish their mission. They would pause briefly in Yalta, a short journey from their target, to bring on more coal. Given no delays and traveling at full steam to Theodosia, they would have the battleship in their sights by noon the next day, June 23.

But down in the engine room, the stoker, L. Pykhtin, aimed to stop Yanovich from so much as reaching the *Potemkin*. Social Democrats in Sevastopol had learned all about the *Stremitelny*'s mission before it left the naval base — the information came from the maid of the destroyer's former commander; she reported that he had come home after hearing of his dismissal, and he spoke of his distress. Pykhtin, a merchant sailor and revolutionary, worked for the chief mechanic of the steamer *Volga*, P. Kuzyayev. A former naval officer, Kuzyayev had volunteered to join Yanovich. Pykhtin asked his chief mechanic for a job on the *Stremitelny*. Nobody bothered to make a background check of the stoker, who had been fired from Sevastopol's port the year before for subversive activities. From the minute he came aboard, he plotted to sabotage the destroyer. With the help of the torpedo quartermaster Babenko (who had since been dismissed), they had kept the *Stremitelny* from arriving in Constanza before the *Potemkin* left. The effort was not without cost. Their disabling of the torpedoes alerted Yanovich to the possibility that the few sailors he had brought to perform the more grueling tasks of running the destroyer might be working against him.

Even under the officers' close watch, Pykhtin found a new way to spoil the *Stremitelny*'s mission. As it steamed toward the Crimean coast, he and several other sailors fed the furnaces with a type of coal that burned at an extremely high temperature. It would take time, but eventually the intense heat would disable the furnaces, shutting down the engines. The critical question was whether this would occur before they were caught or before the *Stremitelny* found the *Potemkin*.

In Sevastopol, Chukhnin was deliberating what to do about the *Potemkin* now that it was in Theodosia. Yanovich was halfway across the Black Sea and of little use to him for the present moment. Believing he had rooted out his fleet's most rebellious sailors, Chukhnin had ordered Krieger early that morning to lead the squadron to retrieve the *St. George* in Odessa. When he returned, Chukhnin planned on sending his battleships after the *Potemkin* again at Theodosia. But the squadron would not be back until the next day, and he could hardly rely on Krieger to be decisive. Chukhnin had dispatched another destroyer, the *Griden,* to seek out the *Potemkin,* but its commander steamed back to Sevastopol soon after it set off, fearing his crew might mutiny.

Pressure on Chukhnin continued to increase. The tsar and the navy minister refused to hear any more excuses. Nicholas telegraphed, "Resolve this situation and put an end to the *Potemkin*'s roaming from port to port. Do you think you will have the capability to accomplish what we spoke about? Report your results." Admiral Avelan repeated much the same demand: "*Potemkin* demands coal and water from city authorities of Theodosia, threatening bombardment in case of refusal. This is intolerable. The *Potemkin* mutiny must be ended by the most radical measures available. Sink the *Potemkin,* if you can." Throughout the day, Chukhnin also received desperate pleas for help from Theodosia. These telegrams could pile up on his desk until they were a foot high, but Chukhnin knew he was powerless to fulfill their requests. They were all at the mercy of that *damned* ship.

A full moon hung over Theodosia, casting faint shadows across the *Potemkin*'s decks. After midnight, Kovalenko and Feldmann stood on the bridge, contemplating the future. The provincial governor had never arrived, nor had their coal and water, forcing the sailors to send an ultimatum to the mayor. In all likelihood, they would have to shell the city and engage the garrison in the morning.

The prospect burdened the crew and raised many questions: How many troops would they be fighting against, and would these troops be loyal to their officers? Did the garrison have artillery? How would the workers react to the bombardment? Would they join the sailors? How much destruction would they have to inflict before the city's authorities capitulated? And who would be hurt the most by the shelling — surely, the innocent residents of Theodosia?

Attempting to get some answers, Feldmann had sneaked ashore earlier that evening to contact the city's revolutionary groups, but he had failed to locate a single one. As terrible a choice as it was, the sailors were resigned to attacking Theodosia. They had no other option.

For the first time, Kovalenko and Feldmann spoke of the dangers that they had assumed since joining the sailors in their uprising. The newspapers indicated it was known that an officer and several Odessan revolutionaries were participating in the mutiny. If captured, they knew they would face the gallows. Although at first they tried to appear unshaken by the prospect, Kovalenko admitted his fear and thought of what his mother would feel on learning of his death. It was painful to even imagine it. After a while, the two left the bridge to catch a few hours of sleep in a stateroom. They shook hands and parted ways; it was the last time they would converse.

Throughout the battleship, sailors sat quietly and wrote letters to their families in case the worst happened. Some also scribbled notes to Admiral Chukhnin, pleading that they were innocent of participation in the mutiny; they would present these notes if they were captured. Nobody remembered speaking to Matyushenko that night. He walked the decks, hoping that General Pleshkov would abandon his resistance, and if not, that they could find a way to obtain coal, so that the *Potemkin*'s guns could remain silent.

In the city, General Pleshkov remained at headquarters. In the early hours of June 23, he received a telegram from General Volkov, granting his wish. It had been too late to stop the delivery of food supplies, but now his orders were direct: Theodosia was not to send any more aid to the battleship, regardless of the threat of attack. Pleshkov had also received a message from Vice Admiral Chukhnin, who bluntly explained that the Black Sea Fleet was powerless to protect the city in the coming hours; Pleshkov's troops would have to defend it themselves. When the mayor, accompanied by the city council, came to Pleshkov's office to plead for the delivery of coal and water, the general shredded the *Potemkin*'s ultimatum before their eyes. His orders were clear, he told the mayor, and he would make no concessions to the mutineers.

# 22

A S THE SAILORS awakened on the morning of June 23, Theodosia's citizens were already in flight. At 5 A.M. the mayor had posted notices in the streets, warning that the *Potemkin* would begin its bombardment at any moment. Panic followed. Those with the means drove by carriage into the hills, but most families left on foot. Parents bundled their smallest children in their arms; the rest of the family dragged whatever possessions they could transport. Every store and factory in the city closed down, and police nervously patrolled the streets, expecting shells from the battleship at any moment.

As they witnessed this pitiful sight, a chill went through the crew; the men knew they had caused this terror. When the deadline passed, Matyushenko and Feldmann boarded a launch to see if the city's authorities were preparing the delivery of food and coal or if they had rejected their ultimatum outright. In the port, one of the mayor's clerks waited on a quay, obviously expecting them.

"The garrison commander refuses," he said directly. "Wait until eleven o'clock. We've appealed to the governor. He's certain to permit us to give you the coal. For God's sake, wait!"

Feldmann told the clerk they would consider the offer but to understand that the *Potemkin* sailors would follow through on their threat soon. Before the two returned to the battleship, Matyushenko took a circuitous route, searching for stockpiles of coal along the shore and within the harbor's inlet — one last chance. To their surprise, they spotted three barges laden with coal, anchored by a quay at the harbor's northern edge. The barges lay out in the open, all but waiting to be taken — the answer to their needs. Matyushenko steered the launch past one of them. Its captain appeared on deck, and Matyushenko asked a price for the coal.

"I'll give you the coal for nothing," the captain said. "Just don't destroy my barges."

Feldmann and Matyushenko sped back to the *Potemkin* and told the crew of their discovery. Relieved to get coal without attacking Theodosia, thirty sailors volunteered to retrieve the barges. Armed with rifles, they boarded a launch — Matyushenko, Feldmann, Nikishkin, and Koshuba among them. The *Ismail* accompanied the volunteers. They rubbed their hands together, praising their good fortune. When one cocked his rifle, the others kidded him for showing excess caution.

When the launch came alongside one of the barges, most of the sailors clambered aboard to help lift its anchor, so that they could tow the coal back to the *Potemkin*. The nearby quay and shore were deserted; everyone in town apparently had taken to the hills. After laying down their rifles, the sailors strained to lift the anchor, foot by foot, from the harbor's murky depths. When one sailor tired, another willingly took his place.

Just as the anchor cleared the water, a lookout on the launch cried out a warning: "Soldiers! Soldiers are coming!"

Suddenly, a company of soldiers appeared on the shoreline, another on the quay.

"Keep working!" Koshuba told his comrades on the barges. "They won't fire at us."

Before any of them could take cover behind the stacks of coal, shots rang out. The ambush's first salvo cut down three sailors.

"Comrades, take your rifles," Nikishkin yelled over the screams of the wounded men. He took up his own and aimed; by his side, Feldmann did the same. Before Nikishkin could fire, he crumpled, shot in the chest. He staggered at the barge's edge and fell off the side. Feldmann looked around, dazed, as bullets flew around him. Down in the water, Nikishkin stared straight at him, his eyes begging for help. Feldmann plunged feet first into the harbor and wrapped his arms around the stricken man. Others on the barge jumped into the water, only to be shot as they tried to swim away. Several sailors returned fire, taking cover behind the piles of coal, Koshuba among them.

On the launch, two sailors had already fallen. Under a volley of gunshots, Matyushenko gathered as many sailors as he could back on the launch before the two companies of soldiers converged on the quay. The sailors were desperately outnumbered. In sheer cowardice, the sailors on the *Ismail* turned the torpedo boat back toward the *Potemkin,* leaving its guns silent. For many, the torpedo boat offered their only chance at escape, and it was gone. Confusion reigned as those abandoned on the barge called for help. A few simply cursed the *Ismail;* others followed their comrades into the water, swimming for cover behind the barge or underneath the quay. Matyushenko turned the launch around to retrieve a few more sailors. He told those around him to return fire, but they could do little more than duck. Several lay dying on the deck, pressing their wounds to stanch the flow of blood.

A few moments after the launch steered away from the barge, Matyushenko abruptly lost control of it. The launch swung in a circle, heading straight toward the soldiers amassed on the quay. A bullet had disabled the steering. The soldiers aimed at them as Matyushenko scrambled toward the stern. All seemed lost. Somehow, he escaped the barrage of bullets and managed to grab the rudder, turning the launch away from the quay. One shot dislodged his cap, which briefly covered his eyes, but none hit him. With the steering crippled, he could return to the battleship only with those who had already made it on board; he could hear others cry for help behind him. A hail of bullets followed in his wake.

A wounded sailor lying at his feet looked up at Matyushenko and asked, "What's going to happen? Will I die?"

"Don't even worry about it, my dear Vanya," Matyushenko said as cheerfully as he could manage. "You're going to live — you'll be getting married before you know it."

In the water, Feldmann held Nikishkin around the chest as he ferociously paddled toward the retreating launch. Several sailors around him were killed as they swam. His strength waning, Feldmann knew he would not make it back to the ship. As he turned back toward shore, another bullet hit Nikishkin. His body convulsed, his grip on Feldmann weakened, and he sank to the bottom of the harbor. Feldmann swam toward a nearby ship. Grabbing its anchor chain, he rested for a moment to catch his breath. Koshuba and another sailor swam around the stern of the ship.

"Where are you going?" Feldmann gasped.

"To the battleship!" Koshuba answered, breathlessly.

Too tired to follow them, Feldmann held tight to the anchor chain. "Tell the sailors their comrades want vengeance," he said.

Koshuba nodded, and the two sailors swam toward the battleship, rifle fire still cracking out from the quay. They managed to cover a short distance before Koshuba was shot in the hand and had to slow down. A sloop carrying a band of soldiers dragged the two out of the water. A few minutes later, Feldmann was hauled onto the quay and arrested as well. He lost consciousness as they took him away.

On the *Potemkin*, Kirill and Kovalenko had rushed to the forecastle when they heard the first rifle shots. Mayhem broke out on board as the crew tried to figure out what to do. Some loaded the small-caliber guns to fire on the soldiers; others begged them not to shoot for fear they would hit some of their comrades. A few soldiers on the quay aimed at the *Potemkin*, causing more alarm as bullets ricocheted off the steam funnels.

"The launch is coming!" A sailor pointed from the gun deck after Matyushenko had finally regained control of the boat to direct it out of the harbor. "Drop the ladders!"

When Matyushenko swung the launch around to the battleship's side, a somber silence fell on the *Potemkin*. The sailors looked down at their comrades. One lay in a pool of his own blood, his rifle grasped in his hands, his face still with death, eyes open.

"Stretcher," Matyushenko ordered, climbing up the ladder. "Tsyrkunov is dead."

The sailors scrambled down to lift the injured men out of the launch and carry them to the infirmary, though they had no doctor. Only eight of the thirty sailors had returned; the rest were either captured or killed. A convulsion of rage, fear, and desperation seized the crew.

"To the guns, comrades! Death to the traitors!"

"Enough shooting, enough bloodshed! Let's go to Sevastopol!"

"It's better to die than to turn ourselves over to the Russian government!"

"They've put our comrades under arrest! They have them in port!"

"Open fire on Theodosia!"

"To Romania! To Romania!"

Moments later, when the sailors assembled on the quarterdeck, their demands for action had grown only slightly more reasonable. Theodosia lay emptied before them, apart from soldiers, police, and a few stragglers who had not yet made it to the hills. The crew could easily launch an attack, shelling the city into oblivion in retribution for their fallen comrades and then landing an assault party to take the barges. More sailors would die, but success was more than likely. At first, this course of action looked likely.

"Let's go ashore and die honestly, in battle, with our guns in our hands," Kirill declared. "Otherwise, we'll be damned as cowards and as traitors."

To prepare, some sailors rushed to their positions. The battle pennant was raised, the signalman warned all foreign vessels to leave the port, and the twelve-inch guns swiveled to target the train station, where many of the city's most influential people were waiting for transport out of Theodosia.

But before these sailors could launch an attack, other crew members forced them away from the guns. Sailors cursed one another, and fights broke out throughout the battleship. Eventually, though, the pennant was lowered. "There's no support for us anywhere," one sailor said in appeal, expressing what many felt. "In Odessa, the *St. George* betrayed us. Here, the army jeers at us, and we've lost our comrades trying to get a handful of coal. The bravest of us will all be killed, one by one, and the rest will be taken when the *Potemkin*'s captured."

Another sailor stood forward. "There's only one thing left to do: go back to Romania while we still can move."

Matyushenko listened to these words; he also understood Kirill's demand for revenge. He himself had gripped the hand of a dying sailor on his way to the infirmary only minutes before. But to what end would their shells fall? he asked himself. They might destroy some government buildings, and with some luck, kill the officers who had ordered the ambush on the quay, but their fusillade would also murder many soldiers — men who, Matyushenko believed, were in much the same predicament as he was. There was one main difference between them: the soldiers had not yet learned that attacking a worker or a sailor meant striking their own brother. Matyushenko believed that their deaths could be justified only if the revolution's fate hung in the balance.

And this was far from the case, he realized. The *Potemkin*'s revolution was lost. With little more than the workers' tacit support and lacking coordination with revolutionary leaders in the cities, the *Potemkin* was free only to roam the Black Sea, struggling to find coal, water, and food, accomplishing nothing for the cause. This truth crushed Matyushenko, but he finally accepted it.

What could they do now? The engines were on the verge of breakdown, having run continuously since they left Sevastopol twelve days before. The machinists and the stokers charged with keeping them running were exhausted and on the brink of collapse themselves. The rest of the crew was tired and hungry. The strain of braving death almost constantly since the mutiny began had become too much. Now sailor was turning against sailor. On a strictly practical level, Matyushenko knew their ability to engage in battle was deteriorating every moment. Sooner or later the officers' destroyer or the squadron would find the battleship. The sailors who had followed his leadership deserved better than to die needlessly at sea or to face the hangman. Matyushenko knew that most wanted to surrender in Constanza, where there was some hope of freedom.

For once, Matyushenko did not deliver a rousing speech about the need to make sacrifices for the revolution. He did not demand that they continue the crusade and martyr themselves. As much as he was pained to surrender this great battleship, which he had thought could spark the people's revolution, he now resolved to lead the sailors to the safety they had earned. "To Romania!" the crew shouted again. Though he still wished to fight, Matyushenko accepted their calls. "To Romania . . . Let's go to Constanza again . . . Back to Romania . . . It's be better to die there or anywhere else than in front of a naval firing squad . . . Romania!"

At 11:30 A.M., the engine room raised the steam; the sailors promised to chop up the decks and masts for fuel if they ran out of coal. A half-hour later, they raised anchor. As the *Potemkin* left Theodosia's harbor, Kirill persisted in trying to convince Matyushenko and the battleship's other leaders that they should accept the glory of an "honest death" by heading to the Caucasus. His pleas fell on deaf ears. With the *Potemkin* low on coal and fresh water for its boilers, surviving their flight to Romania and escaping Chukhnin's clutches must serve as their final blow against the tsar.

The sailors steered a course first to the southeast to stay far away from Sevastopol; they'd heard reports of destroyers looking for the battleship. The shoreline of Theodosia, then the mountains looming behind, soon disappeared from sight.

It was a warm evening at Peterhof. While Nicholas rode his horse alone through Alexandria Park, the clouds darkened overhead, threatening a downpour. The humiliating *Potemkin* mutiny looked as if it would never end, despite the tsar's prayers to God and his harsh notes to Vice Admiral Chukhnin, both delivered daily. The battleship might have spared Theodosia by leaving the port earlier that day, but now Nicholas was receiving reports that the mutineers were expected to travel to Yalta or to visit their wrath on his Crimean palace at Livadia, where he had stayed with his father during the final hours before Alexander III's death. The admirals also speculated that the sailors might try to connect with revolutionaries in Batumi. No matter. As far as Nicholas was concerned, the *Potemkin* controlled the Black Sea, just as it controlled every conversation in St. Petersburg and every Russian newspaper's front page — his censors had lifted their ban on the story after the release of the official account.

In Nicholas's conservative staple, *Novoye Vremya*, the publisher A. S. Suvorin had delivered a blistering editorial about the mutiny:

> The sons of Russia are tearing apart their own mother — lying, cutting, and shredding her with dull knives to prolong her suffering. This is what we have lived long enough to see, the disgrace and dishonor. . . . Nobody could have imagined this, neither here nor abroad, nor in Japan, which could not have hoped that such a despicable treason would come to its aid, that this revolution would use any means to achieve its purpose. . . . The *Potemkin* treason is mindless, pointless, poor in its shame and monstrously gruesome in its actions.

The reactionary newspaper *Moskovskiye Vedomosti* mirrored these sentiments, then went on to blame the "foreign Jewish press" for exaggerating the *Potemkin*'s significance.

Most other Russian newspapers were far less dismissive of the incident, though it was unlikely that Nicholas ever read them. The widely circulated, progressive *Russkoye Slovo* used the mutiny and Chukhnin's failed attempts to capture the battleship as proof that government reform was critical: "Fear is the sole basis of discipline in the army and the navy, and it will prove as poor an instrument for keeping the rank and file loyal to the throne as it has in the suppression of discontent among the people. The government should learn the lesson that the soldiers and sailors are beginning to awaken as the people have already awakened."

The liberal daily *Nasha Zhizn* was even more pointed: "It was sufficient that two or three agitators appeared and gave a few speeches for normal obedience to yield to open, bloody rebellion. It is obvious this catastrophe was set in motion by society's structure; it is obvious ignorance and passivity can no longer be the basis of social order, and fear is a poor instrument for command. Radical reforms are needed to create harmony between the people's aspirations and the government's actions." This editorial, coming after several reports about the Odessa riots, earned *Nasha Zhizn* a visit from an official of the Interior Ministry, who temporarily locked the newspaper's doors.

What the censors could not squash were the conversations on the streets of St. Petersburg about Cossacks seen firing on a crowd of workers outside the Putilov factory. Nor could they stop the rumors — of a palace coup, of rampant sedition in the army in the Far East, of the tsar's intention to call for a representative assembly soon, of the tsar's outright refusal of the same, and of the tsar's plan to accept, or to reject, peace with Japan. The Black Sea mutiny added fuel to this flurry of speculations, as if the *Potemkin,* much as Bloody Sunday had done before, made the rot in the tsar's regime impossible to ignore. Now everyone was waiting for the push that would topple him from power. "Is it revolution?" was the question on people's lips as well as in newspaper editorials.

As Nicholas neared the Lower Palace, the *Potemkin* infected his thoughts, as it had continually over the past week and a half. The battleship was alone, he reasoned, to reassure himself, without support and far away on the Black Sea; its sailors presented no imminent threat to his hold on power. Nicholas dismounted moments before the clouds finally broke, escaping inside just as the rain descended. The rest of his evening stretched before him: dinner first, then, perhaps, some time in his office riffling through reports about the state of his empire. He simply wanted the damned mutiny to end — was this too much to ask?

In St. Petersburg that same evening, the chief of the naval staff stood outside the Admiralty, thronged by Russian and foreign journalists wanting to know exactly when this would happen. "We can't tell you," Admiral A. A. Wirenus said. "The whole affair is in the hands of Vice Admiral Chukhnin."

"Do you think he'll dispatch the squadron again?" a reporter asked.

"We don't know what he'll do. . . . The situation is grave. The ship is not in the hands of her crew, but under the control of the Revolutionary Committee that went on board at Odessa. They've issued a high-sounding manifesto to the powers. They want to be considered insurgents. . . . They know their heads are forfeit and they'll stop at nothing."

Wirenus then concluded that he wished a destroyer like the *Stremitelny* would torpedo the *Potemkin,* making a grim example of the sailors by sending them to the bottom of the Black Sea.

Late that night, Lieutenant Yanovich was searching along the Crimean coastline for the *Potemkin.* Given the battleship's low coal supplies, the mutineers would have been foolish to stray too far into the open sea.

Delayed by a boiler breakdown on the way to Yalta, Yanovich and the other officers had arrived at Theodosia earlier in the day, eager for battle, only to find that the battleship had already gone. They had missed the *Potemkin* by a mere six hours. Officers of the *Stremitelny* were equally surprised when, arriving ashore, they were detained by soldiers; the garrison commander, Pleshkov, had believed they came from another ship of mutineers. Once the misunderstanding was resolved, and in spite of the crew's exhaustion, the destroyer loaded on more supplies, and Yanovich renewed his chase.

The *Stremitelny* thrust onward at full speed into the early hours of June 24. At 4 A.M., its lookout spotted the faint lights of a vessel to the south. Although the darkness was almost complete, Yanovich could tell that it must be a warship of some sort. He altered the *Stremitelny*'s course to intercept it. A few minutes later, he sighted three funnels;

their spacing and height suggested they belonged to the *Potemkin*. No other battleships were asail in the area, he knew, so the ship in his sights could not be part of Chukhnin's second squadron.

It had happened. He had finally found the mutinous warship, Yanovich thought. He ordered his crew to their battle stations. Quickly, the torpedo tubes were positioned for attack, and the *Stremitelny* steamed a direct path toward the battleship. With the *Potemkin*'s six- and twelve-inch guns, along with its battery of quick firers — weapons whose primary purpose was to repel destroyers — Yanovich and his crew knew they had only the slimmest chance of success in sinking the *Potemkin*. Indeed, it was likely they would perish in the effort.

As they closed in, the battleship in their sights changed course, beating a retreat toward Theodosia; but it was no match for the *Stremitelny*'s speed. An instant before Yanovich gave the order to fire torpedoes, however, he approached close enough to discover that his desired target was actually the old training vessel *Pamyat Mercuriya*. It was evading the *Stremitelny* because its captain believed that the *Potemkin*'s torpedo boat was pursuing him. Since Yanovich, in his rush to leave Sevastopol, had forgotten to bring the naval codebooks with him, the two ships had been unable to identify each other by wireless telegraph.

Sending a message through the semaphore operator, Yanovich requested to come aboard; his hopes of attacking the mutineers had been dashed once again. He and several officers rowed across to the training vessel to see if it had received any recent reports on the *Potemkin*. They had not. Keen to return to his pursuit, Yanovich bid the captain farewell. When he stepped out of the cabin and looked across at his ship, he could barely make it out — it was all but lost in a pall of steam. The coal in the furnaces had finally crippled the destroyer. Pykhtin and the other stokers barely escaped through a hatchway after the pipes burst.

The *Pamyat Mercuriya*'s captain offered to help Yanovich repair the *Stremitelny*, but Yanovich declined. The destroyer needed more than simple repairs. They would have to return to Sevastopol. His hunt was over.

# 23

THE POTEMKIN STEAMED through the darkness; the only sounds to be heard on the battleship were the steady din of the engines and the bow cutting through the waves. The sailors had extinguished all exterior lights. Once or twice a cabin door creaked open, sending a sliver of light across the deck, but then the door was quickly shut again. With clouds concealing the stars and the moon, the darkness seemed impenetrable. One sailor likened the *Potemkin* to a black sea monster moving through the gloom.

Distressed that some sailors, led by the petty officers, might attempt to take over the *Potemkin* before it reached Romania, Matyushenko patrolled the decks with a loaded revolver. Sadly, the mutiny had come to this end, sailor pitted against sailor. On the battleship's stern, he could only vaguely make out the *Ismail*'s outlines, though it followed close behind. Soon after the ship had left Theodosia, some sailors on the torpedo boat had tried to rush the helm, planning to surrender at Sevastopol. Their attempted coup had failed, so now the *Potemkin* was towing the torpedo boat to ensure that it stayed with the battleship.

On the quarterdeck, Matyushenko came across committee member Illarion Shestidesyaty. He was looking out into the darkness.

"Can't sleep, Illarion?" Matyushenko asked.

"Not after what happened this morning. Nightmares."

"Things went terribly in Theodosia. We shouldn't have exposed ourselves to attack in that way. Poor Nikishkin and Koshuba. And the others. They'll all be missed, my dear brother," Matyushenko said.

"But now we must be prepared against the petty officers, do you understand? It's better to die than to return to Sevastopol."

Shestidesyaty volunteered to keep watch, well aware that Chukhnin would pardon the petty officers while showing no mercy to the rest of the crew.

Matyushenko thanked him warmly and left to enlist others to guard key sections of the battleship. He was right to be worried. Down in a secluded corner of the lower decks, forty-five petty officers and sailors plotted to take over the *Potemkin*. None wanted to go to Romania, never to see Russia again. They believed their opportunity had come. The sailor committee had lost much of its influence over the crew. The officers only needed to arrest Matyushenko and other chief instigators of the mutiny for the crew to fall into line behind them, agreeing to return to the Black Sea Fleet's base. At the meeting, the counter-mutineers resolved to kill any revolutionary sailors who resisted.

After disbanding, the petty officers scouted each committee member's location. Unarmed, they knew their best chance was to attack the ship's leaders while they slept. To their surprise, they discovered most of them awake and stationed throughout the battleship, many holding revolvers, obviously anticipating a counter-mutiny. Their presence dissuaded the petty officers from taking action, even though they knew this was likely their last chance to take over the *Potemkin* before arriving in Constanza.

At daybreak on June 24, ten days after they had first mutinied, the sailors found themselves, once again, crossing the Black Sea with no land or other ships in sight. Apart from a few squawking, venturesome seagulls, they were alone on the calm waters. Morning passed and the scorching June sun loomed constantly overhead, as if tracking them across the water. On the forecastle, the sailors had little to sing or laugh about as they rested between watches. Most talked among themselves, sullen and reflective. "Everyone wondered what the future might bring," sailor Lychev later recounted. "What awaited us in a strange, unknown land? An unfamiliar language and customs of a distant country. This upset everyone."

Many worried about what kind of work they would do and if they would ever see their families again. Even so, they knew a worse fate (hard labor, at best; execution, at worst) awaited them if they returned to Russia. This dilemma, coming after ten days of intense emotion and punishing physical hardship, was too much for some. At one point on the return voyage to Constanza, a sailor rushed onto the spar deck, his face livid and eyes wild. He ran from railing to railing, screaming that they should blow up the battleship. It took several men to restrain him. While being carried to the infirmary, he lost consciousness. Several hours later, he died.

Kirill could scarcely bear to stay on the *Potemkin*, certain the crew had abandoned the revolution for their own safety. If only the sailors had better understood the historical chance the mighty battleship gave them, he thought, then they would have remained true to the cause instead of taking what he saw as the coward's path of escape. So humiliated was he by the retreat, he contemplated taking a small boat loaded with arms and some food and casting off into the sea. He abandoned this idea after realizing that he was unlikely to reach the shore. Kirill brooded alone in a stateroom, dejected and blaming himself for not doing more. Lost in depressed thoughts, he missed the ceremony that took place that afternoon aboard the *Potemkin*.

The sailors had already held funerals for two of the sailors who returned with Matyushenko after the ambush in Theodosia, wrapping their bodies in canvas shrouds, stitching them shut, and then dropping them into the sea. Now the crew met on the quarterdeck to bury the revolutionary flag. A sailor lowered from the mast the large red flag they had stitched with the words LIBERTY, EQUALITY, FRATER-NITY. Solemnly, Matyushenko and the others brought it to the railing. Then they let it fall from their hands, overboard. "It was tragic to watch the flag disappear," Matyushenko later recalled. "And then it suddenly rose in the ship's wake, as if urging all the sailors to carry on the struggle."

He knew, however, that there was no such hope for them now. Looking back on the past days, he lamented how close they had come to succeeding. In Odessa, after the confrontation with the squadron, they could have moved on the city, capturing Kakhanov's arsenal and transferring it to the workers. But then Dr. Golenko and the *St. George*'s crew had betrayed them, throwing their plans into disarray and sending them around the Black Sea on a fruitless search for help. Matyushenko imagined that other revolutionaries would reproach them with scornful words for returning to Romania — "You pitiful cowards! What an enormous and powerful fortress you surrendered." Although he accepted blame for their failure, he felt that the people whose liberty they had attempted to win had abandoned them. "Why were you asleep?" he later wrote. "Why were you asleep for eleven days when we searched for fresh water throughout the Black Sea? You know well that no one can drink saltwater or run a battleship without coal. Why didn't you help us?" The best Matyushenko could do now was to make sure the crew reached Constanza and won their own freedom.

By dusk, the placid sea became choppy. As the sailors traveled westward through the night, a developing storm sent waves crashing against the battleship's side. Upon heavy rolling seas, with uncertain steps, the machinists and stokers labored in the holds to keep the engines running; the boilers were all but ruined by saltwater. Coal stocks were perilously low as well. A couple of hours from the Romanian coast, a towering wave severed the towline connecting the *Ismail*. The *Potemkin* turned back to search for the torpedo boat in the rough seas and the darkness. After making contact, the *Ismail* stayed close to the battleship for shelter.

At 11 P.M. the ships finally approached Constanza; the waves eased as they came closer to shore. The *Potemkin*'s searchlights panned the waters for marker buoys as the ship navigated into the harbor. Its crew assembled on the forecastle, looking out at the brightly lit city in the distance — a welcome sight after two days at sea. The engines were cut, and the battleship drifted forward until it barely cut a wake. In the silence, the sailors heard faint sounds of music coming from the port. It pained them to think of how their dire predicament compared to the carefree evening enjoyed by the people of Constanza.

"Drop anchor!" came the order from the bridge, piercing the quiet. The anchor splashed into the water, its heavy chain clanging and screeching as it traveled through the hawsehole. By the time the sailors had secured the anchor, the music had ceased in the port, and the lights from the Romanian cruiser *Elizaveta* shined in their eyes.

Shortly after midnight, Captain Negru, Constanza's port commander, strode down the quay to meet the *Potemkin*'s launch. He was clueless about the crew's intentions in returning to the city, but newspaper reports that Krieger's squadron had sunk the mutineers were, obviously, false. The day before, Negru had finished drafting his report to the Romanian foreign minister about the *Potemkin*'s first visit. Now, once again, he faced a force that he had no ability to repel.

Among the sailors in the launch, he recognized Matyushenko, whom Negru had described to his superiors as the "soul of the mutiny."

"What do you want here?" Negru asked him stiffly.

"Have you seen the *Sinop* or the *Ekaterina II*?" Matyushenko asked, explaining that in Theodosia they had heard of revolts aboard the two Russian battleships.

"They haven't come into this port," Negru said, sensing that the sailors clearly harbored some hope that others had joined their struggle.

"Then we've decided to surrender," Matyushenko announced.

No doubt it took Negru a moment to believe the good fortune the sailor's statement represented, but he recovered quickly. He asked the sailors to meet him at the old lighthouse on the end of Constanza's promontory. Before Negru left, Captain Banov of the Russian transport ship *Psezuape* came to the quay to ask to attend the discussions. Negru told him his services were not needed. Too much was at stake for Negru to play diplomat — nor did he have much patience left for the Russians.

When Negru arrived at the lighthouse an hour later, General G. Angelesku, the commander of the troops, and several other city officials joined him. They made it clear to Matyushenko that the crew must surrender the battleship and all arms before coming ashore. They were prohibited from conducting political propaganda campaigns while in Romania. In exchange, the entire crew would be granted asylum and allowed to live freely within the country. Under no circumstances, General Angelesku assured Matyushenko, would his government deport them to Russia. The sailors promised to take the offer to the crew for a final vote. Then they returned to the battleship.

Once the *Potemkin* had appeared again in the Romanian port, telegrams burned up the wires between Constanza, Bucharest, St. Petersburg, and Sevastopol about how to manage this latest turn of events in the crisis. The Russian diplomat charged with Romanian affairs sent a curt early morning message to General Yacob Lagovari, King Carol's foreign minister, with a thinly veiled threat:

> I have the honor to ask the Imperial Government not to let the crews of the *Potemkin* and *Ismail* to come ashore, nor to supply them with coal or provisions. At the same time, I have the obligation to inform you as per orders of my government that the crews of these ships have stained them with murders and robberies.

General Lagovari knew that if he followed the tsar's instructions, the *Potemkin* crew would be left with few options other than to shell his chief port. Then again, he could not allow the sailors everything they wanted, which would anger Nicholas. His third option, the one he had sanctioned Negru to take, was to offer the sailors the same terms he had during their first stopover. Then, in a deft diplomatic maneuver, the foreign minister would feign not to have received the Russian diplomat's request until after he had negotiated the *Potemkin*'s surrender. Then he would advise St. Petersburg that it was too late to change the terms. But the Russians shouldn't be too unhappy with that. After all, Nicholas had praised these very measures when the *Potemkin* left Constanza four days before — Lagovari would take pleasure in reminding the Russians of that.

In Sevastopol, Chukhnin's staff awakened him with a report that the *Potemkin* had finally been located and wanted to surrender in Constanza. He immediately dispatched Rear Admiral Pisarevsky, the commander of the training detachment, to take two battleships and four torpedo boats to capture the *Potemkin* before the sailors abandoned the ship or decided to take off again. Pisarevsky would likely arrive too late, however, reaffirming Avelan's rebuke to Chukhnin, delivered after the *Potemkin* had retreated from Theodosia, that the fleet was always a "step behind" the mutineers.

Chukhnin had not had much sleep before he was disturbed with this news. The previous night, he had worked late, writing to Nicholas and describing how impossible he found it to explain the deep crisis with the Black Sea Fleet, but that harsher measures would need to be taken to restore authority, including stripping his officers of their present ranks. One can only imagine that Chukhnin feared he might well receive that same punishment.

On June 25, the sun rose over the Black Sea, bathing the Romanian coastline in a soft iridescent light. For all its beauty, the sailors looked toward the land with little affection. Once they committed themselves to stepping onto that shore, most knew they would likely never return to their homeland.

The crew made their way to the quarterdeck to vote on the surrender. Matyushenko explained the terms they had settled with Captain Negru. Then he said, "Comrades, you all know the situation. There's no coal. Our fresh water ran out a long time ago. We're out of food. Sailing to Sevastopol and confessing means to admit failure. The tsar will subject us to the harshest punishment. Now the Romanians have refused us coal, water, and provisions, but they've guaranteed our safety."

"How can you be sure they won't turn us over to the tsar?" a sailor asked.

"That's doubtful," Matyushenko said. "King Carol's no friend to Nicholas, and the Romanian people, I think, would never allow that betrayal. The main point to know is that we'll be free, and this means we will be free to fight."

"Better to surrender to the Romanians than to the Russian government!" another sailor declared. The majority of the crew agreed.

Before Matyushenko left to inform Negru, an oar boat pulled alongside the *Potemkin* carrying a man with a flower in his jacket buttonhole. After stepping aboard, he announced that he was a Social Democrat and then handed his visiting card to Matyushenko. It read "Doctor Rakovsky." Several members of the sailor committee drew him aside. Christian Rakovsky, a Bulgarian-born socialist revolutionary who was close to Georgy Plekhanov and lived in Constanza, promised he would find a way to supply the battleship if the crew could hold out for several more days. But the sailors doubted his ability to obtain what they needed, particularly since they had failed themselves over the whole past week. Furthermore, their low supplies made waiting with the engines running, even for a day, nothing short of impossible. They explained to Rakovsky that the crew was already committed to leaving the battleship. Dropping the discussion, he reassured them the Romanians would stand by any agreement. He offered to help the mutiny's leaders when they came ashore. Then he went down to the infirmary to check on the wounded sailors. It was the most help the sailors had been offered from the Social Democrats since the mutiny began.

Once Negru learned of the *Potemkin*'s acceptance of his terms, he set off for the battleship. He arrived on board at noon with several soldiers at his side and a Romanian flag. He asked the sailors to lower the St. Andrew's flag from the mast. The crew removed their caps and bowed their heads, to avoid seeing the blue, yellow, and red vertical tricolor raised on the mast. Afterward, a signal from the port gave them permission to enter the harbor and disembark. The anchor was weighed. The *Potemkin* moved slowly forward. Several minutes later, the order came to cast anchor for the final time. When the battleship was secure, one of the boatswains cried out in anguish, "This is where we end up, comrades. We're no longer sailors, but free men deprived of their homeland."

The sailors gathered their belongings. Some stripped the battleship of anything of value they could find — binoculars, chronometers, and officer uniforms — an act that Matyushenko and the other revolutionaries abhorred but did not stop. While the landing boats were lowered into the waters, the sailors bid farewell to one another and their home at sea.

As the men left the battleship, the torpedo boat *Ismail* weighed anchor and cut smoothly out of the harbor. Its crew, always reluctant supporters of the mutiny and bound by the threat of sinking if they abandoned the battleship, had decided to return to Sevastopol to seek the tsar's mercy. Distracted by the disembarkation and knowing the loss of the *Ismail* made no difference now, the *Potemkin*'s crew let the torpedo boat leave unscathed.

Throughout the afternoon, a flotilla of boats ferried the sailors from the battleship into the port. As one sailor remembered it, "There was no joking, no laughter, no conversation. Nothing was heard." Many of the crew would recall for the rest of their lives the solemn moment they cast away from the battleship.

Ensign Alekseyev and the petty officers were among the first to come ashore. They went straight to the Russian consul to beg for return passage to Sevastopol. Signalman Vedenmeyer, who had betrayed the crew in Odessa when the guns were fired on the city, guaranteed for himself the tsar's pardon by taking the *Potemkin*'s secret naval codebooks before the Romanians could confiscate them.

The ship's leaders disembarked last. Kovalenko wore civilian clothes. He had packed his uniform, officer dagger, and engineer medals, planning to give them away once he landed. That life was over for him. Even so, although he knew the sailors had little choice but to surrender, he was reluctant to depart the *Potemkin*. Kirill was so overwhelmed with despair that in his long memoir about his participation in the mutiny, he wrote only that the episode was too emotional to recount. Matyushenko bid farewell to his "brave little ship" and descended into a launch, resigned to abandoning the *Potemkin* but not bitterly dejected. True, he thought, the men were giving up a powerful force that might have been used for the revolutionary cause; nevertheless, for eleven days, they had shaken the very foundation of the tsar's hold over Russia.

Stepping onto the quay, carrying duffel bags with their few possessions, the sailors found themselves in the midst of an astonishing scene. Rather than walking into a trap, as some had expected, the men were engulfed by hundreds of Romanians, offering them a hero's welcome. The people of Constanza shook hands with the sailors and clapped them on the back. Some invited crew members into their homes; others wanted to exchange their hats for sailor caps. Cheers rang out for the *Potemkin* as the sailors threaded through the crowd. Matyushenko was deeply moved by this heartfelt reception.

The sailors gathered in a city square near the port. Matyushenko had brought twenty-four thousand rubles from the battleship's safe, and, with the help of several others, he distributed the money evenly among the men (they received roughly half a year's pay). When this was done, he stepped forward to address the crew for the final time. His voice was clear and strong:

> Dear comrades! We've shaken the dust of our dear motherland from our feet and have stepped onto the soil of a foreign country. Russia, our fathers and mothers, our wives and our children are left across the Black Sea. We didn't abandon our motherland. Rather, those

who oppress our people took it away from us. We struggled fairly. We wanted to achieve freedom not only for ourselves but for all the people. But nothing came of it. We didn't make it, but those who are left in Russia, millions of workers and peasants, will succeed. And one day we'll be back in Russia to build a new life. Don't forget these great days. Don't forget each other. Farewell!

Then Matyushenko disappeared into the crowd; the Russian secret police were already on his trail. Over in the harbor, seawater gushed into the *Potemkin*'s lower holds. Resolved to keep their revolutionary battleship out of the tsar's hands, Matyushenko had ordered several sailors to open the seacocks before they disembarked. The *Potemkin* sank steadily.

# Epilogue

The revolutionary is a doomed man.

— MIKHAIL BAKUNIN, *Revolutionary Catechism*

BEFORE MIDNIGHT, Matyushenko, Kirill, and Kovalenko boarded a train to Bucharest. Given their role in the mutiny, they feared the port was too dangerous a place to remain in, particularly since the Russian fleet was on its way to Constanza. They were accompanied by Dr. Rakovsky and Russian émigré Professor Arbore-Ralli, who lived in Bucharest and had offered to share his small house with the men until they decided what to do with their freedom. Matyushenko already knew: he would persist in his fight against the tsar. Death alone would stop him.

In Constanza, many sailors spent their first evening off the *Potemkin* in a state of bittersweet celebration. They had escaped the tsar's clutches but had left their homeland, possibly for good, and they needed to find work and new homes. Some got drunk, trying to release eleven days of intense pressure by finding the bottom of a vodka bottle. Others spent the night recounting their adventure to the city's workers before finding their way to the soldier barracks that General Angelesku had cleared for them on the city's outskirts. Of the entire crew, only forty-seven, including Ensign Alekseyev and most of the petty officers, had gone to the Russian consulate, pleaded their innocence, and requested to be returned to Sevastopol. They would not find the welcome they thought they deserved from the Black Sea Fleet commander.

Immediately on learning of the battleship's surrender, Vice Admiral Chukhnin telegrammed the tsar with the good news: the *Potemkin* would soon return to Sevastopol in loyal hands. Relieved that the nightmare had finally ended, Nicholas managed to play his first game of tennis in weeks, a sufficiently momentous occasion to receive mention in his diary at the mutiny's end. Nonetheless, the diplomatic and political fallout from the *Potemkin* had only just begun.

Controversy surrounded the simple act of regaining control of the battleship. When Rear Admiral Pisarevsky reached Constanza with his squadron early on the morning of June 26, he found the *Potemkin* half sunk in the harbor and flying the Romanian flag. After deriding Captain Negru for this offense, he alternated between demanding the battleship's release and insisting that Jews were responsible for the entire affair. Negru calmly told him that he would see what he could do about the former. Over the next several hours, the diplomatic wrangling rose to the highest levels of both governments. King Carol settled the matter. He agreed to release the battleship without further delay, but Romania would not renege on its agreement with the *Potemkin* sailors and deport them.

Later that day, Pisarevsky raised the St. Andrew's flag over the battleship and a priest splashed holy water on its deck to drive away "the revolutionary demons." Lieutenant Yanovich then took command of the battleship, having arrived with the squadron. He would have preferred the glory of sinking the *Potemkin* rather than overseeing its return to the naval base, an assignment that required pumping water out of the battleship's hull and then slowly towing it back to Sevastopol, since its engines were crippled.

While these events unfolded, Russian and international newspapers weighed in on the mutiny's import. A letter published in *Russkoye Slovo* argued that the *Potemkin* revealed the reasons for the Tsushima disaster: the tsar's navy was a pathetic folly. Challenging the censors again, *Nasha Zhizn* concluded that the mutiny "shows that the sea of Russian life is restless to its very depths and that the rift between the government and the people has reached deeper into the masses." Its liberal cousin, *Russkiye Vedomosti*, denied official claims that the *Potemkin* was merely the result of propaganda efforts of "student-Jews," likening this explanation to blaming the flame for the fire. Loyalist papers tried to hold the line, one opining that "There were no true Russian sailors on the *Potemkin.* . . . The Russian military will always be outside politics." A *Novoye Vremya* editorial called for better naval staffing and the need for counter-revolutionary forces to rally in defense of the monarchy. The only laggards were the socialist journals, whose writers were still preparing their screeds about the *Potemkin*'s revolutionary significance.

The foreign press offered no such delay, reporting the mutiny's end side by side with news that the Japanese were successfully invading Sakhalin Island. The British *Daily Telegraph* now judged the mutiny "the broadest of broad farces," which would not change the Russian government's position on either peace or reform. The leftist French paper *Temps Nouveaux* countered that the mutiny revealed that the revolution was entering an "acute stage." Several German newspapers debated whether the Romanians were right to provide the Russian sailors safe harbor in their country. A *New York Times* editorial said they were but, more important, reckoned that "the moral for Russia of these disastrous events is to agree with her adversary [Japan] quickly and so save what she still has left, in Europe as well as in Asia."

This was not a decision for Chukhnin to make. Besides, he was already frantically occupied with holding on to his command, especially after Nicholas replaced Admiral Avelan with Vice Admiral Aleksei Birilev the day after the *Potemkin*'s surrender. To stave off the same fate, Chukhnin cast a wide net of blame for the mutiny, from Vice Admiral Krieger and Rear Admiral Vishnevetsky, whom he dismissed, down to the newest recruits. He purged hundreds of sailors from the fleet, sending them to the army or to distant posts. In a note to Birilev, he also suggested mandatory retirement for many of his commanders, calling them "weak, indecisive, lazy, and incompetent." Only Chukhnin himself emerged as blameless. Although several naval officers appealed to Birilev to institute serious reforms, including reduced terms of service and improved living conditions for sailors, the new naval minister largely disregarded them.

Instead, the Admiralty focused on punishing the mutineers. After saving his own skin, Chukhnin made this his sole mission as Black Sea Fleet commander. Sevastopol became as much a prison as a naval base. Sailors were held in the fortress cells and on the training vessel *Prut.* While his prosecutors prepared the *Potemkin* investigation and pressed King Carol to return the mutiny's ringleaders, the court-martial of forty-four *Prut* sailors proceeded apace. Begun on July 20 in an aerial balloon hanger on Sevastopol's outskirts, the trials were guarded by a battalion of soldiers and two torpedo boats in the bay. Aleksandr Petrov and three other ringleaders proudly declared their guilt, earning themselves death sentences. Sixteen others received hard labor, eight prison, and the rest were acquitted. Chukhnin had insisted that the entire crew be prosecuted, but the tsar and his naval minister wanted a swift trial, so Chukhnin dropped his demand.

Denying appeals for clemency, the Black Sea Fleet commander held the executions outside the fortress on August 24. Gendarmes tied Petrov, Titov, Adamenko, and Cherny to stakes and cast canvas hoods over them. Then they gave a line of sailor recruits rifles and surrounded these men with soldiers. If the recruits hesitated to execute the convicted, an officer warned, the soldiers would shoot *them*. Before the officer dropped his handkerchief to signal fire, Titov managed to remove his hood with his teeth so he could stare down the firing squad. Under his hood, Petrov yelled defiantly, "You will have accomplished nothing. Thousands will come to take our place." They were his last words.

In the same month, Chukhnin tried seventy-five *St. George* sailors, including Koshuba, who had been transferred from Theodosia. Koshuba and two others were awarded death sentences to be carried out in front of the entire fleet. Nineteen of their crewmates were sentenced to a total of 185 years of hard labor. Without deliberation, Chukhnin rejected their appeals as well.

When Matyushenko heard of the executions of his comrades, it only furthered his determination to strike against the tsar's regime once again. After his first meeting with Lenin in Geneva, the two had sat down a few more times. Lenin expounded on how a close-knit band of revolutionaries was needed to topple the tsar from his throne, no matter the cost in blood or wrecked lives. Matyushenko never fell under his spell, and he refused to join his nascent Bolshevik Party. By August he had returned to Bucharest, having won only promises for money and weapons to support his actions. He had no plans to go back to Switzerland. He wrote to a friend, "Understand that the whole polemic among the parties was swallowing me up. Had I stayed, I would have been completely enveloped in the strife and quarrel."

At meetings held in the small vineyard next to Arbore-Ralli's house, Matyushenko organized a committee of sailors to coordinate the revolutionary work of his former crewmates. In the months since the mutiny's end, the sailors had spread throughout Romania. Some lived in Bucharest and Constanza, working at factories. Others left for the countryside to farm, forming communes of seventy to eighty men. Matyushenko traveled frequently to meet with them, but spent the lion's share of his time in Constanza, planning another Black Sea Fleet rebellion and sending propaganda into Russia.

Okhrana informants reported to Sevastopol that Matyushenko was orchestrating a plot to assassinate Vice Admiral Chukhnin and, more worryingly, had been overheard in September, saying, "There will be a mutiny in the Black Sea Fleet again, and it will be colossal." Periodically, those watching Matyushenko lost his trail. He was suspected, accurately so, of slipping in and out of Sevastopol and Odessa at will. Despite his surreptitious movements his intentions were clear. That autumn, the sailor sent an open letter to the Russian naval officers, warning them, "Change will come soon to Russia. If you think it is far off, you're mistaken. I repeat, it is coming very soon."

Four days after the *Potemkin* surrendered in Constanza, Nicholas invited Sergei Witte — who had likened the mutiny to a grand fable — to Peterhof and offered him the post of chief plenipotentiary to the peace negotiations with Japan. Muravyev, the ambassador to Rome, had withdrawn, and the tsar needed the war concluded. Although feeling, as Witte told another government minister, that he had been called only when "a sewer needed to be cleaned," he was a patriot and the person most qualified for the job. Mandated to secure peace, Witte traveled to Portsmouth, New Hampshire, where President Theodore Roosevelt served as intermediary. (For his self-proclaimed role of "knocking their heads together," Roosevelt won the Nobel Peace Prize.) Despite Japan's superior negotiating position, Witte secured a deal by mid-August that required no indemnity for Russia and the loss of much less territory than expected. To reward Witte for his success, Nicholas made him a count.

Simultaneous with these efforts, Nicholas took steps to quell another critical source of Russia's unrest: the call for government reform. Since February, Interior Minister Bulygin had been convening with grand dukes, ministers, and privy councilors over what kind of representation and rights to offer the people. In early July, a secret conference chaired by the tsar discussed a final proposal. The participants remained divided on how much, if any, reform was needed. Then Count A. P. Ignatyev spoke. A well-known reactionary, he had recently returned from a trip to Odessa and the Black Sea region in the mutiny's wake. To everyone's surprise, he stated that without serious reform the autocracy was finished. On August 6, a month of vacillation later, Nicholas agreed to what would be known as the Bulygin Constitution, promising the creation of an elected State Duma.

As much as Nicholas now believed he had done everything he needed to quiet the rebellions that had started in January and recently erupted in the Black Sea, the worst was yet to come. The war's execution had already marshaled resistance to the tsar and had shown his rule to be corrupt and inept. After all, he had overseen the first loss of a European power against an Asian country in modern history. The new reforms provided for only a consultative body, dismissible at Nicholas's discretion, and its stringent voter restrictions guaranteed that most workers would be excluded. Liberals and revolutionaries alike derided the tsar's halfhearted proposal. Further, he had done nothing to help peasants or workers.

In September, Nicholas and his family took a long Baltic Sea cruise aboard his yacht, the *Polar Star*. During the day, they enjoyed picnics on sandy island beaches and sailed the blue waters. At night, they lit fireworks or settled around the piano to listen to the tsarina play Beethoven. Nicholas was as happy as he had been since his childhood. On September 19, he reluctantly returned to Peterhof, dreading the burdens of state. They came all too quickly.

That same day a strike, a minor affair at a Moscow printing shop, ushered in a national uprising. Twenty-four hours later, printers throughout the city walked out. Over the next few days, workers struck at factory after factory. When the police tried to force the city's bakers to return to work, worried that Moscow would go hungry without bread, a scuffle ensued. Cossack soldiers had to be called in to suppress the unrest. This incident brought Moscow University students into the fray. Workers marched in the streets, more confrontations occurred, and on October 2, a council ("soviet") of workers was assembled to lead the strikes.

Just as the unrest began to lose steam, Prince Trubetskoy died. In St. Petersburg and Moscow, thousands of mourners came out to demonstrate for the liberal hero who in early June had appealed to the tsar for reform, saying, "Do not linger, sire. . . . Great is your responsibility before God and Russia." The crowds waved red flags and sang the "Marseillaise." In front of the Winter Palace, marchers dropped to their knees and quietly honored those who had fallen on Bloody Sunday.

More strikes followed. Printers, steelworkers, woodworkers, shipbuilders, *droshky* drivers, postal workers, and even the Mariinsky ballet dancers — they all participated. Then the railwaymen struck, tipping the scales. Train lines shut down, first the Moscow-Kazan route, then scores of others. Russia stood still. Food prices doubled, then tripled; banks and offices closed; ministers were stuck in their homes; schools were canceled; and telegraph lines and the power supply went dead. In the capital, a lone searchlight above the Admiralty shone at night.

Workers organized more soviets. Revolutionaries — Mensheviks, Bolsheviks, and Socialist Revolutionaries alike — agitated and encouraged more strikes. Apart from the very busy twenty-six-year-old Leon Trotsky, however, Lenin and the revolution's other leaders were in their Geneva remove, far from the swelling, spontaneous insurrection that fanned out across the empire. For the most part, the liberals supported the strikes, announcing as much in the newspapers, but they also feared that the workers would align themselves too closely with the socialists and call for "continuous revolution."

The movement's scale and strength shocked Nicholas, who, as one court steward wrote, had been "living in an utter fool's paradise, thinking that he is as strong and all-powerful as ever." With the *Polar Star* on call outside Peterhof in case the tsar needed to escape the country, he prepared to unleash General Trepov, whose mantra was "spare no cartridges and use no blanks," on the crowds. But even this strong measure offered no guarantee of calming the people. On October 9, with Russia standing on the brink of chaos, Witte cornered the tsar in his Peterhof study and told him he had only two choices to prevent revolution from "sweeping away a thousand years of history": install a military dictatorship and decorate the streets with blood or create a constitutional government as the liberals had proposed. Witte outlined these points in a manifesto prepared in advance of their conversation.

Over the next eight days, as the protests intensified, Nicholas consulted everyone from his wife to his uncles and his ministers. As always, there was division, but most, including Trepov, sided with Witte that much more reform was needed — now. Nicholas finally consented. But on October 17, minutes before signing the manifesto to mandate civic freedom, rule of law, and the creation of a truly representative State Duma, he hesitated. Then he called for his uncle Grand Duke Nikolai, a strong-willed veteran soldier with a physical presence and roaring voice akin to Alexander III, to invest him with dictatorial powers. Before meeting with his nephew, Nikolai told Baron V. B. Fredericks, the minister of court, "You see this revolver" — he withdrew a revolver from his jacket — "I'm going now to the tsar and I will beg him to sign the manifesto. Either he signs or in his presence, I shall send a bullet through my head."

Nicholas signed. Two days later, he lamented to his mother, "My dearest Mama, you can't imagine what I went through before that moment. . . . From all over Russia they cried for it, they begged for it, and around me many — very many — held the same views. . . . There was no other way out than to cross oneself and give what everyone was asking for. My only consolation is that such is the will of God, and this grave decision will lead my dear Russia out of the intolerable chaos she has been in for nearly a year." While the tsar whined to his mother that he had violated his sacred oath to uphold the autocracy, the Russian people rejoiced. The October Manifesto, as the document came to be called, was read in churches and city squares. Strangers embraced one another in the street and threw champagne-soaked parties, celebrating. "The greatest moment in Russian history," one diarist recorded. Rallies in support drew tens of thousands in St. Petersburg, Moscow, Kiev, Odessa, Tiflis, Baku, Minsk, and other cities throughout the empire.

Then true mayhem erupted. Witte took over as president of the Council of Ministers, and the tsar's government attempted to work out the details of these new freedoms. Liberals debated how far to push the reforms and whether or not to support Witte, splitting their ranks. Given an inch, the revolutionaries now battled for more power. Lenin, Martov, and other socialist leaders planned on returning to Russia to foment further rebellion. The soviets organized more strikes, increasingly allowing revolutionaries to dominate their leadership and push toward an armed insurrection. Sensing the government's weakness, soldiers and sailors staged their own protests, and peasants ransacked their landlords' estates.

Fearing the autocracy's downfall, right-wing monarchists fought back with the tacit (and sometimes overt) support of the tsar and his ministers. In the streets, the Black Hundreds, a motley collection of monarchists, marched against liberals, socialists, and the Jews, whom they perceived as the wellspring of Russia's advance toward democracy. In gangs reinforced by common criminals and spurred on by the police, they attacked workers, students, and, most zealously, Jews. In the two weeks after the October Manifesto was announced, a reported three thousand Jews were killed in 690 separate pogroms. The greatest tragedy occurred in Odessa. After the *Potemkin* mutiny, General Kakhanov had been replaced by an even worse type, Baron A. V. Kaulbars, who assisted the Black Hundreds in an orgy of barbarity. Rallying under the cry "Beat the kikes," they torched Jewish homes, pillaged their stores, tossed Jews from rooftops, shot them at point-blank range, mowed them down with machine guns, disemboweled them, and raped them. Over three days, they murdered 800 Jews, wounded 5,000, and left over 100,000 homeless.

Hand in hand with this violence, the Russian people experienced six weeks of what became known as the "Days of Liberty." Unions multiplied. The soviets expanded their reach, especially in St. Petersburg, and they formed militias. Newspapers of every political viewpoint "increased like mushrooms," and nearly absolute freedom of assembly held sway.

These days vanished in early December after the Bolsheviks, prompted by Lenin and mildly encouraged by the Mensheviks and Socialist Revolutionaries, decided to launch an insurrection in Moscow. Though they lacked the population's general support and held misguided hopes that the military's rank and file would come to their side, they were intoxicated by their own fiery words. Lenin said at the time, "Victory, that for us is not the point at all. . . . We should not harbor any illusions. . . . The point is not about victory but about giving the regime a shake and attracting the masses to the movement."

After announcing a general strike and arming some workers, the revolutionaries, led in part by Vasilyev-Yuzhin (the same Bolshevik whom Lenin had sent to connect with the *Potemkin*), seized railway stations and erected barricades in several parts of the city. Over the next few days, a street war developed against the police and soldiers, shutting down Moscow. The governor-general of Moscow then petitioned the tsar for more troops. Sensing that Moscow could fall if the revolutionaries moved on the Kremlin, Nicholas authorized a ruthless repression, bolstered by advice from Witte and Trepov. Soldiers descended on the city with orders to "exterminate the gangs of insurgents." With artillery barrages and a hail of machine-gun bullets, the uprising was put down. Over one thousand Muscovites died.

Emboldened by the military's success, Nicholas then endorsed a widespread terror campaign against his opposition. Socialists were hunted down and killed. Workers and students were whipped with rods and thrown in jail. Peasant villages were torched to the ground. The new interior minister, P. N. Durnovo, instructed his provincial governors that "it is impossible to judge hundreds of thousands of people. I propose to shoot the rioters and in cases of resistance to burn their homes." Over the next five months, the campaign crushed the revolutionary parties, dispirited the liberals, filled the jails, ruined the economy, and left thousands more dead.

Nonetheless, the reforms Nicholas mandated in October could not be dismissed. For the first time, the Russian people had enjoyed the gift, as one observer wrote, "to think and talk freely." This they would not forget. For the first time, the tsar of Russia had agreed to relinquish absolute control over the country, setting in motion the creation of a popularly elected representative body. The people's voice *would* be heard, and Russia would never be the same again.

On April 27, 1906, the State Duma's elected deputies attended a reception at the Winter Palace before they opened their first session. In the vast Coronation Hall, the old and new leaders of Russia stood across from one another, divided by the gold and crimson throne, which was draped with an ermine imperial cloak. To the right stood finely dressed, wizened ministers and state councilors, medal-strewn and gold-braided admirals and generals, and bejeweled ladies in waiting — aristocracy, all of them. To the left stood the recently elected deputies, some in handsome evening clothes befitting their noble rank or wealth, but others in peasant frocks, worker blouses, and priest's cassocks. The two groups stared at one another like enemies across a battlefield.

At 1 P.M., the minister of ceremonies struck the floor with his staff and the doors opened. In came Nicholas, dressed in his Preobrazhensky Guards Regiment uniform. His mother and wife accompanied him at his left and right. A church choir chanted as they strode to the throne, lips pursed, crossing themselves as if on their way to a funeral. With his voice trembling at first, Nicholas read a prepared text from the throne, which promised an exalted future for Russia. He concluded with the hope that the deputies would "prove themselves worthy of the confidence bestowed by tsar and people." Then he bowed and solemnly left the hall, not having cast even a glance at the deputies throughout the ceremony. His court applauded enthusiastically. The deputies did not.

Afterward, they all filed out of the palace to the Neva River, where several small steamboats waited to transport them to the Tauride Palace, the seat of the new State Duma. The sun shone brilliantly as they made their way up the river. People lined the banks and covered the bridges, showing support for their new representatives. They slowed down as they passed the infamous Kresty Prison, where many who had fought for this day remained imprisoned. The deputies waved their hats in salute. Finally they arrived outside the expansive neoclassical palace erected by Catherine the Great to honor her lover and favorite general, Prince Potemkin. With great ambition and resolve, the State Duma opened.

Matyushenko and his crewmates were far from forgotten during these momentous events. A day after the signing of the October Manifesto, the Black Sea sailors joined with soldiers and port workers to demand the imprisoned members of *Potemkin*'s crew be released. Led by Lieutenant Pyotr Schmidt, who brazenly declared himself to be against the government, they broke into the prison and freed the men. Some were killed in pursuit, and Schmidt was arrested. This was the prologue to a fleetwide mutiny that broke out several weeks later (as

Matyushenko had promised and had fought to foment). On November 12, sailors and soldiers alike struck in Sevastopol and marched through the streets. Cowed by the size of the protest, the police and naval officers offered little resistance. Sailors broke into the fortress armory; others took control of several battleships and torpedo boats in the harbor and raised red flags on their masts. The next day, Lieutenant Schmidt, freed from prison, took command of the armored cruiser *Ochakov*, with several former *Potemkin* sailors at his side. They threatened to take over the entire base.

Once again, Vice Admiral Chukhnin appeared to lose the Black Sea Fleet. With little other recourse, he ordered the fortress to fire on the mutinous ships. The bombardment set afire the *Ochakov*, crippled several other ships, killed and injured dozens, and forced the sailors to capitulate. Chukhnin arrested over two thousand sailors and had Schmidt executed for his trouble, but the incident proved that the *Potemkin*'s rebellious spirit lived on in the navy. As a military force, it was ruined.

In the aftermath of Schmidt's revolt, Chukhnin again demanded that the Romanian government extradite the "nest of sailor revolutionaries" living in that country, blaming them for the spread of unrest within his fleet. Still the Romanians spurned him. Chukhnin then turned his attention to the court-martial of the imprisoned *Potemkin* sailors. Their continued presence at the base was too much of a threat.

On January 26, 1906, the trial finally opened. The proceedings lasted less than two weeks. Three crew members caught in Theodosia received death sentences, but these were commuted to fifteen years of forced labor after the prosecutors realized the punishment violated a clemency agreement in the October Manifesto. Three others earned lesser sentences of hard labor. Thirty-one sailors were imprisoned for two years, and the court discharged Officers Alekseyev and Golenko from service. As for Konstantin Feldmann, he had escaped from prison before the trial, masquerading as a soldier.

These results hardly satisfied a vengeful Chukhnin, but he could do nothing unless the mutiny's chief instigators returned to Russia and were captured. He would never see that day. The day after the *Potemkin* trial commenced, a Socialist Revolutionary — the daughter of a naval admiral — entered the Black Sea commander's Sevastopol dacha and shot him four times with a Browning pistol before turning the gun on herself. Miraculously, Chukhnin survived. Five months later though, a sailor named Yakov Akimov, employed as one of the dacha's gardeners, slipped a rifle onto the grounds and fired a single shot at the vice admiral, killing him. The tsar declared Chukhnin a national hero and had him laid to rest alongside Russia's most heralded admirals in Sevastopol's St. Vladimir Cathedral. In an adjacent cemetery, Captain Golikov, whose body had eventually washed ashore, was buried. His epitaph reads as follows: "God, have mercy on their souls. They know not what they do."

Matyushenko knew exactly what he had done and what he wanted to do, but by the start of 1906, he had lost his Romanian base of operations. The police there arrested him on suspicion of spreading socialist propaganda. Defying protests staged by over one hundred *Potemkin* sailors that Matyushenko be released, a Romanian court deported him to Austria-Hungary, from whence he traveled through Switzerland to France. Viewing him as a man without a home, wanted by few countries because of his high profile as a revolutionary, the French then sent him away. In June 1906, he stayed briefly in London before immigrating to the United States. He took a job at the Singer Sewing Machine factory in New York and reestablished ties with other Russian revolutionaries. That September, he met with Maxim Gorky, who helped him publish a memoir about the mutiny. Throughout his time in the city, Matyushenko campaigned tirelessly for the tsar's overthrow, gathering a band of devoted followers in his Lower East Side neighborhood, but he longed for action.

By year's end, he made his way back to France and organized a revolutionary group among the Parisian unemployed. His patience for debates and socialist tracts had worn even thinner, and he began to favor the anarchist views of his friend Arbore-Ralli. "Is there such a thing as a force for good?" Matyushenko wrote him from Paris. "Can a law be written to reflect what my heart and reason desire? My unfettered reason, my conscience, my pure desires — these are laws."

In January 1907 he prepared to return to Russia. He could not stand being away from his homeland, and more acutely, at a distance from his fight against the tsar. His comrades warned him not to go, sure that the manhunt pursuing him had not ended. But Matyushenko was determined. "I can't stay. I'm suffering here bitterly," he told one. In Geneva, he obtained a fake passport and a weapon. Unbeknownst to him, the Russian secret police already suspected that he might be coming.

Since the mutiny's end, Okhrana had continued the pursuit of Matyushenko as one of Russia's most wanted criminals. Although his trail had often gone cold, they had tracked him down over the past two years as he moved from country to country — Romania, Switzerland, France, Austria-Hungary, England, and the United States — but they were unable to win his extradition. Then, in May 1907, a report from a police agent in Paris informed Okhrana that Matyushenko was rumored to be heading to Russia. On June 6, his photograph was widely disseminated to border guards and police, with instructions to do everything possible to arrest him.

Still Matyushenko slipped undetected across the Russia-Romania border at the Dunay River, disguised as a fisherman. He arrived in Odessa on June 28 and rendezvoused with some revolutionaries. By chance, the house was under surveillance. The following day, Matyushenko left for the neighboring Black Sea port of Nikolayev, with the police following. They had no idea who he was, but since he kept the company of men who might have been involved in the recent theft of fifty thousand rubles from a Russian steamship, they considered it worth keeping an eye on him.

While Matyushenko was speaking to a sailor on a park bench in Nikolayev, the police moved in and arrested him. The report stated that he was found carrying a pistol, two spare cartridges, a notebook, a pamphlet titled "The Soldier," as well as papers that gave his name as Fedorenko from Poltava. It would be ten days before the police realized, from the word of an informant, that the documents were forged and that they had, in fact, captured Matyushenko himself.

The subsequent interrogation succeeded in revealing little more than the sparest of facts about his background. He admitted to being born on May 2, 1879, into a peasant family in a village near Kharkov, Ukraine. He had three brothers and two sisters. He had two years of schooling. He worked as a machinist before serving in the Russian navy. He was single and said he did not know if his parents were alive.

The colonel whose job it was to interrogate Matyushenko must have marveled at him. Could this be the man who had brought the Black Sea Fleet to its knees?

On October 11, Matyushenko was delivered to the Sevastopol prison. One of the inmates recalled seeing him for the first time: "Two dozen guards, with revolvers and bare sabers, conducted a man in a black suit. His calm and clear gaze bore witness to his iron will and unshakable resolve. A whisper was heard in the ensuing silence: It's Matyushenko . . . Matyushenko . . . Matyushenko."

He was forbidden visitors; nor could he receive or send messages — such was the fear that he could incite a rebellion on command. A week after his arrival, he was put on trial, charged with killing an officer. No fewer than one hundred guards conveyed him from his cell to the courtroom and back again. He offered no defense, pleading guilty to the charge. His sentence was death. The October Manifesto had banned executions of revolutionaries, but the tsar wanted this *one* hanged, despite a public outcry, and the judges ordered it so. Matyushenko refused to appeal and, as a reward, was allowed to smoke a cigarette.

The next evening, the guards carried a coffin into the courtyard. Word spread throughout the prison that Matyushenko would be hanged the following morning. Yefim Bredikhin was one of those who heard the news. A fellow *Potemkin* sailor, he had also recently been caught in Moscow. He had been transferred to Sevastopol and sentenced to fifteen years' hard labor. He was unable to sleep; like many others whose cells looked out onto the prison courtyard, Bredikhin began burrowing a spy hole in the wall underneath his cell window. At 5:30 A.M., a guard came to his door. Matyushenko wanted to bid him farewell.

Bredikhin followed the guard through the prison corridors to the sentry's room. He was instructed not to say a word during the meeting. Then they led him through several locked doors to Matyushenko's cell. He found his friend surrounded by naval officers of various ranks, there to observe him in his last hours as if he were some kind of rare animal. Leaning against the far wall of his barren cell, Matyushenko eyed the officers steadily, his face stripped of emotion. Bredikhin felt tears well up in his eyes. Matyushenko stepped toward his comrade and hugged him close, whispering into his ear, "It's not worth crying." He handed Bredikhin the golden cross from around his neck, the one given to him at his baptism. Engraved on the cross were the words SAVE AND PRESERVE. When Bredikhin asked Matyushenko to whom he should give the cross, the guards grabbed his shoulders and dragged him out of the cell. He realized too late that he should not have spoken.

Minutes later, Matyushenko, wearing a heavy wool coat, was led to his death. When he stepped into the prison courtyard, all was quiet. Two companies of Cossacks and dragoons guarded the grounds, and a number of naval officers had come to watch the execution. The sun had yet to rise, and the single electrical light cast the long shadow of the hangman on the courtyard wall. The makeshift gallows consisted of a heavy pole fixed in the ground and a table. A naval captain read out Matyushenko's crimes against the state. It took over an hour. Twice, Matyushenko spat to his side, but otherwise he stood still. At the end of the reading, he called out to the sailors in the guard, "Farewell, comrades!" When he tried to speak again, the captain screamed at him to be quiet. Calmly, Matyushenko asked, "Why are you yelling?" A priest came over to offer a final absolution, but Matyushenko brushed him aside and walked straight to the gallows.

The sky began to fill with light.

There were four hangmen, each with their collars up to hide their faces, fearing reprisal for executing a man who was hero to so many. The judge at the trial had told the lead executioner, a broad-shouldered mammoth, that he should take special care with Matyushenko, as he was dangerous. The hangman had replied, "I've dealt with some that were ripping their chains to shreds; I can handle this one."

But Matyushenko did not have to be wrestled into position. He stepped onto the table, still in his chains and manacles, and told those officers who were gathered around him, "Hang me, you cowards. But know, the time will come when it will be you hanging from the lampposts in the street."

The lead executioner stepped up on a stool to loop the noose around Matyushenko's neck. He brought up the slack in the rope secured to the pole, stepped down, and without pausing, kicked the table out from underneath Matyushenko. The rope went bolt straight.

Drums rolled. Matyushenko twisted and swayed several feet from the ground for the next fifteen minutes. The drums stopped.

The hangmen brought down Matyushenko. They struggled to take off the manacles because he had wrenched out several of his joints during his struggle for breath. Finally, they put his twenty-eight-year-old body into the coffin and carried him away to the same make-shift cemetery where the sailors of the November 1905 mutiny had been buried.

Alone outside Matyushenko's former cell, Bredikhin had neither heard the charges nor seen the hanging. In their brief exchange, Matyushenko had managed to pass him a note. It simply read, "Today the sentence will be carried out. I am proud to die for the truth, as a revolutionary should."

In the end, the *Potemkin* mutiny and the struggles of 1905 failed to remove Nicholas from the throne. That would take another twelve years and a river of blood.

Seventy-two days after the State Duma opened its first session, the tsar ordered its dissolution after the deputies made demands, including the freeing of all political prisoners, for which he would not stand. Nicholas still held the reins of control and, despite his October Manifesto, he still believed in his divine right to rule the Russian Empire as he pleased. New duma elections were held; new deputies were elected; and this new body was soon dissolved as well. By 1908, Nicholas had effectively broken every key promise of reform. A lack of coordination among the opposition, the army's sustained loyalty, and feints at political change that quieted the masses and further drove the wedge between liberals and socialists — these had kept Nicholas in power.

What caused the *Potemkin* mutiny to fail? Sailor memoirs and socialist polemics list many specific reasons, including its premature launch without the rest of the fleet, the difficult logistics of obtaining coal and water, a diffuse leadership structure, the betrayal of the *St. George,* an absence of support from those on land, and an unwillingness to remove the petty officers. But even if the crew had managed to endure for longer and bring more of the Black Sea Fleet to their side, their chances of instigating a mass uprising beyond the region looked doomed from the start, particularly given the overall impediments to revolution in Russia at the time.

For their efforts, Matyushenko and Vakulenchuk lost their lives, as did Petrov, Koshuba, and several other Tsentralka members. Of the entire *Potemkin* crew, some of whom returned to Russia in the years before Nicholas abdicated, 173 were court-martialed. Collectively, they earned 322 years of prison and forced labor in Siberia.

Most remained in exile, staying in Romania or scraping out a new existence in Switzerland, Argentina, Canada, Australia, the United States, England, Ireland, and elsewhere. Lieutenant Kovalenko became a schoolteacher in Geneva. Kirill and Feldmann followed similar paths, writing memoirs of their time aboard the *Potemkin* and then dying during Stalin's great purges in 1937. Some sailors returned to Russia after the tsar's fall in 1917, but only a few held positions in Lenin's new state, most notably committee member Lychev, who became an ambassador to Great Britain. For all of them, their eleven days of mutiny on the Black Sea marked the rest of their lives.

The battleship *Potemkin* itself fought no more for revolution. Not wanting to hear the battleship's name again, Nicholas had the *Potemkin* rechristened the *Panteleimon* ("all merciful"). The tsar's admirals used it to attack Turkish ships during World War I. Later, during the civil war that followed the Russian Revolution, embroiling the entire country, its engines were blown up so that it would not fall into Bolshevik hands. By 1925, the *Potemkin* had been ignobly scrapped for metal. A portion of its mast was even used for a lighthouse.

No doubt the mutiny fell short of its lofty goals, and the sailors suffered from this result, but this does not diminish the *Potemkin*'s significance, much as the failure of the 1905 Revolution overall did not preclude its impact on Russia's future. The Black Sea uprising struck at the heart of the tsar's pillar of support: the military. This came at a critical point in 1905, when Nicholas was contemplating peace with Japan and mandating a reform proposal developed by his interior minister, Bulygin. Although Nicholas never spelled out why he agreed to end the war and approve the August 1905 consultative duma, which then led to the October Manifesto, the mutiny affected him too deeply not to have influenced his thoughts.

The tsar and his allies dreaded a repeat of the mutiny and the wholesale loss of the military to revolution's side. As one monarchist said, "Each time the Black Sea Fleet sails, I fear lest another *Potemkin* be among them, and another Matyushenko amongst its crew." In February 1917, carrying on the *Potemkin*'s legacy, mutinies at the

Petrograd garrison and Kronstadt naval base proved to be the decisive blow that forced Nicholas from the throne. The gunshot from the light cruiser *Aurora,* signaling the Bolshevik military coup in October, punctuated the part played by sailors in the Russian Revolution from 1905 to 1917.

In the Soviet Empire, the *Potemkin* mutiny became one of the revolution's most symbolic and seminal moments. The government awarded the sailors medals and lauded them as heroes. Monuments were built and a litany of books were published about the events. Most famously, Sergei Eisenstein dramatized the story in his landmark film *Battleship Potemkin,* seen and studied throughout the world. Curiously, Feldmann played a cameo role in the film as a sailor.

Lenin called the 1905 revolution a "dress rehearsal"; it confirmed that he would need ruthless methods to seize control of Russia in the 1917 uprising. After his success, history was written and filmed to serve him. The Bolsheviks hijacked the *Potemkin* story for their own propaganda, asserting their party's pivotal role on the battleship. Lenin and his faithful leveled bitter invective at Matyushenko, who had openly rejected their party, marginalizing his efforts and accentuating any missteps that he had made. According to many histories, the mutiny ended in surrender because Matyushenko was not the bold Bolshevik leader that the crew needed. These political accounts aside, the sailors who participated in the Black Sea uprising did not mutiny to bring about the repressive Soviet state dominated by Lenin and his successor, Josef Stalin.

British historian Orlando Figes aptly characterized the Russian Revolution as "the people's tragedy" in a monumental survey of the period in his book of the same name. Part of this tragedy was that men, such as Matyushenko and his fellow crewmates, who sought freedom and a better life, died in a revolutionary struggle that resulted in a Russia they would have despised as much as the one they fought against.

The truth of their lives, and the reasons they sacrificed them, are worth recovering.

Dramatis Personae

Acknowledgments

Research Notes and Bibliography

Notes

Index

# Dramatis Personae

To assist the reader in navigating the many names in the story, the author has highlighted a number of the key individuals — although this list is certainly not comprehensive:

## Potemkin Mutineers

P. V. Alekseyev — sailor committee member who participated in the mission to buy meat in Odessa

A. P. Berezovsky ("Kirill") — Odessan revolutionary, a Menshevik, who became a member of the battleship's leadership

E. R. Bredikhin — sailor committee member, an anarchist, who was close to Matyushenko

S. A. Denisenko — sailor committee member who ran the engine room during the mutiny

I. A. Dymchenko — sailor committee member and one of the lead agitators

K. I. Feldmann — Odessan revolutionary, a Menshevik, who came on board the battleship when it first arrived in the port city

V. P. Kulik — machinist and sailor committee member, who was part of the funeral deputation to General Kakhanov

I. A. Lychev — sailor committee member and a close friend of Vakulenchuk

A. N. Matyushenko — Tsentralka member and "the soul of the mutiny," as one witness described him

F. V. Murzak — senior boatswain who was elected second officer by the sailor committee

F. Z. Nikishkin — stoker and one of the better agitators, who fired the first shot to start the mutiny

E. K. Reznichenko — sailor committee member who commanded the *Smely* to reconnaissance the squadron

G. N. Vakulenchuk — Tsentralka member and leader of the *Potemkin* revolutionaries

F. A. Vedenmeyer — senior signalman and sailor committee member

## Potemkin Officers

Ensign D. P. Alekseyev — elected by the sailor committee to act as captain after the mutiny

Lieutenant I. I. Gilyarovsky — second officer on the *Potemkin,* known as one of the cruelest of the "dragons"

Dr. A. S. Golenko — assistant ship surgeon, who elected to stay on the *Potemkin* after the mutiny

Captain E. N. Golikov — first officer of the *Potemkin*

Lieutenant I. M. Kovalenko — engine room officer, who elected to join the revolutionaries and became one of the ship's leaders

Ensign A. N. Makarov — supply officer who purchased the maggot-infested meat in Odessa

Dr. C. G. Smirnov — senior doctor on board the *Potemkin*

Lieutenant V. K. Ton — weapons officer who directly supervised Matyushenko

## Other Black Sea Fleet Sailors

S. P. Deinega — *St. George* revolutionary who helped launch the mutiny on his battleship

I. T. Yakhnovsky — founder of the revolutionary movement within the Black Sea Fleet

D. P. Koshuba — Tsentralka member who led the mutiny on the *St. George*

A. O. Kuzmenko — senior boatswain, who was elected to captain *St. George* after its mutiny

L. Pykhtin — stoker and saboteur on *Stremitelny*

A. M. Petrov — Tsentralka member who led the mutiny on the training ship *Prut*

M. L. Volgin — revolutionary sailor on the battleship *Twelve Apostles*

I. Babenko — torpedo quartermaster on the destroyer *Stremitelny*

## Other Black Sea Fleet Officers

Captain N. N. Banov — commanded the Russian transport ship *Psezuape,* which was in Constanza at the time of the mutiny

Captain A. P. Baranovsky — commanded the training ship *Prut*

Vice Admiral G. P. Chukhnin — head of the Black Sea Fleet and chiefly responsible for suppressing revolutionary unrest and the mutiny itself

Colonel P. P. Eikhen — commanded the military transport ship *Vekha*

Captain I. E. Guzevich — commanded the battleship *St. George*

Lieutenant A. A. Yanovich — volunteered to lead the destroyer *Stremitelny,* manned by officers, to hunt down the *Potemkin*

Lieutenant P. M. Klodt von Yurgensburg — commanded the torpedo boat *Ismail* before the mutiny

Captain M. N. Kolands — commanded the battleship *Twelve Apostles*

Vice Admiral A. H. Krieger — chief flag officer of the Black Sea Fleet who led the flagship *Rostislav* in the squadron sent after the *Potemkin* in Odessa

Rear Admiral S. Pisarevsky — head of the Black Sea Fleet training detachment, who retrieved the *Potemkin* after the mutiny's conclusion

Rear Admiral F. F. Vishnevetsky — led the battleship *Three Saints* and was second in command of the squadron sent to Odessa to sink the *Potemkin*

## Odessa Officials

General S. V. Kakhanov — military governor

General K. A. Karangozov — adjunct to Kakhanov

Mayor D. B. Neidhardt — head of civilian leadership

Brigadier General V. P. Pereleshin — head of the commercial port

N. I. Romanenko — port official and assistant to Pereleshin

## Constanza and Theodosia Officials

Mayor L. A. Durante — head of civilian leadership in Theodosia

Captain N. Negru — port commander of Constanza and lead negotiator with the *Potemkin* in Romania

General F. Pleshkov — garrison commander in Theodosia

## Key St. Petersburg Figures

Nicholas Romanov — tsar of all the Russias

Admiral F. K. Avelan — naval minister

A. G. Bulygin — interior minister

D. F. Trepov — deputy interior minister, a hardliner who proposed martial law be instituted in Odessa and surrounding regions

S. Iu. Witte — former finance minister and plenipotentiary to the Japan-Russia peace talks

P. N. Milyukov — historian and one of the leaders of Russian liberalism

S. N. Trubetskoy — rector of Moscow University who represented the *zemstvos* assembly to Nicholas II to promote government reform

# Acknowledgments

I am very grateful for my team of translators who helped decipher the mysteries of the Russian language (Matvei Yankelvich, Margaret Weiss, Olga Parno, Sergey Levchin, Zlata Akilova, Dima Dubson, Ludmilla Sheffer, Tanya Bass, Noam Primak, Efrem Yankelevich, and Christina Sever); the wisdom of Earl Dille and John Haley, who read the manuscript in advance and offered many improvements; the librarians at the New York Public Library, Slavic and Baltic Division, as well the archivists at the Russian State Naval Archive — your contribution to history should never go unrecognized; Elihu Rose, who illuminated me on the true nature of mutiny; my researchers in St. Petersburg and Moscow, Igor Kozyr and Irina Krivaya, who worked tirelessly by my side, cast the light down corridors I never would have discovered alone, and offered much needed guidance throughout; my friend Brett Forrest, who opened many doors in Russia; the kindness and generosity of Dr. Robert Zebroski, who provided me access to his voluminous research on the Black Sea Fleet, without which this would have been a much lesser book; the keen little red pen of Liz O'Donnell, the best of line editors, and my wonderful copyeditor, Susanna Brougham; the great representation and support of Scott Waxman and his comrade-in-arms Farley Chase; the finest editor and champion of my writing, Susan Canavan, and her team at Houghton Mifflin (with special mention for Megan Wilson and Reem Abu-Libdeh); my wife, Diane, for so many untold gifts that I almost blush at the thought of how lucky I am; and my baby daughter, Charlotte, who has taught me the meaning of joy. Finally, this book is dedicated to my grandparents, one of whom my family sadly lost during the course of my writing. His passing reminded me of how much we owe those who first help us stand on our own two feet.

# Research Notes and Bibliography

When writing *Red Mutiny,* I kept by my side a quotation from a historian of the French Revolution, Albert Mathiez: "The historian has a duty both to himself and to his readers. He has to a certain extent the cure of souls. He is accountable for the reputation of the mighty dead, whom he conjures up and portrays. If he makes a mistake, if he repeats slanders on those who are blameless, or holds up profligates or schemers to admiration, he not only commits an evil action; he poisons and misleads the public mind."

In my attempt at discovering the truth behind the events of the *Potemkin* mutiny, I had the boon and bane of a tremendous amount of research material. Many participants in the mutiny wrote memoirs, including Matyushenko, Kovalenko, Feldmann, Lychev, and Kirill. In addition to these, I had access to accounts written by Chukhnin, Kakhanov, Negru, and Krieger, as well as scores of other government officials, enabling me to tell both sides of the story. Further, during the court-martial investigations of the Black Sea mutinies in 1905, interviews were conducted with hundreds of sailors and officers who witnessed the events. Then there are the reams of telegrams and correspondence that passed back and forth between the Admiralty, the squadron, Nicholas II, Chukhnin, Kakhanov, Avelan, and officials in Odessa, Theodosia, and Constanza. For many of these latter documents (among others), I am indebted to Dr. Robert Zebroski, who provided copies of the research he conducted for his fine doctoral dissertation, "The Making of a Sailors' Revolution in the Black Sea Fleet, 1902–1905."

My own visits to the Russian archives, particularly the Naval Archives in St. Petersburg, uncovered fascinating source material, including ship logs of the *Stremitelny* and those battleships involved in the squadron sent after the *Potemkin.* Supporting this research, I found many contemporary newspaper and journal accounts of the events as well as several extensive document collections, such as Nevsky's *Vosstaniye na bronenostse Knyaz Potemkin Tavrichesky*. And finally, I enjoyed the benefit of countless histories by Russian scholars of the *Potemkin*, each offering new details and insights. Most important were Gavrilov's *V borbe za svobodu: Vosstaniye na bronenostse Potemkin* and Kardashev's *Burevestniki, revolyutsii v Rossii i flot*. The only published English-language version account of the mutiny, Richard Hough's Potemkin *Mutiny* (1960), was also helpful, although he lacked access to the Russian archives.

The difficulty in the scale and breadth of this amount of material resides in two factors: (1) the first-person accounts often contradict one another, whether because of the failings of memory or attempts to slant recollections for one's own benefit, and (2) many document collections and much of Russian scholarship have been influenced to accentuate the role of Lenin and the Bolshevik Party. In *Red Mutiny*, my challenge was to identify the most trustworthy first-person accounts, balance these against the whole, and discern fact from revisionism in histories written after 1917. I hope that my efforts have proved worthy, and any errors or misjudgments are wholly my own.

Finally, in 1905, the Russian Empire used the Julian calendar, which was thirteen days behind the Gregorian calendar used in the West. Throughout the book and notes section, I employ the Russian calendar. The sole exception to this rule is the use of the Gregorian calendar in the notes when referring to the dates of Western newspapers or magazines. The author, assisted by Yaroslav Gorbachov, has employed a conventional transliteration of Russian names, one based on the BGN/PCGN system.

## Archives in Russia*

Central State Archive of the October Revolution, Moscow — TsGAOR
Central State Historical Archive, St. Petersburg — TsGIA
Central State Military Historical Archive, Moscow — TsGVIA
Central State Historical Archive, Moscow — TsGIA(M)
Central State Archive of the Military Naval Fleet, St. Petersburg — TsGAVMF

## Contemporary Newspapers and Journals

*Chicago Tribune*
*Daily Telegraph* (London)

---

* Please note that I have used former designations of these archives since many documents were culled from research by Dr. Zebroski in 1988–89, when these were the applicable names.

*Iskra*
*Journal de St. Petersburg*
*Manchester Guardian*
*Moskovskiye Vedomosti*
*Nasha Zhizn*
*New York Herald Tribune*
*New York Times*
*Novoye Vremya*
*Osvobozhdeniye*
*Proletary*
*Russkiye Vedomosti*
*Russkoye Slovo*
*Times* (London)
*Washington Post*

## Books and Articles

Adoratsky, V. V., ed., *Krasny arkhiv,* 1925, vol. 8, pp. 250–53

Alekseyev, P. B., *Vosstaniye na bronenostse Knyaz Potemkin Tavrichesky* (Odessa, 1926)

Alexinsky, Gregor, *Modern Russia* (Charles Scribner's Sons, 1913)

Alzona, Encarnacion, *French Contemporary Opinion of the Russian Revolution of 1905* (Studies in History and Economics and Public Law, Columbia University, 1967)

Anthony, Irvin, *Revolt at Sea: A Narration of Many Mutinies* (G. P. Putnam's Sons, 1937)

Arbenina, Stella, *Through Freedom to Terror* (Hutchinson and Company, 1927)

Arbis Art Publishers, *Peterhof: The Great Palace* (St. Petersburg, 2001)

Ascher, Abraham, *The Revolution of 1905: Russia in Disarray* (Stanford University Press, 1988)

Ascherson, Neal, *Black Sea* (Hill and Wang, 1995)

Balmuth, Daniel, *The Russian Bulletin: A Liberal Voice in Tsarist Russia* (Peter Land, 2000)

Barkovets, A., *Dinastia Romanovyh: Tsarevich Alexi* (St. Petersburg, 2004)

Baron, Samuel, *Plekhanov: The Father of Russian Marxism* (Stanford University Press, 1963)

Baumann, Joachim, and Moosburger, Uwe, *Odessa: Facets of a Changing City* (Verlag Friedrich Pustet, 2003)

Baylen, Joseph, *The Tsar's Lecturer General: W. T. Snead and the Russian Revolution of 1905* (Georgia State College, 1969)

Bell, Christopher, and Elleman, Bruce, eds., *Naval Mutinies of the Twentieth Century: An International Perspective* (Frank Cass, 2003)

Belomor, A., *Vice-Admiral G. P. Chukhnin* (St. Petersburg, 1909)

Bennett, Geoffrey, "The *Potemkin* Mutiny" (*U.S. Naval Institute Proceedings*, September 1959), pp. 58–66

Berezovsky, Anatoly, *Odinnadtsat dney na Potemkine* (St. Petersburg, 1907)

Bernstein, Herman, ed., *The Willy-Nicky Correspondence* (Alfred A. Knopf, 1918)

Bind, Edward, *The Secret Letters of the Last Tsar* (Longmans, Green, and Company, 1938)

*Black Sea Coast of the Soviet Union: A Short Guide* (Foreign Languages Publishing House, 1957)

Bliznyuk, A. M., "Reis Stremitelnogo" (*Voprosy Istory*, no. 6, 1975), pp. 212–14

Bogachev, P. M., ed., *Revolyutsionnoye dvizheniye v chernomorskom flote v 1905–1907 gg* (Moscow, 1956)

British Admiralty, *The Black Sea Pilot* (Hydrographic Department, 1942)

Brooks, Jeffrey, *When Russia Learned to Read: Literacy and Popular Literature* (Princeton University Press, 1985)

Bullocke, J. G., *Sailors' Rebellion: A Century of Naval Mutinies* (Eyre and Spottiswoode, 1938)

Bulow, Prince Von, *Memoirs of Prince Von Bulow*, vols. 1 and 2 (Little, Brown and Company, 1931)

Busch, Noel, *The Emperor's Sword: Japan vs. Russia in the Battle of Tsushima* (Funk and Wagnalls, 1969)

Bushnell, John, *Mutiny amid Repression: Russian Soldiers in the Revolution of 1905–1906* (Indiana University Press, 1985)

———, *The Tsarist Officer Corps, 1881–1914: Customs, Duties, Inefficiency* (American Historical Review, October 1981)

Byrnes, Robert F., *Pobedonostsev: His Life and Thought* (Indiana University Press, 1968)

Cecil, Lamar, *Wilhelm II: Emperor and Exile: 1900–1941*, vol. 2 (University of North Carolina Press, 1996)

Chernenko, A. M., and Shlyakhov, A. B., "P. M. Matyushenko" (*Ukrains'kyy Istorychnyy Zhurnal*, no. 10, 1989), pp. 136–41

Chernov, Yu, *Myatezhny Bronenosets* (Moscow, 1990)

Curtis, William, *Around the Black Sea* (Hodder and Stoughton, 1911)

Delbruck, Hans, *The Barbarian Invasions*, vol. 2 of *History of the Art of War* (University of Nebraska Press, 1990)

Dennett, Tyler, *Roosevelt and the Russo-Japanese War* (Peter Smith, 1959)

Deutscher, Isaac, *The Prophet Armed: Trotsky, 1879–1921* (Oxford University Press, 1954)

Dillon, E. J., *The Eclipse of Russia* (George H. Doran Company, 1918)

*Dispatches from U.S. Consuls in St. Petersburg, 1803–1906* (National Archives and Records Service, 1963)

Don Levine, Isaac, ed., *Letters from the Kaiser to the Czar* (Frederick Stokes Company, 1920)

Ducamp, Emmanuel, *The Winter Palace* (Alain du Gourcuff Editeur, 1995)

Dugdale, E. T. S., ed., *German Diplomatic Documents, 1871–1914,* vol. 3 (Methuen and Company, 1928)

Elchaninov, A., *The Tsar and His People* (Harper and Brothers, 1890)

Emelin, Y., *Naval Officers Killed During Time of Revolution, 1905–1907* (St. Petersburg, 2003)

Erickson, Carolly, *Alexandra: The Last Tsarina* (St. Martin's Press, 2001)

Essad-Bey, Mohammed, *Nicholas II: Prisoner of the Purple* (Funk and Wagnalls Company, 1937)

Esthus, Raymond, *Double Eagle and Rising Sun* (Duke University Press, 1988)

Fedorov, A. M., *Revolyutsionnyye vosstaniia v chernomorskom flote v 1905g* (Moscow, 1946)

Feldmann, K. I., *The Revolt of the* Potemkin, translated by Constance Garnet (W. Heineman, 1908)

Figes, Orlando, *A People's Tragedy: The Russian Revolution* (Penguin, 1996)

Fischer, George, *Russian Liberalism: From Gentry to Intelligentsia* (Harvard University Press, 1958)

Fischer, Louis, *The Life of Lenin* (Harper and Row, 1964)

Fisher, Alan, *The Crimean Tatars* (Hoover Institution Press, 1978)

Fox, Ralph, *Lenin: A Biography* (Harcourt, Brace and Company, 1934)

Fuller, William, *Civil-Military Conflict in Imperial Russia* (Princeton University Press, 1985)

Galai, Shmuel, *The Liberation Movement in Russia, 1900–1905* (Cambridge University Press, 1973)

Gasiorowski, Waclaw, *Tragic Russia* (Cassell and Company, 1908)

Gautier, Theophile, *Russia* (Arno Press, 1970)

Gavrilov, B. I., *V borbe za svobodu: Vosstaniye na bronenostse Potemkin* (Moscow: Mysl, 1987)

——, "Vosstaniye na 'Georgy Pobedonosets'" (*Voprosy Istorii,* no. 6, 1975), pp. 120–28

Genkin, I., *Vosstaniye na bronenostse "Potemkin Tavrichesky": K dvadtsatiletiyu vosstaniya* (Moscow-Leningrad, 1925)

George, Arthur, *St. Petersburg: Russia's Window to the Future* (Taylor Trade Publishing, 2003)

George, James, *History of Warships: From Ancient Times to the Twenty-first Century* (Naval Institute Press, 1998)

Gerasimov, A., *Krasny bronenosets: Vooruzhennoye vosstaniye v 1905 godu na bronenostse "Potemkin Tavrichesky"* (Leningrad, 1925)

Getzler, Israel, *Martov: A Political Biography of a Russian Social Democrat* (Cambridge University Press, 1967)

Grand Duke Cyril, *My Life in Russia's Service — Then and Now* (Selwyn and Blount, 1939)

Grishin, P. P., *Uroki "Potemkina" i taktika vooruzhennogo vosstaniya* (Moscow-Leningrad, 1932)

Gurko, V. I., *Features and Figures of the Past* (Stanford University Press, 1939)

Guttridge, Leonard, *Mutiny: A History of Naval Insurrection* (Naval Institute Press, 1992)

Gwynn, Stephen, ed., *The Letters and Friendships of Sir Cecil Spring Rice* (Greenwood Press, 1929)

Hagerman, Herbert, *Letters of a Young Diplomat* (Rydal Press, 1937)

Hall, Coryne, *Little Mother of Russia: A Biography of the Empress Marie Feodorovna* (Holmes and Meier, 2001)

Hamburg, G. M., *Politics of the Russian Nobility* (Rutgers University Press, 1984)

Hamm, Michael, ed., *The City in Late Imperial Russia* (Indiana University Press, 1986)

Hammond, Nicholas, *Alexander the Great: King, Commander, and Statesman* (Noyes Press, 1980)

*Handbook for Travellers: Russia, Poland, and Finland* (John Murray, 1888)

Hapgood, Isabel, *Russian Rambles* (Houghton Mifflin, 1895)

Harcave, Sidney, *Count Sergei Witte and the Twilight of Imperial Russia* (M. E. Sharpe, 2004)

———, *First Blood: The Russian Revolution of 1905* (Macmillan Company, 1964)

———, ed., *The Memoirs of Count Witte* (M. E. Sharpe, Inc., 1990)

Hardinge, Lord of Penshurst, *Old Diplomacy* (John Murray, 1947)

Harrison, W., *The British Press and the Russian Revolution of 1905* (Oxford Slavonic Papers, vol. 7, 1974), pp. 74–95

Hathaway, Jane, ed., *Rebellion, Repression, Reinvention: Mutiny in Comparative Perspective* (Praeger, 2001)

Healy, Ann, *The Russian Autocracy in Crisis* (Archon Books, 1976)

Herlihy, Patricia, *Odessa: A History, 1794–1914* (Harvard University Press, 1986)

Herwig, Holger, *The German Naval Officer Corps: A Social and Political History* (Clarendon Press, 1973)

Hitchens, Keith, *Rumania, 1866–1947* (Clarendon Press, 1994)

Hone, Joseph, *Duck Soup in the Black Sea: Further Collected Travels* (Hamish Hamilton, 1988)

Hough, Richard, *The Fleet That Had to Die* (Birlinn, 1958)

———, *The Potemkin Mutiny* (Pantheon Books, 1960)

Howe, M. A. Dewolfe, *George von Lengerke Meyer* (Dodd, Mead and Company, 1920)

Ignatyev, A. A., *A Subaltern in Old Russia* (Hutchinson and Company, 1944)

Inozemtsev, M., ed., "Bronenosets 'Knyaz Potemkin Tavrichesky' v Odesse" (*Krasny arkhiv*, nos. 69–70, 1935), pp. 72–100

Iroshnikov, Mikhail, *Before the Revolution: St. Petersburg in Photographs* (Harry Abrams, 1991)

Jane, Fred, *Imperial Russian Navy* (Thacker and Company, 1904)

Joubert, Carl, *The Truth About the Tsar* (Eveleigh Nash, 1905)

Judge, Edward, *Plehve: Repression and Reform in Imperial Russia* (Syracuse University Press, 1983)

Kagan, Frederick, and Higham, Robin, eds., *The Military History of Tsarist Russia* (Palgrave, 2002)

Kanatchikov, Semyon Ivanovich, *A Radical Worker in Tsarist Russia* (Stanford University Press, 1986)

Kardashev, Iu., *Burevestniki, revolyutsii v Rossii i flot* (Moscow, 1987)

——, "Nesostoyavshayasya Kazn" (*Sovetskiye Arkhivy*, no. 5, 1970), pp. 64–67

——, "Novyye Svedeniya o Vosstanii na Bronenostse Potemkin" (*Voprosy Istorii*, no. 11, 1965), pp. 57–65

Karsten, Peter, *The Naval Aristocracy: The Golden Age of Annapolis and Emergence of Modern American Navalism* (Free Press, 1972)

Keegan, John, *The Price of Admiralty* (Penguin Books, 1990)

Keep, J. L. H., *The Rise of Social Democracy in Russia* (Clarendon Press, 1963)

——, *Soldiers of the Tsar: Army and Society in Russia, 1462–1874* (Clarendon Press, 1985)

Kennan, George F., *Russia Leaves the War* (Princeton University Press, 1956)

Kennard, Howard, *The Russian Peasant* (J. B. Lippincott Company, 1908)

King, Charles, *The Black Sea: A History* (Oxford University Press, 2004)

King, Greg, *The Court of the Last Tsar: Pomp, Power, and Pageantry in the Reign of Nicholas II* (John Wiley and Sons, 2006)

Klado, Captain Nicolas, *The Battle of the Sea of Japan* (Hodder and Stoughton, 1906)

——, *The Russian Navy in the Russo-Japanese War* (Hurst and Blackett, 1905)

Klier, John D., ed., *Pogroms: Anti-Jewish Violence in Modern Russian History* (Cambridge University Press, 1992)

Kokovtsov, Count, *Out of My Past* (Stanford University Press, 1935)

Korostovetz, J. J., *Pre-War Diplomacy: The Russo-Japanese Problem* (British Periodicals Limited, 1920)

Kovalenko, A. M., "Odinnadtsat dney na bronenostse Knyaz Potemkin Tavrichesky," *Byloe* (no. 1[13]), 1907), pp. 88–113; (no. 2[14] 1907), pp. 124–41; (no. 3[15] 1907), pp. 46–68

*Krasny arkhiv,* "Vosstaniye na bronenostse *Georgy Pobedonosets*" (vols. 11–12, 1925), pp. 231–62

Kravchinsky, Serge, *The Russian Peasantry* (Swan Sonnenschein, 1894)

Krupskaya, Nadezhda, *Reminiscences of Lenin* (Lawrence and Wishart, 1960)

Lenin, V. I., *Collected Works,* vol. 8 (Foreign Languages Publishing House, 1962)

Lieven, Dominic, *Nicholas II: Emperor of All Russias* (John Murray, 1993)

Lincoln, W. Bruce, *In War's Dark Shadow: The Russians Before the Great War* (Dial Press, 1983)

———, *Sunlight at Midnight: St. Petersburg and the Rise of Modern Russia* (Basic Books, 2000)

Los, F. E., ed., *Revolyutsiya 1905–1907 rokiv na Ukraine* (Kiev, 1955)

———, *Revolyutsionnaya borba na Ukraine v period pervoy russkoy revolyutsii. 1905g.* (Kiev, 1955)

Lychev, I. A., *Potemkintsy* (Moscow, 1954)

Lyubimov, D. N., "Russkaya Smuta" (Bakhmeteff Archive of Russian and East European History and Culture, Columbia University, n.d.)

MacDonogh, Giles, *The Last Kaiser: William the Impetuous* (Weidenfeld and Nicolson, 2000)

Mahan, A. T., *Types of Naval Officers* (Little, Brown and Company, 1901)

Manning, Roberta, *The Crisis of the Old Order in Russia* (Princeton University Press, 1982)

Massie, Robert, *Dreadnought: Britain, Germany, and the Coming of the Great War* (Random House, 1991)

———, *Nicholas and Alexandra* (Atheneum, 1968)

———, *Peter the Great: His Life and World* (Alfred A. Knopf, 1980)

*Master Roll of the Marine Department and Naval Fleet* (St. Petersburg, 1907)

Matyushenko, A. N., "Pravda o Potemkine," *Vosstaniye na bronenostse Potemkin Tavrichesky,* Nevsky, V. I., ed, Part VII — Matrosy chernogo morya (Moscow, 1923)

Maud, Renee Elton, *One Year at the Russian Court: 1904–1905* (John Lane Company, 1918)

Maylunas, Andrei, and Mironenko, Sergei, *A Lifelong Passion: Nicholas and Alexandra, Their Own Story* (Weidenfeld and Nicolson, 1996)

Maynard, John, *The Russian Peasant and Other Studies* (Collier Books, 1962)

McCormick, Frederick, *The Tragedy of Russia in Pacific Asia* (Outing Publishing Company, 1907)

McCully, Newton, *The McCully Report: The Russo-Japanese War* (Naval Institute Press, 1977)

McFarland, Philip, *Sea Dangers: The Affair of the Somers* (Schocken Books, 1985)

McGuffie, T. H., *Stories of Famous Mutinies* (Arthur Baker Limited, 1966)

McNeal, Robert H., *Tsar and Cossack, 1855–1914* (Macmillan, 1987)

McReynolds, Louise, *The News Under Russia's Old Regime* (Princeton University Press, 1991)

Mehlinger, Howard, and Thompson, John, *Count Witte and the Tsarist Government in the 1905 Revolution* (Indiana University Press, 1972)

Melnikov, P. M., *Bronenostse Potemkin* (St. Petersburg: Sudostroeniye, 1980)

Milyukov, Paul, *Political Memoirs: 1905–1917* (University of Michigan Press, 1967)

Mishanov, Valentin, *The Navy of the Russian Empire* (Slavia Art Books, 1996)

Mitchell, Donald, *A History of Russian and Soviet Sea Power* (Macmillan Publishing, 1974)

Mitchell, Mairin, *The Maritime History of Russia, 848–1948* (Sidgwick and Jackson, 1949)

Morison, Elting, *The Letters of Theodore Roosevelt* (Harvard University Press, 1951)

Mossolov, A. A., *At the Court of the Last Tsar* (Methuen and Company, 1935)

*Nagel Travel Guides: Rumania* (Nagel Publishers, 1967)

Naida, S. F., ed., *Revolyutsionnoye dvizheniye v tsarskom flote, 1825–1917* (Moscow, 1948)

———, *Voennyye moryaki v period pervoy russkoy revolyutsii 1905–1907* (Moscow-Leningrad, 1955)

National Archives and Records Service, "Dispatches from U.S. Consuls in Odessa, 1834–1906," vol. 13, February 25, 1903–August 14, 1906 (1963)

Neuberger, Joan, *Hooliganism: Crime, Culture, and Power in St. Petersburg* (University of California Press, 1993)

Nevinson, Henry, *The Dawn in Russia, or Scenes in the Russian Revolution* (Harper and Brothers, 1906)

Nevsky, V. I., ed., *Vosstaniye na bronenostse "Knyaz Potemkin Tavrichesky": Vospominaniya materialy i dokumenty* (Moscow-Petrograd, 1924)

*1905 god. Revolyutsionnoye dvizheniye v Odesse i Odesshchine* (Odessa, 1925)

Nish, Ian, *The Origins of the Russo-Japanese War* (Longman, 1985)

*Nominal Roll of Lieutenants and Midshipmen* (St. Petersburg, 1904)

Novikoff-Priboy, A., *Tsushima* (Alfred A. Knopf, 1937)

O'Connell, Robert L., *Sacred Vessels: The Cult of the Battleship and the Rise of the U.S. Navy* (Westview Press, 1991)

Oldenburg, S. S., *Last Tsar: Nicholas II, His Reign, and Russia* (Academic International Press, 1977)

Olgin, Moissaye, *The Soul of the Russian Revolution* (Henry Holt and Company, 1917)

Oliphant, Laurence, *The Russian Shores of the Black Sea* (Konemann, 1998)

Paleologue, Maurice, *Three Critical Years: 1904–1906* (Robert Speller and Sons, 1957)

Pares, Bernard, *My Russian Memoirs* (AMS Press, 1931)

*Parliamentary Debates: The 6th Session of the 27th Parliament of the United Kingdom of Great Britain and Ireland,* vol. 148 (Wyman and Sons, 1905)

Payne, Robert, *The Life and Death of Lenin* (Simon and Schuster, 1964)

——, *The Terrorists* (Funk and Wagnalls Company, 1957)

Pipes, Richard, *The Russian Revolution* (Vintage Books, 1991)

——, *Struve: Liberal on the Left, 1870–1905* (Harvard University Press, 1970)

Platonov, A. P., ed., *Vosstaniye v chernomorskom flote v 1905g* (Leningrad, 1925)

Pleshakov, Constantine, *The Tsar's Last Armada: The Epic Journey to the Battle of Tsushima* (Basic Books, 2002)

Pleskov, V. A., ed., *Tsarsky Flot pod Krasnym Styagom* (Moscow, 1931)

Plotto, Alexandre V., *Au Service du Pavillon de Saint Andre* (Paris, 1998)

Pobedonostsev, Konstantin, *Reflections of a Russian Statesman* (University of Michigan Press, 1965)

Pokrovsky, M. N., ed., *Armiya v pervoy revolyutsii: Ocherki i materialy* in series 1905: *Materialy i dokumenty* (Moscow-Leningrad, 1927)

Politovsky, Eugene, *From Libau to Tsushima* (John Murray, 1906)

Ponomarev, I. I., *Geroyi Potemkina* (Moscow, 1955)

Popov, M., "Potemkin v Feodosii" (*Voenno-Istorichesky Zhurnal,* no. 22[6], 1980), pp. 64–67

Prokhorov, A. M., ed., *Great Soviet Encyclopedia* (Macmillan, 1973)

*Proletarskaya revolyutsiya,* no. 12 (147), 1925.

Pyatnitsky, O., *Memoirs of a Bolshevik* (International Publishers, 1933)

Radzinsky, Edvard, *The Last Tsar: The Life and Death of Nicholas II* (Doubleday and Company, 1992)

Rawson, Don, *Russian Rightists and the Revolution of 1905* (Cambridge University Press, 1995)

Reichman, Henry, *Railwaymen and Revolution: Russia, 1905* (University of California Press, 1987)

*Revolyutsionny bronenosets. Vosstaniye v chernomorskom flote* (Po materialam "Iskra" i "Sotsialdemokrata") (Geneva, 1905)

Rice, Christopher, *Russian Workers and the Socialist-Revolutionary Party Through the Revolution of 1905–1907* (Macmillan, 1988)

Riha, Thomas, *A Russian European: Paul Miliukov in Russian Politics* (University of Notre Dame Press, 1969)

Rivet, Charles, *The Last of the Romanofs* (E. P. Dutton and Company, 1918)

Robbins, Richard, *The Tsar's Viceroys* (Cornell University Press, 1987)

Romanov, Alexander, *Once a Grand Duke* (Farrar and Rinehart, 1932)

Romanov, Nicholas, *Dnevnik Imperatora Nikolaia II, 1890–1906* (Moscow, 1991)

Rose, Elihu, "Anatomy of Mutiny" (*Armed Forces and Society*, 1982), pp. 561–74

———, "Mutiny on the *Potemkin*" (*Military History Quarterly*, Autumn 1988), pp. 105–113

Rosen, Baron, *Forty Years of Diplomacy* (Alfred A. Knopf, 1922)

Rostotskaya, N., *Potemkinskie dni v Odesse* (Odessa, 1906)

Sablinsky, Walter, *The Road to Bloody Sunday* (Princeton University Press, 1976)

Salisbury, Harrison, *Black Night, White Snow: Russia's Revolutions, 1905–1917* (Doubleday and Company, 1978)

Sanders, Jonathan, "The Union of Unions" (dissertation, Columbia University, 1985)

Saul, Norman, *Sailors in Revolt: The Russian Baltic Fleet in 1917* (Regents Press, 1978)

Schwarz, Solomon, *The Russian Revolution of 1905* (University of Chicago Press, 1967)

Selivanov, V. I., *Matros Matyushenko* (Moscow, 1931)

———, *Matros Petrov* (Moscow, 1931)

Service, Robert, *Lenin: A Biography* (Harvard University Press, 2000)

Shanin, Teodor, *Russia, 1905–1907: Revolution as a Moment of Truth* (Yale University Press, 1986)

Shlyakhov, A. B., "Potemkintsy v Sevastopolskom Vosstanii" (*Voprosy Istorii*, no. 11, 1985), pp. 178–80

Singleton, Esther, ed., *Russia as Seen and Described by Famous Writers* (Dodd, Mead and Company, 1904)

Smith, Edward, *The Young Stalin: The Early Years of an Elusive Revolutionary* (Farrar, Straus and Giroux, 1967)

Spector, Ivar, *The First Russian Revolution: Its Impact on Asia* (Prentice Hall, 1962)

Spector, Ronald, *At War, at Sea: Sailors and Naval Combat in the Twentieth Century* (Viking, 2001)

Stern, Leo, *Die Russische Revolution von 1905–1907 im Spiegel der Deutschen Presse* (Rutten and Loening, 1961)

Stockdale, Melissa, *Paul Miliukov and the Quest for a Liberal Russia* (Cornell University Press, 1996)

Subtelny, Orest, *Ukraine: A History* (University of Toronto Press, 1988)

Surh, Gerald, *1905 in St. Petersburg: Labor, Society, and Revolution* (Stanford University Press, 1989)

Thompson, Arthur, and Hart, Robert, *The Uncertain Crusade: America and the Russian Revolution of 1905* (University of Massachusetts, 1970)

Tomilov, S. A., *Bronenosets Potemkin* (Odessa, 1975)

Tomitch, V. M., *Battleships*, vol. 1 of *Warships of the Imperial Russian Navy* (BT Publishers, 1968)

Treadgold, Donald, *Lenin and His Rivals: The Struggle for Russia's Future* (Frederick Praeger, 1955)

Treptow, Kurt, *A History of Romania* (Columbia University Press, 1996)

Trotsky, Leon, *My Life: An Attempt at an Autobiography* (Charles Scribner's Sons, 1931)

——, *1905* (Random House, 1971)

Troyat, Henri, *Daily Life in Russia Under the Last Tsar* (Stanford University Press, 1959)

Tyrkova-Williams, Ariadna, *Cheerful Giver: The Life of Harold Williams* (Peter Davies, 1935)

Urossov, Serge Dmitriyevich, *Memoirs of a Russian Governor* (Harper and Brothers, 1908)

U.S. Department of State, *Papers Relating to the Foreign Relations of the United States* (1906)

Valentinov, Nikolay, *Encounters with Lenin* (Oxford University Press, 1968)

Valk, S. N., et al., *1905 god v Peterburge* (Leningrad-Moscow, 1925)

Van der Kiste, John, and Hall, Coryne, *Once a Grand Duchess: Xenia, Sister of Nicholas II* (Sutton Publishing, 2002)

Van Dyke, Carl, *Russian Imperial Military Doctrine and Education, 1832–1914* (Greenwood Press, 1990)

Vasilyev-Yuzhin, M. I. V., *V ogne pervoy revolyutsii* (Moscow, 1955)

Vassili, Count Paul, *Behind the Veil at the Russian Court* (John Lane Company, 1914)

Verner, Andrew, *The Crisis of Russian Autocracy: Nicholas II and the 1905 Revolution* (Princeton University Press, 1990)

Vilensky, V., ed., *Katorga i ssylka*, no. 5, vol. 18 (Moscow, 1927)

Villari, Luigi, *Russia Under the Great Shadow* (T. Fisher Unwin, 1905)

Viroubova, Anna, *Memories of the Russian Court* (Macmillan Company, 1923)

Vorres, Ian, *The Last Grand Duchess: Her Imperial Highness Grand Duchess Olga Alexandrovna* (Charles Scribner's Sons, 1964)

Walkin, Jacob, *The Rise of Democracy in Pre-Revolutionary Russia* (Frederick Praeger, 1962)

Wallace, Donald Mackenzie, *Russia* (Henry Holt and Company, 1908)

Warner, Denis, and Warner, Peggy, *The Tide at Sunrise: A History of the Russo-Japanese War* (Frank Cass, 2002)

Warth, Robert, *Nicholas II: The Life and Reign of Russia's Last Monarch* (Praeger, 1997)

Washburn, Stanley, *The Cable Game: The Adventures of a Press Boat During the Russian Revolution of 1905* (Andrew Melrose, 1913)

Weber, Max, *The Theory of Social and Economic Organization* (Free Press, 1997)

Weinberg, Robert, *The Revolution of 1905 in Odessa* (Indiana University Press, 1993)

Wells, David, and Wilson, Sandra, *The Russo-Japanese War in Cultural Perspective, 1904–1905* (St. Martin's Press, 1999)

Westwood, J. N., *Russia Against Japan, 1904–1905: A New Look at the Russo-Japanese War* (State University of New York Press, 1986)

———, *Witnesses of Tsushima* (The Diplomatic Press, 1970)

White, John, *The Diplomacy of the Russo-Japanese War* (Princeton University Press, 1996)

Wieczyneki, Joseph, ed., *Modern Encyclopedia of Russian and Soviet History,* vol. 24 (Academic International Press, 1981)

Wildman, Allan, *The End of the Russian Imperial Army* (Princeton University Press, 1980)

Williams, Harold Whitmore, *Russia of the Russians* (Pitman and Sons, 1914)

Wilson, H. G., *Battleships in Action,* vol. 1 (Scholarly Press, 1969)

Wintringham, Thomas, *Mutiny: Being a Survey of Mutinies from Spartacus to Invergordon* (Stanley Nott, 1936)

Witte, Count Sergei, *Memoirs of Count Witte* (Howard Fertig, 1967)

Wolfe, Bertram, *Three Who Made a Revolution* (Delta Books, 1964)

Woodward, David, *The Russians at Sea: A History of the Russian Navy* (Frederick A. Praeger, 1965)

Wynn, Charters, *Workers, Strikes, and Pogroms: The Donbass-Dnepr Bend in Late Imperial Russia* (Princeton University Press, 1992)

Yegorov, I. "Potemkin Tavrichesky" (*Morskoy sbornik,* nos. 6–7, 1925), pp. 3–16

Zadneprovsky, N., and Sokolov, N., *Afanasy Matyushenko* (Kharkov, 1958)

Zebroski, Anthony, "The Making of a Sailors' Revolution in the Black Sea Fleet, 1902–1905," dissertation (State University of New York at Stony Brook, 1994)

# Notes

*page* PROLOGUE

xiii   *"History does nothing":* Marx, as quoted in Wolfe, front matter, n.p.

*At 91 rue de Carouge:* Service, p. 164; Valentinov, pp. 79–80, 146–47; Krupskaya, p. 120; Salisbury, pp. 138–39.

*It was the end:* Chernenko and Shlyakhov; Selivanov, *Matros Matyushenko,* pp. 29–30.

*When he spoke:* Valentinov, p. 146.

*One day he would:* Salisbury, p. 151.

xiv   *"The Rubicon has":* Lenin, *Collected Works,* vol. 8, p. 562. In a long article about the *Potemkin* written directly after the mutiny, Lenin wrote, "No reprisals no partial victories over the revolution can diminish the importance of this event. The first step has been taken. The Rubicon has been crossed."

*To many stories:* Feldmann, pp. 17–19; Hough, *Potemkin Mutiny,* pp. 23–26; Ponomarev, p. 53; Selivanov, *Matros Matyushenko,* p. 10.

*"he lived not":* Selivanov, *Matros Matyushenko,* p. 9.

*After the mutiny's end:* Chernenko and Shlyakhov; Selivanov, *Matros Matyushenko,* pp. 27–30; TsGIA(M), f. 102, op. 00, d. 1667, p. 5; Hough, *Potemkin Mutiny,* pp. 223–26.

*While in Switzerland:* Krupskaya, pp. 117–19.

xv   *"It's not for me":* Chernenko and Shlyakhov.

*These intellectual leaders:* Selivanov, *Matros Matyushenko,* pp. 29–30.

*That afternoon, Matyushenko:* ibid.; Chernenko and Shlyakhov; Krupskaya, pp. 117–18.

PART I

1   *"Where there is":* Mitchell, M., p. 37.

*"Shine out in all":* Kennan, p. 3.

CHAPTER 1

3   *The Neva River:* Gautier, pp. 139–43; Erickson, pp. 150–53; Kennan, pp. 3–4; Hapgood, pp. 56–57.

*Nicholas II began:* Pleshakov, p. 183; Gurko, pp. 339–42; Harcave, *First Blood,* p. 78; Ascher, p. 75; Erickson, pp. 150–53; Hagerman, pp. 90–93; Maud, pp. 107–11; Van der Kiste and Hall, p. 59; Hardinge, p. 112; Vorres, pp. 113–14; Hall, pp. 205–6; Lincoln, *In War's Dark Shadow,* p. 286; Rosen, pp. 253–54; Hapgood, pp. 57–58; *Daily Telegraph,* January 20, 1905. The events of the Blessing of the Waters have been widely documented in memoirs by court individuals, who remembered the occasion in great detail.

4  *Icons of the patron saints:* Ducamp, p. 68; King, G., pp. 172, 307–8.
  *"in the coming year":* Salisbury, p. 115.
  *The city of St. Petersburg:* Lincoln, *Sunlight at Midnight,* pp. 20–21.

5  *In his private life, Nicholas:* Figes, p. 12.
  *In this St. Petersburg:* Olgin, pp. 15–17; Ascher, pp. 20–24; Kanatchikov, pp. 83–84.
  *Across the breadth:* Massie, *Nicholas and Alexandra,* p. 3; Kennard, pp. 6–7; Wolfe, p. 11.
  *None of these people:* Figes, p. 11.

6  *"more rolling and peculiarly warlike":* Gurko, p. 341.
  *His younger sister:* Vorres, p. 114.
  *Murder had been the fate:* Gasiorowski, p. 247.
  *After all, Nicholas was born:* Pleshakov, pp. 253–54.

7  *At 4 P.M., Nicholas left:* Romanov, N., January 6, 1905.
  *His hope for such:* Esthus, p. 31.
  *His Second Pacific Squadron:* Hough, *The Fleet,* p. 33; Warner and Warner, p. 483.
  *"Tell them I wish":* ibid., p. 482.

8  *"His broad shoulders":* Novikoff-Priboy, p. 20. It should be noted that *Tsushima* by A. Novikoff-Priboy is actually a novel, but its author participated in these events, and he has been sourced in numerous accounts of the Battle of Tsushima as providing an accurate recollection of what occurred. Out of caution, the author has used only his descriptive passages regarding individuals and action, rather than rely on his account for a specific course of events.
  *Rozhestvensky had excelled:* Pleshakov, pp. 37–41; Hough, *The Fleet,* pp. 17–18.
  *"We're now doing":* Westwood, *Russia Against Japan,* p. 138.
  *ostensibly, asserting territorial control:* Figes, pp. 18, 168; Don Levine, p. 96; Judge, p. 158; Wells and Wilson, pp. 4–9.

9  *When war broke out:* Arbenina, p. 19; Salisbury, p. 90; Fuller, pp. 131–33; Figes, p. 169; McCormick, vol. 2, p. 205; Ascher, p. 52; Fuller, p. 132.
  *"iron monsters":* Pleshakov, p. 116.
  *Forbidden to stop:* Warner and Warner, pp. 423–26.

9  *Other horrors included:* Politovsky, p. 84; Hough, *The Fleet Had to Die,*
p. 77; Westwood, *Witnesses of Tsushima,* pp. 115–18.

10 *Rozhestvensky was crushed:* Politovsky, pp. 132–201; Warner and Warner,
pp. 484–87; Hough, *The Fleet,* pp. 96–110; Pleshakov, pp. 173–95.

11 *Unbeknownst to him:* Kagan and Higham, pp. 198–99.
*"Enemy squadron square":* Busch, prologue; Warner and Warner, pp. 500–
501; Woodward, pp. 146–47.

12 *"She'll never get":* Woodward, pp. 158–61.
*"To the health":* Westwood, *Witnesses of Tsushima,* p. 165.
*At ten miles' distance:* Wilson, pp. 243–45; Klado, *The Battle,* pp. 27, 30–37.
*From the day's beginning:* Westwood, *Russia Against Japan,* pp. 146–48;
Warner and Warner, pp. 504–6; Mitchell, D., pp. 252–56; Wilson, p. 247;
Hough, *The Fleet,* pp. 163–68; Spector, R., pp. 14–15.

13 *Within minutes:* Novikoff-Priboy, pp. 185–96; Westwood, *Witnesses of
Tsushima,* p. 184.

14 *Admiral Togo stood unprotected:* Hough, *The Fleet,* p. 67; Warner and
Warner, p. 505.
*In the* Suvorov's *cylindrical:* Wilson, pp. 248–54; Novikoff-Priboy,
pp. 178–81; Westwood, *Witnesses of Tsushima,* pp. 181–83, 189–90;
Hough, *The Fleet,* pp. 170–75; Warner and Warner, pp. 508–11; Spector,
R., pp. 15–19; Pleshakov, pp. 269–72; Busch, pp. 154–57.

15 *At 2:50 P.M.:* Novikoff-Priboy, pp. 185–96; Westwood, *Witnesses of
Tsushima,* pp. 183–89; Hough, *The Fleet,* pp. 177–79; Westwood, *Russia
Against Japan,* p. 148; Busch, pp. 159–60.
*By 7 P.M. the battle:* Mitchell, D., pp. 262–65.

16 *From the quays:* Williams, p. 404.
*Fifteen miles south:* Massie, *Nicholas and Alexandra,* pp. 111–12.

17 *His naval minister:* "World Politics," *North American Review* (July 1905);
*Chicago Daily Tribune,* May 29, 1905.
*Wild rumors ran:* Pleshakov, pp. 309–11; *Daily Telegraph,* May 31, 1905;
Romanov, N., May 16, 1905.
*On January 9:* Figes, pp. 173–81; Ascher, pp. 90–93.
*"Strikes are rolling":* Olgin, p. 118.

18 *History has recorded:* Bind, p. 175; Vassili, p. 217; Essad-Bey, p. 132;
Massie, *Nicholas and Alexandra,* p. 89.
*Yet in his diary:* Romanov, N., May 16–19, 1905.

CHAPTER 2

20 *Now covered with cypress:* Curtis, pp. 292–303; Villari, pp. 136–39; *Hand-
book for Travellers,* pp. 367–71.
*"Do you have any water?":* Ponomarev, pp. 52–53.
*Vice Admiral Grigory Chukhnin:* TsGAVMF, f. 920, op. 6, d. 410, p. 74.

21  *He ordered frequent:* ibid., p. 1.
    *"And now, my child":* Ponomarev, p. 44.
    *While many of the captains:* Naida, *Voyennyye moryaki,* p. 416; TsGAVMF,
    f. 417, op. 2, d. 771, p. 3.
    *Latrine pipes:* Nevsky, p. 23.
    *"No entry to dogs":* Ponomarev, p. 7.
    *"If we must sacrifice":* Berezovsky, p. 30.
22  *"Enough blood":* Naida, *Revolyutsionnoye dvizheniye,* p. 113.
    *Usually at these gatherings:* Berezovsky, pp. 19–21; Vilensky, p. 28.
    *On occasion, they would draft:* TsGAVMF, f. 243, op. 1, d. 9731, p. 213;
    Gavrilov, *V borbe za svobodu,* p. 199.
    *"the revolution can't be made":* Naida, *Revolyutsionnoye dvizheniye,* p. 363.
    *A radical from Sevastopol:* Ponomarev, p. 65.
23  *Tall, with a broad, square face:* Selivanov, *Matros Petrov,* pp. 9–15.
    *"We see how difficult":* *Proletarskaya revolyutsiya,* no. 12, 147, 1925. This
    speech was recounted by Petrov in a letter to his sister days before he was
    executed by firing squad on August 24, 1905.
    *Many others echoed:* Gavrilov, *V borbe za svobodu,* pp. 26–28.
    *"To delay means":* Ponomarev, p. 65.
    *"Why wait for":* ibid.
    *But he was:* Gavrilov, *V borbe za svobodu,* p. 27.
24  *"Here's to the tsar":* ibid., p. 66.
    *In 1879, in a hut:* Selivanov, *Matros Matyushenko,* p. 7; Zadneprovsky and
    Sokolov, p. 3.
    *He shared the living quarters:* Olgin, pp. 24–26; Kennard, pp. 11–15;
    Kravchinsky, pp. 233–34. In the two biographies on Matyushenko, his fam-
    ily's living quarters and village were described as typical of the region.
    Therefore, the author took the liberty of using these sources to show stan-
    dard village life in the Ukraine.
    *The grant of freedom:* Olgin, p. 32.
25  *When Afanasy was:* Selivanov, *Matros Matyushenko,* pp. 7–8; Zadneprovsky
    and Sokolov, pp. 3–4.
    *There he experienced:* Kanatchikov, pp. 83–84; Figes, pp. 111–15; Olgin,
    pp. 8–15.
    *A decent dinner:* *Handbook for Travellers,* p. 65.
    *The conditions crippled:* Lincoln, *In War's Dark Shadow,* p. 121.
    *There he found:* Selivanov, *Matros Matyushenko,* p. 8; Zadneprovsky and
    Sokolov, pp. 5–7.
26  *"It's not possible":* Zadneprovsky and Sokolov, pp. 6–7.
    *There was a world:* Kardashev, "Novyye Svedeniya."
27  *Several months later:* Zadneprovsky and Sokolov, pp. 7–8; Matyushenko,
    pp. 285–92; Kanatchikov, pp. 1–200; Reichman, pp. 90–108. Little is
    known of Matyushenko's life in the Far East other than the bare facts of

where and how long he lived in Vladivostok. I have drawn elements of his thought process from his writings about the oppression of workers, as well as sentiments expressed in the autobiography of Kanatchikov, whose background was remarkably similar to Matyushenko's. Kanatchikov brilliantly expressed his thoughts in his book.

27 *"We're not even"*: Figes, p. 116.

*They invited him:* Zadneprovsky and Sokolov, p. 8; Pyatnitsky, p. 17; Rice, pp. 42–46.

28 *These nobles:* Figes, p. 123. Orlando Figes's *A People's Tragedy* is one of the best books written on the development of the Russian Revolution, including its section on the history of revolutionary thought in Russia.

*Early radicals:* ibid., pp. 131–41; Wolfe, pp. 24–27, 91–94; Deutscher, pp. 1–4; Pipes, *Russian Revolution*, pp. 135–43.

*But Russia had not:* Figes, p. 146; Baron, pp. 262–63; Wolfe, pp. 91–94.

29 *Never a cohesive group:* Figes, pp. 148–50; Shanin, pp. 216–19; Wolfe, p. 120.

*A young firebrand:* Figes, pp. 149–52; Wolfe, pp. 289–97; Gurko, pp. 389–91; Getzler, p. 70.

30 *In an abstract way:* Zadneprovsky and Sokolov, p. 8.

*Bound by conscription laws:* Lychev, pp. 15–17; Kanatchikov, p. 159; Joubert, pp. 69–70; Subtelny, pp. 202–3.

*"naked, exposed, and trembling":* Kanatchikov, p. 159.

*The next day:* Lychev, pp. 16–17; Zadneprovsky and Sokolov, p. 9.

31 *"I promise and do":* Figes, p. 55.

*"dislodge every last":* Lychev, p. 21.

*First he became:* Wildman, p. 35; Figes, p. 57; Lychev, pp. 18–20; McNeal, p. 90; Zadneprovsky and Sokolov, pp. 11–12.

*In the Russian navy:* Fedorov, p. 11.

32 *"Breakfast of porridge":* TsGAVMF, f. 417, op. 2, d. 771, p. 3.

*At dinner, the borscht:* Nevsky, p. 24.

*If a sailor complained:* TsGAVMF, f. 417, op. 2, d. 771, p. 4.

*In the six hours:* Wildman, p. 35; Figes, p. 57; Lychev, pp. 18–20.

*Almost to a rule:* Manning, pp. 30–34; Fuller, pp. 13–15.

*Those who chose:* Zebroski, pp. 70–100. Zebroski's dissertation on the Black Sea Fleet reveals great sociological insight into the struggles between sailors and officers within the Russian navy.

*Naturally, there was plenty:* Bushnell, *The Tsarist Officer Corps*. One of the best studies on the subject.

*Many officers were boorish:* Naida, *Voyennyye moryaki*, p. 414.

*Matyushenko weathered:* Zadneprovsky and Sokolov, p. 13; Selivanov, *Matros Matyushenko*, p. 9; Zebroski, p. 119.

33 *Just like the radical:* Figes, p. 114.

*He despised how peasants:* Matyushenko, pp. 285–90; Zebroski, pp. 477–88.

*Ivan Yakhnovsky had:* Ponomarev, pp. 11–16; Platonov, pp. 137–45; Vilensky, pp. 23–27.

*The Russian navy required:* Saul, pp. 16–17; Zebroski, pp. 37–60.

34  *Furthermore, the nature:* Zebroski, p. 54.

*He openly befriended:* Zadneprovsky and Sokolov, pp. 13–14; Ponomarev, p. 53.

*"What truth could":* Matyushenko, p. 291. This quotation is from the beginning of Matyushenko's account of the *Potemkin* mutiny, a long essay about the exploitation of workers, peasants, and sailors and how difficult it is to discover the source of freedom and equality within a system focused on suppressing the same. The author has taken the liberty of drawing from this to exemplify the passionate talks Matyushenko gave.

*Matyushenko energetically took:* Melnikov, p. 147.

*They smuggled aboard:* Lychev, pp. 28–32; Nevsky, p. 320; Platonov, pp. 31–32.

35  *The leaders of each:* Lychev, p. 32; Platonov, p. 34; Gavrilov, *V borbe za svobodu,* pp. 21–25.

*Throughout, Matyushenko maintained:* Lychev, p. 60; Ponomarev, p. 53.

*Much of Tsentralka's work:* Berezovsky, p. 23.

*"To me every party":* Gavrilov, *V borbe za svobodu,* p. 51.

*Once when a petty officer:* Ponomarev, p. 53.

36  *"he would go through fire":* ibid.

*With his distinguished:* ibid.

*When Matyushenko and the others:* ibid., p. 66.

*Crew members:* Gavrilov, *V borbe za svobodu,* p. 34; Feldmann, p. 31; Ponomarev, p. 24; Fedorov, pp. 150–51. The percentage of politically reliable sailors aboard the *Potemkin* has been an item of debate since the mutiny itself. Even the government, after an intensive investigation, could never arrive at a specific list. Numbers ranged from as few as fifty to as many as four hundred. Matyushenko declared once that "there are three hundred socio-democrats ready to die" aboard the *Potemkin.* Taking arguments from several sources, the author came to an approximation of two hundred sympathetic sailors, fifty devoted ardently to the cause.

*"self-seekers":* Lychev, p. 33.

*The next day:* Ponomarev, p. 66; Gavrilov, *V borbe za svobodu,* pp. 29–33.

37  *Late that evening:* Platonov, pp. 42–44; TsGIA, f. 102, op. 00, d. 1667, pp. 278–79; Gavrilov, *V borbe za svobodu,* p. 32; Feldmann, pp. 30–31; Berezovsky, pp. 37–39.

CHAPTER 3

38 *Down in the bowels:* TsGAVMF, f. 1025, op. 2, d. 35, p. 149; Kardashev, *Burevestniki revolyutsy,* p. 8; Berezovsky, p. 36; Nevsky, p. 259.

*The cavernous engine room:* Massie, *Dreadnought,* p. 475; Grand Duke Cyril, pp. 47–48; Novikoff-Priboy, pp. 215–16.

*"Anchor is starting!":* interview with Igor Koyzr.

*Fifty-one years old: Master Roll,* pp. 606–9; TsGAVMF, f. 417, op. 5, d. 361, p. 13–31; ibid., f. 432, op. 5, d. 5783, pp. 13–31.

*"Remember, the hour":* Berezovsky, p. 34.

39 *The day before:* ibid., p. 33.

*Meanwhile, three of Golikov's:* Nevsky, p. 231.

*A crowd had assembled:* TsGAVMF, f. 1025, op. 2, d. 35, p. 149; Kardashev, *Burevestniki revolyutsy,* p. 8; Berezovsky, p. 36; Nevskii, p. 259.

*The* Potemkin *moved:* British Admiralty, pp. 242–47.

40 *Ever since the Minoans:* Mitchell, D., pp. 26–29; George, J., pp. 11–65; Karsten, p. 340; O'Connell, p. 66; Spector, R., pp. 46, 22–23.

*Nicholas doubled:* Mitchell, D., pp. 192–203; Mitchell, M., p. 320.

*The battleship* Potemkin: Melnikov, Part I. Melnikov provides the best description of the construction and armament of the battleship *Potemkin,* absolutely superior to any other source in terms of the ship's physical characteristics.

41 *The* Potemkin *was:* Anthony, p. 8.

*In October 1903:* Melnikov, Part I.

*Born into a high-ranking: Master Roll,* pp. 606–9; TsGAVMF, f. 417, op. 5, d. 361, pp. 13–31; TsGAVMF, f. 432, op. 5, d. 5783, pp. 13–31.

*At that time, professors:* Ignatyev, p. 269.

*He studied mathematics:* Plotto, n.p.

42 *In his new position:* Platonov, p. 15; Jane, pp. 472–73.

*"half-educated Godless traitors":* TsGAVMF, f. 920, op. 6, d. 410, p. 269.

*Golikov was told:* ibid., p. 270; Fedorov, p. 21.

*"So to arms":* TsGAVMF, f. 243, op. 1, d. 9731, p. 117.

43 *An old campaigner:* Plotto; Belomor.

*"revolutionary hooligans":* TsGAVMF, f. 928, op. 6, d. 410, p. 71; ibid., f. 417, op. 1, d. 3457, p. 94.

*Four months into:* TsGIA, f. 102, op. 5, 1905, pp. 104–6; Platonov, p. 18; Feldmann, pp. 26–28.

*Thirty-six sailors:* Fedorov, pp. 15–25; Bogachev, p. 165.

*Those suspected:* Zebroski, p. 167; TsGAVMF, f. 243, op. 1, d. 9731, p. 244.

44 *"mighty victory":* Platonov, p. 149.

*"pernicious traitors":* Belomor, pp. 164–68.

*When Chukhnin sent hundreds:* TsGAVMF, f. 417, op. 4, d. 6826, p. 1.

*As Chukhnin noted: Washington Post,* December 25, 1904.
*"in ten days":* Guttridge, p. 74.

45 *Chukhnin was burdened:* Berezovsky, p. 31.
*Few sailors escaped:* ibid, p. 14; Gavrilov, *V borbe za svobodu,* p. 18.
*"It took nine years":* Nevsky, p. 229.
*"This is what happens":* Berezovsky, p. 32.
*Decorated for bravery:* Kovalenko, p. 47; *Master Roll,* pp. 63–64; TsGAVMF, f. 417, op. 2, d. 786, p. 80; Emelin, p. 69.

46 *"Do you know":* Berezovsky, pp. 14–15.
*Late that night:* Melnikov, p. 149.
*Then they turned:* Naida, *Voyennyye moryaki,* p. 85; Zadneprovsky and Sokolov, p. 12; Feldmann, p. 32; Platonov, p. 13.

47 *"Taking care":* Berezovsky, pp. 30–31.
*"It's not the tsar's":* Ponomarev, pp. 69–70.
*Because of the firing:* Nevsky, p. 259.
*"We've got to start":* Ponomarev, p. 70.

48 *One of nine children:* ibid., p. 7.
*"If I'm to suffer":* ibid., p. 19.
*"Believe Vakulenchuk":* Lychev, p. 25.
*One afternoon, the mounted police:* ibid., pp. 26–27.

49 *The ship's movement:* Melnikov, p. 149.
*"stars of the nation":* Pleshakov, p. 117.

CHAPTER 4

50 *Early morning on June 13:* Kovalenko, p. 88; Nevsky, pp. 231–32, 259.
*Apart from a black-and-white-banded:* British Admiralty, pp. 225–27.
*Connected to the Mediterranean:* King, C., pp. 5–17; Ascherson, pp. 2–7.
*Called Pontos Axeinos:* King, C., p. xi.
*"Import a typhoon":* Washburn, pp. 73–74.

51 *On these perilous waters:* Mitchell, M., pp. 143–44.
*Golikov sent an ensign:* Nevsky, pp. 231–32, 259; TsGAVMF, f. 1025, op. 2., d. 35, p. 149; *1905 god,* p. 210.
*One among them:* Ponomarev, p. 60.
*The* Ismail *steamed:* Gavrilov, *V borbe za svobodu,* p. 35. Most sources refer to the torpedo boat as No. 267, its official designation by the Black Sea Fleet. For ease of reading, I have chosen to use its former name.
*The port district hummed:* Herlihy, p. 194.

52 *In 1794, only a Tatar:* King, C., p. 163; Hough, *Potemkin Mutiny,* p. 42.
*Connecting the port:* Herlihy, p. 140; Ascherson, pp. 142–43.
*Over the decades:* Weinberg, p. 1. Robert Weinberg's *The Revolution of 1905 in Odessa* and Patricia Herlihy's *Odessa: A History, 1794–1914* offer two of the best English-language examinations of Odessa, and I highly rec-

ommend that readers investigate these books for further details on the history and social framework of this fascinating city.

52 *"the Russian jostles":* Herlihy, p. 123.

53 *Despite its cosmopolitan:* Weinberg, p. 22.

*Impressive colonnaded mansions:* Herlihy, p. 194.

*"Could we even":* Isaac Babel, as quoted in Herlihy, p. 128.

*Overall, those of the Jewish faith:* Weinberg, p. 11.

*Although thousands had:* ibid., pp. 18–19; Herlihy, pp. 253–57.

*Similarly, police:* Herlihy, p. 304; Inozemtsev, pp. 75–76. In numerous reports from this period, time and again officials targeted the Jews as responsible for the unrest. In this latter reference from the Red Archive, General Kakhanov, the military commander of Odessa, blames Jewish individuals for the early June unrest five times in the span of two pages.

54 *Furthermore, the revolutionaries:* Gavrilov, *V borbe za svobodu,* pp. 55–58; Platonov, pp. 56–60; Keep, *The Rise of Social Democracy in Russia,* pp. 74–75, 161–75.

*Although Odessan revolutionaries:* Feldmann, pp. 3–5; Nevsky, pp. 8–13; Weinberg, pp. 110–14.

*Then in May:* Nevsky, pp. 15–16; Weinberg, pp. 115–20.

*Their frustrations peaking:* Berezovsky, pp. 64–65; Weinberg, p. 127.

55 *"Down with the police!":* ibid.; Nevsky, pp. 19–20; Berezovsky, pp. 69–70.

*The night before: Revolyutsionny bronenosets,* p. 29.

*At 8 A.M., Anatoly:* Berezovsky, pp. 67–70; TsGIA(M), f. 102, op. 00, d. 1667, pp. 29–30.

*Walking farther:* Berezovsky, pp. 70–72.

56 *This factory employed:* Weinberg, p. 128.

*An hour later: Russkiye Vedomosti,* June 21, 1905; Berezovsky, pp. 72–76; Feldmann, pp. 5–6; Hough, *Potemkin Mutiny,* pp. 50–51; Ponomarev, pp. 72–73. This entire scene, including the dialogue and excerpted descriptions, is drawn from these sources.

58 *Behind the high walls:* Inozemtsev, pp. 74–76; Hough, *Potemkin Mutiny,* pp. 49–50.

*At sixty-three years of age: Russky Invalid,* August 19, 1908.

*Since the beginning:* Inozemtsev, pp. 74–75.

59 *Under his command:* Hough, *Potemkin Mutiny,* pp. 49–50.

*He had ordered:* Inozemtsev, p. 75.

*Supply officer Makarov: 1905 god,* p. 210; Nevsky, p. 232; TsGAVMF, f. 1025, op. 2, d. 35, p. 149; Weinberg, p. 129.

CHAPTER 5

61 *Two bells struck:* interview with Igor Kozyr; Novikoff-Priboy, p. 141; Pleshakov, pp. 119–20; Hough, *Potemkin Mutiny,* pp. 20–21.

62 *As the sun rose:* Berezovsky, p. 41; Nevsky, p. 230; Lychev, p. 52.

*"Attention! Present arms!":* interview with Igor Kozyr; Pleshakov, pp. 119–20.

*As Golikov disappeared:* Berezovsky, p. 41; Hough, *Potemkin Mutiny,* p. 16; Ponomarev, pp. 73–74; Matyushenko, p. 294.

*It was an unusually hot: Journal de St. Petersburg,* June 15, 1905.

*"Don't you remember":* Berezovsky, p. 41.

63 *Several others cursed:* ibid.; TsGAVMF, f. 1025, op. 2, d. 35, p. 149; Hough, *Potemkin Mutiny,* pp. 15–17.

*Tall, trim, and through-and-through:* Hough, *Potemkin Mutiny,* p. 16; Melnikov.

*"Now. What's all this":* Berezovsky, pp. 41–42; Matyushenko, p. 293; TsGAVMF, f. 1025, op. 2, d. 35, p. 149.

64 *Later that morning:* Berezovsky, pp. 42–43; Gavrilov, *V borbe za svobodu,* p. 36; Ponomarev, p. 73; Bogachev, p. 39; Zebroski, pp. 216–17. There is some discrepancy in the accounts as to when this discussion took place on the ship. Gavrilov and Ponomarev suggest that they had this discussion immediately on the return of the torpedo boat at 5 A.M. But the sailor revolutionaries could not have known of the widespread response about the tainted meat until after the morning striking of the colors, when the sailors had a chance to inspect it on their own and then received word from Smirnov that nothing would be done about it. In Berezovsky's memoir, he accounts for this meeting after the confrontation with Dr. Smirnov, which the author has decided is the most likely scenario.

*A couple of years before:* Berezovsky, p. 44.

*"First in St. Petersburg":* Ponomarev, p. 73.

*With each passing day:* Bogachev, p. 39.

65 *"We won't eat":* Berezovsky, p. 42.

*Even Golikov had complained:* Gavrilov, *V borbe za svobodu,* p. 18; Kovalenko, p. 47; *Master Roll,* pp. 63–64; TsGAVMF, f. 417, op. 2, d. 786, p. 80; Emelin, p. 69.

*Gilyarovsky came across:* Matyushenko, p. 293; *New York Herald Tribune,* June 30, 1905.

*"Why aren't you serving":* Matyushenko, p. 294; Hough, *Potemkin Mutiny,* p. 19.

66 *"The crew refuses":* Kovalenko, p. 89.

*"We have to teach":* TsGAVMF, f. 1025, op. 2, d. 17, p. 46; Gavrilov, *V borbe za svobodu,* p. 37.

*Golikov called Dr. Smirnov:* Hough, *Potemkin Mutiny,* p. 21; Kovalenko, pp. 89–90.

67 *The sailors stood stiffly:* Matyushenko, p. 294; Berezovsky, pp. 45–46; Zebroski, p. 220; Feldmann, p. 34; Nevsky, p. 233; Lychev, p. 54; Bogachev, pp. 47–48.

67  *"It seems you":* ibid.
68  *Matyushenko knew:* Berezovsky, p. 46.
    *A few boatswains:* Feldmann, p. 34.
    *As long as they stayed:* Matyushenko, p. 294.
    *"Come on!":* Berezovsky, p. 46.
    *"Eat it yourself":* Kardashev, *Burevestniki revolyutsii,* p. 17.
    *Golikov looked out:* Matyushenko, p. 294, Feldmann, pp. 34–35; Hough,
    *Potemkin Mutiny,* p. 24; Bogachev, p. 54; Lychev, p. 54; Berezovsky,
    pp. 46–47. Concerning this stage of the mutiny, the sources contradict one
    another as to whether the sailors held fast in their protest or began to break
    ranks. It is clear from Matyushenko's memoir that the sailor-revolutionaries
    made their move once it began to look as if they were being singled out. If
    the crew remained together, this seemed unlikely to have occurred. There-
    fore, the author believes Matyushenko moved to the turret once it looked as
    if the sailors were beginning to follow Golikov's command.
69  *Trying to stop complete:* Berezovsky, p. 47.
    *"Those who record":* Gavrilov, *V borbe za svobodu,* p. 38.
    *"So it's mutiny":* Hough, *Potemkin Mutiny,* p. 25.
    *The order sent:* Berezovsky, pp. 48–49.
    *by regulation:* Hough, *Potemkin Mutiny,* p. 22.
    *While several guards:* Berezovsky, p. 48; Gavrilov, *V borbe za svobodu,* p. 38;
    Feldmann, p. 36; Matyushenko, p. 294; *1905 god,* p. 211; TsGIA(M), f.
    102, op. 00, d. 1667, p. 279; Platonov, p. 47; Ponomarev, pp. 75–76;
    Nevsky, p. 233; Lychev, p. 54. In most popular Russian accounts and sailor
    memoirs published after the release of Sergei Eisenstein's film, the tarpau-
    lin was brought forward and thrown over the sailors, who then awaited
    death. However, sailor testimony and memoirs prior to the film recorded
    the order to bring forward the tarpaulin but made no mention of its cover-
    ing the sailors and/or being placed on the deck. In Eisenstein's memoir, he
    makes it clear that the use of the tarpaulin to cover the sailors was entirely
    his invention and that consulting Russian officers had told him that this
    never would have been done. The tarpaulin would have been ordered
    solely to prevent blood from staining the deck. Nonetheless, Eisenstein
    went ahead with the dramatic image, and this has obviously influenced sail-
    ors' memories and histories of this event ever since. The Russian historian
    Gavrilov was the first to question the validity of the tarpaulin myth, and the
    author has carefully looked through memoirs and court-martial testimony
    and agrees that the canvas was never used in the way it has been popular-
    ized. Nonetheless, calling for the tarpaulin to cover the deck is equally
    chilling by any standard.
70  *"Those who will":* Hough, *Potemkin Mutiny,* p. 25.
    *"Sir, don't shoot":* Gavrilov, *V borbe za svobodu,* p. 39.
    *The rage that had gathered:* Matyushenko, pp. 294–95.

"*Brothers! What are they doing*": ibid., p. 295; Bogachev, p. 39.

Matyushenko and Vakulenchuk: Matyushenko, p. 295; TsGAVMF, f. 1025, op. 2, d. 35, p. 149; Bogachev, pp. 39–40.

71  "*What are you doing?*": Matyushenko, p. 296.

*This was the decisive:* ibid. This is a paraphrase of Matyushenko's description of this critical moment during the mutiny, one whose import he knew was life or death.

72  *Then Gilyarovsky ordered:* ibid.; Bogachev, pp. 40–56; Nevsky, p. 234; Gavrilov, *V borbe za svobodu,* p. 39; Kardashev, *Burevestniki revolyutsii,* p. 13 (sailor court-martial records). As with other details of these confusing moments, memoirs and histories contradict one another. Some place Vakulenchuk as part of the guard detail or underneath the tarpaulin itself. Others had shots fired first, then the move to the armory. In this case, the author has relied on Matyushenko's account of the events, which is aligned most closely with court-martial documents.

*They hesitated:* Bogachev, p. 40; Feldmann, p. 35.


PART II

73  "*A man-of-war*": Karsten, p. 140.

"*I'm awfully fond*": Gorky, as quoted in Maynard, p. 19.


CHAPTER 6

75  *For the summer:* Barkovets, p. 17; King, G., pp. 206–9; Massie, *Peter the Great,* p. 610; Lieven, p. 62; Hall, p. 92.

*Nicholas began each day:* Elchaninov, pp. 11–15; Verner, p. 62; Massie, *Nicholas and Alexandra,* pp. 111–22; King, G., pp. 214–15.

76  *The rest of his day:* Romanov, N., June 14, 1905. The schedule detailed for June 14 was typical for Nicholas II, as conveyed in earlier references. However, for accuracy's sake, it is worth mentioning that in the afternoon of this day, Nicholas took his daughter Marie on a special picnic for her birthday. Nonetheless, the schedule did not deviate to any great degree.

*The conservative: Novoye Vremya,* June 14, 1905.

77  *Nicholas preferred:* Balmuth, p. 238.

*The uncensored truth: Daily Telegraph,* June 27–28, 1905; *Washington Post,* June 27–28, 1905.

*The first of the Romanovs:* Lieven, pp. 1–7; Figes, pp. 6–7.

78  *For more than 250 years:* ibid.

*Alexander III took easily:* Lieven, pp. 23–25; Warth, pp. 1–3.

*A timid, small boy:* Figes, pp. 16–17; Warth, p. 4; Massie, *Nicholas and Alexandra,* pp. 13–15.

79  *From a young age:* Warth, pp. 5–6.

79 *A gaunt figure:* Byrnes, p. 312; Essad-Bey, pp. 10–12; Massie, *Nicholas and Alexandra,* p. 14.
   *At their conclusion:* Essad-Bey, p. 13.
   *Nicholas preferred:* Figes, pp. 17–19; Essad-Bey, p. 19; Warth, pp. 6–8.
80 *"Sandro, what am I going":* Romanov, A., pp. 168–69.
   *"The heir is":* Ascher, p. 14.
   *At twenty-six years:* Essad-Bey, pp. 69–73; Lincoln, *In War's Dark Shadow,* pp. 282–83; Salisbury, pp. 56–57.
81 *"It has come to":* Vassili, pp. 254–55.
   *"Nicholas spent the first":* Essad-Bey, p. 87.
   *The tsar's wife, Alix:* Figes, p. 20.
82 *First, he refused:* ibid., pp. 21–23; Warth, pp. 24–25; Romanov, A., pp. 138–39; Verner, p. 57.
   *"There were as many":* Urossov, p. 137.
   *"The Sovereign listens":* Warth, p. 34.
   *Alexander III had pushed:* Salisbury, p. 43.
   *Their peasant families:* Olgin, p. 32.
   *The landed nobles:* Figes, pp. 35–54.
83 *The great famine of 1891:* ibid., pp. 158–61; Walkin, p. 186.
   *In the aftermath:* Figes, pp. 164–65.
   *"The power of revolution":* Walkin, p. 186.
   *And some* zemstvos *nobles:* ibid., p. 192.
   *Plehve, his reactionary interior minister:* Judge, p. 234.
84 *the tsar's selection:* Ascher, pp. 55–66; Verner, p. 113; Figes, pp. 171–73.
   *A month later:* Salisbury, pp. 120–27; Sablinsky, pp. 344–47.
85 *"I adhere to autocracy":* Verner, p. 113.
   *"a sergeant major":* Harcave, *Memoirs of Count Witte,* p. 132.
   *The first castigated:* Gurko, pp. 368–69.
   *Over the next three:* Figes, p. 191; Harcave, *First Blood,* pp. 144–50.
   *"The war has been":* Lenin, *Collected Works,* vol. 8, p. 483.
86 *"We talked while":* Stockdale, p. 136.
   *"Peace at all costs":* Ascher, p. 129.
   *"For 200 years we":* Daily Telegraph, May 19, 1905.
   *"There is no time":* Manchester Guardian, May 19, 1905.
   *"I don't even have":* Esthus, p. 38.
   *"ends the chances":* Don Levine, p. 172.
   *"The time has come":* Oldenburg, p. 130; Morison, p. 1206.
87 *"It is essential":* Pares, p. 82; Oldenburg, pp. 132–33; Fischer, G., pp. 189–91; Galai, pp. 251–53.
   *"I personally do not":* Dispatches from U.S. Consuls, letter dated February 9, 1905, from Mr. Ethebert Watts to Frank Loomis, assistant secretary of state.
   *On June 14, as Nicholas:* Romanov, N., June 14, 1905.

CHAPTER 7

88  *On the* Potemkin: Rose, "Mutiny on the *Potemkin.*"
   *But that afternoon:* Matyushenko, p. 296; Berezovsky, pp. 51–53; Gavrilov, *V borbe za svobodu,* pp. 39–42; Feldmann, p. 36; Nevsky, p. 234; Lychev, pp. 55–56; Vorres, p. 34.
89  *"I know you":* Matyushenko, p. 296.
90  *"Enough of this":* Lychev, p. 55.
   *He also sent:* Vilensky, p. 30.
   *"Hunt them all down!":* Hough, *Potemkin Mutiny,* p. 29.
   *In contrast:* Nevsky, p. 260; Kovalenko, p. 90.
   *In the midst:* Berezovsky, p. 52.
91  *Slim, with a clean-shaven:* Kovalenko, p. 88; *Osvobozhdeniye,* July 6, 1905.
   *A Ukrainian nationalist:* Subtelny, p. 296.
   *Kovalenko looked around:* Kovalenko, p. 90.
   *"This would never":* ibid., p. 91.
93  *Within seconds:* ibid., pp. 91–93.
   *Barricaded within:* Nevsky, p. 262.
   *A group of sailors found:* Kardashev, *Burevestniki revolyutsii,* p. 22.
   *"Let me die":* Matyushenko, p. 298; TsGAVMF, f. 1025, op. 2, d. 35, p. 150; Bogachev, p. 60; Lychev, pp. 57–58.
   *Down in the coal-hold:* Vilensky, pp. 32–34.
94  *Torpedo officer:* Berezovsky, p. 54; Matyushenko, p. 297; Feldmann, p. 37; Zebroski, p. 231.
   *"We haven't found":* Hough, *Potemkin Mutiny,* p. 33.
95  *Then a sailor:* Lychev, p. 56; TsGAVMF, f. 1025, op. 2, d. 17, pp. 24–25.
   *"Man the guns":* Hough, *Potemkin Mutiny,* p. 38.
   *Lieutenant Pyotr Klodt:* Berezovsky, p. 58.
   *"What can we":* ibid.
   *The forty-one-year-old:* Melnikov; *Nominal Roll,* p. 168.
96  *Instead Klodt watched:* Berezovsky, p. 58; Ponomarev, pp. 246–47.
   *Finally, twenty minutes:* Ponomarev, p. 78; Gavrilov, *V borbe za svobodu,* p. 42; Nevsky, pp. 262–63; Hough, *Potemkin Mutiny,* p. 39.
   *Revolutionary sailor Alekseyev: 1905 god,* p. 212.
   *Meanwhile, several more:* Gavrilov, *V borbe za svobodu,* p. 42.
97  *The sailors found:* Kardashev, *Burevestniki revolyutsii,* p. 14.
   *While the sailors:* Kovalenko, pp. 93–94.
98  *With the hollers:* Ponomarev, p. 79; TsGAVMF, f. 1025, op. 2, d. 35, pp. 149–50; Lychev, p. 57, Berezovsky, pp. 55–57; Bogachev, p. 60; Hough, *Potemkin Mutiny,* pp. 35–36; Gavrilov, *V borbe za svobodu,* p. 41.
99  *"Enough blood":* Matyushenko, p. 297; Nevsky, p. 237.
100  *"I was stricken":* Gavrilov, *V borbe za svobodu,* p. 47.
   *Leaning against the ship's railing:* Vilensky, pp. 32–33.

CHAPTER 8

102  *"Who will lead":* Ponomarev, p. 80; Melnikov, p. 152.
     *After checking on the engine room:* Vilensky, p. 34.
     *He called for a drumroll:* ibid.; Feldmann, p. 41; Ponomarev, p. 80.
     *"All of Russia is waiting":* Hough, *Potemkin Mutiny,* p. 58.

103  *"Matyushenko had a rare intuition":* Feldmann, pp. 18–19. Feldmann also
     wrote, however, that this was Matyushenko's downfall as a leader, saying
     that while he was "full of boiling energy when the temper of the crowd was
     rising, he sank into apathy as soon as it dropped."
     *Known as "the Preacher":* Berezovsky, p. 26.
     *It would control:* Feldmann, p. 41.
     *The committee included:* TsGAVMF, f. 1025, op. 2, d. 19, p. 166;
     *Revolyutsionnyi bronenosets,* p. 51.

104  *"Not all of us":* Vilensky, p. 34; Hough, *Potemkin Mutiny,* pp. 40–41.
     *Although drawn from every quarter:* Gavrilov, *V borbe za svobodu,* pp. 44–
     49. Gavrilov's study provides the most comprehensive look into the politi-
     cal affiliations of the sailors both for and against the mutiny.
     *The committee members left:* Ponomarev, p. 81; Berezovsky, p. 61.
     *The twenty-five sat:* Berezovsky, pp. 97–98, 114; Kardashev, *Burevestniki
     revolyutsy,* p. 24.
     *"And you, Your Excellency":* Kardashev, p. 97.
     *First they settled:* Lychev, pp. 61–62.
     *Then came the question:* ibid., p. 58.

105  *"What do we need":* Ponomarev, pp. 86–88.
     *Matyushenko also raised:* ibid.; Feldmann, p. 41; Hough, *Potemkin Mutiny,*
     pp. 61–62; Ponomarev, p. 82.
     *A couple of hours:* Rostotskaya, p. 13; Kardashev, *Burevestniki revolyutsy,*
     p. 22; Lychev, p. 58.

106  *"Murzak was a typical sea wolf":* Lychev, p. 59.
     *"But what of the flag?":* Ponomarev, pp. 81–82.
     *The young officer had agreed:* Nevsky, pp. 264–66.

107  *"You might need this":* Selivanov, *Matros Matyushenko,* p. 18.
     *The French coined the word:* Hathaway, p. 13; Wintringham, p. 9.
     *The Roman historian:* Delbruck, pp. 178–85.
     *The new emperor:* Rose, "Anatomy of Mutiny"; Weber, p. 156.
     *In the sixteenth century:* Guttridge, p. 6.
     *In 1790 the Royal Navy:* McGuffie, pp. 37–42.
     *In 1852 on the U.S. brig-of-war:* McFarland, pp. 138–39.
     *Short of a death sentence:* Guttridge, pp. 8–10.

108  *In 1910, Afro-Brazilian sailors:* Bell and Elleman, pp. 32–33.
     *Over a century before:* Bullocke, pp. 189–209.
     *Only a few months:* Mahan, p. 367.

*The British navy's:* Guttridge, p. 7.

*Russia's code of military:* Bushnell, *Mutiny amid Repression*, p. 75.

*As the* Potemkin *steamed:* Berezovsky, p. 104; Feldmann, p. 44; Ponomarev, p. 82.

109 *Afterward Matyushenko wandered:* Kovalenko, p. 96.

110 *They had first met:* Zadneprovsky and Sokolov, p. 17.

*After roaming the ship:* Kovalenko, p. 96.

111 *"Can a sailor":* ibid., p. 101.

112 *On the evening of June 14:* Berezovsky, p. 88.

*That morning, workers: Revolyutsionnyi bronenosets*, pp. 29–30; Inozemtsev, p. 76; Rostotskaya, pp. 10–11; Weinberg, pp. 129–31.

113 *"bloody hills of flesh": Revolyutsionnyi bronenosets*, p. 30.

*A couple of hours:* Berezovsky, pp. 81–94.

114 *From Primorsky Boulevard:* Feldmann, p. 15.


CHAPTER 9

115 *A mile out:* Kovalenko, p. 103.

*Shortly after the* Potemkin: Nevsky, p. 238; Berezovsky, p. 101.

116 *By 4 A.M. the committee:* Gavrilov, *V borbe za svobodu*, p. 52; Berezovsky, pp. 98–100; Matyushenko, p. 299.

*"we will raze":* Feldmann, pp. 45–47; Bogachev, p. 57.

117 *"Citizens of Odessa!":* TsGVIA, f. 400, op. 5, d. 31, p. 73.

*The sailors lowered:* Matyushenko, p. 300; TsGVIA, f. 400, op. 5, d. 31, p. 73; Ponomarev, p. 92; Pleskov, p. 32.

*The crowd was stunned:* Matyushenko, p. 300.

118 *Then Matyushenko boarded:* Gavrilov, *V borbe za svobodu*, p. 62.

*The launch neared:* TsGVIA, f. 400, op. 5, d. 31, p. 73; Vilensky, pp. 36–37; *1905 god*, p. 213; Berezovsky, p. 103.

119 *"Where are you going?":* Hough, *Potemkin Mutiny*, p. 80.

*At the same time:* Berezovsky, pp. 94–95; Rostotskaya, p. 12.

120 *"We may have lacked":* Kardashev, *Burevestniki revolyutsii*, p. 25.

*On several merchant ships:* Gavrilov, *V borbe za svobodu*, p. 62.

*"There are thousands":* Berezovsky, p. 95; Hough, *Potemkin Mutiny*, p. 72.

*Minutes later, fifty:* TsGVIA, f. 400, op. 5, d. 31, p. 74; *Revolyutsionnyi bronenosets*, p. 38; Gavrilov, *V borbe za svobodu*, p. 60; Gerasimov, p. 125.

121 *He needed to convince:* Berezovsky, p. 96.

*On his approach:* Novikoff-Priboy, pp. 48, 89–90; Berezovsky, p. 107.

*Dymchenko, the committee member:* ibid., p. 110.

122 *"You might at any moment":* Feldmann, p. 64. As Feldmann did not include in his memoir the speech that he gave at the forecastle in the morning (but rather one given a few hours later), the author has used the later

speech, since according to Feldmann's description, it touched on similar topics.

122  *Seated at a long bench:* ibid., p. 53.
123  *A couple of hours before:* Rostotskaya, p. 12.
     *"Will the workers follow":* ibid., pp. 12–14; *Revolyutsionnyi bronenosets,* p. 38; Ponomarev, pp. 94–96; Lychev, pp. 62–65; Berezovsky, pp. 114–16; Gavrilov, *V borbe za svobodu,* p. 64.
124  *The members of the joint commission:* Rostotskaya, p. 13.
     *"If we go ourselves":* Berezovsky, p. 117.
     *As the committee:* Ponomarev, p. 96.
125  *The very thought:* TsGAVMF, f. 417, op. 1, d. 3023, p. 98.
     *Less than an hour:* Inozemtsev, p. 77; Witte, p. 263.
     *At 10:30 A.M., the head:* ibid.; TsGVIA, f. 400, op. 5, d. 31, p. 74.
126  *Even before the* Potemkin: Inozemtsev, pp. 77–80.
     *The Potemkin could launch:* Hough, *Potemkin Mutiny,* p. 70.
     *Kakhanov felt trapped:* Inozemtsev, pp. 79–80.
127  *At 12:30 P.M., Kakhanov:* TsGIA(M), f. 601, op. 1, d.105, p. 3.


CHAPTER 10

128  *The morning papers: Novoye Vremya,* June 15, 1905.
     *"Your Imperial Majesty":* Kardashev, "Novyye Svedeniya."
     *In his message:* Essad-Bey, p. 150; Vassili, pp. 355–56.
     *At first, Nicholas simply refused:* Romanov, N., June 15, 1905. In his diary that night, Nicholas wrote, "The sailors on the battleship *Potemkin* have revolted, killed the officers, and seized the ship, threatening riots in the city! Unbelievable."
     *The Romanovs had always:* Pipes, *Russian Revolution,* p. 81. Pipes quotes Sergei Witte, who said, concerning the Russian military, "Who has created the Russian Empire? . . . only the power of the army's bayonet. The world bowed not to our culture, not to our bureaucratized church, not to our wealth and prosperity. It bowed to our might."
129  *As a child:* Wildman, pp. 6–8; Verner, pp. 22–25; Fuller, pp. 40–41.
     *"regarded himself as a soldier":* Fuller, pp. 40–41.
     *Over the past two:* Bushnell, *Mutiny amid Repression,* pp. 234–35. Bushnell lists every mutiny that occurred in 1905. Before June 14, 1905, eight incidents of mutiny had taken place within the Russian Empire, but none of the scale, longevity, or threatening significance of the *Potemkin.*
     *Beyond his own romance:* Keep, *Soldiers,* pp. 378–81.
     *Although the War Ministry:* Fuller, p. 130. Fuller lists 3,893 actions by the military in 1905 to actively suppress unrest. He points out that in 7.9 percent of these actions, violent force was used.
     *He approved an ukaz:* Kardashev, "Novyye Svedeniya."

*The tsar also instructed:* Kardashev, *Burevestniki revolyutsii,* p. 30.

*"Immediately take the most severe":* ibid.

130  *"Where is the chief":* TsGIA, f. 601, op. 1, d. 105, p. 1; TsGAVMF, f. 417, op. 1, d. 3023, p. 54.

*the Admiralty Building:* Lincoln, *Sunlight at Midnight,* pp. 108–9; Gautier, p. 107.

*Behind its walls: Journal de St. Petersburg,* June 16, 1905.

*At 1 P.M., a telegram:* TsGAVMF, f. 417, op. 1, d. 3023, p. 34.

*A huge chamber:* Melnikov, p. 180.

*Avelan, the privileged son:* Ioffe, pp. 178–79; Romanov, A., pp. 90–99, 216–23; *Washington Post,* October 30, 1893.

*Grigory Chukhnin:* TsGAVMF, f. 406, op. 9, d. 4636; Ioffe, pp. 210–11; Belomor; *Washington Post,* December 25, 1905; *Daily Telegraph,* May 30, 1905.

132  *He suspected right away:* Belomor, pp. 22–24.

*In the first, Krieger:* TsGAVMF, f. 417, op. 1, d. 3023, p. 53; Platonov, pp. 155–56.

133  *The telegrams exasperated:* Belomor, p. 23.

*"Proceed to Odessa":* TsGIA(M), f. 52, op. 1, d. 316, p. 11; Platonov, pp. 155–56; Kardashev, *Burevestniki revolyutsii,* p. 32.

*They also sent:* TsGIA(M), f. 52, op. 1, d. 316, p. 12.

*"For God's sake":* Kardashev, *Burevestniki revolyutsii,* pp. 29–30.


CHAPTER 11

134  *"There are about one hundred":* Melnikov, p. 154; Ponomarev, pp. 97–98; Vilensky, p. 37. There is some confusion among the sources whether this speech was given on June 16, prior to the firing on Odessa, or in this particular scene. It is clear that Matyushenko gave dramatic speeches in both situations, and it is likely that he used threats similar to "We will line up."

135  *The sailors went enthusiastically:* Berezovsky, pp. 115–21; Feldmann, p. 55.

*"What have you come":* Feldmann, p. 55.

*Feldmann ran to the admiral's stateroom:* ibid., pp. 46–47.

136  *"Comrades," one of the soldiers said:* ibid., pp. 55–56; Berezovsky, p. 121.

*When he rushed:* Kovalenko, p. 106.

*Baron P. P. Eikhen:* TsGAVMF, f. 1025, op. 2, d. 17, pp. 17–20.

137  *"You're under arrest":* ibid.; Feldmann, pp. 58–59.

*When the colonel had disappeared:* TsGAVMF, f. 1025, op. 2, d. 17, p. 18.

138  *The Vekha's sailors:* ibid., pp. 60–62; Kovalenko, p. 107; Lychev, pp. 66–67.

*"judged for all":* Feldmann, p. 60.

*By late afternoon:* TsGVIA, f. 400, op. 5, d. 31, p. 74; Weinberg, p. 135.

139 *Then, a few minutes after:* Weinberg, p. 75.

*As the crowd at the scene:* ibid.

*"It's freedom we need":* ibid., p. 135.

*"Comrades, there are heaps":* Revolyutsionnyi bronenosets, p. 40.

*The first curls of smoke:* TsGIA(M), f. 52, op. 1, d. 316, p. 74.

*Hundreds started breaking:* Revolyutsionnyi bronenosets, p. 33; Rostotskaya, p. 20–22; Bogachev, p. 128.

140 *General Kakhanov resisted:* TsGVIA, f. 400, op. 5, d. 31, p. 75.

*He even refused to push:* 1905 god, p. 218.

*"state of war":* Chicago Daily Tribune, June 30, 1905.

*Kakhanov was certain:* Inozemtsev, p. 80.

*"Let them gather":* ibid., p. 93; Gavrilov, V borbe za svobodu, p. 71. There is no doubt that Kakhanov allowed the riots to occur, and Karangozov's statement reveals the almost unimaginable cruelty with which they viewed the situation. That said, historians such as Gavrilov further argue that the police sent in agents disguised as vagrants to set fires and stir the crowds to increased violence, including inciting a pogrom. Although this author certainly does not put this past the Odessan officials — as they would later exercise these techniques in the fall of 1905 — there is not enough proof to conclude that they directly motivated these acts on June 15, 1905. That said, several individuals (Glotov among them) in the port tried to incite anti-Semitic violence. Several were killed in their attempts, according to Robert Weinberg's fine history *The Revolution of 1905 in Odessa*, p. 139.

*But over the next two hours:* Daily Telegraph, June 30, 1905; Rostotskaya, pp. 21–22; TsGVIA, f. 400, op. 5, d. 31, pp. 75–77; *Revolyutsionnyi bronenosets,* pp. 33–35; National Archives and Records Service, letter from Odessan consul to United States Embassy in St. Petersburg, June 29, 1905; Bogachev, pp. 127–31. The last reference from Bogachev's collection of documents pertains to a letter sent from I. G. Korolenko to his older brother, Vladimir, the noted Russian journalist. It was written as the events occurred. His description of the events of that night in Odessa remains one of the most poignant.

141 *At midnight, Kakhanov:* Inozemtsev, p. 82.

142 *Kakhanov gave the order:* Hough, *Potemkin Mutiny,* pp. 77–80; Bogachev, p. 131; Inozemtsev, p. 95; *New York Daily Tribune,* June 30, 1905. In Richard Hough's history of the *Potemkin* mutiny, he provides the best description of the slaughter that occurred on the Richelieu Steps. But, as with Sergei Eisenstein's film, which made this scene famous, his book mistakenly situates this slaughter as taking place during the day. Although violence definitely occurred on the steps in the first stages of the riot as people tried to escape the port, the Cossacks and soldiers did not move in force until midnight, on Kakhanov's order.

*In the city streets:* Bogachev, p. 129.

143 *As the fires began:* Kovalenko, pp. 107–11.

144 *"Listen, Matyushenko":* ibid., pp. 110–11; Feldmann, pp. 68–69.

145 *"Fire! The city's on fire!":* Feldmann, pp. 70–73; Berezovsky, pp. 128–30; Ponomarev, pp. 102–3.

*Gathered to avoid: Revolyutsionnyi bronenosets,* p. 15; Berezovsky, pp. 130–31; Gavrilov, *V borbe za svobodu,* p. 74.

146 *"Whom will we be killing?":* Nevsky, p. 241.

CHAPTER 12

147 *Feldmann and several* Potemkin *sailors:* Feldmann, pp. 74–77; Hough, *Potemkin Mutiny,* pp. 102–4.

148 *Everywhere lay corpses:* ibid.; *Revolyutsionnyi bronenosets,* p. 34; Kardashev, *Burevestniki revolyutsii,* p. 24; *Chicago Daily Tribune,* July 2–5, 1905.

*Feldmann and the others:* Feldmann, pp. 77–79.

149 *While Feldmann and the sailors:* Nevsky, p. 264.

150 *"We ask all Cossacks":* Grishin, p. 63.

*Fewer than forty-eight hours:* Hough, *Potemkin Mutiny,* pp. 110–11.

*"Is it true":* Berezovsky, p. 138.

151 *Then he recounted:* Kovalenko, pp. 125–27. According to Kovalenko, this idea of escaping to Romania was initiated in the stateroom where the officers were held, and then Ensign Alekseyev began speaking of it on June 16.

*The two left:* ibid., p. 128; Berezovsky, p. 137. The two accounts of this conversation, and the time it took place, contradict each other, but the author has attempted to reconcile the differences to clarify the deep concern among the ship's leaders that support for the mutiny was in jeopardy.

*Matyushenko dismissed any suggestion:* Kovalenko, p. 128.

*Matyushenko had been busy:* Berezovsky, pp. 132–39; Ponomarev, pp. 104–5; Gavrilov, *V borbe za svobodu,* p. 77.

152 *"He's still new":* Ponomarev, pp. 104–5.

*"They are the most rotten":* Berezovsky, pp. 134–35.

*Matyushenko moved:* ibid.

*Feldmann returned with:* Feldmann, p. 84.

153 *"There's a big military conference":* Hough, *Potemkin Mutiny,* p. 111; Feldmann, pp. 85–86. The author has drawn this conversation from Hough's account, but for one change: the time of the meeting. Hough stipulates that the military conference was to be held during the funeral, but this contradicts the timeline of when the *Potemkin* actually fired on the city.

*That very morning:* Baylen, pp. 29–31, 49–50.

*Before midnight on June 15:* Belomor, p. 172; Kardashev, "Novyye Svedeniya."

*First, the transport ship:* TsGAVMF, f. 417, op. 1, d. 3023, p. 62.

154　*Second, the squadron :* ibid., p. 53; Platonov, pp. 73–74; Gavrilov, *V borbe za svobodu,* p. 87.

　　*Finally, reports had reached: New York Herald Tribune,* June 30, 1905; *Daily Telegraph,* June 30, 1905; Saul, p. 25.

　　*In fact, Chukhnin: Journal de St. Petersburg,* June 10–11, 1905.

　　*"Go to Sevastopol today":* Ponomarev, p. 103; Kardashev, "Novyye Svedeniya"; Gavrilov, *V borbe za svobodu,* p. 87. Whatever else was said at the meeting has been lost to history. None of the three recorded the details of their discussion in their diaries or correspondence, as if writing it down would remind them of this nadir in their lives. Yet the commands that followed reveal much.

　　*When Chukhnin returned:* Kardashev, "Novyye Svedeniya"; Belomor, p. 173; Kardashev, *Burevestniki revolyutsii,* pp. 32–33; Romanov, N., June 16, 1905.

　　*He also sent a message:* Kardashev, "Nesostoyavshayasya Kazn."

155　*He was anxious:* Belomor, p. 174.

　　*After his admirals left:* Gavrilov, *V borbe za svobodu,* p. 87.

　　*Over the past sixteen hours:* Nevsky, pp. 363–66.

　　*"expended 1,510 bullets":* 1905 god, p. 220; Gavrilov, *V borbe za svobodu,* p. 72; TsGVIA, f. 400, op. 5, d. 31, p. 15.

　　*In truth, the violence:* Bushnell, *Mutiny amid Repression,* p. 62; Ascher, p. 172.

　　*The tsar had other concerns: Daily Telegraph,* June 29–30, 1905. *Chicago Daily Tribune,* June 29–30, 1905.

　　*Trepov was cracking down:* Robbins, pp. 224–27; Surh, pp. 269–71.

　　*Further, a conference:* Manning, p. 111.

156　*And, finally, rumors: New York Herald Tribune,* June 30, 1905; *Daily Telegraph,* June 30, 1905. The author hesitated to include these rumors about mutiny in the army, but in almost every paper he read, they were repeated. Even if they were only such — rumors — Nicholas read foreign papers and would have been apprised of them, deepening his concern.

　　*Prior to the Battle of Tsushima:* White, pp. 210–11; Esthus, pp. 26–35; Dennett, pp. 174–88.

　　*On May 25:* Howe, pp. 156–62; "Letter from Roosevelt to Lodge, June 16, 1905," Morison, pp. 1221–32.

　　*"Russia is so corrupt":* Morison, pp. 1221–32.

　　*In the two weeks:* "Letter from Roosevelt to George Meyer, June 19, 1905," ibid., pp. 1241–42.

　　*Towering in height:* Essad-Bey, p. 94; Harcave, *Memoirs,* pp. 418–19; Harcave, *Count Sergei Witte,* pp. 142–43; Korostovetz, pp. 18–19.

157　*"Only not Witte!":* Korostovetz, p. 11.

　　*Instead the tsar chose:* White, p. 233; U.S. Department of State, pp. 814–15.

　　*That afternoon, June 16:* Dillon, p. 229.

　　*"Fate of the Empire": Chicago Daily Tribune,* June 29, 1905.

*"Czar's Warship in": New York Times,* June 29, 1905.

*"There is always": Daily Telegraph,* June 29, 1905; Harrison, pp. 75–80.

*The* Times *of London: Times,* June 29, 1905; Harrison, pp. 75–80.

158 *"It had been hoped": Petit Journal,* as quoted in *Daily Telegraph,* June 30, 1905.

*"a flashlight revealing": Tageblatt,* as quoted in *New York Times,* July 1, 1905.

*"What is left for the autocracy": Nichi Nichi Shimbun,* as quoted in *Daily Telegraph,* July 1, 1905.

*In the realm of finance: Daily Telegraph,* June 30, 1905; *New York Herald Tribune,* June 30, 1905.

*"It seems difficult": Parliamentary Debates,* p. 546.

*The potential consequences:* Alzona, pp. 5–23; White, pp. 194–95; Lieven, pp. 92–93; Gwynn, pp. 469–70; Bulow, pp. 143–47.

159 *The sultan of the Ottoman Empire:* Spector, I., p. 61.

*"preposterous little creature":* Dennett, p. 188.

*Yet Roosevelt was a realist:* ibid., pp. 54–55.

*The French ambassador:* Paleologue, pp. 258, 265.

*Wilhelm II persistently urged:* Dugdale, p. 206.

*British ambassador Charles Hardinge: British Reports,* report from Charles Hardinge, July 4, 1905 (FO 65/1701).

*American ambassador Meyer:* Howe, pp. 173–75.

*Sultan Abdul Hamid II:* Spector, I., p. 62.

*"Japan has had the luck":* Esthus, p. 56.

160 *From his small Geneva apartment:* Service, p. 164; Valentinov, pp. 79–80, 146–47; Krupskaya, p. 120; Salisbury, pp. 138–39.

*With his bald, egglike head:* Wolfe, p. 55; Fischer, L., p. 6; Valentinov, p. 13.

*"What is there for me":* Fischer, L., p. 17.

*His first influences:* Payne, *The Life,* pp. 76–77.

*Lenin also fell under the spell:* Figes, pp. 145–46; Fischer, L., p. 40.

161 *In 1893, Lenin passed:* Fischer, L., pp. 18–35.

*There he followed a road:* Payne, *The Life,* pp. 148–51.

*In July 1903:* Figes, pp. 153–54; Wolfe, pp. 240–43.

*"Of such dough":* Trotsky, *My Life,* p. 163.

*After the meeting:* Salisbury, pp. 142–43; Payne, *The Life,* pp. 176–78.

*"A military collapse":* Payne, *The Life,* p. 182.

162 *"Squads must arm themselves":* Lenin, *Collected Works,* vol. 8, p. 237; Fischer, L., p. 44.

*Lenin labored:* Wolfe, pp. 288–89; Salisbury, pp. 140–41; Lenin, *Collected Works,* vol. 8, pp. 144–47; ibid., vol. 34, pp. 296–300.

*However, on the morning: La Tribune de Genève,* June 29, 1905; Krupskaya, p. 110. The author has taken the liberty of selecting this newspaper as the one from which Lenin learned of the news. In his wife's recollections of Lenin's time in Geneva, she wrote, "We lived at one with all the Russian political emigrants in Geneva — from one number of the *Tribune* to the next." This was how Lenin learned of Bloody Sunday.

162 *This was the beginning:* Lenin, *Collected Works,* vol. 8, pp. 560–73.

*"You'll leave for Odessa":* Vasilyev-Yuzhin, pp. 68–71; Fox, pp. 124–26; Prokhorov, p. 526; Keep, *The Rise,* p. 174. In places, this conversation between Lenin and Vasilyev-Yuzhin hints of Bolshevik revisionism, but the sources are clear that Lenin did in fact send Vasilyev-Yuzhin to Odessa. The author has eliminated a few of the more overreaching comments attributed to Lenin, including, most outrageously, the statement that once Vasilyev-Yuzhin commandeered the battleship, he was to send a torpedo boat to get Lenin, to bring him to Russia.

163 *It was more than likely:* Bushnell, *Mutiny amid Repression,* pp. 58–62.

CHAPTER 13

164 *An Orthodox priest led:* Gerasimov, pp. 130–31; Nevsky, p. 323; Berezovsky, pp. 140–44; Matyushenko, pp. 315–19; *New York Herald Tribune,* June 30, 1905.

*Matyushenko had come:* Matyushenko, p. 318.

165 *"Keep moving":* Berezovsky, p. 141.

*"Long live freedom!":* ibid.; Ponomarev, p. 106.

*Before the ceremony:* Matyushenko, pp. 315–18; Berezovsky, pp. 140–44.

166 *With thousands of troops:* ibid.; TsGAVMF, f. 417, op. 1, d. 3023, p. 40; *Washington Post,* June 30, 1905.

167 *When Kakhanov had authorized:* Inozemtsev, pp. 83–85.

*If so, then ambushing the sailors:* ibid. In the long report that Kakhanov wrote about his actions during the *Potemkin* mutiny, he did not attribute to himself the plan to ambush the sailors on their return from the funeral. But given that, directly after the failed ambush, the *Potemkin* bombarded the city, one can imagine his hesitancy in accepting blame. The plot was obviously organized, and the author believes that the officers on the ground would not have risked the effort without Kakhanov's authorization. Therefore, the author has done his best to re-create the reasoning behind the ambush, particularly given the thoughts that Kakhanov was having during this time, as evidenced in his long report on the *Potemkin*.

*At 5:20 P.M., the battleship:* Krasny arkhiv, St. George Mutiny, p. 235; TsGAVMF, f. 920, op. 6, d. 428, p. 5.

168 *given the unreliability:* Platonov, p. 75.

*Vishnevetsky planned to send:* Krasny arkhiv, St. George Mutiny, p. 235; TsGAVMF, f. 920, op. 6, d. 428, p. 53.

*on board the Twelve Apostles:* Pleskov, p. 19.

*"The question's whether"*: ibid., p. 20.

169 *Throughout the squadron:* TsGAVMF, f. 1025, op. 2, d. 37, p. 96.

*"I have no intention"*: Platonov, p. 178.

170 *On the* St. George: Gavrilov, *V borbe za svobodu,* p. 88.

*late that afternoon:* Platonov, p. 101.

171 *Although the sailor committee:* Feldmann, p. 87; Nevsky, p. 242.

*"Here, lads, a good man"*: Feldmann, pp. 87–89; Berezovsky, p. 145.

172 *"Stay, brothers! We must"*: Feldmann, p. 90; Berezovsky, pp. 146–48; Nevsky, p. 241; Rostotskaya, p. 29.

173 *"We will die together"*: Berezovsky, p. 148.

*"Weigh anchor and get up steam"*: Gavrilov, *V borbe za svobodu,* pp. 80–83; Feldmann, pp. 90–93; Hough, *Potemkin Mutiny,* pp. 116–19; Berezovsky, pp. 149–51; Kovalenko, pp. 131–52; Lychev, p. 69; Nevsky, p. 241; Platonov, pp. 69–71; Selivanov, *Matros Matyushenko,* pp. 20–23. The sources contradict one another as to the reason for and timing of the firing on the city. Some remark that the shelling began as the funeral party was still in the city, but this contradicts the viable account of Matyushenko, whose details of the funeral are vivid and clear. Since he gave the speech that inspired the crew to launch the attack — and he attended the funeral — the author believes the attack came afterward. More important, the sources give numerous reasons for the shelling: the ambush on the funeral party, Kakhanov's preventing the resupply of the ship, the slaughter on June 15, the military council meeting. The author weaves most of these reasons into the decision to shell Odessa.

174 *With the firing:* Matyushenko, p. 302.

*"Get it right this time"*: Hough, *Potemkin Mutiny,* p. 118.

175 *In Odessa's streets: Russkoye Slovo,* June 24, 1905; National Archives and Records Service, letter from Consul Heenan to George Meyer, American ambassador in St. Petersburg, July 4, 1905.

176 *"A white flag!"*: Ponomarev, p. 108.

*"We've fired two shells"*: Feldmann, pp. 94–102.

*He found Kakhanov:* Inozemtsev, p. 85.

177 *"The commander in chief"*: Feldmann, pp. 94–102.

*When two representatives:* Rostotskaya, pp. 23–24.

178 *Even before the battleship:* Ponomarev, p. 56; Nevsky, p. 274.

*"Keep up the bombardment"*: Gavrilov, *V borbe za svobodu,* p. 83.

CHAPTER 14

179 *A few hours after midnight:* Berezovsky, pp. 155–58.

*"We intercepted a telegram"*: ibid., pp. 158–59.

180 *"What if the squadron"*: Ponomarev, p. 110; Kovalenko, pp. 134–35; Feldmann, p. 104; Nevsky, pp. 242–43.

181  *Matyushenko ended the meeting:* Kovalenko, p. 134; Hough, *Potemkin Mutiny*, pp. 152–57.
*"Distinctly visible":* Feldmann, p. 106.
*Kirill suggested:* Kovalenko, p. 135; Hough, *Potemkin Mutiny*, p. 155.

182  *"Where's the doctor?":* Kovalenko, p. 136.
*"Cut steam. Will sink you":* Gavrilov, *V borbe za svobodu*, p. 92; TsGAVMF, f. 1025, op. 2, d. 35, p. 151.

183  *"Give the order":* Hough, *Potemkin Mutiny*, pp. 133–34.
*"The Black Sea crews":* Platonov, p. 79.
*The* Potemkin *began:* Kovalenko, p. 137; Ponomarev, p. 112; Berezovsky, pp. 162–63; Hough, *Potemkin Mutiny*, pp. 134–35.

184  *"Apparently it's no fun":* Kovalenko, p. 137.
"Three Saints, *what is keeping":* Gavrilov, *V borbe za svobodu*, p. 93.
*When he discovered:* Hough, *Potemkin Mutiny*, p. 134.
*He had never expected: Krasny arkhiv, St. George Mutiny*, p. 236.

185  *As usual, Koshuba:* Feldmann, p. 147.
*They had witnessed:* ibid., p. 108.
*His task was to persuade:* Pleskov, p. 22. It is also clear from the account of Volgin that the *St. George*'s revolutionaries did not limit their efforts at propaganda to their battleship alone. *St. George* sailors assigned to the steam launches spread the idea of revolt to those on other ships as well.
*Meanwhile, on the* Rostislav: Gavrilov, *V borbe za svobodu*, p. 94; Hough, *Potemkin Mutiny*, p. 137.
*"The tsar himself":* Hough, *Potemkin Mutiny*, p. 137.
*"This is the shame":* Pleskov, p. 23.

186  *Gathered on rooftops: Russkoye Slovo,* June 24, 1905.
*Even the city's revolutionaries:* Rostotskaya, pp. 24–28.
*After sending away:* TsGAVMF, f. 417, op. 1, d. 3023, p. 112; Gavrilov, *V borbe za svobodu*, p. 90.
*"What can the* Potemkin *do":* Kardashev, *Burevestniki revolyutsii*, p. 37; Inozemtsev, p. 85.
*Still, he was optimistic:* Hough, *Potemkin Mutiny*, p. 149.

187  *When the* Potemkin *dropped anchor:* Berezovsky, p. 164; *Journal de St. Petersburg,* June 18, 1905.
*"We knew they would":* Hough, *Potemkin Mutiny*, p. 135.
*"Ah, how glad I am":* Kovalenko, p. 137; Feldmann, p. 109.
*In the wardroom:* Nevsky, p. 243; Feldmann, pp. 110–11, 139; Gavrilov, *V borbe za svobodu*, p. 94.

188  *"I'll fix a powder":* Berezovsky, pp. 162–63.
*"Send representatives":* Gavrilov, *V borbe za svobodu*, p. 94.
*The jokes and songs ended:* Nevsky, p. 243.

189  *At 12:05 P.M.:* ibid.
*"This will decide things":* Hough, *Potemkin Mutiny*, p. 138.

CHAPTER 15

190 *"See over there?"*: TsGAVMF, f. 1025, op. 2, d. 37, p. 4.

*The squadron had twenty:* Kardashev, *Burevestniki revolyutsii,* p. 33.

*If the* Potemkin *was to have:* Klado, *The Battle,* pp. 54–55.

*No wonder then:* Kovalenko, p. 138.

191 *"Black Sea sailors"*: Ponomarev, p. 113; Kardashev, *Burevestniki revolyutsii,* p. 38; Feldmann, pp. 110–11.

*The flagship commanded:* Tomitch, pp. 47–53.

*"We won't fire!"*: TsGAVMF, f. 870, op. 1, d. 33043, pp. 24–25.

*"Five thousand meters"*: ibid.; Berezovsky, p. 169; Lychev, p. 71; Nevsky, p. 143; Hough, *Potemkin Mutiny,* p. 139; Kovalenko, pp. 138–39.

192 *With the squadron:* Feldmann, p. 113.

193 *"It was the kind of scene"*: Kardashev, *Burevestniki revolyutsii,* p. 38.

*Desperate to get the squadron:* Nevsky, p. 243; Gavrilov, *V borbe za svobodu,* p. 97. Ensign Alekseyev testified to officials that he countermanded this order, preventing the collision. Given, however, that the officer was feigning sickness during the mute battle, the author finds his account self-serving and unlikely, though Russian historian Gavrilov believes differently.

*The* Potemkin *crossed:* Kardashev, *Burevestniki revolyutsii,* pp. 38–39.

194 *"Gun crews!"*: Kovalenko, p. 139; Pleskov, p. 26.

*"This was the moment"*: Matyushenko, p. 304.

*"Officers of the squadron"*: Kovalenko, p. 139.

195 *Krieger hoped the mutineers would:* Platonov, p. 162.

*As the* Potemkin *passed:* Berezovsky, p. 169; Melnikov, p. 164.

*Then Krieger signaled:* Pleskov, pp. 27–29; Gavrilov, *V borbe za svobodu,* p. 99; Ponomarev, p. 114.

196 *"Why are there so many"*: Gavrilov, "Vosstaniye na 'Georgii.'"

*From the moment:* Krasny arkhiv, *St. George Mutiny,* pp. 246–50.

197 *"Stop the engines"*: TsGAVMF, f. 1025, op. 2, d. 37, p. 2; TsGVIA, f. 400, op. 5, d. 31, p. 37; Gavrilov, "Vosstaniye na 'Georgii'"; Platonov, pp. 83–84; *Krasny arkhiv, St. George* Mutiny, pp. 242–51; Gavrilov, *V borbe za svobodu,* pp. 101–5.

198 *At most, Koshuba:* Krasny arkhiv, *St. George Mutiny,* pp. 252–59.

*"The . . . crew . . . of"*: Gavrilov, "Vosstaniye na 'Georgy.'"

*A wave of joy:* Feldmann, p. 115.

*To avoid a trap:* Gavrilov, "Vosstaniye na 'Georgii.'"

*Stirred to action:* ibid.; *Krasny arkhiv, St. George Mutiny,* pp. 240–45; Berezovsky, pp. 173–78; Feldmann, pp. 115–18.

200 *he no longer felt:* Kovalenko, p. 141.

*Once back on the* Potemkin: Matyushenko, pp. 304–5.

201 *Kovalenko imagined:* Kovalenko, p. 49.

201  *"Looking at the sailors":* Berezovsky, pp. 182–83.

*Sixteen miles southeast:* Melnikov, pp. 165–66; Platonov, pp. 89–90, 162; Kardashev, *Burevestniki revolyutsii,* p. 41.

202  *Since even this meager attempt:* TsGAVMF, f. 417, op. 1, d. 3023, p. 117. According to the archives, Krieger also sent a telegram to Avelan before the departure of torpedo boat No. 272, informing him of his plan for a night attack on the *Potemkin.* But apparently the meeting with the captains convinced him that this plan was foolish.


CHAPTER 16

203  *Apart from a horseback ride:* Romanov, N., June 17, 1905.

*Finally, in the early evening:* TsGIA(M), f. 601, op. 1, d. 105, p. 8.

*"After a most prompt investigation":* Kardashev, "Nesostoyavshayasya Kazn."

*At a city concert hall: Daily Telegraph,* July 3, 1905.

*Russian aristocrats: Washington Post,* June 30, 1905; *Times,* June 30, 1905; *Chicago Daily Tribune,* July 1, 1905.

204  *"the last support":* Los, *Revolyutsionnaya borbe,* pp. 67–69.

*"Soldiers! Follow the example":* Valk, pp. 253–54.

*Inspired by the mutiny:* Surh, pp. 269–72; Brooks, pp. 183–87.

*Of course, a series of strikes:* Rice, pp. 78–79. According to Rice, this committee, which formed during the *Potemkin* mutiny, endured until the October 1905 strikes.

*Among the liberal opposition:* Ascher, pp. 175–76; Stockdale, pp. 138–39; Sanders, pp. 901–2, 930.

*Regardless of how often: Chicago Daily Tribune,* June 30, 1905; *Daily Telegraph,* June 30, 1905; *Manchester Guardian,* June 30, 1905; *New York Herald Tribune,* June 30, 1905; Alzona, pp. 52–55.

205  *The Parisian* Temps: *Daily Telegraph,* July 1, 1905.

*"Not since the insurrection": Los Angeles Times,* July 1, 1905.

*"God knows what's happening":* Maylunas and Mironenko, p. 277.

*"What is happening to Russia?":* ibid., p. 278.

*Nelidov, his first choice:* White, pp. 232–33; Harcave, *Count Sergei Witte,* p. 144; Kokovtsov, pp. 52–54, 551.

206  *Meanwhile, he stalled:* ibid., p. 45.

*The comforts of the private railcar:* interview with St. Petersburg Railway Historical Museum.

*He was impatient:* Belomor, p. 173.

*The first one repeated:* Kardashev, "Novyye Svedeniya."

207  *The day before:* Gavrilov, *V borbe za svobodu,* p. 93.

*Chukhnin was most troubled:* Belomor, p. 174.

*As the train hurtled:* Platonov, pp. 90–92; Melnikov, p. 169.

208 *Odessans fled on whatever transport:* Russkoye Slovo, June 24, 1905; *Daily Telegraph,* July 1, 1905; *Manchester Guardian,* July 1, 1905.
*"The train station":* Gavrilov, *V borbe za svobodu,* p. 109.
*Despite the futility:* Inozemtsev, p. 86.
*While he delivered his orders:* ibid.; National Archives and Records Service, letter from Consul Heenan to Ambassador Meyer, June 21, 1905; *Russkiye Vedomosti,* June 21, 1905.

209 *"We're not afraid":* Berezovsky, p. 182.
*"Another act of heroism":* Matyushenko, p. 307.
*On the* St. George: Gavrilov, "Vosstaniye na 'Georgy.'"
*He found it strange:* Feldmann, p. 121.
*After the prayer:* Krasny arkhiv, *St. George Mutiny,* p. 241.

210 *"Tomorrow we want coal":* Matyushenko, p. 307; Inozemtsev, p. 96.
*"dull, feral, and aloof":* Kovalenko, p. 46; Feldmann, p. 119.

211 *Then they settled:* Berezovsky, pp. 184, 196.
*As the crews retired:* Gavrilov, *V borbe za svobodu,* p. 110; Feldmann, p. 124.
*In the peaceful night:* Kovalenko, p. 49; Feldmann, p. 124.

212 *He could not:* Matyushenko, p. 307; Berezovsky, pp. 187–88. This conclusion about his state of mind can be inferred from Matyushenko's brazen behavior the next day, marching into Odessa unarmed and speaking to a general as if that officer was an underling.
*Kirill and Feldmann:* Feldmann, pp. 126–27.
*None of them knew:* Gavrilov, *V borbe za svobodu,* p. 111.

CHAPTER 17

213 *At 8 A.M., Matyushenko:* Berezovsky, pp. 187–88; Feldmann, pp. 128–31.
214 *"What's happened?":* Kovalenko, p. 50.
*They left Kovalenko's cabin:* ibid.; Matyushenko, p. 307.
215 *As the launch was prepared:* Platonov, p. 95.
*"Our crew no longer wishes":* Kovalenko, pp. 51–52.
216 *"If the* Potemkin": Nevsky, p. 245; Berezovsky, p. 191.
*"I'm the son of a peasant":* Platonov, pp. 95–96; Zebroski, pp. 338–39.
217 *Golenko slipped off:* Gavrilov, *V borbe za svobodu,* pp. 112–13.
*"Our committee shouldn't":* ibid., pp. 112–14.
*The launch cast off:* Kovalenko, pp. 54–55; Feldmann, pp. 132–33.
218 *After they left:* Inozemtsev, p. 87.
*A crew led by Kirill:* Feldmann, p. 134; Gavrilov, "Vosstaniye na 'Georgy.'"
219 *When Dr. Golenko revisited:* Gavrilov, *V borbe za svobodu,* p. 115.
*Boatswain Kuzmenko:* Krasny arkhiv, *St. George Mutiny,* p. 242.
*"Most of the* Potemkin": Platonov, pp. 95–96; Gavrilov, "Vosstaniye na 'Georgii.'"

220  *"Kill the traitors!":* Melnikov, p. 167.
     *A sailor ran:* TsGAVMF, f. 1025, op. 2, d. 35, pp. 151–52; Matyushenko,
     p. 308; Feldmann, pp. 136–38; Berezovsky, pp. 197–99; Gavrilov, *V borbe
     za svobodu,* pp. 117–18; Nevsky, p. 246.
222  *On the* Potemkin's *bridge:* Ponomarev, p. 123.
     *While the* Potemkin: TsGAVMF, f. 920, op. 6, d. 428, p. 51.
     *"The doctor's a traitor":* Kovalenko, pp. 56–57; Matyushenko, p. 308;
     Melnikov, p. 168.
     *Standing on the bridge:* Matyushenko, p. 308.
223  *"Brothers, comrades":* Feldmann, p. 139.
     *Although fear gripped the crew:* Matyushenko, pp. 308–9; Melnikov, p. 26.
224  *"How come you want to go":* Berezovsky, p. 201.
     *"This is what we'll do":* Feldmann, p. 149.
     *The* Vekha *struck a further blow:* TsGAVMF, f. 1025, op. 2, d. 17, p. 19.
     *"It appears that we're lost":* Feldmann, p. 143; Berezovsky, p. 202.
225  *Kovalenko could barely stand:* Kovalenko, p. 57.
     *across the battleship:* Lychev, p. 77.
     *The journey to Romania: Revolyutsionnyi bronenosets,* p. 21.
     *The only voice:* Feldmann, pp. 143–44.
     *In Odessa that evening:* Inozemtsev, pp. 87–88.
226  *The citizens of Odessa:* National Archives and Records Service, letter from
     Consul Heenan to George Meyer, American ambassador in St. Petersburg,
     July 4, 1905; *Chicago Daily Tribune,* July 3, 1905; *Russkoye Slovo,* June 21,
     1905.
     *At 11 P.M., General Karangozov:* Inozemtsev, p. 88; TsGAVMF, f. 417,
     op. 1, d. 3023, p. 120.
     *Three hours later:* Nevsky, p. 368; TsGAVMF, f. 920, op. 6, d. 428, p. 51.
     *He had traveled:* Vasilyev-Yuzhin, pp. 68–77.

PART III

229  *"We must dare":* Vasilyev-Yuzhin, p. 76.
     *"What tragic poetry":* Melnikov, p. 175.

CHAPTER 18

231  *On the afternoon:* Feldmann, p. 153.
     *Before the meeting started:* ibid., p. 144.
     *The committee believed:* Hitchens, pp. 1–50; Treptow, p. 319.
232  *"Maybe they'll let us":* Berezovsky, p. 218.
     *"After we get fuel":* Ponomarev, p. 130; *Revolyutsionnyi bronenosets,*
     pp. 21–22.
     *It was unanimous:* Berezovsky, pp. 208–18; Feldmann, p. 155.
233  *"Comrades, there's a significant reason":* Berezovsky, pp. 216–18.

*"We need to let the workers":* Ponomarev, p. 131.

234 *In Nikolayev, a port:* Melnikov.
*Chukhnin had arrived:* Belomor, pp. 176–77.
*Later that same afternoon:* Platonov, p. 162; Gavrilov, *V borbe za svobodu,* p. 141.
*"I am afraid the sea":* TsGAVMF, f. 417, op. 1, d. 3023, p. 67.

235 *Chukhnin ordered Captain Guzevich:* Belomor, p. 175.
*"The squadron has returned":* Los, *Revolyutsiya 1905–1907,* p. 373.
*The governor-general:* Kardashev, *Burevestniki revolyutsii,* p. 35.
*In other seaside cities:* Zebroski, p. 295.
*Chukhnin was scheduled:* Nevsky, pp. 364–65; Belomor, p. 176; TsGAVMF, f. 920, op. 6, d. 428, p. 8, p. 41; Gavrilov, *V borbe za svobodu,* p. 150.
*Throughout the day:* Los, *Revolyutsiya 1905–1907,* p. 373; Kardashev, "Nesostoyavshayasya Kazn"; Kardashev, *Burevestniki revolyutsii,* pp. 46–47; TsGAVMF, f. 920, op. 6, d. 428, p. 68; ibid., f. 417, op. 1, d. 3023, p. 79.

236 *But Chukhnin placed his faith:* Bliznyuk; Hough, *Potemkin Mutiny,* pp. 151–52.
*The thirty-two-year-old:* TsGAVMF, f. 406, op. 9, d. 4969, p. 9; ibid., f. 417, op. 4, d. 3831, pp. 1–21; Chernov, p. 351; *Nominal Roll,* p. 270.

237 *Chukhnin readily accepted:* Bliznyuk; TsGAVMF, f. 870, op. 1, d. 149, p. 154; Hough, *Potemkin Mutiny,* p. 152.
*At 9:30 A.M.:* Ponomarev, pp. 291–92; Naida, *Voennyye moryaki,* p. 371.
*Unknown to Baranovsky:* Selivanov, *Matros Petrov,* pp. 9–15.

238 *"Come on, boys":* Naida, *Voennyye moryaki,* p. 372.
*Early on June 15:* Gavrilov, *V borbe za svobodu,* pp. 143–46; Naida, *Voennyye moryaki,* pp. 370–72; Platonov, pp. 100–104.
*Several minutes into:* Ponomarev, pp. 292–95.

239 *"Where do you think":* Zebroski, ref 179, 181; Platonov, pp. 103–4.
*A short time later:* Platonov, pp. 103–4; Ponomarev, p. 293.
*During the journey:* Ponomarev, p. 296.
*With no shells:* Naida, *Voennyye moryaki,* p. 366.
*Less than an hour:* ibid., p. 374.

240 *Onshore in Odessa:* TsGAVMF, f. 920, op. 6, d. 428, p. 61.
*"Orthodox fellow believers!":* Kardashev, *Burevestniki revolyutsii,* p. 48. This bottle eventually washed ashore in the Crimea and was sent to Zubchenko's wife.
LIBERTY, EQUALITY, FRATERNITY: Gavrilov, *V borbe za svobodu,* p. 126.
*"To the Whole Civilized World":* ibid., p. 199; Grishin, pp. 64–66; Feldmann, pp. 157–58; Berezovsky, p. 219. The historical documents contradict one another as to whether Kirill wrote the declaration to the "Civilized World" and Feldmann to "European Monarchs" or vice versa.

241  *"We are not pirates":* Ponomarev, p. 132.

    *Feldmann then stood:* Los, *Revolyutsionnaya borba,* p. 66.

242  *Constructed on a low promontory:* British Admiralty, pp. 168–71; *Nagel Travel Guides,* pp. 281–85.

    *"A bad sign":* Kovalenko, p. 58.


CHAPTER 19

243  *"Guard, attention!":* Berezovsky, pp. 222–24; Ponomarev, pp. 133–34; Feldmann, pp. 159–62; Bogachev, pp. 20–22.

    *Negru shook his head:* TsGAVMF, f. 417, op. 1, d. 3023, p. 270; Bogachev, pp. 19–20; Kovalenko, p. 58.

244  *"Most of all":* Bogachev, p. 21; Ponomarev, p. 133; Berezovsky, p. 226.

    *"I have to ask":* Bogachev, p. 21; Ponomarev, p. 133.

245  *"They want to conspire":* Berezovsky, p. 224.

    *"Officer coming":* Matyushenko, p. 309; Nevsky, p. 280; Feldmann, pp. 161–62.

246  *After Banov skittered:* ibid., pp. 163–64.

    *Dusk had fallen:* Kovalenko, pp. 63–64.

    *"We didn't come":* Matyushenko, p. 310.

247  *On the* Potemkin: Kovalenko, p. 61; Bogachev, p. 21; Berezovsky, p. 226.

    *In Constanza, Captain Negru:* Bogachev, pp. 19–25.

248  *With his sharp features:* Chernov, p. 351.

    *The day before:* Bliznyuk; TsGAVMF, f. 870, op. 1, d. 149, pp. 154–55.

    *"Have you seen":* Gavrilov, *V borbe za svobodu,* pp. 148–49; Ponomarev, p. 292.

    *At first light:* *Times* (London), July 4, 1905; *Manchester Guardian,* July 4, 1905.

249  *In Odessa, Yanovich:* Bliznyuk; TsGAVMF, f. 870, op. 1, d. 149, pp. 154–55.

    *In the throne room:* King, G., p. 205; Abris Art Publishers, pp. 12–14. Although historical documents do not stipulate this, the author has assumed that Nicholas met the delegation in the throne room, a hall ordinarily used by Nicholas to receive official visitors at Peterhof.

    *Along with other monarchists:* Lyubimov, p. 277; Rawson, pp. 83–85; Manning, pp. 112–13.

    *But he likely paid:* Verner, p. 194.

250  *Anyway, his thoughts:* Romanov, N., June 20, 1905.

    *"Krieger must be":* Gavrilov, *V borbe za svobodu,* p. 151.

    *For nearly a week:* *Chicago Daily Tribune,* June 30, 1905; *Times* (London), July 3, 1905; *New York Times,* July 3, 1905.

    *With the* Potemkin: *Parliamentary Debates,* p. 773; TsGAVMF, f. 920, op. 6, d. 428, p. 160.

*Talk that the army:* Gavrilov, *V borbe za svobodu,* p. 169.

*"The* Potemkin *uprising":* Kardashev, *Burevestniki revolyutsii,* p. 50.

251  *"Under the present conditions":* Dillon, p. 299.

*"I feel compelled":* ibid., p. 300.

*Nicholas was finally learning:* Fuller, p. 160; U.S. Department of State, p. 816; *Chicago Daily Tribune,* July 4, 1905.

*"A state is only powerful":* Verner, p. 197.

*"The devil only knows":* Romanov, N., June 20, 1905.

252  *At 7:30 A.M. on June 20:* Hough, *Potemkin Mutiny,* p. 205.

*"I've received instructions":* Bogachev, pp. 22–23.

*"Try to persuade":* Berezovsky, p. 227.

253  *"Are we really":* Ponomarev, pp. 134–35.

*"How about Poti?":* Feldmann, pp. 167–70; Berezovsky, pp. 228–29.

*Then Denisenko proposed:* Smith, pp. 135–37.

254  *"We hope the Ottoman":* Berezovsky, p. 231.

*"Every country has":* Feldmann, p. 170.

*"The cause you fight for":* Kovalenko, p. 61.

*When he returned:* Bogachev, p. 23.

CHAPTER 20

256  *"Despite the offer":* Hough, *Potemkin Mutiny,* p. 196.

*Chukhnin's preparations:* Kardashev, "Nesostoyavshayasya Kazn."

*His spies had already learned:* Platonov, pp. 54–55.

257  *"The crews despise you":* Belomor, p. 177.

*On the deck of each ship:* ibid., p. 178.

*He brought in additional troops:* Gavrilov, *V borbe za svobodu,* pp. 150–51; Melnikov, p. 171; Zebroski, pp. 367–68.

*Delayed by repairs:* TsGAVMF, f. 870, op. 1, d. 149, p. 160; Hough, *Potemkin Mutiny,* pp. 205–6.

258  *After two fruitless days:* Platonov, pp. 118–20.

*"A regrettably shameful":* Daily Telegraph, July 5, 1905.

*The foreign press offered:* The author studied the following English-language newspapers during this period, many of which carried quotations from newspapers in Germany, France, Austria, and Japan: *The Times* (London), *Manchester Guardian, Daily Telegraph, New York Times, New York Herald Tribune, Washington Post, Los Angeles Times,* and *Chicago Daily Tribune.* Furthermore, the author reviewed studies such as "French Contemporary Opinion of the Russian Revolutions of 1905," by Encarnacion Alzona; *The Uncertain Crusade,* by Arthur Thompson and Robert Hart; and *Die Russische Revolution von 1905–1907 im Spiegel der Deutschen Presse,* by Dr. Leo Stern, to understand the change in opinion on the sailors.

259  *"They are practically pirates"*: *Chicago Daily Tribune*, July 4, 1905.
     *The* New York Times *argued:* Thompson and Hart, p. 51.
260  *"coming into a cage"*: *Times* (London), July 4, 1905.
     *"They were willing"*: Alzona, pp. 53–54.
     *The Bulgarians promised:* Spector, I., p. 62.
     *Almost daily, President Roosevelt:* Thompson and Hart, p. 60.
     *"Heretofore, I have"*: Howe, p. 176.
     *"We have lately"*: *Daily Telegraph*, July 3, 1905.
261  *"Comrades, now it's our turn"*: Valk, p. 258.
     *In Geneva, the revolution's :* Getzler, pp. 96–106.
     *Lenin did write:* Lenin, *Collected Works,* vol. 8, pp. 544–46, 555.
     *"One cannot overstate"*: ibid., p. 572.
262  *Nowhere was the situation worse:* Feldmann, pp. 176–77.
     *The machinists and stokers:* Kovalenko, pp. 62–63; Gavrilov, *V borbe za svobodu,* p. 130; Berezovsky, p. 237; Feldmann, pp. 172–78.
     *Standing on the bridge:* Matyushenko, p. 310.
263  *Like Kovalenko:* Kovalenko, p. 63.
     *"What do you think"*: Vilensky, pp. 36–38.
264  *Before the sun set:* Feldmann, p. 178.


CHAPTER 21

265  *At 8 A.M. on June 22:* Hough, *Potemkin Mutiny,* pp. 174–75.
     *Located on the southern Crimean:* Curtis, p. 217; Ascherson, pp. 16–18, 95–96; King, C., pp. 84–86, 92, 115–17, 162; *Black Sea Coast,* pp. 98–100; Fisher, pp. 64–93; *Handbook for Travellers,* pp. 395–96.
266  *The crew lowered a launch:* Berezovsky, pp. 239–44.
267  *"the duty of every citizen"*: Feldmann, p. 180.
     *Then Matyushenko stood:* Popov.
     *"Gentlemen, please have mercy"*: Berezovsky, p. 248.
268  *On his return: Revolyutsionnyi bronenosets,* p. 49.
     *"Don't disgrace Theodosia"*: Nevsky, p. 266.
     *As soon as the battleship:* TsGAVMF, f. 920, op. 6, d. 428, pp. 112–18.
     *Volkov ordered the garrison:* Popov.
     *"Having just returned"*: *Revolyutsionnyi bronenosets,* p. 49.
269  *Although Pleshkov and the police chief:* Popov; Nevsky, p. 266.
     *"I was summoned"*: ibid.
     *At his headquarters:* ibid.
     *Under the glare:* Feldmann, p. 182.
270  *At 3 P.M., a barge:* ibid., pp. 184–85; Matyushenko, p. 311.
     *"Have you heard anything"*: Berezovsky, pp. 250, 254.
271  *"Don't let them"*: ibid., pp. 251–55.

272 *"We're now fighting":* Revolyutsionnyi bronenosets, p. 49.
*When they returned:* Ponomarev, p. 137; Popov; Matyushenko, p. 311.
*Across the Black Sea:* TsGAVMF, f. 870, op. 1, d. 149, pp. 161–65; Bliznyuk; Platonov, pp. 118–19.
273 *But down in the engine room:* Bliznyuk.
*In Sevastopol, Chukhnin:* TsGAVMF, f. 920, op. 6, d. 428, p. 150; Gavrilov, *V borbe za svobodu*, p. 131.
274 *"Resolve this situation":* TsGIA(M), f. 601, op. 1, d. 105, p. 40.
*"Potemkin demands coal":* Gavrilov, *V borbe za svobodu*, p. 131.
*Throughout the day:* TsGAVMF, f. 920, op. 6, d. 428, p. 127.
*A full moon hung:* Berezovsky, p. 260; Feldmann, p. 186.
275 *Throughout the battleship:* Nevsky, p. 269; Matyushenko, p. 311.
*In the city:* Popov; TsGAVMF, f. 920, op. 6, d. 428, p. 118.


CHAPTER 22

279 *As the sailors awakened:* Popov; Matyushenko, pp. 311–12; Feldmann, pp. 187–96; Berezovsky, pp. 216–67; Kovalenko, pp. 66–67, Nevsky, pp. 268–69; Ponomarev, pp. 138–39.
280 *"Let's go ashore":* Berezovsky, p. 264.
*To prepare, some sailors:* Gavrilov, *V borbe za svobodu*, p. 136.
*"There's no support":* Kovalenko, p. 66.
*Matyushenko listened:* Matyushenko, pp. 312–13; Selivanov, *Matros Matyushenko*, pp. 25–26; Berezovsky, p. 264; Hough, *Potemkin Mutiny*, p. 179.
*They steered a course:* Gavrilov, *V borbe za svobodu*, pp. 136–37.
282 *It was a warm evening:* Romanov, N., June 23, 1905.
*The humiliating Potemkin mutiny:* ibid.; *Chicago Daily Tribune*, July 6, 1905.
*"The sons of Russia":* *Novoye Vremya*, June 22, 1905.
*The reactionary newspaper:* *Moskovskiye Vedomosti*, June 23, 1905.
283 *"Fear is the sole basis":* *Russkoye Slovo*, June 23, 1905; *Chicago Daily Tribune*, July 6, 1905.
*"It was sufficient":* *Nasha Zhizn*, as quoted in *Russkoye Slovo*, June 23, 1905.
*What the censors:* *Times* (London), July 6, 1905; *Daily Telegraph*, July 8, 1905.
*As Nicholas neared:* Romanov, N., June 24, 1905.
284 *"We can't tell you":* *New York Times*, July 7, 1905.
*Late that night:* TsGAVMF, f. 870, op. 1, d. 149, pp. 164–68; Bliznyuk; Melnikov, pp. 119–20.
*The Stremitelny thrust onward:* Hough, *Potemkin Mutiny*, pp. 183–85; Bliznyuk; Platonov, p. 120; TsGAVMF, f. 870, op. 1, d. 149, p. 167.

CHAPTER 23

286 *The* Potemkin *steamed:* Berezovsky, p. 268.
   *"Can't sleep, Illarion?":* Ponomarev, pp. 140–41.
287 *He was right:* Lychev, pp. 81–82.
   *"Everyone wondered":* ibid., p. 81.
288 *This dilemma, coming:* Berezovsky, pp. 271–72.
   *Kirill could scarcely bear:* ibid., pp. 268–75.
   *"It was tragic":* Matyushenko, p. 313.
289 *"You pitiful cowards":* ibid.
   *By dusk, the placid sea:* Lychev, p. 82.
   *At 11 P.M. the ships:* Berezovsky, pp. 275–76.
   *Shortly after midnight:* Bogachev, p. 24.
290 *"soul of the mutiny":* Selivanov, *Matros Matyushenko,* p. 262.
   *"What do you want":* Bogachev, p. 24; Nevsky, p. 272; Berezovsky, p. 276;
   Matyushenko, p. 313.
   *When Negru arrived:* Nevsky, pp. 272, 283; Lychev, p. 83.
291 *"I have the honor":* Hough, *Potemkin Mutiny,* p. 207.
   *General Lagovari knew:* ibid., pp. 207–10.
   *He immediately dispatched:* Platonov, p. 166.
   *Pisarevsky would likely arrive:* TsGAVMF, f. 417, op. 1, d. 3023, p. 207.
   *The previous night:* ibid., p. 237; Nevsky, p. 365.
292 *On June 25, the sun rose:* Lychev, p. 82.
   *"Comrades, you all know":* Ponomarev, p. 143.
   *Before Matyushenko left:* Matyushenko, p. 314; Platonov, p. 121.
293 *Once Negru learned:* Ponomarev, p. 143; Matyushenko, p. 314.
   *"This is where":* Lychev, p. 82.
   *The sailors gathered:* TsGAVMF, f. 417, op. 1, d. 3023, p. 273;
   Matyushenko, p. 314; Nevsky, p. 273.
   *As one sailor:* ibid.
   *"There was no joking":* Lychev, p. 84.
   *Ensign Alekseyev and the petty officers:* ibid.; Platonov, p. 170.
294 *Kovalenko wore civilian clothes:* Kovalenko, pp. 67–68.
   *Kirill was so overwhelmed:* Berezovsky, p. 278.
   *Matyushenko bid farewell:* Matyushenko, p. 314; Feldmann, p. 133.
   *Stepping onto the quay:* Gavrilov, *V borbe za svobodu,* p. 139; Nevsky,
   pp. 272–73.
   *The sailors gathered:* Nevsky, p. 273.
   *"Dear comrades":* Kardashev, *Burevestniki revolyutsii,* p. 52.
295 *Over in the harbor:* Hough, *Potemkin Mutiny,* p. 183; TsGAVMF, f.417,
   op. 1, d. 3023, pp. 270–79; *Chicago Daily Tribune,* July 11, 1905.

EPILOGUE

296 *"The revolutionary"*: Bakunin, as quoted in Radzinsky, p. 13.
   *Before midnight, Matyushenko:* Nevsky, pp. 276–77; Lychev, p. 95.
   *In Constanza:* TsGVIA, f. 400, op. 5, d. 21, p. 111; Platonov, p. 170;
   Nevsky, pp. 273–77; Lychev, pp. 89–90.
   *Immediately on learning:* TsGAVMF, f. 920, op. 6, d. 428, p. 171.

297 *Relieved that the nightmare:* Romanov, N., June 25, 1905.
   *When Rear Admiral Pisarevsky:* Bogachev, p. 25.
   *Over the next several hours:* ibid.; Hough, *Potemkin Mutiny,* pp. 209–15.
   *"the revolutionary demons":* Gavrilov, *V borbe za svobodu,* p. 154.
   *Lieutenant Yanovich then:* Platonov, pp. 168–70.
   *A letter published: Russkoye Slovo,* June 25, 1905.
   *"shows that the sea":* Gavrilov, *V borbe za svobodu,* p. 174.
   *Its liberal cousin:* ibid.
   *"There were no true":* ibid.

298 *"the broadest of broad": Daily Telegraph,* July 10, 1905.
   *"acute stage":* Alzona, p. 53.
   *Several German newspapers:* Stern, pp. 464–71.
   *"the moral for Russia": New York Times,* July 11, 1905.
   *Besides, he was:* Romanov, N., June 26, 1905.
   *To stave off:* Platonov, p. 155.
   *"weak, indecisive, lazy":* ibid., p. 172; Zebroski, p. 441.
   *Although several naval officers:* TsGAVMF, f. 417, op. 2, d. 852, p. 247.

299 *Begun on July 20:* Platonov, pp. 125–26; Gavrilov, *V borbe za svobodu,*
   pp. 155–57; TsGAVMF, f. 407, op. 1, d. 166, pp. 46–48; Kardashev,
   "Novyye Svedeniya."
   *In the same month:* TsGAVMF, f. 1025, op. 2, d. 27, pp. 261–71; Gavrilov,
   *V borbe za svobodu,* p. 157.
   *When Matyushenko heard:* Lychev, pp. 98; Krupskaya, pp. 117–18;
   Chernenko and Shlyakhov.
   *"Understand that the whole":* ibid.

300 *In the months:* Shlyakhov.
   *"There will be a mutiny":* TsGIA(M), f. 102, op. 00, d. 1667, pp. 15–16;
   Shlyakhov.
   *"Change will come soon":* Nevsky, pp. 336–38.
   *Four days after:* Harcave, *Memoirs,* pp. 422–23; Thompson and Hart,
   p. 61; Dillon, p. 298.
   *"a sewer needed":* Esthus, p. 63.

300 *Simultaneous with these efforts:* Ascher, pp. 177–89; Harcave, *First Blood,*
   pp. 162–65; Figes, pp. 186–87.

301  *In September, Nicholas:* Salisbury, pp. 150–51.
     *Twenty-four hours later:* ibid., pp. 151–55; Harcave, *First Blood,* pp. 176–91; Howe, pp. 231–41; Lincoln, *In War's Dark Shadow,* pp. 297–99.
302  *For the most part:* Ascher, p. 237.
     *"living in an utter":* Figes, p. 191.
     *"sweeping away a thousand":* ibid.
303  *Witte outlined these points:* Mossolov, pp. 89–90; Essad-Bey, pp. 164–70; Salisbury, pp. 154–57.
     *"My dearest Mama":* Bind, pp. 183–86.
     *While the tsar whined:* Essad-Bey, pp. 170–71; Healy, pp. 16–17.
     *Then true mayhem erupted:* Harcave, *First Blood,* pp. 199–205.
304  *In the streets:* Healy, pp. 15–17; Figes, pp. 196–97; Klier, pp. 224–25; Ascher, p. 258.
     *The greatest tragedy:* Weinberg, pp. 166–69.
     *Hand in hand:* Lincoln, *In War's Dark Shadow,* pp. 306–9; Ascher, pp. 275–303.
     *"Victory, that for us:* Figes, p. 199.
305  *After announcing a general strike:* Ascher, pp. 304–25.
     *"exterminate the gangs":* Ascher, p. 321.
     *"it is impossible":* Figes, p. 201.
     *Over the next five months:* Ascher, pp. 341–42.
     *On April 27, 1906:* Essad-Bey, pp. 174–77; Healy, pp. 148–52; Tyrkova-Williams, pp. 55–57; Vassili, pp. 343–45; Nevinson, pp. 320–26; Howe, pp. 285–87.
306  *A day after the signing:* Shlyakhov; Harcave, *First Blood,* pp. 203, 221–22; Trotsky, *1905,* pp. 198–207.
307  *"nest of sailor revolutionaries":* TsGIA(M), f. 102, op. 00, d. 1667, p. 5.
     *On January 26, 1906:* TsGAVMF, f. 1025, op. 2, d. 19, p. 31.
     *The proceedings lasted:* Gavrilov, *V borbe za svobodu,* p. 158; TsGAVMF, f. 1025, op. 2, d. 35, p. 34.
     *As for Konstantin Feldmann:* Feldmann, pp. 273–93.
     *He would never see:* Plotto; Gavrilov, *V borbe za svobodu,* p. 160; TsGAVMF, f. 417, op. 1, d. 3457, pp. 21, 94.
308  *"God, have mercy":* Chernov, p. 351; TsGAVMF, f. 417, op. 5, d. 361, pp. 13–31.
     *Matyushenko knew exactly:* Chernenko and Shlyakhov; Selivanov; Guttridge, p. 141.
309  *Since the mutiny's end:* Chernenko and Shlyakhov; TsGAOR, f. 102, op. 8, d. 1221, pp. 173–77, 205, 251, 313.
     *On June 6, his photograph:* TsGAOR, f. 102, op. 8, d. 1221, p. 205.
     *Still Matyushenko slipped:* Nevsky, pp. 327–29; Chernenko and Shlyakhov; TsGIA(M), f. 102, op. 00, d. 1667, p. 9.

310 *"Two dozen guards"*: Chernenko and Shlyakhov.

*He was forbidden:* Platonov, pp. 131–36; Adoratsky, pp. 250–53; Zebroski, pp. 484–85; Nevsky, pp. 31–32; Chernenko and Shlyakhov. The events and description of Matyushenko's execution are primarily based on the observances of Bredikhin, who later conveyed them in a letter to Arbore-Ralli. This letter, and other details of his last days, are found in these five sources.

312 *Seventy-two days:* Lieven, p. 60.

*A lack of coordination:* Figes, pp. 202–04.

*What caused the* Potemkin: Bogachev, pp. 14–15; Rostotskaya, p. 32; Lychev, p. 86; Berezovsky, pp. 8–9, 279; Feldmann, p. 199; *Proletary*, July 4, 1905; Platonov, p. 41; *Revolyutsionnaya Rossiya,* July 1, 1905; *Revolyutsionny bronenosets.*

313 *Of the entire* Potemkin: Zebroski, p. 466.

*Most remained in exile:* ibid., pp. 185–93.

*The battleship* Potemkin: Gavrilov, *V borbe za svobodu,* p. 194.

*"Each time the Black Sea Fleet":* ibid., p. 193.

# Index

Adamenko, I., 238, 239, 299
Akimov, Yakov, 308
Aleksandr Mikhailovich (Grand Duke), 80, 81
Alekseyev, Dmitry P. (officer), 97–99, 137, 253–54, 262, 318
    as replacement captain on *Potemkin*, 105–6, 112, 151, 172–73, 183, 190–91, 198, 209, 217, 222, 233, 359n193
    and Odessa, 145–46, 151, 152, 191
    after surrender, 293–94, 296, 307
Alekseyev, Pyotr V. (mutineer), 317
    in Odessa, 51, 60, 116, 123
    on *Potemkin*, 64, 96, 103
Alexander I (tsar), 28
Alexander II (tsar), 6, 24, 42, 78, 79, 81
Alexander III (tsar), 3–7, 24, 42, 82, 129, 156, 303
    naval expenditures by, 40
    as autocrat, 78–79, 81
    death of, 80, 282
    conditions under, 82–83
*Alexander* (Russian ship), 18
Alexandra ("Alix"; Nicholas II's wife), 4, 80, 81
Alexis (Grand Duke), 4, 82
*Almaz* (Russian cruiser), 18
anarchists, 54, 64, 104–5, 308
Angelesku, G., 290, 296
Arbore-Ralli, Zik, xiv, 296, 300, 308
army (soldiers; troops), 166–67, 204, 305

peasants and workers in, 30–31, 241
and *Potemkin* mutineers, 136, 148–50, 153, 171, 178, 213–14, 250
mutinous rumblings in, 156, 159, 304
Matyushenko's ambush by, 165–66, 277–78, 356n167
in Odessa, 210, 211, 213–14, 223
in Theodosia, 269, 271–72, 280–81
*See also* Cossacks; military; *specific officers*
Atamasov, I., 238
*Aurora* (Russian cruiser), 40, 314
Austria-Hungary, 159, 232, 308, 309
Avelan, Fyodor K., 6, 17, 130–33, 202, 319
    and Nicholas II, 153–55, 157
    and Chukhnin, 207, 235, 236, 274, 291
    replacement of, 298

Babel, Isaac., 53
Babenko, I., 249, 273, 318
Bakunin, Mikhail, xiv
Balfour, A. J., 158
Banov, N. N., 244–46, 255, 290, 318
Baranovsky, A. P., 237–39, 318
*Battleship Potemkin* (film), x, 314, 344n70, 352n142
Batumi (Georgia), 104, 227, 253, 264, 282
Beckendorf, Aleksandr, 250
*Berezan* (Russian cruiser), 64

Berezovsky, A. P. ("Kirill"). *See* "Kirill"
Bessalayev, Stefan, 48
Birilev, Aleksei, 298
Bismarck, Otto von, 83
Black Hundreds, 304
Black Sea, ix, xii, 50–51, 158, 235, 236
Black Sea Fleet, 19, 40, 338n32
  sailors' hopes for fleetwide mutiny
    in, ix, 37, 48, 102, 104, 116, 124,
    126, 134, 135, 149–51, 182–85,
    187, 192, 194, 197, 198–201, 290
  mutinous conditions in, ix–x, 20–24,
    36, 42–45, 133, 154, 168, 169–
    70, 195–201, 207, 234–36, 249,
    251–52, 256–58, 260, 274, 300,
    306–7, 313
  Sevastopol as base for, 101
  pursuit and confrontation of
    *Potemkin* by, 140, 179–84, 190–
    96
  as not joining *Potemkin* mutineers,
    179, 262–63, 280, 281, 312
  weapons of, 190, 191
  eventual fleetwide mutiny in, 306–7
  *See also* Chukhnin, Grigory P.; mili-
    tary; *officers, sailors, and ships in*
Bloody Sunday (St. Petersburg, 1905),
    17, 44, 54, 64, 84–85, 162, 204,
    216, 261, 283, 302
Boisman (*Eriklik* captain), 154–55, 249
Bolsheviks, 30, 54, 103, 123, 134, 160–
    62, 299
  uprisings by, x, 302, 304–5, 313, 314
Boris (Odessan Bolshevik), 134, 136,
    187
Borodin, Zakhary, 196
Bosphorus Strait, 44, 50, 159, 250, 260
Bredikhin, Yefim, 64, 90, 103, 105,
    116, 310–12, 317
Bucharest (Romania), 296, 299, 300
Bulgaria, 256, 258, 260
Bulygin, A. G., 85, 301, 313, 319
Bulygin Constitution, 301
Bundists, 54, 122, 123
Carol I (Romanian king), 232, 252,
    259, 291, 292, 297, 299

Catherine the Great (tsar), 52, 266,
    306
Caucasus (Russia), 50, 58, 235
  plans to spread revolution to, 23,
    201, 253, 264, 281
*Chema* (Russian ship), 154
Cherny (*Prut* mutineer), 299
Chernyshevsky, Nikolai, 160
*Chicago Daily Tribune,* 157, 258–59
Chukhnin, Grigory P., 186, 233, 300,
    318
  on revolutionaries, 20–22, 35, 43–
    44, 132
  and *Potemkin*'s officers, 39, 65
  reputation of, 41
  background of, 43–46, 130–32
  orders pursuit of *Potemkin*, 104,
    116, 124, 167, 206–8, 246, 256–
    58, 260, 272–74, 282–84
  and Nicholas II, 153–55, 157, 203,
    234, 274, 282, 291–92, 297, 308
  plans for mutineers' punishment by,
    155, 249, 256, 296–98
  and Avelan, 207, 235, 236, 274,
    291
  and *St. George*'s crew, 214–19
  on *Potemkin*'s supplies, 268
  as unable to protect Theodosia, 275
  on *Potemkin*'s surrender, 291–92
  and fleetwide mutiny, 307
  assassination of, 307–8
conscription, 9, 30, 31, 34, 48, 67, 155,
    205, 241
Constantinople (Turkey), 255, 258
Constanza (Romania)
  *Potemkin* heads to, for coal and pro-
    visions, 223–25, 231–33, 240–42,
    262–63
  *Potemkin* at, 243–47, 250, 251–55,
    259, 260, 267
  *Stremitelny* in, 257–58, 273
  *Potemkin* heads to, to surrender,
    281–82, 286–89
  *Potemkin*'s surrender in, 290–95
  *Potemkin* exiles in, 300
  *See also* Romania

constituent assembly (duma)
  revolutionaries' calls for, 22, 241
  liberals' calls for, 29, 54, 76, 83–87,
    155–56, 204, 249, 303–4
  establishment of, 301, 303, 305–6
Cossacks
  as guarding Nicholas II, 4, 16, 56
  in Odessa, 56–57, 59, 60, 114, 120–
    21, 125, 139–42, 146, 148–50,
    164–66, 176, 218
  in Libau, 154
  Matyushenko's ambush by, 165–66,
    356n167
  in Nikolayev, 234, 238
  in St. Petersburg, 283
  in Moscow, 301–2
Council of Ministers, 303
counter-mutiny
  on St. George, 217–20, 251, 262,
    271, 280, 312
  on Vekha, 224, 235
  attempted, on Ismail, 286
Cranby (British steamer), 248–49
Crimean Peninsula, 50, 265, 272
Crimean War, 20, 24, 40, 266
Deinega, Simon P., 196, 210, 318
Denisenko, Stefan A., 69, 317
  as Potemkin revolutionary, 64, 90,
    93–94, 103, 106–7, 253, 263–64
Dergachi (Russia), 24, 26, 27, 30
Dorrer, V. F., 249, 251
"dragons." See officers
duma. See constituent assembly
Durante, L. A. (mayor of Theodosia),
  266–70, 274–76, 319
Durnovo, P. N., 305
Dymchenko, I. A., 173, 181, 182, 317
  on sailors' committee, 103, 121–23,
    171
  and St. George, 198, 214

Eikhen, P. P., 136–38, 319
Eisenstein, Sergei, x, 314, 344n70,
  352n142
Ekaterina II (Russian ship), 22, 23,
  154, 234, 237, 271, 290

Elizaveta (Romanian cruiser), 243, 244,
  246–47, 289
Emerans (collier), 118, 119, 121, 139
England, 308, 309, 313
  navy of, 40, 107
  Articles of War in, 108
  on mutiny, 157–59, 250, 260
Eriklik (Russian ship), 154–55
Evpatoria (Crimea), 254

Feldmann, Konstantin I., 187, 217,
  317
  as Odessa revolutionary, 114
  joins Potemkin mutineers, 119, 122,
    134–36, 138, 180, 184, 192, 223–
    25, 233
  on Odessa fire, 145, 147
  and Vakulenchuk's burial, 147–49,
    152–53
  on shelling Odessa, 171–72, 174
  takes ultimatum to Kakhanov, 176
  on board St. George, 200, 209, 212
  writes international proclamation,
    240–41, 363n241
  in Constanza, 245
  and Theodosia, 253–54, 263, 270,
    274–79
  after surrender, 307, 313, 314
Figes, Orlando, 314, 338n28
France, 40, 157–59, 308, 309
  revolutions in, x, 26, 28, 84
Fredericks, V. B., 303

Gapon, Georgy, xiv, 84
Geneva (Switzerland), 313
  Lenin in, xiii–xv, 160, 162, 261,
    299–300
  Matyushenko in, xiii–xv, 299–300,
    308, 309
George III (British king), x, 108
Gerasimov (official), 118–19, 126
Gerasimov (revolutionary), 168–69
Germany. See Wilhelm II
Gilyarovsky, Ippolit I., 62, 216, 318
  reputation of, 41, 45–46, 65, 69–70
  and meat boycott, 65–70, 72, 91

killing of, 88–90, 98, 109, 138
wife and child of, 137, 138, 143, 213
Glotov, Nikita, 139
Golenko, A. S. (Dr.), 147, 173, 318
  and meat-buying trip, 51
  as meat inspector, 60, 66–67, 218
  during *Potemkin* mutiny, 89, 109,
    144, 145
  disappearance of, 182, 218
  return of, 187
  on *St. George*, 215–19
  and *St. George* counter-mutiny, 217–
    22, 288
  discharged from military, 307
Golikov, Y. N. (captain), 61, 62, 102,
    105, 111, 205, 216, 318
  suspects mutineers on his ship, 36,
    38–39, 41, 43, 66, 68
  background of, 41–42, 46
  sailors' disciplining by, 45, 67–68
  at Tendra Island, 51
  and rotten meat, 63, 65, 66–71
  and Gilyarovsky, 65, 69
  tries to flee *Potemkin* mutineers, 88,
    94, 95, 97
  death of, 98–100, 106, 109, 150,
    236, 245
  burial of, 308
Gorky, Maxim, 84, 308
*Griden* (Russian destroyer), 274
Grigorkov, K. K., 197, 200
Grigoryev, N. F., 91–93
Gulyayev, Pavel, 226
Guzevich, Ilya E., 170, 184, 191, 196–
  98, 200, 209, 235, 319

Hardinge, Charles, 159
Hellville (off Madagascar), 7, 10, 11
Herzen, Aleksandr, 28
*Holy Trinity* (Russian ship), 22
Howe, Richard, 108

Ignatyev, A. P., 301
Imperial Guard, 4, 7, 236
*The Influence of Sea Power upon History* (Mahan), 40

Ismail (*Potemkin*'s torpedo boat), 63,
  181, 341n51
  on meat-buying trip, 51–52, 60
  officers try to flee on, 88, 95–97
  in Odessa's harbor, 115, 117–19,
    211, 218
  and *St. George*, 198, 200, 202, 222,
    223
  in Constanza, 252, 291
  heads to Theodosia, 261–64
  in Theodosia, 277, 278
  attempted counter-mutiny on, 286
  surrender of, 286, 289, 293
Ivan the Terrible (tsar), 6, 78, 81

Japan
  Nicholas II in, 8
  on mutiny, 158, 260–61
  *See also* Russo-Japanese War
Jewish Bund, 54, 122, 123
Jews, 53–54, 59, 114, 139, 282, 297,
  304, 342n53

Kakhanov, Semyon V., 58, 319
  and Odessa workers' uprisings, 58–
    59, 113
  as Odessa's military governor, 125,
    126–27, 133, 140, 152, 172, 208,
    213, 218, 223, 253, 288
  Nicholas II's orders to, 129–30, 138
  and Odessa port uprising, 140–43,
    352n140
  and Vakulenchuk's funeral, 148, 149,
    153, 164–67, 356n167
  *Potemkin*'s ultimatums to, 175–77,
    210, 211
  and Black Sea squadron's flight, 186,
    208
  reports from, of *Potemkin*'s surren-
    der, 203, 206, 208
  on *Potemkin* supplies, 218, 219
  *St. George* surrenders to, 225–26,
    234
  on *Prut* sighting, 240
  replacing of, 304
Kaluzhny, P. V., 144–45, 262

Karangozov, K. A., 140, 176–77, 226,
    319, 352n140
Kaulbars, A. V., 304
*Kazarsky* (Russian cruiser), 167, 185
Kharkevich, A. N., 91, 93, 97
Kharkov (Russia), 33, 76, 77, 143, 201
    workers' conditions in, 24–27
    Matyushenko in, 30–31, 98, 309
"Kirill" (Anatoly P. Berezovsky), 187,
    188, 217, 288, 317
    and Odessa, 55–58, 112–14, 124,
        145–46
    joins *Potemkin* mutineers, 119–23,
        134–36, 138, 150–52, 223–25
    on shelling Odessa, 171–74
    and Black Sea squadron, 179–81,
        184, 192–93, 195
    on *St. George,* 198, 199–201, 212,
        214–15
    Odessa ultimatum written by, 211
    on international law on mutiny, 232,
        233
    international proclamation written
        by, 240–41, 363n241
    and Theodosia, 253–54, 266–67,
        269–72, 279–81
    after surrender, 294, 296, 313
Klodt von Iurgensburg, Pyotr M., 51–
    52, 95–96, 319
Kokovtsov, Vladimir, 251
Kolands, M. N., 169, 185–86, 193,
    195–96, 319
Konstantin Konstaninovich (Grand
    Duke), 205
Korea, 8, 77
Koshuba, Dorofey P., 170, 318
    on *St. George,* 184–85, 196–99, 209–
        11, 214, 217–21
    joins *Potemkin,* 222, 224, 253
    in Theodosia, 266, 270, 277, 278–
        79, 286
    punishment for, 299, 313
Kostenko, M. M., 190, 192–94
Kovalenko, Aleksandr, 116, 117, 210,
    211, 318
    on Golikov, 45

and mutiny on *Potemkin,* 91–93, 97,
    110–12, 254, 263
    joins mutineers, 143–45
    on Ensign Alekseyev, 151, 152
    and shelling of Odessa, 173, 174–75
    on Black Sea squadron, 180–82,
        192, 194
    on *St. George,* 200, 201, 214–16
    and *St. George* counter-mutiny, 214–
        16, 218, 225
    fears of, about Dr. Golenko, 218
    in Constanza, 241–44, 247
    in Theodosia, 267, 274–75, 279
    after surrender, 294, 296, 313
Krieger, A. H., 169, 234, 235, 290,
    319
    Chukhnin's view of, 132–33, 155,
        207, 236, 274
    delays by, 154, 168
    at captains' meeting, 184–86, 201–2
    *Potemkin*'s plans to provoke, 187
    in showdown with *Potemkin,* 190–
        95, 203, 206, 207, 226, 259
    and *St. George* mutiny, 196–98
    warns *Prut* captain, 237, 238
    Nicholas II reprimands, 250
    retrieves *St. George,* 274
    dismissal of, 298
Kronstadt (Russia), 203–4, 314
Krupskaya, Nadezhda, 160, 161
Kulik, Vasily, 148, 149, 198, 241, 317
Kursk province (Russia), 249, 251
Kuzmenko, A. O., 209, 210, 215–17,
    219–22, 318
Kuzyayev, P., 273

Lagovari, Iacob, 291
Lenin, Vladimir Ilyich, x, 313
    and Matyushenko, xiii–xv, 299, 314
    revolutionary views of, 29–30
    on Russo-Japanese War, 86
    background of, 160–61
    representatives of, 161–62, 226–27,
        261
    and 1905 uprisings, 302, 304–5,
        314, 334n

Libau (Russia), 9, 12, 154, 203–4, 260
liberals, 157
    duma sought by, 18, 29, 54, 76, 83–
        87, 155–56, 204, 249, 303–4
    naval officers' opposition to, 45–46
    Nicholas II's rejection of, 83–85,
        204–6, 283, 302
    revolutionaries' view of, 161
    nobles' opposition to, 249
    on mutineers, 261
    on Nicholas II's duma, 301
    on workers' strikes, 302
Livadia (Crimea), 282
Liventsev, N. Y., 63, 65, 69, 89, 93
Lodz, 77, 155, 260, 261
London *Times,* 157, 259–60
Louis XVI (French king), x, 158
Lower Palace (Peterhof), 75, 154, 283–
    84
Lvov, Georgy (prince), 83
Lychev, Ivan A., 31, 103, 106, 232,
    287, 313, 317

Madagascar, 7, 10, 11
Magellan, Ferdinand, 107
Mahan, Alfred Thayer, 40
Makarov, Aleksandr N., 89, 318
    and meat, 51–52, 59–60, 63
    and mutineers, 96, 99, 103
Manchuria, 8, 11, 77, 128, 203, 241
    *See also* Port Arthur
Maria (Nicholas II's daughter), 87
Marie (Nicholas II's mother), 4, 79, 80,
    129, 303
Martov, Julius, 161, 162, 261, 304
Martyanov, Iosif, 103
Marx, Karl, xiii, xv, 27, 28–29, 161
Matyushenko, Afanasy Nikolayevich,
    51, 211–12, 317
    Russian secret police following, xiii,
        xiv, 128, 295, 300, 309
    as *Potemkin* revolutionary leader,
        xiii–xv, 20–24, 35–36, 46–49, 70–
        71, 286–89, 313, 339n34
    after surrender, xiv, 296, 299–300,
        306–12

    background of, xiv, 24–28, 30–35,
        110, 309
    arrests of, 26, 98, 308, 309–10
    and *Potemkin*'s rotten meat, 61–72
    and killing of officers on *Potemkin,*
        88–90, 94–95, 98–101
    as sailors' committee head, 102–6,
        116, 123–26, 134–38, 143–46,
        151–53, 179, 209–10, 217, 252–
        55, 263–64, 286–87
    and Vakulenchuk's death and fu-
        neral, 108–10, 117–19, 164–66,
        356n167
    observes Odessa fire, 145–46
    and shelling of Odessa, 170–77
    and Black Sea squadron, 179–84,
        187–95
    and *St. George,* 198–201, 209, 214–
        15, 217–25
    in Constanza, 241–47, 252–55
    in Theodosia, 267, 269–70, 272,
        275–82
    and *Potemkin*'s surrender, 281–82,
        290, 292–95
    execution of, 310–12
Medvedev, Fyodor, 56–57
Mensheviks, 30, 54, 103, 123, 160–62
    Lenin's attack on, xiii, 261
    Kirill as, 55, 113
    uprisings by, 302
Meyer, George, 156, 159, 251, 260
Michael (first Russian autocrat), 77
*Mikasa* (Japanese ship), 11, 13, 14
military (Russian)
    mutinies in, as threatening state, x,
        xiv, 107, 157–58, 205, 307, 313,
        350n129
    peasants and workers conscripted
        into, 9, 30–31, 33–34, 241
    nobles as officers in, 32, 41, 58, 65,
        95, 105, 130, 131
    skilled workers in, 33–34, 104
    salaries and promotions in, 42, 129,
        132
    tsar as dependent on, 87, 128–29,
        157, 161–62, 350n129

military (Russian) (*cont.*)
  Russian press on, 205, 283
  *See also* army; Black Sea Fleet; con-
    scription; Cossacks; mutiny; of-
    ficers; Russo-Japanese war; sail-
    ors; *specific officers and ships*
Milyukov, Pavel N., 83, 86, 204, 319
Mirsky, P. D. (prince), 84–85
Moscow (Russia), 53, 80–82, 201
  strikes in, 155, 204, 301–2, 304–5
Mukden (Manchuria), 11, 77
Muravyev, Nikolai V., 206, 251, 300
Murzak, F. V., 105–6, 224, 272, 317
mutiny
  general punishment for, ix, 100,
    107–8, 116, 122, 130, 133, 150,
    155, 172, 235, 284
  significance of *Potemkin*'s, ix–xi, xiii–
    xv, 313–14, 334n
  as revolution precursor, x, xiv, 107,
    157, 158, 205, 307, 313, 350n129
  threats of, in Black Sea Fleet, 20–24,
    36, 42–45, 133, 154, 168, 169–
    70, 195–201, 207, 234–36, 249,
    251–52, 258, 260, 274, 300, 313
  threats of, on *Berezen,* 64
  on *Potemkin,* 67–72, 88–90, 258
  history of, 107–8, 350n129
  Nicholas II on, 129, 203
  on *St. George,* 196–202, 206, 207,
    251, 258, 271
  international law on, 232
  on *Prut,* 237–40
  *See also* counter-mutiny; military;
    *Potemkin;* punishment
Naval Cadet School, 41, 43, 131, 132
Nechayev, Sergei, xiv, 28, 29
Negru, Nikolai, 243–45, 247, 252, 254–
    55, 267, 319
  and *Potemkin*'s surrender, 289–93,
    297
Neidhardt, Dmitry B., 125, 319
Nelidov, A. I., 157, 205–6
Nelson, Horatio, 44–45
Neupokoyev, L. K., 71, 88, 89
Neva River, 3–7, 16–17, 130, 306

Nicholas II (tsar), 12, 24, 41, 104
  weakness of regime of, ix, xiii–xiv,
    203–5, 258–61, 282–83, 297–98,
    301, 312, 313
  and Neva River ceremony, 3–7
  and Bloody Sunday, 17, 44, 64
  draftees' oath of loyalty to, 31
  Matyushenko's view of, 33, 172, 174
  plans to bring down, 37
  naval expenditures by, 40
  background and character of, 75–87,
    159
  reform resisted by, 83–85, 204–6,
    283, 302
  Ukrainian nationalists on, 91, 92
  hears of *Potemkin* mutiny, 127, 128–
    30, 350n128
  and Chukhnin, 153–55, 157, 203,
    234, 274, 282, 291–92, 297, 308
  orders of, about mutineers, 154,
    185–86, 203–6, 256
  and *St. George*'s counter-mutiny,
    226
  meets with nobles, 249–52
  makes naval changes, 298
  reforms under, 301–6, 312, 313
  forcing of, from throne, 314
  *See also* military; October Manifesto;
    press; Russo-Japanese War; *names
    of specific ships and palaces of*
Nikishkin, Fyodor Z., 36, 103, 173,
    220, 263, 317
  starts *Potemkin* mutiny, 72, 88, 150–
    51
  and Vakulenchuk's death, 108, 109,
    117
  death of, 277, 278, 286
Nikolai (Grand Duke), 303
Nikolayev (Russia), 40, 46, 131, 206,
    257
  revolutionary plans in, 23, 34
  *Vekha* in, 136
  martial law in, 155
Nikolayev (Russia) (*cont.*)
  martial unrest in, 234, 238
  Chukhnin in, 234–37

*Prut* ordered to, 238, 248
Matyushenko arrested in, 309
nobles
    constitutional rule urged by, 28
    military officers as, 32, 41, 58, 65,
      95, 105, 130, 131
    and news of *Potemkin* mutiny, 203
    support for Nicholas II from, 249–50
    *See also* liberals; *zemstvos*
*Novoye Vremya*, 76, 86, 128, 282, 298

*Ochakov* (Russian cruiser), 307
October Manifesto, 303–7, 310, 312,
    313
Odessa (Russia)
    plans for revolution in, 23, 64, 104,
      113–14, 123–25, 128, 146, 201,
      261, 288
    Matyushenko in, 27, 300, 309
    meat-buying in, 51–52
    history of, 52–55, 266, 341n52
    workers' uprisings in, 52–55, 64, 76,
      77, 104, 112–14, 120–21, 123–
      26, 134, 135–36, 164, 165, 269
    Vakulenchuk's body and funeral in,
      109, 116–20, 147–49, 164–66
    *Potemkin* in harbor of, 113–16, 208–
      24, 226, 260
    *Potemkin*'s threat to shell, 116, 121,
      133, 135, 150–53, 166, 167, 211,
      219, 223
    mutineers joined by revolutionaries
      in, 123–26, 134, 284
    port access to, closed, 126–27
    martial law in, 128–30
    looting in, 139–40, 142
    fires in, 139–43, 145–47, 153, 155,
      158, 173, 204, 258, 283, 352n140
    massacre in, 140, 141–42, 146, 148,
      176, 352n142
    maps of, 151–52, 171, 174, 178, 187
    military conference to be held in,
      153, 164, 171, 173, 175
    deaths and damages in, 155, 205,
      258, 260
    Vasilyev-Yuzhin in, 162–63, 226–27

*Potemkin*'s shelling of, 170–77, 258,
    259, 357n174
*Potemkin* and *St. George* at, 200–
    201, 208–12
*St. George* turns against *Potemkin* at,
    222–23, 280, 288
*St. George* surrenders in, 225–26,
    234–35
*Prut* heads toward, 238, 239–40
*Stremitelny* in, 247–49, 257
mutineers' execution planned in, 256
pogroms in, 304
*See also* Kakhanov, Semyon V.
officers
    killing of, on *Potemkin*, ix, 88–90,
      93–97, 108, 116, 121–22, 128,
      169, 204, 245, 258, 260
    backgrounds of, 32, 33–34, 41–46,
      58, 65, 95, 105, 130, 131
    *Potemkin* mutineers' plans for, 37,
      100
    salaries and promotions of, 42, 77,
      129, 132
    conditions for, 49, 64
    and mutiny on *Potemkin*, 88, 91–93,
      95–97, 110–12, 118, 205
    number of, on *Potemkin*, 88
    on *Potemkin* after mutiny, 105–6
    of *Vekha*, 136–38, 143
    releasing of, 143–45, 149–51, 209
    as Kakhanov informers, 167
    cowardice of, 185, 190–91, 193–94,
      197, 198, 222, 359n193
    on *St. George*, 197–200
    on *Stremitelny*, 237, 247–48, 271
    *See also* petty officers; *specific indi-*
      *viduals*
Okhrana (Russian secret police), xiii,
    xiv, 128, 295, 300, 309
O'Laughlin, John Callan, 157
*Oslyabya* (Russian ship), 13–15, 18
Ottoman Empire, 50, 159, 232, 254,
    259, 260

Paleologue, Maurice, 159
pamphlets. *See* propaganda

*Pamyat Mercuriya* (Russian ship), 285
Parashchenko (police chief), 56, 57
Parmen, Father, 61, 91, 93, 115, 148,
    149
peasant(s)
    Matyushenko's background as, xiv,
        24–27, 30–33, 309
    conditions of, 5, 24–25, 33, 46, 82,
        339n34
    conscription of, 9, 30, 31, 241
    uprisings of, 17, 76, 77, 83, 304
    communal leadership of, 24, 103
    hopes for, as revolutionaries, 28, 29,
        102, 201
    at Nicholas II's coronation, 81
    Vakulenchuk's background as, 165
    no reforms for, 301
    terror campaign against, 305
    *See also* serfs
Pereleshin, V. P., 125–26, 210, 319
Perelygin, Kuzma, 146
Peresyp (Odessa district), 55–59, 114,
    138, 208, 256
Peterhof (tsar's dacha), 75–77, 87, 128,
    153, 155, 203, 206, 249–51, 282–
    84, 301, 302
Peter the Great (tsar), 4, 40, 41, 91
Petrov, Aleksandr M., 23, 48, 237–40,
    299, 313, 318
Petrov, Vladimir, 28
petty officers
    Matyushenko on, 35, 106
    and *Potemkin* mutiny, 37, 93, 99–
        100, 111, 233, 240, 263
    conditions of, 106
    release of some, after mutiny, 116,
        179
    as working to foil mutiny, 152, 170,
        212, 214–18, 233, 240, 263, 286–
        87, 312
    on *St. George*, 210, 212, 214–19,
        221
    after surrender, 293–94, 296
Pisarevsky, S., 236, 291, 297, 319
Plehve, Vyacheslav von, 83–84
Plekhanov, Georgy, 29, 161, 292

Pleshkov, F., 268–70, 272, 275, 284,
    319
Pobedonostsev, Konstantin, 79
pogroms, 304, 352n140
    *See also* Jews
Poland, 77, 85
*Polar Star* (tsar's yacht), 33, 301, 302
Port Arthur (Manchuria), 7, 9, 62–63,
    90, 207
Potemkin, Grigory (prince), 40, 104,
    266, 306
*Potemkin* (Russian battleship)
    significance of mutiny of, ix–xi, xiii–
        xv, 313–14, 334n
    killing of some officers on, ix, 88–90,
        93–97, 108, 116, 121–22, 128,
        169, 204, 245, 258, 260
    rotten meat on, ix, 62–72, 91, 93,
        111, 117, 145, 258
    as Black Sea ship chosen for mutiny,
        23, 37
    plans of revolutionaries on, to extend
        sea revolution to land, 23, 64,
        104, 113–14, 116–18, 120, 122–
        24, 134, 146, 167, 201, 288
    Matyushenko assigned to, 33
    number and kinds of sailors on, 36,
        88, 339n36
    hopes on, to start fleetwide revolu-
        tion, 37, 48, 102, 104, 116, 124,
        126, 134, 135, 149–51, 182–85,
        187, 192, 194, 197, 198–201, 290
    departs from Sevastopol, 38–39
    description of, 40–41, 340n41
    weapons and ammunition on, 41, 47,
        102, 120, 123, 126, 133, 172, 180
    mutiny on, 67–72, 88–101, 125,
        205, 238
    crew divided on, 100, 105, 122,
        124–25, 134, 138, 150–52, 170–
        72, 188, 219, 223, 225, 231, 233,
        247, 263, 270, 275, 280, 281,
        286, 339n36
    mutineers' options for, 102, 105
    coal and provisions needed for, 104,
        116, 118, 119, 121, 138, 139,

210, 211, 218, 231–33, 244–45, 247, 261–62, 266–68, 274, 276–81, 289, 292, 312
arrives in Odessa's harbor, 113–14
Odessan revolutionaries join mutineers on, 123–26, 134, 284
Russian command's willingness to sink, 133, 154, 169, 187, 193, 274
international response to mutiny on, 133 157–60, 204–5, 244, 245, 258–60, 271, 275, 284, 297–98
Lenin learns of mutiny on, 162–63, 261
Odessa blocks coal and provisions for, 168, 169
news of mutiny on, brought to other ships, 169
*St. George* joins, 197–201, 208–12
*St. George* turns against, 222–23, 280, 288
heads to Constanza for coal and provisions, 223–25, 231–33, 240–42, 262–63
international proclamations from, 233, 240–41, 254–55, 258
and piracy, 241, 253, 259, 263, 265
in Constanza, 241–47, 250, 251–55, 259, 262, 289–91
Constanza refuses coal and provisions for, 252–54, 263
heads to Theodosia, 253–55, 261–64
in Theodosia, 265–76
Theodosia refuses coal and water for, 270, 272, 274–78
heads to Romania to surrender, 281–82, 286–89
surrender of, 290–95
attempted sinking of, by departing mutineers, 295, 297
towing of, back to Sevastopol, 297
reasons for failure of, 312
history of ship, after mutiny, 313
*See also* Black Sea Fleet; Matyushenko, Afanasy Nikolayevich; sailors; sailors' committee (on *Potemkin*); Vakulenchuk, Grigory N.; *specific sailors and officers on*
Poti (Georgia), 253
Preobrazhensky Guards Regiment, 3–7, 79–80, 125, 129, 306
press, 19, 76–77, 79, 86, 365n259
international, on mutiny, ix, 133, 157–60, 162, 204–5, 244, 245, 258–61, 271, 275, 284, 297–98
revolutionary, xiv, 86, 161–62, 304
on Tsushima Battle, 19, 76–77, 86, 297
on tsar's government, 77, 84, 128
Nicholas II's censorship of, 83, 129, 203, 283
on Odessa fire, 142–43
official report of mutiny by, 258
Russian, on mutiny, 282–83, 297–98
on Russian strikes, 302
proclamations
Vishnevetsky's, 169–70
*Potemkin*'s, 233, 240–41, 254–55, 258, 267, 284
Nicholas II's, 269–70
propaganda
punishment for those with, 21, 34
on ships, 36, 42–45, 62, 204, 238, 358n185
among workers, 55, 56–57, 204
mutineers mentioned in revolutionaries', 204, 261
Nicholas II's, 269–70
mutineers prohibited from distributing, in Romania, 290
Matyushenko's post-*Potemkin* spreading of, 300, 308
Soviet, about *Potemkin,* 314
*See also* proclamations
*Prut* (Russian ship), 171, 237–40, 248–51, 258, 271
as a prison, 257, 298–99
*Psezuape* (Russian ship), 244, 245, 247, 290
Psiol, I. N., 201–2

Pushkin, Aleksandr, 28
Pykhtin, L., 273, 285

Rakitin, Grigory, 246, 247
Rakovsky, I. Christian, 292–93, 296
"Resolution of the Black Sea Sailors,"
    22
*Retvizan* (Russian ship), 40
"Revolt of the Lash," 108
Reznichenko, Y. K., 181, 182, 317
    on sailors' committee, 103, 105, 123,
        137, 233
    in Theodosia, 266, 270–72
Richelieu Steps (Odessa), 52, 126, 213
    massacre on, 140, 141–42, 146, 148,
        176, 352n142
Romanenko, Nikolai I., 210, 219, 220–
    22, 226, 319
Romania, 50, 236, 307
    independence of, from Russian tsar,
        xiv, 231–32, 292
    some *Potemkin* crew members as
        wanting to surrender in, 150–52,
        222–25, 231, 280
    *Potemkin* heads to, for coal and pro-
        visions, 223–25, 231–33, 240–42,
        262
    *Potemkin* in, 243–47, 250, 251–55,
        259
    reasons for *Potemkin*'s going to, 244
    offers to buy *Potemkin* from muti-
        neers, 246–47
    ordered not to aid mutineers, 256,
        259, 260, 263, 291
    *Stremitelny* in, 257–58, 273
    *Potemkin* heads to, to surrender,
        281–82, 286–89
    *Potemkin*'s surrender in, 290–95
    press on, 298
    *See also* Carol I; Constanza
Romanov family, 7, 41, 77–87, 128–29,
    205
    *See also* military; *specific tsars*
Roosevelt, Theodore, 86, 156, 157,
    159, 260, 300

*Rostislav* (Russian ship), 23–24, 37,
    181, 184, 185, 191–93, 196, 257
Rostov-on-Don (Russia), 27, 30
Rozhestvensky, Zinovy P., 43, 237
    and Tsushima Battle, 7–18, 21, 85,
        130, 187
Russian Empire, 5, 10, 50, 82, 83, 232
    plans to spread revolution from
        *Potemkin* to entire, 23, 64, 104,
        113–14, 116–18, 120, 122–24,
        134, 146, 167, 201, 288
    history of revolutionary activity in,
        28–30
    history of mutinies in, 350n129
    *See also* military; mutiny; nobles;
        peasant(s); sailors; workers; *spe-
        cific places, tsars, ships, and revo-
        lutionaries in*
Russian Orthodox Church, 4, 78, 79
Russian Revolution, x, xiv, 84
*Russkiye Vedomosti*, 77, 86, 297
*Russkoye Slovo*, 86, 283, 297
Russo-Japanese War, 3–4, 7–11, 17, 18,
    20, 35, 40, 85, 128
    Nicholas II's vacillation about end-
        ing, ix, 86–87, 156–57, 159, 205–
        6, 250–51, 259, 313
    Tsushima Battle of, 11–16, 18–19,
        21, 45, 130, 156, 187, 335n8
    as Russian loss, 42, 46, 76, 83, 85–
        87, 158–60, 259
    Chemulpo Battle in, 45
    domestic effects of, 53, 155–57, 203,
        204, 260, 282, 301
    revolutionaries on, 241
    peace negotiations on, 300
    *See also* Nicholas II
Russo-Turkish War, 8, 41–42, 58, 131,
    191
Ryzhy, Nikolai, 104

sailors (Russian)
    mutinous sentiments among, ix–x,
        20–24, 36, 42–45, 133, 154, 168,
        169–70, 191, 195–201, 207, 234–36,

249, 251–52, 256–58, 260, 274, 300, 304, 306–7, 313
  conditions of, x–xi, 9–10, 21, 31–34, 42–47, 62–64, 67, 111, 117, 339n34
  training of, 31–32, 34
  number of revolutionaries on Potemkin among, 90, 339n36
  in Nikolayev, 234, 238
  on Stremitelny, 248, 249
  Chukhnin addresses, 257
  after Potemkin's surrender, 296, 298, 300
  See also Black Sea Fleet; military; mutiny; officers; petty officers; sailors' committee; Tsentralka; names of specific ships and sailors
sailors' committee (on Potemkin)
  establishment of, 102–6, 259
  plans of, 115–16, 135–36, 145
  Odessan revolutionaries join, 135–36, 138, 143–45, 259
  releases officers in Odessa, 138, 143–45, 149–50, 179
  decree from, to Kakhanov, 150
  on divisions among crew, 151–53
  on shelling Odessa, 171, 174
  on Black Sea squadron, 180–81, 192
  on supplies in Odessa, 187
  on St. George traitors, 217–18
  plans of, while heading to Constanza for coal and provisions, 231–33
  writes international proclamations, 233, 240–41
  plans to head to Theodosia, 252–55, 263–64
  in Theodosia, 267–68, 270, 272
sailors' committee (on Prut), 239
sailors' committee (on St. George), 209–11
St. George (Russian ship), 167, 170, 183, 190, 191
  revolutionaries on, 184–85, 194, 195–201, 358n185
  mutiny on, 196–202, 206, 207, 251, 258, 271
  crew divided on, 198–99, 210, 212, 214–20, 225
  in Odessa harbor, 208–12, 220
  sailors' committee on, 209–11
  counter-mutiny on, 217–20, 251, 262, 271, 280, 312
  turns against Potemkin, 222–23, 280, 288
  surrender of, 225–26, 234–35, 251
  punishment of mutineers from, 271
St. Petersburg (Petrograd), 6–7, 44, 201, 203, 314
  workers' conditions in, 5, 53
  strikes in, 155, 204, 205, 259, 283
  soviets in, 304
  See also Bloody Sunday; Imperial Guard; Winter Palace
Sakhalin Island, 156, 250–51, 259, 298
Sakharov, Vladimir, 155, 251
Schmidt, Pyotr, 306, 307
Schultz, I. A., 91, 112, 149
serfs, 24, 31, 82
  See also peasant(s)
Sergei (Grand Duke), 17, 82, 206
Sevastopol (Russia), 20, 21, 24, 104
  revolutionaries in, 20–24, 31–33, 35, 110, 232, 273, 300
  mutinous behavior in, 22–23, 154, 256–57, 306–7
  revolutionaries' plans to capture, 37
  Potemkin sails from, 38–39
  Chukhnin as based in, 43–44, 307–8
  censorship about Potemkin mutiny in, 71, 90, 95, 96
  Black Sea Command based in, 101, 126, 132, 133, 140, 153–55, 235, 237, 240, 255, 273–74
  part of Potemkin crew wants to return to, 102, 124, 134–35, 150, 222, 224, 279, 293–94, 296
  martial law declared in, 155
  Krieger's squadron retreats to, after

Sevastopol (Russia) (*cont.*)
Potemkin showdown, 196–98, 201–2, 206, 259
plans to prevent *Potemkin* from taking, 207, 236
part of *St. George* crew wants to return to, 214–16, 219
*St. George* heads toward, after counter-mutiny, 220–21
as *Potemkin*'s presumed destination after *St. George* counter-mutiny, 226
*Stremitelny* sails from, 248
location of, 253–54
*Stremitelny* returns to, 285
part of *Ismail* crew wants to surrender in, 286–87
*Potemkin* mutineers' reasons for not surrendering in, 292
prisons in, 298–99, 310
*See also* Tsentralka
Shestidesyaty, Illarion, 286–87
Shott, Aleksandr, 40
Simferopol (Russia), 268, 269
*Sinop* (Russian ship), 184, 194, 195
mutiny attempts on, 201, 257, 271, 290
*Smely* (steamer), 181, 182
Smirnov, Sergei (Dr.), 63, 65–67, 91, 93, 318
Social Democratic Party, 227, 292–93
splits in, xv, 29–30, 54, 55, 161, 261
Russian sailors in, 28, 33, 35, 48, 57, 168–69, 273
Kirill and Feldmann in, 119, 121, 122
propaganda by, 204, 238, 261
terror campaign against, 305
*See also* study circles
Socialist Revolutionaries, 29, 54, 55, 104, 123, 204, 302, 307
soldiers. *See* army; Cossacks; military
*Somers* (American ship), 107
Soviet Union, 314
Stalin, Josef, 253, 313, 314

Stolypin, Pyotr, 125
*Stremitelny* (Russian torpedo boat), 237, 247–49, 256–59, 262, 271–73, 284–85
strikes (in Russia), 10, 17, 83, 84, 304
in Odessa, 54–59, 104, 112–14
in Moscow, 155, 204, 301–2
in St. Petersburg, 155, 204, 205, 259
in Theodosia, 269
Struve, Pyotr, 83, 204
study circles, 27–28, 30, 34–35, 48, 103
Sukhumi (Caucasus), 235
surrender
*St. George*'s, 225–26, 234–35, 251
Romanian officials urge *Potemkin* to, 245, 252–53, 260
terms of *Potemkin*'s, from Romania, 252, 281, 290, 292
Matyushenko on, 254
*Potemkin*'s, 281–82, 290–95
*Ismail*'s, 286–87, 293
Suvorin, A. S., 282
*Suvorov* (Russian ship), 13–16, 18, 112
*Svetlana* (Russian cruiser), 45
Sweden, 75, 77
Syrox, Aleksei, 98, 99
Tendra Island, 167, 184–85
Black Sea Fleet's maneuvers off, 23, 154, 196, 237–38
*Potemkin* at, 39, 41, 46, 50, 51, 55, 60, 91
Theodosia (Crimea)
*Potemkin* heads to, 253–55, 261–64
*Potemkin* in, 265–72, 274–76
*Stremitelny* in, 284–85
*Three Saints* (Russian ship), 167, 184
*Potemkin*'s pursuit by, 180, 182, 183, 185, 188, 191–93, 201
Titov, D., 238–39, 299
Tkachev, Pyotr, 160–61
"To All European Monarchs" (*Potemkin*'s proclamation), 241, 254–55, 258, 363n241
"To All Sailors on Patrol" (pamphlet), 42–43

"To All the Civilized World"
(*Potemkin*'s proclamation), 233,
240–41, 254–55, 258, 267, 284
Togo Heihachiro, 11–17, 45, 187
Ton, Wilhelm K., 94, 98, 318
torpedo boats (Russian)
in pursuit squadron, 167, 168, 182,
184, 185, 190, 191, 194, 199,
201–2
Chukhnin's orders to, in Sevastopol,
207
*Stremitelny*'s "suicide squad" in,
237, 246–47, 256–59, 262, 271–
73
*See also* Ismail
Treaty of Berlin (1878), 232
Treaty of Paris (1856), 44, 250
Trepov, Dmitry F., 85, 128–30, 155,
203, 302, 303, 305, 319
Trotsky, Leon, 302
Trubetskoy, S. N., 86–87, 302, 319
Tsarskoye Selo (Russia), 7, 16–17, 75,
131
Tsentralka (revolutionary sailor organization), 110, 232
mutiny plans of, 20–24, 36, 71, 100,
104, 124, 185
work of, 35
*Potemkin* revolutionaries' report to,
37, 116
execution of members of, 313
Tsushima Battle, 11–16, 18–19, 21, 45,
130, 156, 187, 335n8
press on, 76–77, 297
revolutionaries on, 85–86
aristocrats' reaction to, 203, 204
Tsvetkov, N. Y., 94
Tsyrkunov (sailor), 279
Turkey, 236, 250, 254, 256, 259, 260
*See also* Russo-Turkish War
*Twelve Apostles* (Russian ship), 167–70,
180, 183, 185–86, 193, 195–96,
201

Ukraine, 24, 91, 143–45
Union of Liberation, 83

Union of Russian Men, 249
Union of Unions, 86
United States, x, 131, 308, 309
reaction of, to mutiny, 157, 159
consul from, in Odessa, 226
*See also* Meyer, George; Roosevelt,
Theodore
*Ural* (Russian cruiser), 18

Vakhtin, B. V., 93, 109
Vakulenchuk, Grigory N., 51, 60, 318
at Tsentralka meeting, 23
as *Potemkin*'s top revolutionary
leader, 35–37, 46–48, 70–71, 106,
124, 172, 179, 223, 312
background of, 48, 110, 165
and meat, 62, 64–65, 69, 70–71
wounding and dying of, 88–90, 101,
108–9
lying in state of, 116–20, 128, 138,
148
funeral for, 145, 153, 164–67
Varna (Bulgaria), 258, 272
Vasilyev-Yuzhin, Mikhail, 162–63, 226–
27, 261, 305
Vedenmeyer, Frederick A., 103, 105,
174, 176, 177–78, 294, 318
*Vekha* (Russian ship)
follows *Potemkin,* 136–39, 143, 154
as hospital ship, 181, 182, 187, 218
counter-mutiny on, 224, 235
Vishnevetsky, F. F., 132, 154, 319
*Potemkin* recovery strategy of, 167–68,
182, 183–86, 195, 201, 207, 210
proclamation by, 169–70
*Potemkin*'s plans to provoke, 187
dismissal of, 298
Vladivostok (Russia), 11, 12, 18, 27,
98, 132
*Volga* (Russian steamer), 273
Volgin, Mikhail L., 168–69, 195, 318,
358n185
Volkov, E. N., 268, 269, 275

Warsaw, 76, 77, 155, 261
Watts, Ethelbert, 87

White, E. J., 157

Wilhelm II (German kaiser), 8–9, 86, 158–59

Winter Palace (St. Peterburg), xiv, 3–7, 10, 17, 44, 84, 85, 130, 302
  Duma received at, 305–6

Wirenus, A. A., 284

Witte, Sergei, 76, 82, 156–57, 206, 300, 302–3, 305, 319, 350n129

workers (urban)
  conditions of, 5, 24–27, 33, 46, 82–83, 339n34
  conscription of, 9, 31, 33–34
  hopes for, as revolutionaries, 28–29, 102, 312
  uprisings of, in Odessa, 53–60, 64, 76, 77, 104, 112–14, 120–21, 123–26, 134, 135–36, 164, 165, 269

  no reforms for, 301
  soviets formed by, 302, 304
  terror campaign against, 305
  *See also* strikes (in Russia)

Yakhnovsky, Ivan T., 33–35, 37, 318

Yalta (Russia), 273, 282, 285

Yanovich, Andrei A., 236–37, 247–49, 257–58, 272–73, 284–85, 297, 319

Zagoskin, M., 269

Zaushkevich, S. A., 91–93

*zemstvos,* 78, 81–86

*Zhutky* (Russian torpedo boat), 248

Zubchenko, M., 240